Edna Forrest.

CONSTITUTIONAL DOCUMENTS
OF THE REIGN OF JAMES I

Cambridge University Press
Fetter Lane, London

New York
Bombay, Calcutta, Madras
Toronto
Macmillan

Tokyo
Maruzen Company, Ltd

Constitutional Documents of the Reign of James I
A.D. 1603–1625
with an historical commentary

by

J. R. TANNER, Litt.D.

Fellow and formerly Tutor of
St John's College, Cambridge

Cambridge
at the University Press
1930

PRINTED IN GREAT BRITAIN

PREFACE

THIS collection of constitutional documents for the reign of James I has been prepared as a companion volume to the editor's *Tudor Constitutional Documents*, the first edition of which was published in 1922. The arrangement of the earlier work has been closely followed, and as far as possible the same principles have determined the selection of matter for inclusion. The historical commentary which deals with the more important constitutional problems of the reign has been taken mainly, although not exclusively, from the first three lectures of the writer's *English Constitutional Conflicts of the Seventeenth Century 1603–1689*, published in 1928, but sections have been added on the Secretary of State, the Privy Council, the Star Chamber, and the High Commission Court; and Finance has been treated rather more fully than in the work on the Tudors. As before, the texts selected have been chosen mainly for their accessibility to students in the University and College Libraries of Cambridge.

In collections of this kind there is a danger that too much may be omitted. Considerations of space sometimes lead an editor to present only the bare bones of documents, and to omit as mere verbiage all that clothes the skeleton and makes it live. But the phrases of old documents express the mentality of the age to which they belong, and even verbiage has its share in creating for the student the atmosphere of the period in which his work lies. In the present volume, therefore, the editor has endeavoured to limit his omissions to the following categories, although he has reluctantly to admit that this is of the nature of a counsel of perfection, and it has not been possible to apply the principles uniformly and in every case. (1) Whole passages have been omitted which refer only to matters of secondary constitutional importance. (2) In the discussion of legal questions, as for instance in the debate on impositions in 1610, where arguments are supported by an array of precedents and illustrations, it has been thought sufficient to make a selection from these instead of including them all. (3) In Acts of Parliament, where sentences which are common form recur with wearisome iteration, it has not been thought necessary to print them more than once. With these exceptions it is generally true to say that the documents are given in full.

Thanks are due to the following for permission to print copyright material: To the Controller of His Majesty's Stationery Office for extracts from the *Calendar of State Papers* and from the *Acts of the Privy Council for the Reign of James I.* To the President and Council of the Royal Historical Society for Sir Julius Caesar's discourse on the Great Contract of 1610, printed in *Parliamentary Debates in 1610,* ed. S. R. Gardiner, Camden Society, 1861. To Mr Anthony Spedding and General E. W. Spedding for permission to quote freely from the late Mr James Spedding's edition of Bacon's *Works* and from his *Letters and Life of Bacon.* Finally, to Messrs Longmans, Green, & Co., the publishers of the *English Historical Review,* for permission to reprint Nicholas Faunt's 'Discourse touching the office of Principal Secretary of Estate, etc.'

The writer also desires to acknowledge the kindness of Professor F. G. Marcham of Cornell University in allowing him to include a missing passage in the Speaker's claim of privilege in 1604, and to thank Professor J. E. Neale for calling his attention to an extract from William Roper's *Life of Sir Thomas More* bearing on the earlier history of the Speaker's claim.

J. R. T.

18 *July* 1930

CONTENTS

LIST OF DOCUMENTS

(A) STATUTES

(B) CASES

(C) EXTRACTS

(D) MISCELLANEOUS DOCUMENTS

The Succession Question and Divine Right

LIST OF BOOKS

*_** *The following are the full titles and editions of the works referred to in an abbreviated form in the footnotes and in the text.*

ANSON, Sir WILLIAM. The Law and Custom of the Constitution. Fourth edition. 1909.

BACON, Sir FRANCIS, Viscount St Albans. Works. Ed. James Spedding. 1857–9.

—— Letters and Life. Ed. James Spedding. 1861–74.

BARLOW, WILLIAM, afterwards Bishop of Lincoln. The Sum and Substance of the Conference...at Hampton Court, January 14, 1603[–4]. Edition of 1625.

BURN, J. S. The Star Chamber. 1870.

Calendar of State Papers, Domestic [contracted as *Cal. S. P. Dom.*].

Calendar of State Papers, Venetian.

CARDWELL, E. Documentary Annals of the Reformed Church of England 1546–1716. 1839.

—— Synodalia. 1842.

CARLYLE, E. I. Committees of Council under the Earlier Stuarts. In English Historical Review, xxi, 673.

COKE, Sir EDWARD. Fourth Institute (*c.* 1628). Edition of 1669.

—— Twelfth Report. In The Reports of Sir Edward Coke.... Edition of 1777.

Commons' Journals.

COWELL, Dr JOHN. The Interpreter.... 1607.

CREIGHTON, MANDELL, Bishop of Peterborough, and afterwards of London. Queen Elizabeth (1896). Edition of 1900.

DASENT, Sir E. R. Acts of the Privy Council. *See also* Privy Council.

DICEY, A. V. The Law of the Constitution. 1885.

Dictionary of National Biography [contracted as *D.N.B.*]. First edition, 1885– .

DIETZ, F. C. Elizabethan Customs Administration. In English Historical Review, xlv, 35.

DOWELL, S. A. A History of Taxation and Taxes in England. Edition of 1884.

DUNCAN-JONES, A. S. Archbishop Laud. Great English Churchmen Series. 1927.

EDWARDS, I. ab O. A Catalogue of Star Chamber Proceedings relating to Wales. 1929.

ELLIS, Sir HENRY. Original Letters illustrative of English History.... 1824–46.

English Historical Review [contracted as *E.H.R.*].

EVANS, FLORENCE M. G. The Principal Secretary of State 1558–1680. 1923.

FIGGIS, J. N. The Divine Right of Kings. Second edition. 1914.

FILMER, Sir ROBERT. *Patriarcha*: or the Natural Power of Kings. Written 1642; published 1680.

FIRTH, Sir C. H. The House of Lords during the Civil War. 1910.

FORSTER, JOHN. Sir John Eliot: a Biography. Edition of 1872.

FRERE, W. H., afterwards Bishop of Truro. A History of the English Church in the Reigns of Elizabeth and James I, 1558–1625. 1904.

FROUDE, J. A. The Reign of Elizabeth. Everyman Library.

FULLER, THOMAS. The Church History of Britain. Edition of 1837.

—— The History of the Worthies of England. Ed. P. A. Nuttall. 1840.

GARDINER, S. R. History of England 1603–1642. Edition of 1883–4.

—— Cromwell's Place in History. 1897.

—— Parliamentary Debates of 1610. Camden Society. 1861.

—— Reports of Cases in the Star Chamber and High Commission. Camden Society. 1886.

GEE, H. and HARDY, W. J. Documents illustrative of English Church History. 1896.

GOLDWIN SMITH. The United Kingdom: a Political History. 1899.

GOOCH, G. P. English Democratic Ideas in the Seventeenth Century. Cambridge Historical Essays. 1898.

GOODMAN, GODFREY, Bishop of Rochester. The Court of King James. *c.* 1650.

GWATKIN, H. M. Church and State to the Death of Queen Anne. 1917.

HALLAM, HENRY. The Constitutional History of England from the Accession of Henry VII to the Death of George II. Edition of 1876.

HALLIWELL, J. O. Letters of the Kings of England.... 1848.

HOLDSWORTH, Sir W. S. A History of English Law. Third edition. 1922– .

HUDSON, WILLIAM. A Treatise of the Court of Star Chamber. Written *c.* 1633. Printed in *Collectanea Juridica*, 1792.

HUNT, JOHN. Religious Thought in England from the Reformation.... 1870.

JAMES I. Works. Edition of 1616.

LODGE, EDMUND. Illustrations of British History.... 1838.

Lords' Journals.

MANWARING, ROGER, afterwards Bishop of St David's. Sermons on Religion and Allegiance. 1627.

MAXWELL-LYTE, Sir H. C. The Great Seal of England. 1926.

MAY, Sir T. ERSKINE. Parliamentary Practice. Tenth edition. 1893.

MILTON, JOHN. Prose Works. 1848–53.

MONTAGUE, F. C. The Political History of England 1603–1660. 1907.

MORLEY, JOHN, afterwards Viscount Morley. Oliver Cromwell. 1900.

NICHOLS, JOHN. The Progresses...of King James I. 1828.

Parliamentary History. Ed. William Cobbett. 1806–20.

PARSONS, ROBERT (writing under the pseudonym of R. Doleman). A Conference about the next Succession to the Crown of England.... 1594.

PETYT, WILLIAM. *Jus Parliamentarium.* 1739.

PIKE, L. O. A Constitutional History of the House of Lords. 1894.

Privy Council, Acts of the, in the Reign of James I. *See also* Dasent.

PROTHERO, Sir G. W. Select Statutes and other Constitutional Documents, 1558–1625. Third edition. 1906.

RALEIGH, Sir WALTER. Works. Edition of 1829.

RELF, FRANCES H. Notes of the Debates in the House of Lords....1621, 1625, and 1628. Royal Historical Society. 1929.

ROPER, WILLIAM. The Life of Sir Thomas More. 1626.

RUSHWORTH, JOHN. Historical Collections. Vol. 1. 1659.

RYMER, THOMAS. *Foedera*. Edition of 1704–35.

SCOFIELD, CORA L. A Study of the Court of Star Chamber. 1900.

SEELEY, Sir J. R. The Growth of British Policy. 1895.

SIBTHORP, ROBERT. Sermon on Apostolic Obedience. 1627.

State Trials. Ed. Thomas Bayly Howell. 1809.

Statutes of the Realm.

STRYPE, JOHN. Annals of the Reformation. Edition of 1824.

—— The Life of Archbishop Whitgift. Edition of 1718.

TANNER, J. R. Tudor Constitutional Documents 1485–1603. Second edition. 1930.

—— English Constitutional Conflicts of the Seventeenth Century, 1603–1689. 1928.

TOMLIN, T. E. Law Dictionary. Fourth edition. 1835.

TRAILL, H. D. Social England. 1893–7.

TREVELYAN, G. M. England under the Stuarts. 1904.

TURNER, E. R. Parliament and Foreign Affairs 1603–1760. In English Historical Review, xxxiv, 172.

—— The Privy Council of England in the Seventeenth and Eighteenth Centuries, 1603–1784. 1927–8.

USHER, R. G. The Rise and Fall of the High Commission. 1913.

CONSTITUTIONAL DOCUMENTS OF THE REIGN OF JAMES I A.D. 1603–1625 WITH AN HISTORICAL COMMENTARY

Introductory

IT has been said that as we pass from the sixteenth to the seventeenth century, we appear to emerge into a new age.

(1) It is said that the Tudor period reconstructed English civilisation. The two great powers in which medieval civilisation had centred had been the Church and the Baronage, and both these had been overthrown by the Tudor Kings. The Dissolution of the Monasteries was a visible social revolution; and scarcely less of a revolution was involved in the more silent and gradual subsidence of the baronial power. The fresh industrial energy of the towns was everywhere replacing the declining industrial energy of the monastic foundations; and as the Reformation swept away the monasteries, so the Civil War was about to dismantle the baronial strongholds,—now only relics of a military power which had long since spent itself. The danger from great lords and retainers had completely passed away; the King's writ ran everywhere; the long arm of the Privy Council reached into every corner of the kingdom. What men needed now was not protection from the great lords, but protection from tyrannical abuse of its authority on the part of the power by which the great lords had been overthrown.

(2) The same strong dynasty which had thus accomplished a social revolution had also achieved an ecclesiastical revolution. The Reformation had been carried through; on the whole, its results were accepted; and the crusade of the Catholic powers against it had had the effect of identifying the cause of national independence with the repudiation of the claims of Rome. The long reign of Elizabeth, by bringing the greater part of the nation into the fold of the national Church, had put an end to the danger of a war of religion within the realm. The adherents of Rome had ceased to be dangerous. They were a small minority which could organise an assassination but could not raise a rebellion.

(3) The Tudors had also lifted the fear of foreign invasion from the English mind. It was not only that the Spanish Armada had been defeated; but also that there had been an immense improvement in the defensible position of England. The success of the United Provinces against Spain had placed the ports of Holland—the natural base for a flank attack upon the English coasts—in the hands of a friendly power. Somewhat the same thing had happened in Ireland—the most vulnerable point in the dominions of Elizabeth. 'Ireland hath very good timber and convenient havens,' says a letter-writer of 1580[1]; 'if the Spaniard might be master of them, he would

[1] Thomas Bawdewyn to the Earl of Shrewsbury (Edmund Lodge, *Illustrations of British History*, ii, 231).

in short space be master of the seas.' This was clearly understood by Spanish statesmen, and as long as Ireland was full of semi-independent chieftains who were hostile to the Reformation, it was easy for Spain to stir up and co-operate in rebellions. But the relentless suppression of rebellions by Elizabeth's vigorous viceroys had, at any rate, closed the door to foreign intervention. And now at last the accession of James VI of Scotland to the throne of England had barred another road, and had deprived another foreign power of its traditional opportunity for intervention. The alliance between France and Scotland, which had weighed heavily upon the judgments of English statesmen, was now determined in the course of nature, and ceased to affect the direction of English policy. England was finally delivered from the nightmare of the North.

One result of this new security was a change of emphasis in politics. In the reign of Elizabeth it was foreign policy that was of transcendent importance, and determined the issues of national life and death. The causes which governed foreign policy lay for the most part outside England, and the whole matter was, from its very nature, bound to be in the hands of the Queen and the group of experts in diplomacy which surrounded her. But in the reign of James the greatest foreign questions had been already settled, and it was therefore possible for constitutional questions to come to the front. Foreign affairs were a region where statecraft might exercise itself, but they no longer involved issues that were vital; the subtle and discerning instinct of the political classes saw that they need no longer eclipse all other questions. 'Just as after the Napoleonic wars,' says Seeley[1], 'a period of reform set in, and the kind of stagnation in which legislation had fallen was broken up, so at the end of the Spanish war, Parliament was relieved from a pressure which had paralysed it.'

James I was a scholar rather than a statesman. Like his predecessors the Tudors, he had been precocious, being able at the age of ten 'extempore to read a chapter out of the Bible out of Latin into French and out of French after into English,' and exhibiting a 'surprising command of general knowledge.'[2] This precocity was the forerunner of a genuine interest in things of the mind, but ever since the days of Pope and the *Dunciad* it has been the fashion to call him a pedant.

> O, cried the goddess, for some pedant reign!
> Some gentle James to bless the land again;
> To stick the doctor's chair into the throne,
> Give law to words, or war with words alone,
> Senates and Courts with Greek and Latin rule,
> And turn the Council to a grammar-school!

It is true that James belonged to an age when scholarship was often pedantic; it would, however, be nearer the mark to speak of him as a scholar.

Although there was nothing about James I to inspire devotion, or to strengthen the hold of the monarchy upon the nation, his ability and learning were both real, and they raised him to a level at which he was capable of

[1] *Growth of British Policy*, i, 258.
[2] *Dictionary of National Biography*, xxix, 161.

appreciating large ideas and taking a statesmanlike view[1]. On two important questions, in particular, he was far in advance of his time,—on a union with Scotland which should be real as well as personal, and on toleration for the Roman Catholics. It is true that he was inclined to over-value himself: 'I am neither a god nor an angel,' he thought it necessary to inform his Council, 'but a man like any other,'[2] but in the monarchical age in which he lived this defect was not as serious as it seems. Where James really failed was in his want of steadiness of purpose; in his imperfect understanding of his English Parliaments due to his Scotch upbringing and early experience; and, above all, in his unfortunate weakness for favourites. Someone says of him that he suffered from a 'partiality to worthless Scotsmen, if only they were sprightly and active,'[3] and of this the promotion of Robert Carr is the most important instance. But Carr was not so dangerous as Buckingham, for he left affairs in the hands of the trained administrators, while Buckingham, 'brilliant, ambitious, vain-glorious, impulsive, and passionate, with just capacity enough to go splendidly astray,'[4] would be satisfied with nothing less than an effective personal control of both policy and administration. A Government in which the wise Burghley and the wise Burghley's son came to be replaced by men of this type, was certain, sooner or later, to find itself in political difficulties.

[1] *Dictionary of National Biography*, ii, 336. Anyone reading the King's speeches to his Parliaments with a mind free from the influence of a hostile tradition, might very well come to the conclusion that James I has been underrated by historians.
[2] *Ib.* lviii, 328.   [3] *Ib.* xxix, 171.
[4] Goldwin Smith, *The United Kingdom: a Political History*, i, 453.

The Succession Question and Divine Right

A principal danger of the reign of Elizabeth had been the danger of a disputed succession. At one time it must have appeared doubtful whether a disputed succession would not, after all, follow upon Elizabeth's death; for James of Scotland did not appear then in the light in which we are accustomed to regard him now,—as quite the obvious heir. If the succession was to be determined by the will of Henry VIII, the crown would go to the descendants of his younger sister Mary, who had married Charles Brandon, Duke of Suffolk. But if the will of Henry VIII was set aside, and it was held that the descendants of his elder sister Margaret had the prior claim, then it was at any rate arguable that James as an alien could not inherit; and in that case the crown would pass to the descendants of Margaret's second marriage, who were represented by Lady Arabella Stuart. But fortunately for the union between England and Scotland, the advantages which the accession of James would bring were present to the minds of English statesmen, and especially to the mind of the one whose word carried the greatest weight— the aged Queen herself. As death drew near, she abandoned her habitual reserve on the succession question and spoke out plainly in favour of James. 'I told you,' she said to Nottingham and others on March 22, two days before she died, 'my seat had been the seat of Kings, and I will have no rascal to succeed me; who should succeed me but a King?' Cecil asked her what she meant by 'no rascal shall succeed me'; and she replied, 'My meaning was, a King should succeed me; and who should that be but our cousin of Scotland?'[1] Thus it came about that the Stuart House succeeded to the throne of England without opposition; and when their title was once established, there was an end to disputed successions, for the curse of childlessness which had descended upon the House of Tudor spared the House of Stuart. At the time of his accession James had two sons.

The sense of relief with which the nation saw the accession of James is described in one of Bacon's Fragments[2]. It had been generally supposed, he tells us, especially abroad, that when Elizabeth died, 'there must follow in England nothing but confusions, interreigns, and perturbations of estate; likely far to exceed the ancient calamities of the civil wars between the Houses of Lancaster and York, by how much more the dissensions were like to be more mortal and bloody when foreign competition should be added to domestical, and divisions for religion to matter of title to the crown.' But when it fell out that James succeeded without opposition, 'it rejoiced all men to see so fair a morning of a Kingdom, and to be thoroughly secured of former apprehensions; as a man that awaketh out of a fearful dream.' Thus it had come about, as Seeley remarks[3], that 'England in 1620 was not the same State that she had been under the Queen. England and Scotland were united in the person of the King, and united in the Reformation. All those dangerous and terrible discords which in the Queen's time had laid the island open to foreign

[1] Robert Carey's account, quoted in Creighton, *Queen Elizabeth*, p. 302.
[2] 'The Beginning of the History of Great Britain' in *Works* (ed. Spedding), vi, 277.
[3] *Growth of British Policy*, i, 258.

invasion were extinguished. There were no longer two sovereigns in the island, and two evenly balanced religions; no longer two systems of alliance and of royal affinity. The State ruled by James was as much greater than the State ruled by Elizabeth as James himself was less great than Elizabeth.'

The political thought of James I and his contemporaries was coloured by the doctrine of the Divine Right of Kings; but in order to understand how they conceived this, it is necessary to deal first with Prerogative. It has been the fashion with some writers to regard prerogative as if it were something illegitimate and tyrannical; but, strictly speaking, the royal prerogative is neither more nor less than the legal exercise of the royal authority. Its province, at different times in English history, has varied in extent. Before 1377 it had included powers of legislation and taxation. It has always included the power of summoning and dissolving Parliament, of coining money, of creating peers, and of pardoning criminals. In the Tudor period its scope was greatly extended, for by the Reformation the control of the Church fell to it, and it was even strong enough to develop permanent institutions, for the Star Chamber and High Commission Court, although they had a basis in statute were not limited by statute, but were dependent on and controlled by the authority of the Crown. But all this does not exhaust the meaning of prerogative. In every State there must be some ultimate power to deal with emergencies and exceptional situations—the power which modern jurists speak of as 'sovereignty.' This also was prerogative, and in the seventeenth century the emergency power was unquestionably vested in the Crown.

This doctrine of prerogative was essential to the existence of a civilised State; and it came to the Crown by right of inheritance, for in early days, when the State was as yet imperfectly developed and the province of law small, it was to the right 'of *kings* to rule and *princes* to decree justice' that the country owed internal security as well as military glory. And it belonged to the Tudor Kings also because there was no other serious claimant, for in their day no statesman ever dreamed of entrusting emergency powers to an assembly. Thus when James I came to the throne, he succeeded to a prerogative which was stronger than it had ever been before. The Commons read the history of the preceding century rightly when they complained in the *Apology* of 1604 [p. 217]: 'the prerogatives of princes may easily and do daily grow,' although they grossly misrepresented the Parliamentary history of the Tudor period in their next sentence: 'the privileges of the subject are for the most part at an everlasting stand.'

Now this salutary prerogative, when it fell into the hands of literary persons with a taste for broad philosophical conceptions, could easily be transformed from something necessary into something intolerable. It only required a few touches to convert the Tudor doctrine of 'royal prerogative' into the Stuart doctrine of 'absolute power.' Singularly enough, the first thinker and writer to tamper with the idea of prerogative was James I himself. It has been said of him that he lived in an intellectual world of his own[1]. For him 'pompous definitions and sweeping generalities' possessed an 'irresistible fascination.' And so we find him in his *True Law of Free Monarchies*, published anonymously in 1598, claiming an independent legislative power for

[1] *D.N.B.* xxix, 170.

the Crown [p. 9]. Again, in a speech to Parliament in 1610 [p. 14] and in a speech to the judges in 1616 [p. 17] he argues that it is not lawful to dispute the 'absolute prerogative' of the Crown. James himself did not press his own premisses to their logical conclusion—the destruction of the English parliamentary system—but there were others who were quite prepared to do so. In 1607 Dr John Cowell, the Professor of Civil Law in the University of Cambridge, published *The Interpreter* [p. 12], a kind of law dictionary, in which he took occasion to define various political terms. In the article 'King' he wrote: 'He is above the law by his absolute power,' a phrase that at once converted the constitutional doctrine of prerogative, which gave the King powers *outside* the law—to deal with emergencies for which the law made no provision—into a doctrine by the authority of which the King would be enabled to override the law. Under 'Parliament' he stated that 'to bind the Prince' by laws made in Parliament 'were repugnant to the nature and constitution of an absolute monarchy.' Under 'Prerogative' he held it to be incontrovertible that the King of England is an absolute King; and under 'Subsidy' he implied that the King might of his absolute power levy taxes independently of Parliament.

It is not surprising that doctrines such as these were repudiated by the House of Commons, and that Dr Cowell's *Interpreter* was ordered to be burned by the common hangman. But although the House could thus destroy the book, it could not destroy the habit of thought which had produced the book. James himself never went as far as Dr Cowell, for he admitted in a message to Parliament that although 'it was dangerous to submit the power of a King to definition,' yet 'withal he did acknowledge that he had no power to make laws of himself, or to exact any subsidies *de jure* without the consent of his three Estates.' But Archbishop Laud in the next reign taught that it was sacrilege to dispute the King's judgments; and Dr Sibthorp in 1626 and Dr Manwaring in 1627 worked out that further refinement of the doctrine which was to play so important a part between the Restoration and the Revolution as the 'doctrine of non-resistance.' 'If a Prince,' said Sibthorp, 'impose an immoderate, yea, an unjust tax, yet the subject...is bound in conscience to submit.'[1] And Manwaring went further: 'All the significations of a royal pleasure are and ought to be to all loyal subjects in the nature and force of a command....No subject may, without hazard of his own damnation in rebelling against God, question or disobey the will and pleasure of his sovereign.'[2] And the same principles found their way freely into the sermons of the Arminian clergy, who were unable to resist the temptation offered them by the first two verses of the thirteenth chapter of the Epistle to the Romans, lying ready to hand as a text: 'Let every soul be in subjection to the higher powers, for there is no power but of God, and the powers that be are ordained of God. Therefore he that resisteth the power, withstandeth the ordinance of God, and they that withstand shall receive to themselves judgment.' In this body of teaching, which might so easily be turned against the whole parliamentary constitution of the country, we have, as it were, the philosophical cause of the Great Rebellion.

[1] *Sermon on Apostolic Obedience*, p. 16.
[2] *First Sermon on Religion and Allegiance*, pp. 10, 11.

The Divine Right of Kings is closely connected with the doctrine of extraordinary prerogative, but it starts from a different point. In its earlier seventeenth century form it is little more than a right of inheritance,—the right of James to succeed Elizabeth. As her life drew to a close, it came to be realised more clearly than before what possibilities of mischief lay in a disputed succession. Yet in 1594 a Jesuit was proving in an able book how uncertain the succession was[1]. James, he said, was a reigning monarch who was an alien; the whole House of Suffolk was illegitimate, for Charles Brandon had a wife alive when he married the sister of Henry VIII—and so, by a series of plausible disqualifications, he traced the inheritance to a Roman Catholic heir, pronouncing finally in favour of the Infanta of Spain. These arguments had the effect of calling into existence a set of counter-arguments in defence of James's title.

'The King is barred by being an alien,' say the Jesuits; but his hereditary claim overrides this. 'He is barred by the Act of Parliament which gave Henry VIII power to devise the Crown by will'; but his right to the throne is derived from a higher source than an Act of Parliament. Heaven has given him, as next in the succession, an indefeasible Divine Right. Thus the doctrine of Divine Right comes into existence as the only answer which would be a valid one to the Roman Catholic controversialists who attacked James I's title to the throne; and it was supported by the terms of the Succession Act of 1604 [see p. 10] which refers to the King's 'inherent birthright' under 'the laws of God,' and also by the practice of touching for the King's evil, which was to the common people a visible sign of the sanctity of the royal House.

Nor was it long before the doctrine of the Divine Right of inheritance was brought to bear upon the doctrine of extraordinary prerogative and absolute power. If the King succeeded by Divine Right, he held his power of God, and therefore to disobey him was to disobey the ordinance of God. Such a logical inference was all the easier because there was a line of earlier thought which made in the same direction. In the Middle Ages the Popes had claimed sovereignty by Divine Right, disobedience to which was a mortal sin; and this claim had called into existence a counter-claim on behalf of the Emperors— that their authority existed by Divine Right, and had come to them, not by grace of the Pope, but by grace of God alone[2]. It was now easy to make the same claim on behalf of monarchy—in France in defence of Henry IV, and in England in defence of James I, for they both obtained their thrones by right of birth alone, and without the sanction of the Papacy[3].

The development of the principles of Divine Right and absolute power was the special business of the clergy, who were always convinced and earnest supporters of authority. As Fuller puts it: 'In all state alterations, be they never so bad, the pulpit will be of the same wood with the Council Board.'[4] 'Severed from the Roman centre of ecclesiastical authority,' as a

---

[1] *A Conference about the next succession to the Crown of England*, by Robert Parsons writing under the pseudonym of R. Doleman.

[2] J. N. Figgis, *The Divine Right of Kings*, p. 65. 2nd Edition, 1914.

[3] *Ib.* p. 173.

[4] Quoted in G. P. Gooch, *Democratic Ideas in the Seventeenth Century*, p. 62.

modern writer remarks[1], they 'had no support but the throne,' to which they 'clung with a loyalty often servile, giving to the King. . .more than a Catholic in the Middle Ages would have given to the Pope. Jesuitism, with a centre of support above monarchies, had preached tyrannicide: Anglicanism, having no centre of support but the monarchy, preached passive obedience and Divine Right.' The enemies of monarchy and the foes of episcopacy were the same, and 'No Bishop, no King'[2] was one of the wisest of James's *obiter dicta*[3]. If men began to enquire into the origin of monarchy, they were very likely to reach a conclusion which derived its authority from the consent of the governed, and this involved the inference that so far from being a divine institution it was not worth maintaining unless it was useful. But the same critics who were attacking monarchy might very well attack the English episcopacy, using the same weapons; and in fact the Roman Catholic writers had already marshalled their forces, while a different kind of criticism was shaping itself on the Puritan side. It was therefore natural that the clergy, led rather by instinct than by logic, should take a lively interest in the problem of monarchy as it was now being stated afresh. Thus from the principle of the Divine Right of inheritance they were led to enquire into the whole nature of political authority. In opposition to the Roman Catholic writers, who derived power from the people, they argued that resistance, even to an unjust King, was sinful, and they expounded the whole course of Old Testament history in accordance with these views.

It is curious that the most important single contribution to the literature of Divine Right in the seventeenth century should have proceeded from a layman. In 1642 Sir Robert Filmer wrote a treatise called *Patriarcha, or the Natural Power of Kings*, which was published posthumously in 1680 as an argument against the Exclusion Bill. It is difficult to condense Filmer's reasoning without caricaturing it, but it is practically this: Power in its origin was patriarchal. The earliest government was that of Adam over his family, succeeded by that of Noah over his sons. The confusion of tongues was the beginning of *kingly* power, for in all the nations formed at Babel 'God was careful to preserve the fatherly authority by distributing the diversity of languages according to the diversity of families'—as in the Scriptures may be plainly seen. The history of the world was then expounded on the same lines and carried by implication down to Charles I who, although not their 'natural parent,' exercised over his people the same absolute patriarchal power as Noah had exercised over his sons in the ark. But the patriarchs did not receive their power by vote of their children; they derived it direct from God. And so with the power of Kings. It is not derived from the people but is a Divine Right.

We are too ready in these days to regard the whole system of argument by which Divine Right was defended in the seventeenth century as simply absurd, and to think little of the intelligence of the generation which accepted it. But like the equally unhistorical theory of the original contract between King and people, which was the philosophical justification of the

---

[1] Goldwin Smith, i, 429.

[2] 'His Majesty concluded this point. . .and closed it up with this short aphorism, No Bishop, no King' (William Barlow, *The Sum of the Conference*, edition of 1625, p. 36).   [3] W. H. Hutton, in Traill, iv, 18.

Revolution of 1688, Divine Right played a necessary part in the history of political thought[1]. It began by providing a form under which the Reformation could fight the Papal claims to sovereignty; and it gave an intellectual justification to the claims of the Stuart House to the throne. It was only after the Revolution, when all danger from the side of Rome was finally removed, that the theory ceased to be useful, and therefore began to appear absurd. If in the seventeenth century the danger from Rome had been greater, the doctrine might have carried everything before it; but under the Stuarts England was safe.

(1) James I on Monarchy, 1598

James I published the *True Law of Free Monarchies* anonymously in 1598.

*   *   *   *   *   *

The Kings therefore in Scotland were before any estates or ranks of men within the same, before any Parliaments were holden or laws made; and by them was the land distributed (which at the first was wholly theirs), states erected and decerned[2], and forms of government devised and established. And it follows of necessity that the Kings were the authors and makers of the laws and not the laws of the Kings.... And according to these fundamental laws already alleged, we daily see that in the Parliament (which is nothing else but the head court of the King and his vassals) the laws are but craved by his subjects, and only made by him at their rogation and with their advice. For albeit the King make daily statutes and ordinances, enjoining such pains thereto as he thinks meet, without any advice of Parliament or Estates, yet it lies in the power of no Parliament to make any kind of law or statute without his sceptre be to it for giving it the force of a law.... And as ye see it manifest that the King is overlord of the whole land, so is he master over every person that inhabiteth the same, having power over the life and death of every one of them. For although a just prince will not take the life of any of his subjects without a clear law, yet the same laws whereby he taketh them are made by himself or his predecessors, and so the power flows always from himself; as by daily experience we see good and just princes will from time to time make new laws and statutes, adjoining the penalties to the breakers thereof, which before the law was made had been no crime to the subject to have committed. Not that I deny the old definition of a King and of a law which makes the King to be a speaking law and the law a dumb King; for certainly a King that governs not by his law can neither be countable to God for his administration nor have a

---

[1] On this see Figgis, chapter x.   [2] Decreed.

happy and established reign. For albeit it be true, that I have at length proved, that the King is above the law as both the author and giver of strength thereto, yet a good King will not only delight to rule his subjects by the law, but even will conform himself in his own actions thereunto; always keeping that ground, that the health of the commonwealth be his chief law. And where he sees the law doubtsome or rigorous, he may interpret or mitigate the same, lest otherwise *summum jus* be *summa injuria*. And therefore general laws made publicly in Parliament may, upon known respects to the King, by his authority be mitigated and suspended upon causes only known to him....

* * * * * *

James I, *Works* (edition of 1616), pp. 201–3.

(2) Succession Act, 1604

A most joyful and just recognition of the immediate, lawful, and undoubted Succession, Descent, and Right of the Crown

Great and manifold were the benefits, most dread and most gracious Sovereign, wherewith Almighty God blessed this kingdom and nation by the happy union and conjunction of the two noble Houses of York and Lancaster, thereby preserving this noble realm, formerly torn and almost wasted with long and miserable dissension and bloody civil war; but more inestimable and unspeakable blessings are thereby poured upon us because there is derived and grown from and out of that union of those two princely families a more famous and greater union, or rather a reuniting, of two mighty, famous, and ancient kingdoms (yet anciently but one) of England and Scotland under one Imperial Crown in your most Royal Person, who is lineally, rightfully, and lawfully descended of the body of the most excellent Lady Margaret, eldest daughter of the most renowned King Henry the Seventh and the high and noble Princess, Queen Elizabeth his wife, eldest daughter of King Edward the Fourth, the said Lady Margaret being eldest sister of King Henry the Eighth, father of the high and mighty Princess of famous memory, Elizabeth, late Queen of England: In consideration whereof, albeit we your Majesty's loyal and faithful subjects, of all estates and degrees, with all possible and public joy and acclamation, by open proclamations within five hours after the decease of our late Sovereign Queen, acknowledging thereby with one full voice of tongue and heart that your Majesty was our only lawful and rightful liege Lord and Sovereign, by our unspeakable and general rejoicing and applause at your Majesty's most happy Inauguration and Coronation, by the affectionate desire of infinite numbers of us of all degrees to see your Royal Person, and by all possible outward means have endeavoured to make demonstration of our inward love, zeal, and devotion to your most excellent Majesty our undoubted rightful liege Sovereign Lord and King; yet as we cannot do it too often or enough, so can there be no means or way so fit both to sacrifice our unfeigned and hearty thanks to Almighty God for blessing us with a Sovereign adorned with the rarest gifts of mind and body in such admirable peace and quietness, and upon the knees of our hearts to agnize[1] our most constant faith, obedience, and loyalty to your Majesty and your royal progeny as in this High Court of Parliament, where all the whole body of the realm, and every particular member thereof, either in person or by representation (upon their own free elections), are by the laws of this realm deemed to be personally present. To the acknowledgment whereof to your Majesty we are the more deeply bounden and obliged, as well in regard of the extraordinary care and pains which with so great wisdom, knowledge, experience, and dexterity your Majesty (since the Imperial Crown of this realm descended to you) have taken for the continuance and establishment of the blessed peace, both of the Church of England in the true and sincere religion, and of the commonwealth by due and speedy administration of justice, as in respect of the gracious care and inward affection which it pleased you on the first day of this Parliament so lively to express by your own words, so full of high wisdom, learning, and virtue, and so replete with royal and thankful acceptation of all our faithful and constant endeavours, which is and ever will be to our inestimable consolation and comfort. We therefore your most humble and loyal subjects the Lords Spiritual and Temporal and the Commons in this present Parliament assembled, do from the bottom of our hearts yield to the Divine Majesty all humble thanks and praises, not only for the said unspeakable and inestimable benefits and blessings above mentioned, but also that he hath further enriched your Highness with a most royal progeny of most rare and excellent gifts and forwardness, and in his goodness is likely to increase the happy number of them; and in most humble and lowly manner do beseech your most excellent Majesty that (as a memorial to all posterities, amongst the records of your High Court of Parliament for ever to endure, of our loyalty, obedience, and hearty and humble affection) it may be published and declared in this High Court of Parliament, and

[1] *I.e.* recognise.

enacted by authority of the same, that we (being bounden thereunto both by the laws of God and man) do recognise and acknowledge (and thereby express our unspeakable joys) that immediately
upon the dissolution and decease of Elizabeth, late Queen of
England, the Imperial Crown of the realm of England, and of
all the kingdoms, dominions, and rights belonging to the same,
did by inherent birthright and lawful and undoubted succession
descend and come to your most excellent Majesty, as being
lineally, justly, and lawfully next and sole heir of the blood royal
of this realm as is aforesaid, and that by the goodness of God
Almighty and lawful right of descent under one Imperial Crown
your Majesty is of the realms and kingdoms of England, Scotland,
France, and Ireland the most potent and mighty King, and by
God's goodness more able to protect and govern us your loving
subjects in all peace and plenty than any of your noble progenitors;
and thereunto we most humbly and faithfully do submit and
oblige ourselves, our heirs and posterities, for ever, until the last
drop of our bloods be spent, and do beseech your Majesty to
accept the same as the firstfruits in this High Court of Parliament
of our loyalty and faith to your Majesty and your royal progeny
and posterity for ever. Which if your Majesty shall be pleased
(as an argument of your gracious acceptation) to adorn with your
Majesty's royal assent, without which it can neither be complete
and perfect nor remain to all posterity according to our most
humble desire (as a memorial of your princely and tender affection
towards us), we shall add this also to the rest of your Majesty's
unspeakable and inestimable benefits.

1 Jac. I, c. 1; *Statutes of the Realm*, iv, 1017.

(3) Dr Cowell's "Interpreter," 1607

Dr John Cowell's *Interpreter* is usually described as a law dictionary, but it is
not limited to law, as the definitions include GINGER, 'a spice well known, being the
root of a plant that groweth in hot countries'; GROCERS, who are 'merchants that
ingross all merchandise vendible'; GUM, 'a certain clammy or tough liquor that...
issueth out of trees'; LOBBE, 'a great kind of North Sea fish'; and other non-legal terms.

KING....He is above the Law by his absolute power....And
though for the better and equal course in making laws he do
admit the three estates, that is, Lords spiritual, Lords temporal,
and the Commons unto counsel, yet this, in divers learned men's
opinions, is not of constraint but of his own benignity, or by
reason of his promise made upon oath at the time of his coronation.
For otherwise were he a subject after a sort, and subordinate,
which may not be thought without breach of duty and loyalty.

For then must we deny him to be above the law, and to have no power of dispensing with any positive law or of granting especial privileges and charters unto any, which is his only and clear right....

PARLIAMENT.... Touching the great authority of this Court, I find...that Henry the Sixth directing his privy seal to Richard, Earl of Warwick, thereby to discharge him of the Captainship of Calais, the Earl refused to obey the privy seal, and continued forth the said office because he received it by Parliament. But one example cannot make good a doctrine. And of these two one must needs be true, that either the King is above the Parliament, that is, the positive laws of his kingdom, or else that he is not an absolute King....And therefore though it be a merciful policy and also a politic mercy (not alterable without great peril) to make laws by the consent of the whole realm because so no one part shall have cause to complain of a partiality, yet simply to bind the prince to or by these laws were repugnant to the nature and constitution of an absolute monarchy....

PREROGATIVE OF THE KING (*praerogativa regis*) is that especial power, preeminence, or privilege that the King hath in any kind over and above other persons, and above the ordinary course of the common law, in the right of his crown.... Now for those regalities which are of the higher nature (all being within the compass of his prerogative, and justly to be comprised under that title), there is not one that belonged to the most absolute prince in the world which doth not also belong to our King, except the custom of the nations so differ (as indeed they do) that one thing be in the one accounted a regality that in another is none. Only by the custom of this kingdom he maketh no laws without the consent of the three estates, though he may quash any law concluded of by them. And whether his power of making laws be restrained *de necessitate* or of a godly and commendable policy, not to be altered without great peril, I leave to the judgment of wiser men. But I hold it incontrowlable[1] that the King of England is an absolute King....

SUBSIDY (*subsidium*) cometh of the French (*subside*), signifying a tax or tribute assessed by Parliament and granted by the Commons to be levied of every subject, according to the value of his lands or goods, after the rate of 4 shillings in the pound for land and 2 shillings 8 pence for goods, as it is most commonly used at this day. Some hold opinion that this subsidy is granted by the subject to the prince in recompense or consideration that

---

[1] *I.e.* incontrovertible.

whereas the prince of his absolute power might make laws of himself, he doth of favour admit the consent of his subjects therein, that all things in their own confession may be done with the greater indifferency....

Dr John Cowell's *Interpreter*, 1607.

(4) The King's Speech to the Parliament, 1610

This speech was made by James I before Parliament at Whitehall, 21 March, 1610.

...I will reduce to three general and main grounds the principal things that have been agitated in this Parliament, and whereof I will now speak.

First, the errand for which you were called by me, and that was, for supporting of my state and necessities.

The second is, that which the people are to move unto the King: to represent unto him such things whereby the subjects are vexed or wherein the state of the commonwealth is to be redressed, and that is the thing which you call grievances.

The third ground that hath been handled amongst you, and not only in talk amongst you in the Parliament but even in many other people's mouths as well within as without the Parliament, is of a higher nature than any of the former (though it be but an incident), and the reason is, because it concerns a higher point; and this is, a doubt which hath been in the heads of some, of my intention in two things:

First, whether I was resolved in the general to continue still my government according to the ancient form of this State and the laws of this kingdom, or if I had an intention not to limit myself within those bounds, but to alter the same when I thought convenient, by the absolute power of a King.

The other branch is anent the Common Law, which some had a conceit I disliked, and (in respect that I was born where another form of law was established) that I would have wished the Civil Law to have been put in place of the Common Law for government of this people. And the complaint made amongst you of a book written by Doctor Cowell was a part of the occasion of this incident; but as touching my censure of that book, I made it already to be delivered unto you by the Treasurer here sitting, which he did out of my own directions and notes, and what he said in my name that had he directly from me; but what he spake of himself therein, without my direction, I shall always make good, for you may be sure I will be loath to make so honest a man a liar or deceive your expectations: always within very few days my

edict shall come forth anent that matter which shall fully discover
my meaning.

*   *   *   *   *   *

The state of Monarchy is the supremest thing upon earth;
for kings are not only God's lieutenants upon earth and sit upon
God's throne, but even by God himself they are called gods.
There be three principal similitudes that illustrate the state of
Monarchy: one taken out of the Word of God and the two other
out of the grounds of policy and philosophy. In the Scriptures
kings are called gods, and so their power after a certain relation
compared to the Divine power. Kings are also compared to the
fathers of families, for a king is truly *parens patriae*, the politic
father of his people. And lastly, kings are compared to the head
of this microcosm of the body of man.

Kings are justly called gods for that they exercise a manner or
resemblance of Divine power upon earth; for if you will consider
the attributes to God you shall see how they agree in the person of
a king. God hath power to create or destroy, make or unmake, at
his pleasure; to give life or send death; to judge all, and to be
judged nor accomptable to none; to raise low things and to make
high things low at his pleasure; and to God are both soul and body
due. And the like power have kings: they make and unmake
their subjects; they have power of raising and casting down; of
life and of death; judges over all their subjects and in all causes,
and yet accomptable to none but God only. They have power to
exalt low things and abase high things, and make of their subjects
like men at the chess, a pawn to take a bishop or a knight, and to
cry up or down any of their subjects as they do their money. And
to the King is due both the affection of the soul and the service of
the body of his subjects.. ..

As for the father of a family, they had of old under the Law of
Nature *patriam potestatem*, which was *potestatem vitae et necis*, over
their children or family, (I mean such fathers of families as were
the lineal heirs of those families whereof kings did originally
come), for kings had their first original from them who planted
and spread themselves in colonies through the world. Now a
father may dispose of his inheritance to his children at his pleasure,
yea, even disinherit the eldest upon just occasions and prefer the
youngest, according to his liking; make them beggars or rich at
his pleasure; restrain or banish out of his presence, as he finds
them give cause of offence, or restore them in favour again with
the penitent sinner. So may the King deal with his subjects.

And lastly, as for the head of the natural body, the head hath the power of directing all the members of the body to that use which the judgment in the head thinks most convenient. It may apply sharp cures or cut off corrupt members, let blood in what proportion it thinks fit and as the body may spare; but yet is all this power ordained by God *ad aedificationem, non ad destructionem*. For although God have power as well of destruction as of creation or maintenance, yet will it not agree with the wisdom of God to exercise his power in the destruction of nature and overturning the whole frame of things, since his creatures were made that his glory might thereby be the better expressed; so were he a foolish father that would disinherit or destroy his children without a cause or leave off the careful education of them; and it were an idle head that would in place of physic so poison or phlebotomize the body as might breed a dangerous distemper or destruction thereof.

But now in these our times we are to distinguish between the state of kings in their first original and between the state of settled kings and monarchs that do at this time govern in civil kingdoms; for even as God, during the time of the Old Testament, spake by oracles and wrought by miracles, yet how soon it pleased him to settle a Church which was bought and redeemed by the blood of his only Son Christ, then was there a cessation of both; he ever after governing his people and Church within the limits of his revealed will. So in the first original of kings, whereof some had their beginning by conquest and some by election of the people, their wills at that time served for law; yet how soon kingdoms began to be settled in civility and policy, then did kings set down their minds by laws, which are properly made by the King only, but at the rogation of the people, the King's grant being obtained thereunto. And so the King became to be *Lex loquens* after a sort, binding himself by a double oath to the observation of the fundamental laws of his kingdom: tacitly, as by being a King, and so bound to protect as well the people as the laws of his kingdom, and expressly, by his oath at his coronation; so as every just king in a settled kingdom is bound to observe that paction made to his people by his laws in framing his government agreeable thereunto, according to that paction which God made with Noë after the Deluge, 'Hereafter seed-time and harvest, cold and heat, summer and winter, and day and night shall not cease so long as the earth remains.' And therefore a king governing in a settled kingdom leaves to be a king and degenerates into a tyrant as soon as he leaves off to rule according to his laws. In which case the King's conscience may speak unto him as the poor widow said to Philip of Macedon: 'Either govern according to your law, *aut ne Rex sis*. And though no Christian man ought to allow any rebellion of people against their Prince, yet doth God never leave kings unpunished when they transgress these limits, for in that same Psalm where God saith to kings, *Vos Dii estis*, he immediately thereafter concludes, 'But ye shall die like men.' The higher we are placed, the greater shall our fall be. *Ut casus sic dolor*: the taller the trees be, the more in danger of the wind; and the tempest bears sorest upon the highest mountains. Therefore all kings that are not tyrants or perjured will be glad to bound themselves within the limits of their laws, and they that persuade them the contrary are vipers and pests, both against them and the commonwealth. For it is a great difference between a king's government in a settled State and what kings in their original power might do *in individuo vago*. As for my part, I thank God I have ever given good proof that I never had intention to the contrary; and I am sure to go to my grave with that reputation and comfort, that never king was in all his time more careful to have his laws duly observed, and himself to govern thereafter, than I.

I conclude then this point touching the power of kings with this axiom of Divinity, That as to dispute what God may do is blasphemy, but *quid vult Deus*, that divines may lawfully and do ordinarily dispute and discuss, for to dispute *a posse ad esse* is both against Logic and Divinity, so is it sedition in subjects to dispute what a king may do in the height of his power; but just kings will ever be willing to declare what they will do, if they will not incur the curse of God. I will not be content that my power be disputed upon, but I shall ever be willing to make the reason appear of all my doings, and rule my actions according to my laws.

*   *   *   *   *   *

James I, *Works* (ed. of 1616), pp. 528–31.

(5) The King's Speech to the Judges, 1616

This speech was delivered to the judges assembled in the Star Chamber, 20 June, 1616. It not only discusses prerogative, but makes some characteristic observations on recusants and on justices of the peace.

*   *   *   *   *   *

...For the Common Law, you can all bear me witness I never pressed alteration of it in Parliament; but on the contrary, when I endeavoured most an union real, as was already in my person, my desire was to conform the laws of Scotland to the law of England and not the law of England to the law of Scotland, and so the prophecy to be true of my wise grandfather[1] Henry the

---

[1] This could be applied to any male ancestor.

Seventh, who foretold that the lesser kingdom by marriage would follow the greater and not the greater the lesser; and therefore married his eldest daughter Margaret to James the Fourth my great-grandfather.

It was a foolish quirk of some Judges who held that the Parliament of England could not unite Scotland and England by the name of Great Britain, but that it would make an alteration of the laws; though I am since come to that knowledge that an Act of Parliament can do greater wonders, and that old wise man the Treasurer Burghley was wont to say, he knew not what an Act of Parliament could not do in England; for my intention was always to effect union by uniting Scotland to England and not England to Scotland. For I ever meant, being ever resolved, that this law should continue in this kingdom, and two things moved me thereunto: one is, that in matter of policy and State you shall never see anything anciently and maturely established but by innovation or alteration it is worse than it was,—I mean not by purging of it from corruptions and restoring it to the ancient integrity. Another reason was, I was sworn to maintain the law of the land, and therefore I had been perjured if I had altered it; and this I speak to root out the conceit and misapprehension, if it be in any heart, that I would change, damnify, vilify, or suppress the law of this land. God is my judge I never meant it, and this confirmation I make before you all.

To this I join the point of justice, which I call *unicuique suum tribuere*. All my Council, and Judges dead and alive, can and could bear me witness how unpartial I have been in declaring of law....

*   *   *   *   *   *

And though the laws be in many places obscure, and not so well known to the multitude as to you, and that there are many parts that come not into ordinary practice which are known to you because you can find out the reason thereof by books and precedents; yet know this, that your interpretations must be always subject to common sense and reason. For I will never trust any interpretation that agreeth not with my common sense and reason and true logic, for *Ratio est anima Legis* in all human laws without exception; it must not be sophistry or strains of wit that must interpret, but either clear law or solid reason.

*   *   *   *   *   *

Now having spoken of your office in general, I am next to come to the limits wherein you are to bound yourselves, which

likewise are three. First, encroach not upon the prerogative of
the Crown. If there fall out a question that concerns my prerogative or mystery of State, deal not with it till you consult with the
King or his Council or both; for they are transcendent matters,
and must not be slubberly[1] carried with over-rash wilfulness, for
so may you wound the King through the sides of a private person:
and this I commend unto your special care, as some of you of late
have done very well to blunt the sharp edge and vain popular
humour of some lawyers at the bar that think they are not eloquent
and bold-spirited enough except they meddle with the King's
prerogative. But do not you suffer this; for certainly if this liberty
be suffered, the King's prerogative, the Crown, and I shall be as
much wounded by their pleading as if you resolved what they
disputed. That which concerns the mystery of the King's power
is not lawful to be disputed, for that is to wade into the weakness of
Princes and to take away the mystical reverence that belongs unto
them that sit in the throne of God.

Secondly, that you keep yourselves within your own Benches;
not to invade other jurisdictions, which is unfit, and an unlawful
thing.

*   *   *   *   *   *

Keep you therefore all in your own bounds, and for my part I
desire you to give me no more right in my private prerogative than
you give to any subject, and therein I will be acquiescent. As for
the absolute prerogative of the Crown, that is no subject for the
tongue of a lawyer, nor is lawful to be disputed. It is atheism and
blasphemy to dispute what God can do; good Christians content
themselves with his will revealed in his Word. So it is presumption
and high contempt in a subject to dispute what a King can do, or
say that a King cannot do this or that; but rest in that which is
the King's revealed will in his law.

*   *   *   *   *   *

And this you shall find, that even as a King (let him be never
so godly, wise, righteous, and just), yet if the subaltern magistrates
do not their parts under him the kingdom must needs suffer; so
let the Judges be never so careful and industrious, if the justices of
peace under them put not to their helping hands in vain is all
your labour, for they are the King's eyes and ears in the country.
It was an ancient custom that all the Judges, both immediately
before their going to their circuits and immediately upon their

---

[1] The word in the text is 'sliberely'; but the sense is evidently hurriedly or
carelessly.

return, repaired to the Lord Chancellor of England, both to receive what directions it should please the King by his mouth to give unto them, as also to give him an accompt of their labours, who was to acquaint the King therewith; and this good ancient custom hath likewise been too much slacked of late. And therefore, first of all, I am to exhort and command you that you be careful to give a good accompt to me and my Chancellor of the duties performed by all justices of peace in your circuits. Which government by justices is so laudable and so highly esteemed by me, that I have made Scotland to be governed by justices and constables as England is. And let not gentlemen be ashamed of this place, for it is a place of high honour and great reputation to be made a minister of the King's justice in service of the common-wealth.

Of these there are two sorts, as there is of all companies, especially where there is a great number: that is, good and bad justices. For the good, you are to inform me of them, that I may know them, thank them, and reward them, as occasion serves. For I hold a good justice of peace in his country to do me as good service as he that waits upon me in my Privy Chamber, and as ready will I be to reward him; for I accompt him as capable of any honour, office, or preferment about my person, or for any place of counsel or State, as well as any courtier that is near about me or any that have deserved well of me in foreign employments; yea, I esteem the service done me by a good justice of peace three hundred miles, yea, six hundred miles out of my sight as well as the service done me in my presence. For as God hath given me large limits, so must I be careful that my providence may reach to the farthest parts of them; and as law cannot be honoured except honour be given to Judges, so without due respect to justices of peace what regard will be had of the service? Therefore let none be ashamed of this office, or be discouraged in being a justice of peace, if he serve worthily in it.

The Chancellor, under me, makes justices and puts them out; but neither I nor he can tell what they are. Therefore we must be informed by you Judges, who can only tell, who do well and who do ill; without which how can the good be cherished and main-tained and the rest put out? The good justices are careful to attend the service of the King and country for thanks only of the King and love to their country, and for no other respect.

The bad are either idle slow-bellies, that abide always at home, given to a life of ease and delight, liker ladies than men, and think it is enough to contemplate justice, whenas *virtus in actione consistit*: contemplative justice is no justice, and contemplative justices are fit to be put out.

Another sort of justices are busybodies, and will have all men dance after their pipe and follow their greatness, or else will not be content,—a sort of men *qui se primos omnium esse putant, nec sunt tamen*: these proud spirits must know that the country is ordained to obey and follow God and the King, and not them.

Another sort are they that go seldom to the King's service but when it is to help some of their kindred or alliance; so as when they come it is to help their friends or hurt their enemies, making justice to serve for a shadow to faction, and tumultuating the country.

Another sort are gentlemen of great worth in their own conceit, and cannot be content with the present form of government, but must have a kind of liberty in the people, and must be gracious lords and redeemers of their liberty; and in every cause that concerns prerogative give a snatch against a monarchy, through their Puritanical itching after popularity. Some of them have shewed themselves too bold of late in the Lower House of Parliament; and when all is done, if there were not a King they would be less cared for than other men.

*   *   *   *   *   *

As to the charge you are to give the justices, I can but repeat what formerly I have told you; yet in so good a business
      Lectio lecta placet, decies repetita placebit.
And as I began with fulfilling the proverb, *A Jove principium*, so will I begin this charge you are to give to the justices with Church matters; for God will bless every good business the better that he and his Church have the precedence. That which I am now to speak is anent recusants and Papists....

*   *   *   *   *   *

There are three sorts of recusants: the first are they that for themselves will be no recusants, but their wives and their families are; and they themselves do come to church but once or twice in a year, enforced by law or for fashion sake. These may be formal to the law, but more false to God than the other sort.

The second sort are they that are recusants and have their conscience mis-led, and therefore refuse to come to church, but otherwise live as peaceable subjects.

The third sort are practising recusants. These force all their servants to be recusants with them; they will suffer none of their tenants but they must be recusants, and their neighbours, if they would live by them in peace, must be recusants also. These you may find out as a fox by the foul smell a great way round about his hole. This is a high pride and presumption that they for whose souls I must answer to God, and who enjoy their lives and liberties under me, will not only be recusants themselves but infect and draw others after them.

As I have said in Parliament House, I can love the person of a Papist being otherwise a good man and honestly bred, never having known any other religion; but the person of an apostate Papist I hate. And surely for those polypragmatic Papists, I would you would study out some severe punishment for them, for they keep not infection in their own hearts only but also infect others our good subjects. And that which I say for recusants the same I say for priests. I confess I am loath to hang a priest only for religion sake and saying mass; but if he refuse the oath of allegiance which (let the Pope and all the devils in Hell say what they will) yet (as you find by my book and by divers others) is merely civil, those that so refuse the oath and are polypragmatic recusants I leave them to the law; it is no persecution but good justice.

And those priests also that out of my grace and mercy have been let go out of prisons and banished upon condition not to return, ask me no questions touching these; quit me of them and let me not hear of them. And to them I join those that break prison; for such priests as the prison will not hold, it is a plain sign nothing will hold them but a halter: such are no martyrs that refuse to suffer for their conscience. Paul, notwithstanding the doors were open, would not come forth, and Peter came not out of the prison till led by the angel of God; but these will go forth though with the angel of the Devil.

I have given order to my Lord of Canterbury and my Lord of London for the distinction, etc., of the degrees of priests; and when I have an accompt from them then will I give you another charge concerning them....

* * * * * *

James I, *Works* (ed of 1616), pp. 553, 556–7, 563–6.

The Union with Scotland

It was one of the dearest wishes of James I that the personal union between England and Scotland which his accession had established, should be converted into a real union. He expressed this view after his own fashion when he said, 'I am the husband and all the whole isle is my lawful wife.... I hope therefore no man will be so unreasonable as to think that I, that am a Christian king under the Gospel, should be a polygamist and husband to two wives' [p. 26]. But James aimed at too much,—'one worship of God, one kingdom entirely governed, one uniformity of law.'[1] Even unity of government did not come for a hundred years, and Scotland still has a different law and a different worship. One member said that the Scots were pedlars and not merchants[2]. Bacon, who was in favour of naturalisation, had to controvert 'plausible similitudes,' among which was the comparison of England to a rich pasture threatened by the irruption of a herd of famished cattle[3]. Another member indulged in 'invective' against the Scottish nation, 'using many words of scandal and obloquy, ill-beseeming such an audience and not pertinent to the matter in hand'; and, dipping into the history of Scotland, remarked, 'They have not suffered above two kings to die in their beds these 200 years.'[4]

An Act of 1604 appointed commissioners to draw up a scheme of union [p. 31], and a proclamation making the necessary changes in the King's regal style [p. 32] was issued in October of the same year. The question of union was also fully considered in the session of 1606, but the plans of James in spite of his efforts to allay the fears of Parliament [see p. 35] were, to his intense disappointment, wrecked upon the naturalisation question. The lawyers drew a distinction between the *Ante-nati*, born in Scotland before the King's accession to the throne of England, and the *Post-nati*, born after it, and they asked Parliament to pass an Act conferring naturalisation upon the *Ante-nati*, but only declaring it with respect to the *Post-nati*, on the ground that they were already naturalised at common law. The opposition which this proposal met with was partly due to blind hostility to the alien, but there was also a more solid objection. If Philip and Mary had left a son, and he had inherited Spain, would all Spaniards born after his accession be naturalised Englishmen at common law, capable of sitting and voting in Parliament and repealing the penal laws against the Roman Catholics? The lawyers argued in vain: the country gentlemen saw a real danger and refused to pass the Bill, and the only legislative results were an Act of 1607 for the abolition of hostility between the two countries [p. 38], supplemented by an Act of 1610 [p. 43] for the better administration of justice. The whole question of naturalisation was therefore left to be settled by the law-courts, and although the *Ante-nati* had no case, the *Post-nati* brought a collusive action on behalf of a *Post-natus* named Robert Calvin, which was argued before all the judges in the Exchequer Chamber in 1608. It was urged by counsel engaged against the *Post-natus* that the King had two 'ligeances'—the 'ligeance of the King of his kingdom of England' and the

[1] H. M. Gwatkin, *Church and State to the Death of Queen Anne*, p. 265.
[2] *Parliamentary History*, i. 1082.   [3] *Ib.* i. 1086.   [4] *Ib.* i. 1097.

'ligeance of the King of his kingdom of Scotland,' and a person born in one 'ligeance' was an alien in the other. Coke's Report of the case, filling fifty-two closely printed columns in the *State Trials*[1], is a massive achievement of ponderous learning, touching on every subject connected, however remotely, with the matter in hand, from the legal status of the Samaritan leper down to the allegiance due to 'Canutus the Danish King,' with references to Glanville, Fortescue, Skeene, Bracton, Fleta, Littleton, Dyer, Griffith, Justinian, Virgil, Aristotle, Pomponius, 'Tully,' St Luke, and many other authors, but its conclusion is clear enough. The judges held that where a king inherited two kingdoms, though the laws might be different there was only one 'ligeance,' and anyone born within the King's 'ligeance' was his natural-born subject, and no alien in either of his kingdoms.

(1) James I on a Union with Scotland, 1604

This speech was delivered at the opening of the King's first English Parliament, 19 March, 1604, and may be regarded as exhibiting James I at his best. It includes a dissertation on religion.

It did no sooner please God to lighten his hand and relent the violence of his devouring angel against the poor people of this City[2], but as soon did I resolve to call this Parliament, and that for three chief and principal reasons. The first whereof is, ...that you who are here presently assembled to represent the body of this whole kingdom and of all sorts of people within the same, may with your own ears hear, and that I out of mine own mouth may deliver unto you, the assurance of my due thankfulness for your so joyful and general applause to the declaring and receiving of me in this seat (which God by my birthright and lineal descent had in the fullness of time provided for me), and that immediately after it pleased God to call your late Sovereign of famous memory, full of days but fuller of immortal trophies of honour, out of this transitory life. Not that I am able to express by words or utter by eloquence the vive[3] image of mine inward thankfulness, but only that out of mine own mouth you may rest assured to expect that measure of thankfulness at my hands which is according to the infiniteness of your deserts and to my inclination and ability for requital of the same. Shall I ever—nay, can I ever—be able, or rather so unable in memory as to forget your unexpected readiness and alacrity, your ever memorable resolution, and your most wonderful conjunction and harmony of your hearts in declaring and embracing me as your undoubted and lawful King and Governor? Or shall it ever be blotted out of my mind how at my first entry into this kingdom the people of all sorts rid[4] and ran, nay, rather flew to meet me, their eyes flaming nothing but sparkles

---

[1] ii. 611–658.   [2] Probably an allusion to the plague.   [3] Life-like.   [4] Rode.

of affection; their mouths and tongues uttering nothing but sounds of joy; their hands, feet, and all the rest of their members in their gestures discovering a passionate longing and earnestness to meet and embrace their new Sovereign?....

...It is the blessings which God hath in my person bestowed upon you all, wherein I protest I do more glory at the same for your weal than for any particular respect of mine own reputation or advantage therein.

The first, then, of these blessings which God hath, jointly with my person, sent unto you is outward peace, ...which is no small blessing to a Christian Commonwealth, for by peace abroad with their neighbours the towns flourish, the merchants become rich, the trade doth increase, and the people of all sorts of the land enjoy free liberty to exercise themselves in their several vocations without peril or disturbance. Not that I think this outward peace so unseparably tied to my person as I dare assuredly promise to myself and to you the certain continuance thereof; but thus far I can very well assure you, and in the word of a King promise unto you, that I shall never give the first occasion of the breach thereof, neither shall I ever be moved for any particular or private passion of mind to interrupt your public peace except I be forced thereunto, either for reparation of the honour of the kingdom or else by necessity for the weal and preservation of the same; in which case a secure and honourable war must be preferred to an unsecure and dishonourable peace....

But although outward peace be a great blessing, yet it is as far inferior to peace within as civil wars are more cruel and unnatural than wars abroad. And therefore the second great blessing that God hath with my person sent unto you is peace within, and that in a double form. First, by my descent lineally out of the loins of Henry the Seventh is reunited and confirmed in me the union of the two princely roses of the two Houses of Lancaster and York, whereof that King of happy memory was the first uniter as he was also the first ground-layer of the other peace. The lamentable and miserable events by the civil and bloody dissension betwixt these two Houses was so great and so late as it need not be renewed unto your memories; which, as it was first settled and united in him, so is it now reunited and confirmed in me, being justly and lineally descended not only of that happy conjunction but of both the branches thereof many times before. But the union of these two princely Houses is nothing comparable to the union of two ancient and famous kingdoms, which is the other inward peace annexed to my person.

And here I must crave your patiences for a little space to give me leave to discourse more particularly of the benefits that do arise of that union which is made in my blood, being a matter that most properly belongeth to me to speak of as the head wherein that great body is united. And first, if we were to look no higher than to natural and physical reasons, we may easily be persuaded of the great benefits that by that union do redound to the whole island; for if twenty thousand men be a strong army, is not the double thereof, forty thousand, a double the stronger army? If a baron enricheth himself with double as many lands as he had before, is he not double the greater? Nature teacheth us that mountains are made of motes, and that at the first kingdoms being divided, and every particular town or little county, as tyrants or usurpers could obtain the possession, a seignory apart, many of these little kingdoms are now in process of time by the ordinance of God joined into great monarchies, whereby they are become powerful within themselves to defend themselves from all outward invasions, and their head and governor thereby enabled to redeem them from foreign assaults and punish private transgressions within. Do we not yet remember that this kingdom was divided into seven little kingdoms, besides Wales? And is it not now the stronger by their union? And hath not the union of Wales to England added a greater strength thereto? Which, though it was a great principality, was nothing comparable in greatness and power to the ancient and famous kingdom of Scotland. But what should we stick upon any natural appearance, when it is manifest that God by his Almighty Providence hath preordained it so to be? Hath not God first united these two kingdoms both in language, religion, and similitude of manners? Yea, hath he not made us all in one island, compassed with one sea, and of itself by nature so indivisible as almost those that were borderers themselves on the late Borders cannot distinguish nor know nor discern their own limits? These two countries being separated neither by sea nor great river, mountain, nor other strength of nature, but only by little small brooks or demolished little walls, so as rather they were divided in apprehension than in effect; and now in the end and fullness of time united, the right and title of both in my person, alike lineally descended of both the Crowns, whereby it is now become like a little world within itself, being intrenched and fortified round about with a natural and yet admirable strong pond or ditch, whereby all the former fears of this nation are now quite cut off.... What God hath conjoined then, let no man separate. I am the husband, and all the whole isle is my lawful wife;

I am the head and it is my body; I am the shepherd and it is my flock: I hope therefore no man will be so unreasonable as to think that I, that am a Christian king under the Gospel, should be a polygamist and husband to two wives; that I, being the head, should have a divided and monstrous body; or that being the shepherd to so fair a flock (whose fold hath no wall to hedge it but the four seas) should have my flock parted in two.

*   *   *   *   *   *

But neither peace outward, nor peace inward, nor any other blessings that can follow thereupon, nor appearance of the perpetuity thereof by propagation in the posterity, is but a weak pillar and a rotten reed to lean unto, if God do not strengthen and by the staff of his blessing make them durable; for in vain doth the watchman watch the city, if the Lord be not the principal defence thereof; in vain doth the builder build the house, if God give not the success; and in vain (as Paul saith) doth Paul plant and Apollo[s] water, if God give not the increase. For all worldly blessings are but like swift passing shadows, fading flowers, or chaff blown before the wind, if by the profession of true religion, and works according thereunto, God be not moved to maintain and settle the thrones of princes. And although that since mine entry into this kingdom I have, both by meeting with divers of the ecclesiastical estate and likewise by divers proclamations, clearly declared my mind in points of religion, yet do I not think it amiss in this so solemn an audience I should now take occasion to discover somewhat of the secrets of my heart in that matter; for I shall never (with God's grace) be ashamed to make public profession thereof at all occasions, lest God should be ashamed to profess and allow me before men and angels, especially lest that at this time men might presume further upon the misknowledge of my meaning to trouble this Parliament of ours than were convenient. At my first coming, although I found but one religion, and that which by myself is professed, publicly allowed, and by the law maintained, yet found I another sort of religion, besides a private sect, lurking within the bowels of this nation. The first is the true religion which by me is professed and by the law is established; the second is the falsely called Catholics but truly Papists; the third, which I call a sect rather than religion, is the Puritans and Novelists, who do not so far differ from us in points of religion as in their confused form of policy and parity, being ever discontented with the present government and impatient to suffer any superiority, which maketh their sect unable to be suffered in any well-governed commonwealth. But as for my course toward them, I remit it to my proclamations made upon that subject. And now for the Papists, I must put a difference betwixt mine own private profession of mine own salvation and my politic government of the realm for the weal and and quietness thereof. As for mine own profession, you have me your head now amongst you of the same religion as the body is of. As I am no stranger to you in blood, no more am I a stranger to you in faith, or in the matters concerning the house of God. And although this my profession be according to mine education, wherein (I thank God) I sucked the milk of God's truth with the milk of my nurse, yet do I here protest unto you that I would never for such a conceit of constancy or other prejudicate opinion have so firmly kept my first profession if I had not found it agreeable to all reason, and to the rule of my conscience. And I was never violent nor unreasonable in my profession: I acknowledge the Roman Church to be our Mother Church, although defiled with some infirmities and corruptions, as the Jews were when they crucified Christ; and as I am none enemy to the life of a sick man because I would have his body purged of ill humours, no more am I enemy to their Church because I would have them reform their errors, not wishing the down-throwing of the Temple but that it might be purged and cleansed from corruption; otherwise how can they wish us to enter, if their house be not first made clean? But as I would be loather to dispense in the least point of mine own conscience for any worldly respect than the foolishest precisian of them all, so would I be as sorry to strait the politic government of the bodies and minds of all my subjects to my private opinions. Nay, my mind was ever so free from persecution, or thralling of my subjects in matters of conscience, as I hope that those of that profession within this kingdom have a proof since my coming, that I was so far from increasing their burdens with Rehoboam as I have so much as either time, occasion, or law could permit, lightened them. And even now at this time have I been careful to revise and consider deeply upon the laws made against them, that some overture may be proponed to the present Parliament for clearing these laws by reason (which is the soul of the law), in case they have been in times past further or more rigorously extended by judges than the meaning of the law was, or might tend to the hurt as well of the innocent as of guilty persons. And as to the persons of my subjects which are of that profession, I must divide them into two ranks, clerics and laics. For the part of the laics, certainly I ever thought them far more excusable than the other sort, because that sort of religion containeth such an ignorant, doubtful, and implicit kind of faith in the laics grounded upon their Church, as except they do generally believe whatsoever their teachers please to affirm, they cannot be thought guilty of these particular points of heresies and corruptions which their teachers do so wilfully profess. And again, I must subdivide the same laics into two ranks, that is, either quiet and well-minded men, peaceable subjects, who either being old have retained their first drunken-in liquor upon a certain shamefastness to be thought curious or changeable, or being young men through evil education have never been nursed or brought up but upon such venom in place of wholesome nutriment. And that sort of people I would be sorry to punish their bodies for the error of their minds, the reformation whereof must only come of God and the true Spirit. But the other rank of laics who either through curiosity[1], affectation of novelty, or discontentment in their private humours, have changed their coats only to be factious stirrers of sedition and perturbers of the commonwealth, their backwardness in their religion giveth a ground to me the magistrate to take the better heed to their proceeding and to correct their obstinacy. But for the part of the clerics, I must directly say and affirm that as long as they maintain one special point of their doctrine and another point of their practice they are no way sufferable to remain in this kingdom. Their point of doctrine is that arrogant and ambitious Supremacy of their Head the Pope, whereby he not only claims to be spiritual head of all Christians but also to have an imperial civil power over all kings and emperors, dethroning and decrowning princes with his foot as pleaseth him, and dispensing and disposing of all kingdoms and empires at his appetite. The other point which they observe in continual practice is the assassinates and murders of Kings, thinking it no sin but rather a matter of salvation to do all actions of rebellion and hostility against their natural Sovereign Lord if he be once cursed, his subjects discharged of their fidelity, and his kingdom given a prey by that three-crowned monarch, or rather monster, their Head. And in this point I have no occasion to speak further here, saving that I could wish from my heart that it would please God to make me one of the members of such a general Christian union in religion as, laying wilfulness aside on both hands, we might meet in the midst, which is the centre and perfection of all things. For if they would leave and be ashamed of such new and gross corruptions of theirs as themselves cannot maintain, nor deny to

---

[1] *I.e.* a desire for change.

be worthy of reformation, I would for mine own part be content to meet them in the mid-way, so that all novelties might be renounced on either side. For as my faith is the true, ancient, Catholic, and Apostolic faith, grounded upon the Scriptures and express Word of God, so will I ever yield all reverence to antiquity in the points of ecclesiastical policy; and by that means shall I ever with God's grace keep myself from either being an heretic in faith or schismatic in matters of policy. But of one thing I would have the Papists of this land to be admonished, that they presume not so much upon my lenity (because I would be loath to be thought a persecutor) as thereupon to think it lawful for them daily to increase their numbers and strength in this kingdom whereby, if not in my time at least in the time of my posterity, they might be in hope to erect their religion again. No, let them assure themselves that as I am a friend to their persons if they be good subjects, so am I a vowed enemy and do denounce mortal war to their errors; and that as I would be sorry to be driven by their ill behaviour from the protection and conservation of their bodies and lives, so will I never cease, as far as I can, to tread down their errors and wrong opinions. For I could not permit the increase and growing of their religion without, first, betraying of myself and mine own conscience; secondly, this whole isle, as well the part I come from as the part I remain in, in betraying their liberties and reducing them to the former slavish yoke which both had casten off before I came amongst them; and thirdly, the liberty of the Crown in my posterity, which I should leave again under a new slavery, having found it left free to me by my predecessors. And therefore would I wish all good subjects that are deceived with that corruption, first if they find any beginning of instinction[1] in themselves of knowledge and love to the truth, to foster the same by all lawful means and to beware of quenching the spirit that worketh within them; and if they can find as yet no motion tending that way, to be studious to read and confer with learned men and to use all such means as may further their resolution, assuring themselves that as long as they are disconformable in religion from us they cannot be but half my subjects, be able to do but half service, and I to want the best half of them, which is their souls.

*　　*　　*　　*　　*　　*

James I, *Works* (ed. of 1616), pp. 485–97.

[1] Instigation, prompting.

(2) Act for Commissioners of Union, 1604

An Act authorizing certain Commissioners of the Realm of England to treat with Commissioners of Scotland for the weal of both kingdoms

Whereas his most excellent Majesty hath been pleased, out of his great wisdom and judgment, not only to represent unto us by his own prudent and princely speech on the first day of this Parliament how much he desired (in regard of his inward and gracious affection to both the famous and ancient realms of England and Scotland, now united in allegiance and loyal subjection in his Royal Person to his Majesty and his posterity for ever) that by a speedy, mature, and sound deliberation such a further Union might follow as should make perfect that mutual love and uniformity of manners and customs which Almighty God in his Providence, for the strength and safety of both realms, hath already so far begun in apparent sight of all the world, but also hath vouchsafed to express many ways how far it is and ever shall be from his royal and sincere care and affection to the subjects of England to alter and innovate the fundamental and ancient laws, privileges, and good customs of this kingdom, whereby not only his regal authority but the people's security of lands, livings, and privileges (both in general and particular) are preserved and maintained, and by the abolishing or alteration of the which it is impossible but that present confusion will fall upon the whole state and frame of this kingdom. Forasmuch as his Majesty's humble, faithful, and loving subjects have not only conceived the weight of his Majesty's reasons, but apprehend to their unspeakable joy and comfort his plain, clear, and gracious intention to seek no other changes or alteration but of such particular, temporary, or indifferent manner of statutes and customs as may both prevent and extinguish all and every future questions or unhappy accidents by which the perfect and constant love and friendship and quietness between the subjects of both the realms aforesaid may be completed and confirmed, and also perform and accomplish that real and effectual Union already inherent in his Majesty's Royal Blood and Person, and now desired by his Majesty to be performed and brought to an end for the weal of both kingdoms by this course following: Be it therefore enacted by the King's most excellent Majesty, by and with the assent and consent of the Lords Spiritual and Temporal and the Commons in this present Parliament assembled and by authority of the same, [that certain Commissioners named in the Act]...shall by force

of this Act from and after the end of this present session of
Parliament have full power, liberty, commission, and authority at
any time or times before the next session of this Parliament to
assemble and meet, and thereupon to treat and consult with
certain selected Commissioners to be nominated and authorised
by authority of Parliament of the Realm of Scotland, according
to the tenor or purport of their authority or commission in that
behalf, of and concerning such an Union of the said Realms of
England and Scotland, and of and concerning such other matters,
causes, and things whatsoever as upon mature deliberation and
consideration [the said Commissioners]...shall in their wisdoms
think and deem convenient and necessary for the honour of his
Majesty and the weal and common good of both the said realms
during his Majesty's life (which Almighty God long preserve)
and under all his royal progeny and posterity for ever....

1 & 2 Jac. I, c. 2: Statutes of the Realm, iv, 1018.

(3) Proclamation of Union, 1604

Proclamatio pro Unione Regnorum Angliae et Scotiae

As often as we call to mind the most joyful and just recognition
made by the whole body of our realm in the first session of our
High Court of Parliament of that blessing which it hath pleased
God to reserve many years in his Providence to our person, and
now in the fullness of the time of his disposition to bestow upon
us, namely, the blessed Union, or rather reuniting, of these two
mighty, famous, and ancient kingdoms of England and Scotland
under one Imperial Crown, so often do we think that it is our
duty to do our uttermost endeavour for the advancement and
perfection of that work, which is of his beginning, and whereof
he hath given so many palpable signs and arguments as he that seeth
them not is blind and he that impugneth them doth but endeavour
to separate that which God hath put together. For to omit those
things which are evident to sense, that the isle within itself hath
almost none but imaginary bounds of separation, without but one
common limit, or rather guard, of the ocean sea, making the whole
a little world within itself; the nations an uniformity of constitutions, both of body and mind, especially in martial prowesses; a
community of language, the principal means of civil society; an
unity of religion, the chiefest band of hearty union and the surest
knot of lasting peace—what can be a more express testimony of
God's authority of this work than that two mighty nations, having
been ever from their first separation continually in blood each

against other, should for so many years immediately before our succession be at peace together, as it were to that end that their memory being free from sense of the smart of former injuries, their minds might in the time of God's appointment more willingly come together; that it hath pleased him so to dispose that this Union is not enforced by conquest and violence nor contracted by doubtful and deceivable points of transaction, but naturally derived from the right and title of the precedent princes of both kingdoms concurring in our person, alike lineally descended from the blood of both through the sacred conjunction of wedlock, an Union which is the work of God and Nature, and whereunto the works of force or policy cannot attain.

We may add hereunto that which we have received from those that be skilful in the laws of this land, that immediately upon our succession divers of the ancient laws of this realm are *ipso facto* expired.. . .

All which, being matter prepared only by the Providence of Almighty God, and which by human industry could not have been so ordered, we and all our subjects ought first with reverence to acknowledge his handiwork therein and to give him our most humble thanks for the same, and then to further by our endeavours that which his wisdom doth by so many signs point out to be his will, whereof many particularities depending upon the determinations of the States and Parliaments of both Realms, we leave them there to be discussed according to the commissions granted by the several Acts of both Parliaments; and some other things resting in our own imperial power as the Head of both, we are purposed towards the building of this excellent work to do by ourself that which justly and safely we may by our absolute power do; and for a first stone of this work, whereupon the rest may be laid, seeing there is undoubtedly but one Head to both peoples, which is ourself, and that unfeignedly we have but one heart and mind to communicate equally to both States, as lines issuing from one centre, our justice, our favours, and whatsoever else dependeth upon the unity of our supreme power over both, God having ministered to us so just cause to embrace them both with equal and indifferent love, inasmuch as our birth and first part of our life hath been in the one and the later part thereof is like to be for the most part in the other, we think it unreasonable that the thing which is by the work of God and Nature so much in effect one should not be one in name, unity in name being so fit a means to imprint in the hearts of people a character and memorial of that unity which ought to be amongst them indeed.

Wherefore we have thought good to discontinue the divided names of England and Scotland out of our regal style, and do intend and resolve to take and assume unto us, in manner and form hereafter expressed, the name and style of King of Great Britain, including therein, according to the truth, the whole island, wherein no man can imagine us to be led by any humour of vainglory or ambition, because we should in that case rather delight in a long enumeration of many kingdoms and seignories, whereof in our inheritance we have plenty enough if we thought there were glory in that kind of style, but only that we use it as a signification of that which in part is already done, and significant prefiguration of that which is to be done hereafter; nor that we covet any new-affected name devised at our pleasure, but out of undoubted knowledge do use the true and ancient name which God and time have imposed upon this Isle, extant and received in histories, in all maps and cartes[1] wherein this Isle is described, and in ordinary letters to ourself from divers foreign princes, warranted also by authentical charters, exemplifications under seals, and other records of great antiquity giving us precedent for our doing, not borrowed out of foreign nations but from the acts of our progenitors, Kings of this Realm of England, both before and since the Conquest, having not had so just and great cause as we have.

Upon all which considerations we do by these presents, by force of our kingly power and prerogative, assume to ourself by the clearness of our right the name and style of King of Great Britain, France, and Ireland, Defender of the Faith, etc., as followeth, in our just and lawful title, and do hereby publish, promulge, and declare the same, to the end that in all our proclamations, missive foreign and domestical, treaties, leagues, dedicatories[2], impressions[3], and in all other causes of like nature, the same may be used and observed.

And to the end the same may be the sooner and more universally divulged both at home and abroad, our will and pleasure is, that the style be from henceforth used upon all inscriptions upon our current moneys and coins of gold and silver hereafter to be minted.

And for that we do not innovate or assume to us any new thing but declare that which is and hath been evident to all, our will and pleasure is, that in such appellations or nominations as shall be hereafter made by force of these presents, the same shall be expressed in such and the same manner and form and after

---

[1] *I.e.* charts or maps.   [2] *I.e.* dedicatory addresses.   [3] Seals.

such computation as if we had assumed and declared the same the first day of our reign of our Realm of England; forbearing only for the present that anything herein contained do extend to any legal proceeding, instrument, or assurance until further order be taken in that behalf.

Given at our Palace of Westminster the twentieth day of October. *Per ipsum Regem.*

Rymer, Foedera, xvi, 603.

(4) James I on the Union with Scotland, 1607

This speech was delivered 31 March, 1607, on the adjournment of the Houses for the recess. It is one of the King's best efforts, and 'but few traces' are to be seen in it of 'that petulance by which his speeches were usually disfigured' (Gardiner, i, 337).

*   *   *   *   *   *

For myself, I protest unto you all when I first propounded the Union I thought there could have been no more question of it than of your declaration and acknowledgment of my right unto this Crown, and that as two twins they would have grown up together. The error was my mistaking; I knew mine own end but not others' fears. But now, finding many crossings, long disputations, strange questions, and nothing done, I must needs think it proceeds either of mistaking of the errand, or else from some jealousy of me the propounder, that you so add delay unto delay, searching out as it were the very bowels of curiosity, and conclude nothing.

*   *   *   *   *   *

I desire a perfect union of laws and persons, and such a naturalizing as may make one body of both kingdoms under me your King, that I and my posterity (if it so please God) may rule over you to the world's end....For no more possible is it for one King to govern two countries contiguous, the one a great the other a less, a richer and a poorer, the greater drawing like an adamant the lesser to the commodities thereof, than for one head to govern two bodies or one man to be husband of two wives, whereof Christ himself said, *ab initio non fuit sic.*

But in the general union you must observe two things, for I will discover my thoughts plainly unto you; I study clearness, not eloquence. And therefore with the old philosophers I would heartily wish my breast were a transparent glass for you all to see through, that you might look into my heart and then would you be satisfied of my meaning. For when I speak of a perfect union, I mean not confusion of all things: you must not take from

3-2

Scotland those particular privileges that may stand as well with this union as in England many particular customs in particular shires (as the customs of Kent and the royalties of the County Palatine of Chester) do with the common law of the kingdom, for every particular shire almost, and much more every county[1], have some particular customs that are as it were naturally most fit for that people. But I mean of such a general union of laws as may reduce the whole island, that as they live already under one monarch, so they may all be governed by one law.

* * * * * *

There is a conceit entertained, and a double jealousy possesseth many, wherein I am misjudged.

First, that this union will be the crisis to the overthrow of England and setting up of Scotland; England will then be overwhelmed by the swarming of the Scots, who if the union were effected would reign and rule all.

The second is, my profuse liberality to the Scottish men more than the English, and that with this union all things shall be given to them and you turned out of all; to you shall be left the sweat and labour, to them shall be given the fruit and sweet; and that my forbearance is but till this union may be gained.... Some think that I will draw the Scottish nation hither, talking idly of transporting of trees out of a barren ground into a better, and of lean cattle out of bad pasture into a more fertile soil. Can any man displant you unless you will? or can any man think Scotland is so strong to pull you out of your houses? or do you not think I know England hath more people, Scotland more waste ground?

* * * * * *

For the manner of the union presently desired, it standeth in three parts. The first, taking away of hostile laws, for since there can be now no wars betwixt you, is it not reason hostile laws should cease?... The second is community of commerce.... For the third point, of naturalization, all you agree that they are no aliens, and yet will not allow them to be natural.

* * * * * *

And for my part, when I have two nations under my government, can you imagine I will respect the lesser and neglect the greater? Would I not think it a less evil and hazard to me that the plague were at Northampton or Berwick than at London, so near Westminster, the seat of my habitation and of my wife and

---

[1] 'County' must be used here in the sense of 'county palatine'; hence the contrast to 'shire.'

children? Will not a man be more careful to quench the fire taken in his nearest neighbour's house than if a whole town were afire far from him? You know that I am careful to preserve the woods and game through all England, nay, through all the isle; yet none of you doubts but that I would be more offended with any disorder in the Forest of Waltham for stealing of a stag there, which lieth as it were under my nose and in a manner joineth with my garden, than with cutting of timber or stealing of a deer in any forest of the north parts of Yorkshire or the Bishopric[1]. Think you that I will prefer them that be absent, less powerful, and farther off to do me good or hurt, before you with whom my security and living must be and where I desire to plant my posterity? If I might by any such favours raise myself to a greatness, it might be probable. All I cannot draw, and to lose a whole State here to please a few there were madness. I need speak no more of this with protestations. Speak but of wit, it is not likely; and to doubt of my intention in this were more than devilish.

*   *   *   *   *   *

Now to conclude, I am glad of this occasion, that I might *liberare animam meam*. You are now to recede[2]; when you meet again remember, I pray you, the truth and sincerity of my meaning, which in seeking union is only to advance the greatness of your empire seated here in England; and yet with such caution I wish it as may stand with the weal of both States. What is now desired hath oft before been sought when it could not be obtained; to refuse it now, then, were double iniquity. Strengthen your own felicity; London must be the seat of your King, and Scotland joined to this kingdom by a golden conquest but cemented with love (as I said before), which within will make you strong against all civil and intestine rebellion, as without we will be compassed and guarded with our walls of brass. Judge me charitably, since in this I seek your equal good, that so both of you might be made fearful to your enemies, powerful in yourselves, and available to your friends. Study therefore hereafter to make a good conclusion, avoid all delays, cut off all vain questions, that your King may have his lawful desire and be not disgraced in his just ends. And for your security in such reasonable points of restrictions whereunto I am to agree, ye need never doubt of my inclination; for I will not say anything which I will not promise, nor promise anything which I will not swear; what I swear I will sign, and what I sign I shall, with God's grace, ever perform.

James I, *Works* (edition of 1616), pp. 509–25.

[1] *I.e.* the Bishopric of Durham.   [2] Depart.

(5) Act for the Removal of Hostility, 1607

An Act for the utter abolition of all memory of hostility and the dependences thereof between England and Scotland, and for the repressing of occasions of discord and disorders in time to come

I. For the honour, weal, and good of these two mighty, famous, and ancient Kingdoms of England and Scotland, and for the furtherance and advancement of the happy Union already begun in his Majesty's Royal Person: Be it enacted by the King's most excellent Majesty with the assent of the Lords Spiritual and Temporal and the Commons in this present Parliament assembled and by the authority of the same, That one Act made in the fourth year of the reign of King Henry the Fifth, whereby it is enacted that letters of marque or reprisal be granted against the people of Scotland in case where the subjects of England have been spoiled and have complained and not received redress, shall for so much thereof as so concerneth the people of Scotland be utterly repealed and made void; and also that one proviso contained in an Act made in the three and thirtieth year of the reign of King Henry the Eighth, by which proviso the King's Majesty's subjects inhabiting within twelve miles of the Borders of Scotland are allowed and permitted to use cross-bows, hand-guns, hackbuts, or demihakes[1], or to use or keep in his or their houses or elsewhere any such cross-bows, hand-guns, hackbuts, and demihakes, for so much of the said proviso as so concerneth such as shall inhabit within twelve miles of the said late Borders, shall be utterly repealed and made void.

II. And be it further enacted by the authority aforesaid, That these other Statutes hereafter following, that is to say, One Act made in the seventh year of the reign of King Richard the Second whereby it is enacted that no armour, victual, or other refreshment be carried into Scotland upon pain of seizure or forfeiture; And one other Act made in the one and thirtieth year of the reign of King Henry the Sixth whereby it is enacted that March Law be not used out of the circuit of the counties of Northumberland, Cumberland, and Westmorland, or the Town of Newcastle; And one other Statute made in the seventh year of the reign of King Henry the Seventh whereby it is enacted that Scottishmen should avoid out of the Realm of England within a time prefixed; And one other Statute made in the three and twentieth year of the reign of King Henry the Eighth; And a

---

[1] A hackbut was a portable gun, and a demihake was a smaller kind of hackbut.

like Statute made in the first year of the reign of the late Queen Elizabeth whereby the conveying of horses out of England into Scotland is made felony; And one other Statute made in the second and third years of the reign of King Philip and Queen Mary; And the like Statute made in the three and twentieth year of the reign of the late Queen Elizabeth whereby it is enacted that no lands or tenements be let to Scottishmen upon the Borders; shall be utterly abrogated, repealed, and made void: And if there had appeared any other Statute of this Realm of England wherein anything is ordained, enacted, or established expressly and by name against Scottishmen as enemies, or Scotland as an enemy country, to the Kings of this Realm or the State of the same, we should for so much of them as had so concerned Scottishmen or Scotland have utterly abrogated and adnulled the same, seeing all enmity and hostility of former times between the two Kingdoms and people is now happily taken away, and under the government of his Majesty, as under one parent and head, turned into fraternity or brotherly friendship.

III. Provided nevertheless and be it enacted by the authority of this present Parliament, That none of the articles, branches, or clauses abovesaid in this Act before contained and expressed shall take effect or be in force or in any wise be deemed or expounded to take effect or be in force to any intent, construction, or purpose until these Acts of Parliament of the Realm of Scotland hereafter following, that is to say, One Act made in the time of James the First, King of Scotland, by which it was enacted that all persons remaining in England without the King's licence did commit treason; One other Act made in the time of the said King James the First whereby any assurance with Englishmen for taking protection from them for lands or goods is treason; One other Act in the same King's time inhibiting all buying and selling of English goods forbidden, under pain of escheat; One other Act made in the time of James the Second, King of Scotland, that none should pass into England in time of war without licence, under pain of treason; One other Act made in the reign of the said King James the Second, containing that no Englishman come into Scotland without conduct, and that no Scottishman sit under assurance with them; One other Act of the same King's time, that no Scottishman supply Berwick or Roxburgh, under pain of treason; One other Act made in the time of the said King James the Second, that all men be ready for defence of the Realm against England; Two Acts made in the time of James the Third, King of Scotland, for resisting King Edward the Fourth; One other Act made in the time of the said King James the Third concerning the upholding of Berwick and garrisons upon the Borders; One Act made in the reign of Mary late Queen of Scotland by which it was enacted that Scottishmen are charged to leave assurance with Englishmen; One other Act made in the time of the said Queen Mary concerning assured Scottishmen assisting the English army; One Act made in the Parliament of Scotland in the time of the most happy reign of our most gracious Sovereign Lord the King that now is, containing that the Scottish Borderers are discharged[1] to marry English Borderers' daughters; And lastly, one other Act made in the time of our said Sovereign Lord the King, enjoining the Warden to put in a bill the names of all Englishmen that occupy lands in Scotland and seek redress according to the Treaties; shall by Act of Parliament of the said Realm of Scotland be utterly repealed, frustrate, and made void; And until also the said Parliament of the Realm of Scotland shall by their said Act make as full and ample declaration concerning their clear intention and desire of repeal of all other hostile laws of their part not before mentioned, if they were known, as on the part of this Realm of England hath been in this present Act made and expressed.

IV. And be it further enacted by the authority aforesaid, That one Act made in the fifth year of King Richard the Second concerning the restraint of passage of his Majesty's subjects out of this Realm, and every ordinance, provision, article, or clause therein contained, shall be from henceforth utterly repealed.

V. And be it further enacted by the authority of this present Parliament, That no person or persons whatsoever, subject of either Realm, shall be punished, sued, delivered, or remanded, or any way troubled or called in question for life, member, damage, recompense, restitution, or other satisfaction whatsoever, for or by reason of any offences, spoils, wrongs, or trespasses (before the decease of the late Queen Elizabeth of famous memory) which were determinable by the laws or constitutions of the Borders within the courts and jurisdiction of the late Wardens or other-wise, which purported actions of hostility by the sea or land by him or them committed, or whereunto he or they were accessories before or after such offence or fact committed, or privy or aiding to the same, or for or in respect whereof he or they were or are pledged, or otherwise by any way or means whatsoever answerable or chargeable, or else stand charged or chargeable with any promise, contract, bill, bond, bills filed, sentence, decree, or other

---

[1] *I.e.* forbidden.

assurances given or taken for the same only, or for so much only, or such other assurances as was given or is in force for that cause and no other.

VI. And forasmuch as no abolition of hostile laws, or of the memory of hostility or of suit and controversies thereupon depending, can presently and at once extirpate and reform those inveterate evil customs and disorders, as well of feuds and blood as of theft and spoils, wherewith the worst sort of inhabitants near the limits of both Realms were infected and inured[1] although by his Majesty's incessant care and princely policy those parts be already reduced to a more civil and peaceable estate than could in short time have been expected: And whereas experience teacheth that the malefactors of either Realm having committed their offences in the other Realm do forthwith fly and escape many times into their own country, thereby to purchase their impunity, to the great and manifest grievances of the one Realm and the dishonour of the other: And whereas in regard of some difference and inequality in the laws, trials, and proceedings in cases of life between the justice of the Realm of England and that of the Realm of Scotland, it appeareth to be most convenient for the contentment and satisfaction of all his Majesty's subjects to proceed with all possible severity against offenders in their own country according to the laws of the same whereunto they are born and inheritable and by and before the natural born subjects of the same Realm if they shall be there apprehended: Be it therefore enacted by the authority aforesaid, That all offences of conjuration, witchcraft, and dealing with evil and wicked spirits, murder, manslaughter, felonious burning of houses and corn, burglary, robbing of houses by day, robbery, theft...and rape heretofore done and committed since his Majesty's coming to the Crown of England, or hereafter to be done or committed, by any his Majesty's natural born subjects of this Realm of England or the Dominions of the same within the Realm of Scotland and the Dominions thereof, and the accessories of and to the same, shall be from henceforth enquired thereof, heard, and determined before his Majesty's Justices of Assize or his Commissioners of Oyer and Terminer or Gaol Delivery, being natural born subjects within this Realm of England and none other, by good and lawful men of the counties of Cumberland, Northumberland, Westmorland, or any of the said counties at the election of the said Justices of Assizes or Commissioners, in like manner and form to all intents and purposes...as if such offences had been

---

[1] Accustomed.

done and committed within the same shire where they shall be so enquired of, heard, and determined as is aforesaid; At which trials, for the better discovery of the truth and for the better information of the consciences of the jury and Justices, there shall be allowed unto the party so arraigned the benefit of such witnesses only to be examined upon oath that can be produced for his better clearing and justification as hereafter in this Act are permitted and allowed.

*   *   *   *   *   *

XI. And forasmuch as it is intended that an Act like unto this shall be ordained in the Realm of Scotland for the trial and punishment of offenders, being his Majesty's natural born subjects of the same Realm, which shall commit any of the offences aforesaid within the Realm of England or the Dominions thereof, and shall after[1] escape or return back into Scotland: Be it therefore enacted by the authority aforesaid, That upon complaint made by any his Majesty's subjects of the Realm of England to any of the Justices of Assize, Commissioners of Oyer and Terminer or Gaol Delivery, or Justice of the Peace within the precincts of their several commissions respectively, being natural born subjects within the Realm of England, concerning any such offence committed by any his subjects of the Realm of Scotland within the Realm of England in case where the offender is returned into the Realm of Scotland as aforesaid, the said Justice or Commissioner shall have full power and authority to bind over as well the said party complaining or prosecuting as any witness that he shall desire to produce (so as their reasonable charges be first tendered unto them) by recognizance in a convenient sum to his Majesty's use to prosecute and give in evidence within the Realm of Scotland; wherein if default shall be made, and the same proved by certificate or otherwise before the Lord Treasurer, Chancellor, and Barons of the Exchequer, or any of them, in the Exchequer Chamber, and a decree there made that the same recognizance shall stand forfeited, then the Court of Exchequer shall thereupon proceed for the levying of the debt of the said recognizance as if it were adjudged forfeited by the course of the Common Law.

XII. And be it further enacted by the authority aforesaid, That on the other part, every of his Majesty's subjects of the Realm of Scotland, either party grieved or witness, which shall prosecute in any the cases aforesaid within the Realm of England, and thereby shall have occasion to make his repair hither, either

[1] Afterwards.

voluntary or by the like bond as is before expressed on the part of the Realm of England, shall have and enjoy privilege and immunity from all manner of arrests concerning all offences or other causes, as well capital as others, committed, done, or occasioned before he shall so come into England as aforesaid (except treason or wilful murder) so long as he or they shall be necessarily going, coming, or abiding within the said Realm of England for the prosecution of the said offenders.

XIII. Provided nevertheless, That every such offence so committed as aforesaid shall be laid and alleged in the indictment or other declaration to be done and committed in the Realm of Scotland according to the truth of the fact, and not in the counties where the trial is limited to be had and made as aforesaid; Anything in this Act formerly contained to the contrary notwithstanding.

XIV. Provided also and be it further enacted, That if any his Majesty's subjects of the Realm of Scotland shall be proceeded with and tried in the Realm of Scotland upon the prosecution of any party grieved and upon evidence in open court for any offence done or committed within the Realm of England, that no such person shall be eftsoons[1] called in question or proceeded with for the same fact within the Realm of England; but that it shall be lawful for every such person to plead and allege for himself upon his arraignment that he was formerly lawfully acquitted, convicted, or attainted of the same offence within the Realm of Scotland, and that thereupon all further proceedings shall stay until the Court have sufficiently informed themselves, by certificate from the Realm of Scotland or by any other good ways and means, of the truth of the said allegations, which if they shall find true, the said person shall be forthwith discharged of all further impeachment or proceedings.

*   *   *   *   *   *   *

4 & 5 Jac. I, c. 1: *Statutes of the Realm*, iv, 1134.

(6) Act for the better Execution of Justice, 1610

An Act for the better Execution of Justice and suppressing of criminal offenders in the North Parts of the Kingdom of England

I. Whereas in a Statute made in the third session of this present Parliament, entituled An Act for the utter abolition of all memory of hostility and the dependences thereof between England and Scotland, and for the repressing of occasions of discords and

---

[1] *I.e.* a second time.

disorders in time to come, it was amongst other things enacted
that no natural born subject of the Realm of England or the
Dominions of the same should for any high treason, misprison or
concealment of high treason, petty treason, or any other whatsoever offence or cause committed within Scotland, be sent out of
England where he is apprehended to receive his trial until such
time as both Realms should be made one in laws and government,
which is the thing so much desired as that wherein the full
perfection of the blessed Union already begun in his Majesty's
Royal Person consisteth: Since the making of which Statute,
although those parts of the Kingdom of England adjoining and
lying near unto the Realm and Kingdom of Scotland have been
and are by his Majesty's incessant care and princely policy
reduced to a more civil and peaceable estate than could in short
time have been expected or hoped for; yet experience teacheth
that malefactors of either Realm having committed their offences in
the other Realm do forthwith fly and escape into their own country
thereby to purchase their impunity, to the great and manifest
grievance of the one Realm and the dishonour of the other: By
means whereof very many great and heinous offences since the
making of the said Statute have been and are still likely to be
committed without condign punishment; for that since the making
of the said Statute there hath not been any one offender committing
any the offences aforesaid in Scotland that hath been prosecuted
to his trial, judgment, or execution in England by reason or upon
any the branches, laws, or ordinances in the said Statute mentioned
or contained: Whereby it manifestly appeareth that the said
clause in the said Statute contained, and before in this present
Act expressly mentioned, concerning the not sending out of
England any natural born subject of the Realm or Dominions of
the same for any whatsoever offence committed within the Realm
of Scotland to receive his trial for any the said offences, hath not
brought forth that good effect as was hoped for and by the said
law intended, to the great prejudice and dishonour of both Realms:
For the preventing of which apparent and too manifest mischief
and inconvenience be it enacted and by the authority of this
present Parliament established, That if at any time or times after
the end of this present session of Parliament any person or persons
shall commit any offence or offences within the Realm of Scotland
which by the laws of this Realm of England is, are, or shall be
declared or adjudged to be petty treason, murder, manslaughter,
felonious burning of houses and corn, burglary, robbing of houses
by day, robbery, theft, or rape, and do or shall fly or escape into

the Realm of England, and be or shall be apprehended within any the counties of Northumberland, Cumberland, Westmorland, or any parts or members of the same, or within the parts or places lying on the north side of the River of Tyne commonly called or known by the names of Bedlingtonshire, Norhamshire, and Islandshire, the Town and County of Newcastle upon Tyne, and the Town of Berwick upon Tweed, with the bounds and liberties thereof, that then it shall and may be lawful to and for the Justices of Assize or any one of them in the absence of the other, the Justices of Gaol Delivery at their gaol delivery or any four of them, or the Justices of Peace in their General or Quarter Sessions or any four of them, upon due and mature examination of the said offence or offences in open sessions and pregnant proofs of the same, by warrant under their hands and seals to remand and send all and every such offender and offenders into the Realm of Scotland, there to receive their trial for any the offences aforesaid by them there committed; Anything in the said Statute contained to the contrary thereof notwithstanding; This law to continue to the end of the first session of the next Parliament.

II. Provided nevertheless and be it enacted by the authority aforesaid, That [neither] this Statute nor any clause therein contained shall take effect...until a law by Act of Parliament be made and established within the Realm of Scotland for the remanding and sending out of the Realm of Scotland into the Realm of England all and every person and persons born within the Realm of Scotland or the Dominions of the same which shall at any time hereafter commit any the offences aforesaid within the Realm of England, to receive his and their trial in the Realm of England for all and every the said offences by them committed in the said Realm of England.

7 & 8 Jac. I, c. 1: *Statutes of the Realm*, iv, 1156.

Religion

'It is observable in the House of Commons, as their whole story gives it,' wrote Sir John Eliot[1], who knew the House better than any politician of the day except Pym, 'that wherever that mention does break forth of the fears or dangers in religion, and the increase of popery, their affections are much stirred; and whatever is obnoxious in the State, it then is reckoned as an incident to that.' This is visible in the sphere of foreign policy [p. 276], for in the seventeenth century most problems of foreign policy had a religious character, and the foreign policy of the Stuarts sometimes appeared to their Parliaments to imperil Protestantism. It also appears in connexion with a new internal religious discord in which the Crown appeared to Parliament to be taking the wrong side.

§ 1. Puritans and Arminians

On James I's accession, Puritanism in the narrower sense—the rejection of the Prayer Book as a whole, and the complete repudiation of episcopal authority—was only represented by a small minority in the country; but Puritanism in the wider sense—the Puritanism which asked for a further reformation of doctrine and ritual than Elizabeth had been willing to allow—was the creed of the greater part of the members of the Church of England itself. Nor was this at all surprising, for the system of doctrine and the system of discipline associated with Puritanism were the result of the necessity that Protestantism should be systematised[2]. If Protestantism was to fight Rome, it must be something more positive and coherent than a mere negation of Rome; and it acquired coherence through the work of Calvin, who 'shaped the mould in which the bronze of Puritanism was cast,' and 'by his unbending will, his pride, his severity, his French spirit of system, his gift for government, for legislation, for dialectic in every field, his incomparable industry and persistence, had conquered a more than pontifical ascendency in the Protestant world.'[3] The spirit of Calvinism had permeated deeply the Church of Elizabeth, and Hooker himself adhered generally to Calvin's doctrine of election and always spoke of him with respect[4]. We might apply to the public teaching of the Church of Elizabeth some words of Fuller's written in a different connexion: 'The pulpit spake pure Canterbury in the morning, and Geneva in the afternoon.'[5] Thus it had come about that the doctrinal system of Calvin had been very generally taught, both at Cambridge and Oxford, to the rising generation of parish clergy[6], and although his system of discipline had proved unsuitable to the temper of the English people and had failed to take any root, great numbers of religious men

---

[1] John Forster, *Sir John Eliot* (edition of 1872), i, 145.
[2] S. R. Gardiner, *Cromwell's Place in History*, p. 107.
[3] John Morley, *Oliver Cromwell*, p. 47.
[4] *D.N.B.* xxvii, 290.
[5] *Worthies* (ed. P. A. Nuttall, 1840), i, 423.
[6] G. M. Trevelyan, *England under the Stuarts*, p. 148.

accepted the doctrine which Calvin had stated, almost as if it were self-evident: that by the decree of God and for the manifestation of His glory some men are predestinated to everlasting life and others fore-ordained to eternal death[1].

But when the days of storm and stress were over—when Protestantism had vindicated its position—it was inevitable that the iron system from the shelter of which the Reformers had defied Rome should now appear to some thinkers in a new light—as a prison confining religious thought and as a check to the free development of religious life. There were many who declined, in time of peace, to live in a fortress under martial law; and thus in the early seventeenth century a new tendency in religion begins to make its appearance in England. The leader of the new school—at any rate in the realm of thought—was Lancelot Andrewes, whose controversial writings 'laid the foundation of the Anglican position' as the seventeenth century understood it[2]. He, and those who followed him, contended that the accepted Calvinistic doctrines were not the doctrines of the Prayer Book, and were therefore not the doctrines of the Church of England. They were disposed to fall back instead to the theology of the early days of the Reformation, before Calvinism had gathered strength—to the view of Cranmer, that nothing must be rejected which was supported by the custom and practice of the Early Church. This appeal to primitive antiquity was the special characteristic of the work of Andrewes, and he applied it, not only to doctrine but also to the worship in which the doctrine was embodied and expressed, for he attached himself to external rites 'as influencing the spiritual conscience, and mellowing the ironclad reasoning of the Calvinistic preacher.'[3] Thus the new interest in early practices, combined with a reawakening of the artistic taste which Calvinism had stifled, led to the revival of a number of Church ceremonies which, under the influence of Calvinism, had fallen into disuse. To this revolt against Calvinism in England a name was given which was drawn from the history of a similar revolt against Calvinism abroad. The Dutch theologian Arminius had preached in opposition to the more rigid of Calvin's doctrines, and those who followed him were called Arminians. From the point of view of doctrine—if we care to use technical terms—Arminianism met Predestination by Free Will; implacable Necessity by merciful Contingency; Man the Machine by Man the Self-determining Agent[4]. From the point of view of worship, at any rate in England, it meant a ceremonial revival in the Church.

According to the Elizabethan theory of the Constitution, this new movement in the Church was the business of the ecclesiastical supremacy—certainly not of Parliament as a whole, and least of all of the House of Commons—but it was clearly a matter with which Government was concerned. In that age it was unthinkable that there should be more than one Church; the discussion centred on the question in whose hands the one

---

[1] 'No one who wishes to think piously will dare simply to deny that predestination by which God adopts some to hope of life and adjudges others to eternal death.... For not all are created to a like condition; *sed aliis vita aeterna, aliis damnatio praeordinatur.*' (Quoted in A. S. Duncan-Jones, *Archbishop Laud*, p. 23.)

[2] W. H. Hutton, in Traill, *Social England*, iv, 25.

[3] Gardiner, *Cromwell*, p. 108.   [4] Morley, *Cromwell*, p. 53.

Church should be. 'Only on the minds of a few lonely thinkers or hunted sectaries had the idea of religious liberty as yet dawned.'[1] Every religious party held that the ideal of the Church was inseparably bound up with the ideal of the rightly ordered State[2], and coercion in religion was applied as a matter of course. The difficulty of the situation was that the Crown and the Parliament were coming to belong to opposite religious parties; for while Parliament was Puritan and Calvinist, the Crown was Arminian. Even James I was disposed to favour the Arminians: it is said that in his reign a courtier with a taste for theological enquiry once asked 'what the Arminians held,' whereupon someone replied that they 'held' all the best bishoprics and deaneries in the kingdom[3]. The position of Charles I may be inferred from the fact that when Archbishop Abbot died in 1633—an ecclesiastic 'stiffly principled' in Puritan doctrines, who saw in the bishops only a superintending pastorate, and not a separate order in the Church[4]—he replaced him by the most famous of the followers of Lancelot Andrewes—William Laud. And this was not all; not only was Laud himself an Arminian, but unlike Bishop Andrewes, who never forced his ceremonies upon others, 'content,' as Fuller said, 'with the enjoying without the enjoining,'[5] he was prepared to go all lengths to establish the Arminian character of the English Church. And in this he was supported by the Crown, for Charles I naturally adopted the universal principle of Europe—that the subject ought to be of the same religion as his sovereign—naturally, because this was the doctrine of his day and after his day; it survived the civil wars, was the main principle of the policy of James II, and was only abandoned when the Revolution of 1688 laid down the converse principle, that the sovereign should be of the same religion as his subjects, and England being Protestant should be governed by a Protestant prince.

It may be convenient to sum up here the principal points of controversy between Arminianism and Calvinism—or, to put it in a different way, between that tendency of thought in the Church which is called Anglican and the other tendency of later origin and wider diffusion which is called Puritan—between those who appealed to the Bible as interpreted by primitive antiquity and those who appealed to the Bible interpreted literally and exactly as it stood.

(1) The great ordinance of Puritanism was preaching, while the great ordinances of Anglicanism were the Sacraments. This difference in their conception of religious life was not a novelty of the seventeenth century, but had its roots further back, in the reign of Elizabeth. The Queen herself hated preaching, and she had a short way with preachers. On Ash Wednesday, 1565, she went to Paul's Cross to hear the Dean of St Paul's preach. The Dean had not proceeded far in his sermon, when he came to the subject of images, which, we are told, he 'handled roughly.' 'Leave that alone,' Elizabeth called from her seat. The preacher did not hear, and went on with his sermon. 'To your text, Mr Dean,' she shouted, 'To your text. Leave that. We have had enough of that.' The Dean was so confused at the interruption that he was not able to go on with his sermon. Archbishop

---

[1] Goldwin Smith, i, 432.   [2] Morley, *Cromwell*, p. 54.
[3] John Hunt, *Religious Thought in England*, i, 148.
[4] *D.N.B.* i, 6.   [5] *Church History* (edition of 1837), iii, 349.

Parker, seeing him 'utterly dismayed,' took him 'for pity home to Lambeth to dinner.'[1] On the other hand it was one of the notable achievements of the Puritan party in Elizabeth's reign that it succeeded in reviving preaching. The Puritans complained bitterly of 'dumb ministers' and the Puritan clergy carefully cultivated the art. The paralysis of the pulpit which was one of the earlier effects of the Reformation was cured by them, and they reaped their reward. Man cannot live by bread alone, and power over the common people fell to the Puritans rather than to the Anglicans. 'What won them most repute,' says Fuller[2], 'was their ministers' painful preaching in populous places; it being observed in England that those who hold the helm of the pulpit always steer people's hearts as they please.' On the other hand one of the preoccupations of authority was the regulation of preaching, and in 1622 James I issued detailed regulations with regard to it [p. 80].

Out of this arose very naturally (2) the Altar Controversy—whether the altar should stand 'tablewise,' in the middle of the church, where men sometimes put their hats upon it, or used it as a writing-table on which to transact parish business; or 'altarwise,' at the east end of the church, covered, and railed about. Connected with this great fundamental question were a number of minor disputes upon various points of ceremonial; and thus, as Bishop Creighton once remarked in another connexion, 'the unfortunate legacy of fighting great principles over outward trifles was bequeathed to the English Church.'[3]

(3) Last of all, the Sabbatarian Controversy [p. 52] is vastly more important than it appears to be at first sight. The fundamental conflict was after all between those who contended for the exclusive authority of the Bible and those who contended for the co-ordinate authority of the Church[4]. This expressed itself in worship when one side argued that no ceremonies might be imposed which were not authorised by the Bible, and the other side maintained that such ceremonies might be imposed by the authority of the Church, provided that they were not in opposition to the spirit of the Bible teaching. It was only another application of their principle when the Puritans claimed for Sunday the characteristics of the Jewish Sabbath, and a Puritan House of Commons in 1621 expelled the member for Shaftesbury for maintaining that the Sabbath meant Saturday, and for pointing out with reference to the legality of dancing, that David danced before the ark[5]. In this matter, as in many others, the Crown declared itself to be anti-Puritan, and in 1618 James I issued a declaration [p. 54]) (which was afterwards embodied in the 'Book of Sports' and commanded it to be read in churches. The Puritan point of view upon this question is indicated by Milton, who accused the bishops of plucking men 'from their soberest and saddest thoughts,' to 'gaming, jigging, wassailing, and mixed dancing,' as did 'the reprobate hireling priest Balaam' draw the Israelites 'from the sanctuary of God to the luxurious and ribald feasts of Baal-peor.'[6]

[1] The story is told in J. A. Froude, *The Reign of Elizabeth* (Everyman Library), i, 472.
[2] *Church History*, iii, 101.   [3] *Queen Elizabeth*, p. 129.
[4] W. H. Frere, *A History of the English Church* 1558–1625, p. 322.
[5] *Commons' Journals*, i. 521, 524–5.
[6] *Of Reformation in England*, Book ii.

The first Parliament of the reign of James met on 19 March, 1604, but trouble was already brewing in the sphere of religion. The Puritan party within the Church of England had a strong hold upon the nation; and soon after the new King's accession the leading clergy of this school made an attempt to obtain from James what Elizabeth had always denied them—a further reformation in doctrine and worship. Their views were set out in the Millenary Petition [p. 56]—so called because a thousand clergy were supposed to have signed it. This Petition, which was the more important because it really emanated, as it professed to do, not from 'factious men, affecting a popular parity in the Church,' nor from 'schismatics aiming at the dissolution of the State ecclesiastical,' but from 'faithful servants of Christ and loyal subjects' of the King—made certain moderate demands which were assigned to four heads: (1) Modifications in *ceremonial*, the most important of which were: the discontinuance of the use of the sign of the cross in baptism, of confirmation, of the ring in marriage, and of the use of the terms 'priest' and 'absolution'; the wearing of the surplice 'not to be urged'; 'church songs and music moderated to better edification'; and the 'long-someness' of the service 'abridged.' (2) *Preaching*: the abridging of the service was only to make more room for the sermon, and in accordance with the Puritan conception of its importance, the petitioners prayed that none be hereafter admitted to the ministry but 'able and sufficient men, and those to preach diligently, and especially upon the Lord's Day.' (3) *Livings*: that bishops be not allowed to hold livings *in commendam* with their bishoprics; and that 'double-beneficed men' be not allowed. (4) *Church discipline*: that excommunication should not be in the name of lay officials; that 'men be not excommunicated for trifles and twelvepenny matters'; that the delays of ecclesiastical courts be restrained; and that 'the oath *ex officio*, whereby men are forced to accuse themselves, be more sparingly used.' The petitioners also asked for greater strictness in keeping the Sabbath.

Bacon, whose statesmanship enabled him to perceive the danger that lay in a breach between the Crown and the Commons[1], was in favour of concessions to the Puritans in order to preserve the unity of English religious life. And James himself, always disposed to be tolerant, read the Petition with sympathy, and called a Conference on 14 January, 1604, at Hampton Court [p. 60], at which a deputation of the Puritan clergy met the bishops and argued the question of Church reform with them in the King's own presence. The ecclesiastical supremacy, regarded hitherto as a defence against Puritan innovations, was deeply concerned in the controversy, and the ultimate decision rested with the theologian on the throne, who took the keenest interest in the discussions. One of the disputants at the Conference incautiously used the word 'presbytery,' and James, rich in experience of Scotland, at once put himself in a passion. 'A Scottish Presbytery,' he said, inverting in his wrath the proper order of the comparison, 'a Scottish Presbytery...agreeth as well with a monarchy as God and the Devil. Then Jack and Tom and Will and Dick shall meet, and at their pleasures censure me and my Council....Stay, I pray you, for one seven years, before you demand that of me; and if then you find me pursy and fat, and my wind-pipes stuffed, I will perhaps hearken unto you.' The bishops were delighted, and

---

[1] See *D.N.B.* ii, 336.

one of them[1] said that 'his Majesty spake by the instinct of the spirit of God.'
The King himself was no less pleased, and in a letter written the day after the
Conference closed he expressed his satisfaction thus: 'We have kept such a
revel with the Puritans here these two days as we never heard the like, where
I have peppered them...soundly.... They fled me so from argument to
argument without ever answering me directly, *ut est eorum mos*, as I was
forced at last to say unto them that if any of them had been in a College
disputing with their scholars, if any of their disciples had answered them in
that sort, they would have fetched him up in place of a reply, and so should
the rod have plied upon the poor boy's buttocks.'[2]

In the end there were a few minor concessions, but the King refused to
meet the petitioners on any of the main points; and the only important
practical result of the Conference grew out of the famous resolution: 'One
uniform translation of the Bible to be made, and only to be used in all the
churches of England.' It is to this that we owe the Authorised Version of
1611. The Conference only shewed the Puritan clergy how little they had to
expect from James, who on these matters was proving himself to be almost as
inflexible as Elizabeth. In a proclamation of 16 July, 1604 [p. **70**], he
warned them that 'what untractable men do not perform upon admonition
they must be compelled unto by authority'; and the enforcement of the
King's policy by Archbishop Bancroft led to the ejection of some 300 clergy
from their livings for refusing to subscribe *ex animo* to the Book of Common
Prayer[3].

The sympathies of the Commons were with the Puritan ministers in
their conflict with the King and the bishops, and in May, 1604, they took
up their cause in a conference with the Lords [p. **69**], although without
success. In the following month, in the *Form of Apology and Satisfaction to be
presented to his Majesty* [p. **217**], they took occasion to state—in opposition
to the ecclesiastical supremacy and to the Tudor position generally—what
may be called the parliamentary position in matters of religion. 'For matter
of religion,' they say, 'it will appear, by examination of truth and right, that
your Majesty should be misinformed if any man should deliver that the
Kings of England have any absolute power in themselves, either to alter
religion (which God defend should be in the power of any mortal man
whatsoever), or to make any laws concerning the same, otherwise than as in
temporal causes, by consent of Parliament.' But the language of the *Apology*
will serve to disabuse our minds of any idea that the ecclesiastical system
which the Commons contemplated allowed of anything of the nature of
religious liberty, or 'toleration.' 'Neither desire we so much that any man,
in regard of weakness of conscience, may be exempted after Parliament from
obedience to laws established, as that in this Parliament such laws may be
enacted as by relinquishment of some few ceremonies of small importance, or
by any way better, a perpetual uniformity may be enjoyed and observed.'
Thus the Commons proposed to take the religious settlement out of the

---

[1] In Barlow's account this remark is ascribed to one of the lords, but Harington,
who was present at the Conference, assigns it to a bishop (Gardiner, i. 157 *n*.); and
Whitgift repeated it on the third day of meeting (*see* p. 68 below).
[2] J. O. Halliwell, *Letters of the Kings of England*, ii, 109.
[3] See also *D.N.B.* iii, 111.

hands of the King, and to make by statute those concessions to the Puritans which he had refused to make by an exercise of the Supremacy; but after that, conformity was to be enforced, and where James chastised with whips, the Commons were prepared to chastise with scorpions. This explains why there was always a minority in the country ready to support the supremacy of the Crown. Thus the wise lawyer Bacon objected to the transfer of power over religion from the King to Parliament, and regarded the Crown as the proper depositary of existing constitutional authority; and on this particular question it was James who represented the future and stood far in advance of his age.

The religious controversy did not end with the *Apology* of 1604; for a Petition from the Commons in 1610 [p. 77] takes up once more the cause of the 'deprived and silenced ministers.' Nor was it the King's first Parliament only that was of a Puritan complexion. The Parliament of 1614 insisted on going in a body to receive the Communion at St Margaret's, Westminster, avoiding the Abbey for fear of 'copes and wafer cakes.'[1] The grievance concerning ceremonies, throughout the reign, poisoned the relations between James I and his Parliaments.

(1) The Sabbatarian Controversy
Dr Bownd's Book, 1595

Dr Nicholas Bownd's famous book, *The Doctrine of the Sabbath*[2], was first published in 1595, and soon set up the earliest disagreement between the Anglicans and the Puritans on a point of doctrine (*D.N.B.* vi, 74). Thomas Fuller's *Church History of Britain*, from which the following summary of Bownd's doctrine is taken, appeared in 1655.

About this time [1595] throughout England began the more solemn and strict observation of the Lord's Day (hereafter both in writing and preaching commonly called the Sabbath) occasioned by a book this year set forth by one P. Bownd, Doctor of Divinity (and enlarged with additions, *anno* 1606) wherein these following opinions are maintained:

1. That the commandment of sanctifying every seventh day, as in the Mosaical Decalogue, is moral and perpetual.

2. That whereas all other things in the Jewish Church were taken away (priesthood, sacrifices, and sacraments), this Sabbath was so changed that it still remaineth.

3. That there is a great reason why we Christians should take

[1] 'The Communion to be received at the Abbey: not at the Abbey, but at the Parish Church. That in the Abbey they administer not with common bread, contrary [to the] 20th Canon and the Book of Common Prayer' (*Commons' Journals*, 13 April, 1614, i, 463). It is from this time that the close connexion between the House of Commons and St Margaret's may be said to date (Gardiner, *History of England 1603–1642*, ii, 237).

[2] See also the extract from Dr Bownd's book printed in *Tudor Constitutional Documents*, pp. 200–1.

ourselves as straitly bound to rest upon the Lord's Day as the Jews were upon their Sabbath; it being one of the moral commandments, where all are of equal authority.

4. The rest upon this day must be a notable and singular rest, a most careful, exact, and precise rest, after another manner than men are accustomed.

5. Scholars on that day not to study the liberal arts, nor lawyers to consult the case nor peruse men's evidences.

6. Serjeants, apparitors, and summoners to be restrained from executing their offices.

7. Justices not to examine causes for the conservation of the peace.

8. That ringing of more bells than one that day is not to be justified.

9. No solemn feasts nor wedding-dinners to be made on that day—with permission, notwithstanding of the same, to lords, knights, and gentlemen of quality, which some conceive not so fair dealing with him.

10. All honest recreations and pleasures, lawful on other days (as shooting, fencing, bowling) on this day to be forborne.

11. No man to speak or talk of pleasures, or any other worldly matter.

It is almost incredible how taking this doctrine was, partly because of its own purity, and partly for the eminent piety of such persons as maintained it; so that the Lord's Day, especially in corporations, began to be precisely kept, people becoming a law to themselves, forbearing such sports as [were] yet by statute permitted; yea, many rejoicing at their own restraint herein. On this day the stoutest fencer laid down the buckler; the most skilful archer unbent his bow, counting all shooting beside the mark; May-games and morris-dances grew out of request; and good reason that bells should be silenced from jingling about men's legs[1] if their very ringing in steeples were adjudged unlawful. Some of them were ashamed of their former pleasures, like children which, grown bigger, blushing themselves out of their rattles and whistles. Others forebore them for fear of their superiors; and many left them off out of a politic compliance, lest otherwise they should be accounted licentious.

Yet learned men were much divided in their judgments about these Sabbatarian doctrines. Some embraced them as ancient truths consonant to Scripture, long disused and neglected, now seasonably revived for the increase of piety. Others conceived

[1] Morris dancers wore small bells attached to their clothing.

them grounded on a wrong bottom; but, because they tended to the manifest advance of religion, it was pity to oppose them, seeing none have just reason to complain, being deceived into their own good. But a third sort flatly fell out with these positions, as galling men's necks with a Jewish yoke, against the liberty of Christians; that Christ, as Lord of the Sabbath, had removed the rigour thereof and allowed men lawful recreations; that this doctrine put an unequal lustre on the Sunday on set purpose to eclipse all other holy days, to the derogation of the authority of the Church; that this strict observance was set up out of faction to be a character of difference, to brand all for libertines who did not entertain it.

Fuller, Church History (edition of 1837), iii, 143–4.

James I's Declaration of Sports, 1618

This Declaration was issued 24 May, 1618, and was afterwards embodied in Charles I's Declaration of Sports of 1633.

The King's Majesty's Declaration to his subjects concerning lawful sports to be used

Whereas upon our return the last year out of Scotland we did publish our pleasure touching the recreations of our people in those parts under our hand, for some causes us thereunto moving we have thought good to command these our directions then given in Lancashire, with a few words thereunto added, and most applyable to these parts of our realms, to be published to all our subjects.

Whereas we did justly in our progress through Lancashire rebuke some Puritans and precise people, and took order that the like unlawful carriage should not be used by any of them hereafter in the prohibiting and unlawful punishing of our good people for using their lawful recreations and honest exercises upon Sundays and other Holy Days after the afternoon sermon or service, we now find that two sorts of people wherewith that country is much infested (we mean Papists and Puritans) have maliciously traduced and calumniated those our just and honourable proceedings. And therefore lest our reputation might upon the one side (though innocently) have some aspersion laid upon it, and that upon the other part our good people in that country be misled by the mistaking and misinterpretation of our meaning, we have therefore thought good hereby to clear and make our pleasure to be manifested to all our good people in those parts.

It is true that at our first entry to this Crown and Kingdom we were informed, and that too truly, that our County of Lancashire abounded more in Popish recusants than any county of

England, and thus hath still continued since, to our great regret, with little amendment, save that now of late in our last riding through our said county we find, both by the report of the judges and of the bishop of that diocese, that there is some amendment now daily beginning, which is no small contentment to us.

The report of this growing amendment amongst them made us the more sorry when with our own ears we heard the general complaint of our people that they were barred from all lawful recreation and exercise upon the Sunday's afternoon after the ending of all Divine Service, which cannot but produce two evils: the one, the hindering of the conversion of many whom their priests will take occasion hereby to vex, persuading them that no honest mirth or recreation is lawful or tolerable in our religion, which cannot but breed a great discontentment in our people's hearts, especially of such as are peradventure upon the point of turning; the other inconvenience is, that this prohibition barreth the common and meaner sort of people from using such exercises as may make their bodies more able for war, when we or our successors shall have occasion to use them, and in place thereof sets up filthy tipplings and drunkenness, and breeds a number of idle and discontented speeches in their ale-houses. For when shall the common people have leave to exercise if not upon the Sundays and Holy Days, seeing they must apply their labour and win their living in all working days?

Our express pleasure therefore is, that the laws of our Kingdom and canons of our Church be as well observed in that county as in all other places of this our Kingdom. And on the other part, that no lawful recreation shall be barred to our good people which shall not tend to the breach of our aforesaid laws, and canons of our Church: which to express more particularly, our pleasure is that the bishop, and all other inferior churchmen and churchwardens shall for their parts be careful and diligent both to instruct the ignorant and convince and reform them that are misled in religion, presenting them that will not conform themselves but obstinately stand out, to our judges and justices; whom we likewise command to put the law in due execution against them.

Our pleasure likewise is, that the bishop of that diocese take the like strait order with all the Puritans and precisians within the same, either constraining them to conform themselves or to leave the country, according to the laws of our Kingdom and canons of our Church, and so to strike equally on both hands against the contemners of our authority and adversaries of our Church. And as for our good people's lawful recreation, our pleasure likewise is, that after the end of Divine Service our good people be not disturbed, letted, or discouraged from any lawful recreation; such as dancing, either men or women, archery for men, leaping, vaulting, or any other such harmless recreation, nor from having of May-games, Whitsun ales, and morris-dances, and the setting up of May-poles and other sports therewith used, so as the same be had in due and convenient time, without impediment or neglect of Divine Service; and that women shall have leave to carry rushes to the church for the decoring[1] of it, according to their old custom. But withal we do here accompt still as prohibited all unlawful games to be used upon Sundays only, as bear and bull-baitings, interludes, and at all times in the meaner sort of people by law prohibited, bowling.

And likewise we bar from this benefit and liberty all such known recusants, either men or women, as will abstain from coming to church or Divine Service, being therefore unworthy of any lawful recreation after the said service that will not first come to the church and serve God: prohibiting in like sort the said recreations to any that, though conform[2] in religion, are not present in the church at the service of God before their going to the said recreations. Our pleasure likewise is, that they to whom it belongeth in office shall present and sharply punish all such as in abuse of this our liberty will use these exercises before the ends of all Divine services for that day. And we likewise straitly command that every person shall resort to his own parish church to hear Divine Service, and each parish by itself to use the said recreation after Divine Service. Prohibiting likewise any offensive weapons to be carried or used in the said times of recreations; and our pleasure is, that this our Declaration shall be published by order from the bishop of the diocese through all the parish churches, and that both our judges of our circuit and our justices of our peace be informed thereof.

Given at our manor of Greenwich, the four and twentieth day of May, in the sixteenth year of our reign of England, France, and Ireland, and of Scotland the one and fiftieth.

God save the King.

James I's *Declaration of Sports* (reprint of 1817).

(2) The Millenary Petition, 1603

The paragraph here printed as a preface to the text of the Petition was written by Thomas Fuller in 1655.

And now, because there was a general expectation of a

[1] Decorating or adorning. [2] *I.e.* conformist.

Parliament suddenly to succeed, the Presbyterian party, that they might not be surprised before they had their tackling about them, went about to get hands of the ministers to a petition, which they intended seasonably to present to the King and Parliament.... This was called the Millenary Petition, as one of a thousand; though indeed there were but seven hundred and fifty preachers' hands set thereunto, but those all collected only out of five and twenty counties. However, for the more rotundity of the number and grace of the matter, it passeth for a full thousand; which no doubt the collectors of the names (if so pleased) might easily have completed. I dare not guess what made them desist before their number was finished; whether they thought that these were enough to do the deed and more were rather for ostentation than use, or because disheartened by the intervening of the Hampton Court Conference they thought that these were even too many to petition for a denial. It is left as yet uncertain whether this Conference was by the King's favour graciously tendered; or by the mediation of the Lords of his Council powerfully procured; or by the bishops, as confident of their cause, voluntarily proffered; or by the ministers' importunity effectually obtained. Each opinion pretends to probability, but the last most likely...(pp. 171–2).

*   *   *   *   *   *

The humble Petition of the Ministers of the Church of England desiring reformation of certain ceremonies and abuses of the Church

To the most Christian and Excellent Prince, our gracious and dread Sovereign James, by the grace of God, etc. We, the ministers of the Church of England that desire reformation, wish a long, prosperous, and happy reign over us in this life, and in the next everlasting salvation.

Most gracious and dread Sovereign, seeing it hath pleased the Divine Majesty, to the great comfort of all good Christians, to advance your Highness, according to your just title, to the peaceable government of this Church and commonwealth of England; we, the ministers of the Gospel in this land, neither as factious men affecting a popular parity in the Church, nor as schismatics aiming at the dissolution of the state ecclesiastical, but as the faithful servants of Christ and loyal subjects to your Majesty, desiring and longing for the redress of divers abuses of the Church, could do no less, in our obedience to God, service to your Majesty, love to his Church, than acquaint your princely Majesty with our particular griefs. For as your princely pen writeth, 'The King, as a good physician, must first know what peccant humours his patient naturally is most subject unto before he can begin his cure.' And although divers of us that sue for reformation have formerly, in respect of the times, subscribed to the Book, some upon protestation, some upon exposition given them, some with condition, rather than the Church should have been deprived of their labour and ministry; yet now we, to the number of more than a thousand, of your Majesty's subjects and ministers, all groaning as under a common burden of human rites and ceremonies, do with one joint consent humble ourselves at your Majesty's feet to be eased and relieved in this behalf. Our humble suit then unto your Majesty is, that of these offences following, some may be removed, some amended, some qualified:

I. *In the Church Service*. That the cross in baptism, inter-rogatories ministered to infants, confirmation, as superfluous, may be taken away: baptism not to be ministered by women, and so explained: the cap and surplice not urged: that examination may go before the communion: that it be ministered with a sermon: that divers terms of *priests* and *absolution*, and some other used, with the ring in marriage, and other such like in the Book, may be corrected: the longsomeness of service abridged: church songs and music moderated to better edification: that the Lord's Day be not profaned, the rest upon holy-days not so strictly urged: that there may be an uniformity of doctrine prescribed: no Popish opinion to be any more taught or defended: no ministers charged to teach their people to bow at the name of Jesus: that the canonical Scriptures only be read in the church.

II. *Concerning Church ministers*. That none hereafter be ad-mitted into the ministry but able and sufficient men, and those to preach diligently, and especially upon the Lord's Day: that such as be already entered and cannot preach, may either be removed and some charitable course taken with them for their relief or else to be forced, according to the value of their livings, to maintain preachers: that non-residency be not permitted: that King Edward's statute for the lawfulness of ministers' marriage[1] be revived: that ministers be not urged to subscribe but, according to the law, to the Articles of Religion and the King's Supremacy only.

III. *For Church livings and maintenance*. That bishops leave their commendams[2],—some holding prebends, some parsonages,

---

[1] 2 & 3 Edw. VI, c. 21 (1549): printed in Gee and Hardy, p. 366.

[2] Livings held *in commendam*—usually by a bishop in addition to his bishopric.

some vicarages with their bishoprics: that double-beneficed men be not suffered to hold, some two, some three benefices with cure, and some two, three, or four dignities besides: that impropriations annexed to bishoprics and colleges be demised only to the preachers incumbents, for the old rent: that the impropriations of laymen's fees may be charged with a sixth or seventh part of the worth to the maintenance of the preaching minister.

IV. *For Church Discipline.* That the discipline and excommunication may be administered according to Christ's own institution; or, at the least, that enormities may be redressed: as namely, that excommunication come not forth under the name of lay persons, chancellors, officials, etc.; that men be not excommunicated for trifles and twelvepenny matters; that none be excommunicated without consent of his pastor; that the officers be not suffered to extort unreasonable fees; that none having jurisdiction or registers' places put out the same to farm; that divers Popish canons (as for restraint of marriage at certain times) be reversed; that the longsomeness of suits in ecclesiastical courts, which hang sometimes two, three, four, five, six, or seven years, may be restrained; that the oath *ex officio*, whereby men are forced to accuse themselves, be more sparingly used; that licences for marriage without banns asked be more cautiously granted.

These, with such other abuses yet remaining and practised in the Church of England, we are able to shew not to be agreeable to the Scriptures, if it shall please your Highness farther to hear us, or more at large by writing to be informed, or by conference among the learned to be resolved. And yet we doubt not but that without any farther process, your Majesty, of whose Christian judgment we have received so good a taste already, is able of yourself to judge of the equity of this cause. God we trust hath appointed your Highness our physician to heal these diseases. And we say with Mordecai to Esther, 'Who knoweth whether you are come to the kingdom for such a time?' Thus your Majesty shall do that which we are persuaded shall be acceptable to God, honourable to your Majesty in all succeeding ages, profitable to his Church which shall be thereby increased; comfortable to your ministers which shall be no more suspended, silenced, disgraced, imprisoned for men's traditions; and prejudicial to none but to those that seek their own quiet, credit, and profit in the world. Thus with all dutiful submission referring ourselves to your Majesty's pleasure for your gracious answer as God shall direct you, we most humbly recommend your Highness to the Divine Majesty, whom we beseech for Christ's sake to dispose your royal heart to do herein what shall be to his glory, the good of his Church, and your endless comfort.

Your Majesty's most humble subjects the ministers of the Gospel, that desire not a disorderly innovation but a due and godly reformation (pp. 193–5).

Fuller, *Church History* (edition of 1837), iii, 171–2, 193–5.

(3) The Hampton Court Conference, 1604

The passages from William Barlow's *Sum and Substance of the Conference* that follow, are selected mainly to illustrate the nature of the King's interventions in the Conference; these were sometimes very much to the point. Barlow's account of the Conference was drawn up at the request of Archbishop Whitgift, and is the principal authority on its proceedings; the author was afterwards Bishop of Rochester and then of Lincoln.

First Day[1]

* * * * * *

After a while his excellent Majesty came in, and having passed a few pleasant gratulations with some of the Lords, he sat down in his chair,...where beginning with a most grave and princely declaration of his general drift in calling this assembly, no novel device, but according to the example of all Christian princes, who in the commencement of their reign usually take the first course for the establishing of the Church, both for doctrine and policy, to which the very heathens themselves had relation in their proverb, *A Jove Principium*; and particularly in this land King Henry the 8 toward the end of his reign; after him, King Edward the 6, who altered more; after him, Queen Mary who reversed all; and last, the Queen of famous memory, so his Highness added (for it is worth the noting that his Majesty never remembered her but with some honourable addition) who settled it as now it standeth: wherein he said that he was happier than they in this, because they were fain to alter all things they found established, but he saw yet no cause so much to alter and change anything as to confirm that which he found well settled already; which state, as it seemed, so affected his royal heart that it pleased him both to enter into a gratulation to Almighty God (at which words he put off his hat) for bringing him into the promised land, where religion was purely professed, where he sat among grave, learned, and reverend men, not as before elsewhere, a King without state, without honour, without order, where beardless boys would brave him to his face, and to assure us that he called not this assembly for any innovation, acknowledging the govern-

[1] 14 January, 1604.

ment ecclesiastical as now it is to have been approved by manifold blessings from God himself, both for the increase of the Gospel and with a most happy and glorious peace; yet because nothing could be so absolutely ordered but something might be added afterward thereunto, and in any State as in the body of man corruptions might insensibly grow, either through time or persons; and in that he had received many complaints since his first entrance into the kingdom, especially through the dissensions in the Church, of many disorders as he heard, and much disobedience to the laws, with a great falling away to Popery; his purpose therefore was, like a good physician, to examine and try the complaints, and fully to remove the occasions thereof if they prove scandalous, or to cure them if they were dangerous, or if but frivolous yet to take knowledge of them, thereby to cast a sop into Cerberus his mouth that he may never bark again: his meaning being, as he pleased to profess, to give factious spirits no occasion hereby of boasting or glory, for which cause he had called the Bishops in severally by themselves, not to be confronted by the contrary opponents, that if anything should be found meet to be redressed it might be done (which his Majesty twice or thrice, as occasion served, reiterated) without any visible alteration.

And this was the sum, so far as my dull head could conceive and carry it, of his Majesty's general speech. In particular he signified unto them the principal matters why he called them alone with whom he would consult about some special points wherein himself desired to be satisfied; these he reduced to three heads: First, concerning the Book of Common Prayer and Divine Service used in this Church. Second, excommunication in the ecclesiastical courts. Third, the providing of fit and able ministers for Ireland....
(pp. 3–7).

*   *   *   *   *   *

...So admirably, both for understanding, speech, and judgment, did his Majesty handle all those points, sending us away not with contentment only but astonishment, and, which is pitiful you will say, with shame to us all that a King brought up among Puritans, not the learnedest men in the world, and schooled by them; swaying a kingdom full of business and troubles; naturally given to much exercise and repast; should in points of Divinity shew himself as expedite and perfect as the greatest scholars and most industrious students there present might not outstrip him. But this one thing I might not omit, that his Majesty should profess, howsoever he lived among Puritans and was kept for the most part as a ward under them, yet since he was of the age of his

son, ten years old, he ever disliked their opinions. As the Saviour
of the world said, Though he lived among them he was not of
them...(pp. 19–20).

Second Day[1]

...The King's Majesty, entering the chamber, presently took
his chair, placed as the day before (the noble young Prince sitting
by upon a stool), where making a short but a pithy and sweet
speech to the same purpose which the first day he made, viz. of
the end of the conference meet to be had, he said, by every King
at his first entrance to the crown; not to innovate the government
presently established, which by long experience he had found
accomplished with so singular blessings of God 45 years as that
no Church upon the face of the earth more flourished than this
of England. But first, to settle an uniform order through the whole
Church. Secondly, to plant unity, for the suppressing of Papists
and enemies to religion. Thirdly, to amend abuses, as natural to
bodies politic and corrupt man as the shadow to the body, which
once being entered, hold on as a wheel his motion once set going.
And because many grievous complaints had been made to him
since his first entrance into the land, he thought it best to send
for some whom his Majesty understood to be the most grave,
learned, and modest of the aggrieved sort, whom being there
present, he was now ready to hear at large what they could object
or say; and so willed them to begin: whereupon they four[2]
kneeling down, Dr Reynolds the foreman, after a short preamble
gratulary, and signifying his Majesty's summons by virtue whereof
they then and there appeared, reduced all matters disliked or
questioned into these four heads:

1. That the doctrine of the Church might be preserved in
purity, according to God's Word.

2. That good pastors might be planted in all churches to
preach the same.

3. That the Church government might be sincerely ministered, according to God's Word.

4. That the Book of Common Prayer might be fitted to more
increase of piety...(pp. 21–3).

* * * * * *

[1] 16 January.
[2] The four divines who represented the Puritan party at the Conference were
John Reynolds or Rainolds, President of Corpus Christi College, Oxford; Laurence
Chaderton, Master of Emmanuel College, Cambridge; Thomas Sparke, Fellow of
Magdalen College, Oxford; and John Knewstub, Fellow of St John's College,
Cambridge.

His Majesty concluded this point first by taxing St Jerome for his assertion that a Bishop was not *Divinae ordinationis* (the Bishop of London thereupon inserting that unless he could prove his ordination lawful out of the Scriptures he would not be a Bishop 4 hours), which opinion his Majesty much distasted, approving their calling and use in the Church, and closed it up with this short aphorism, No Bishop, no King...(p. 36).

*   *   *   *   *   *

Next to this Dr Reynolds complained that the Catechism in the Common Prayer Book was too brief,...requested therefore that one uniform Catechism might be made which, and none other, might be generally received. It was demanded of him whether if to the short Catechism in the Communion Book something were added for the doctrine of the Sacrament, it would not serve? His Majesty thought the Doctor's request very reasonable; but yet so that he would have a Catechism in the fewest and plainest affirmative terms that may be; taxing withal the number of ignorant catechisms set out in Scotland by every one that was the son of a good man, insomuch as that which was Catechism doctrine in one congregation was in another scarcely accepted as sound and orthodox; wished therefore one to be made and agreed upon, adding this excellent, gnomical, and canon-like conclusion, that in reforming of a Church he would have two rules observed: first, that old, curious, deep, and intricate questions might be avoided in the fundamental instruction of a people; secondly, that there should not be any such departure from the Papists in all things as that, because we in some points agree with them, therefore we should be accounted to be in error.

To the former, Dr Reynolds did add the profanation of the Sabbath day, and contempt of his Majesty's proclamation made for the reforming of that abuse, of which he earnestly desired a straiter course for reformation thereof, and unto this he found a general and unanimous assent.

After that, he moved his Majesty that there might be a new translation of the Bible, because those which were allowed in the reigns of King Henry the Eighth and Edward the Sixth were corrupt, and not answerable to the truth of the original.... Whereupon his Highness wished that some especial pains should be taken in that behalf for one uniform translation (professing that he could never yet see a Bible well translated in English, but the worst of all his Majesty thought the Geneva to be), and this to be done by the best learned in both the Universities, after them to be reviewed by the Bishops and the chief learned of the

Church; from them to be presented to the Privy Council; and lastly, to be ratified by his royal authority; and so this whole Church to be bound unto it and none other: marry withal, he gave this *caveat* (upon a word cast out by my Lord of London) that no marginal notes should be added, having found in them which are annexed to the Geneva translation (which he saw in a Bible given him by an English lady) some notes very partial, untrue, seditious, and savouring too much of dangerous and traitorous conceits.... And so concludeth this point, as all the rest, with a grave and judicious advice. First, that errors in matters of faith might be rectified and amended. Secondly, that matters indifferent might rather be interrupted and a gloss added, alleging from *Bartolus de regno* that, as better a King with some weakness than still a change, so rather a Church with some faults than an innovation. And surely, saith his Majesty, if these be the greatest matters you be grieved with, I need not have been troubled with such importunities and complaints as have been made unto me; some other more private course might have been taken for your satisfaction; and withal, looking upon the Lords, he shook his head, smiling...(pp. 44–8).

*   *   *   *   *   *

To the second general point, concerning the planting of ministers learned in every parish, it pleased his Majesty to answer, that he had consulted with his Bishops about that, whom he found willing and ready to second him in it, inveighing herein against the negligence and carelessness which he heard of many in this land; but as *subita evacuatio* was *periculosa*, so *subita mutatio*. Therefore this matter was not for a present resolution, because to appoint to every parish a sufficient minister were impossible; the Universities would not afford them. Again, he had found already that he had more learned men in this realm than he had sufficient maintenance for; so that maintenance must first be provided, and then the other to be required. In the mean time ignorant ministers, if young, to be removed if there were no hope of their amendment; if old, their death must be expected, that the next course may be better supplied: and so concluded this point with a most religious and zealous protestation of doing something daily in this case, because Jerusalem could not be built up in a day...(pp. 53–4).

*   *   *   *   *   *

Here my Lord of London, kneeling, humbly desired his Majesty (because he saw, as he said, it was a time of moving petitions) that he might have leave to make two or three. First, that there might be amongst us a praying ministry another while; for whereas there are in the ministry many excellent duties to be performed, as the absolving of the penitent, praying for and blessing of the people, administering of the Sacraments, and the like, it is come to that pass now that some sort of men thought it the only duty required of a minister to spend the time in speaking out of a pulpit—sometimes, God wot, very undiscreetly and unlearnedly—and this with so great injury and prejudice to the celebration of Divine Service that some ministers would be content to walk in the churchyard till sermon time rather than to be present at public prayer. He confessed that in a Church new to be planted preaching was most necessary; but among us, now long established in the faith, he thought it not the only necessary duty to be performed and the other to be so profanely neglected and contemned. Which motion his Majesty liked exceeding well, very acutely taxing the hypocrisy of our times which placeth all religion in the ear, through which there is an easy passage, but prayer, which expresseth the heart's affection and is the true devotion of the mind, as a matter putting us to overmuch trouble (wherein there concur, if prayer be as it ought, an unpartial consideration of our own estates, a due examination to whom we pray, an humble confession of our sins, with an hearty sorrow for them and repentance not severed from faith) is accounted and used as the least part of religion.

The second was, that till such time as learned and sufficient men might be planted in every congregation, that godly homilies might be read and the number of them increased, and that the opponents would labour to bring them into credit again, as formerly they brought them into contempt. Every man (saith he) that can pronounce well cannot indite well.

The King's Majesty approved this motion, especially where the living is not sufficient for maintenance of a learned preacher; as also in places where plenty of sermons are, as in the City and great towns. In the country villages, where preachers are not near together, he could wish preaching; but where there are a multitude of sermons there he would have homilies to be read divers times: and therein he asked the assent of the plaintiffs and they confess it. A preaching ministry, saith his Majesty, was best, but where it might not be had, godly prayers and exhortations did much good. That that may be done, let it, and let the rest that cannot, be tolerated...(pp. 54–7).

* * * * * *

Mr Knewstub took exceptions to the cross in baptism, being in number two. First, the offence of weak brethren, grounded upon the words of St Paul, Romans 14 and I Corinthians 8, viz. the consciences of the weak not to be offended: which places his excellent Majesty answered most acutely, beginning with that general rule of the Fathers, *Distingue tempora et concordabunt Scripturae*, shewing here the difference of those times and ours: then, a Church not fully planted nor settled, but ours long stablished and flourishing; then, Christians newly called from paganism and not thoroughly grounded, which is not the case of this Church, seeing that heathenish doctrine for many years hath been hence abandoned. Secondly, with a question unanswerable, asking them how long they would be weak? Whether 45 years were not sufficient for them to grow strong? Thirdly, who they were pretended this weakness? For we, saith the King, require not now subscription of laics and idiots but preachers and ministers, who are not still, I trow, to be fed with milk but are enabled to feed others. Fourthly, that it was to be doubted some of them were strong enough, if not headstrong, and howsoever they in this case pretended weakness, yet some in whose behalf they now spake thought themselves able to teach him and all the Bishops of the land...(pp. 67–8).

*   *   *   *   *   *

The next thing which was objected was the wearing of the surplice, a kind of garment which the priests of Isis used to wear. Surely, saith his Majesty, until of late I did not think that it had been borrowed from the heathen because it is commonly termed a rag of Popery in scorn; but were it so, yet neither did we border upon heathenish nations, neither are any of them conversant with us or commorant[1] amongst us who thereby might take just occasion to be strengthened or confirmed in paganism, for then there were just cause to suppress the wearing of it; but seeing it appeared out of antiquity that in the celebration of Divine Service a different habit appertained to the ministry, and principally of white linen, he saw no reason but that in this Church, as it had been for comeliness and for order sake, it might be still continued. This being his constant and resolute opinion, that no Church ought further to separate itself from the Church of Rome, either in doctrine or ceremony, than she had departed from herself when she was in her flourishing and best estate, and from Christ her Lord and Head....

---

[1] Resident.

Dr Reynolds took exceptions at those words in the Common Prayer Book of matrimony, 'With my body I thee worship.' His Majesty looking upon the place, I was made believe (saith he) that the phrase did import no less than Divine worship and adoration; but by the examination I find that it is an usual English term, as a gentleman of worship, etc., and the sense agreeable unto Scriptures, giving honour to the wife, etc. But turning to Dr Reynolds (with smiling, saith his Majesty), Many a man speaks of Robin Hood who never shot in his bow: if you had a good wife yourself you would think all the honour and worship you could do to her were well bestowed.

The Dean of Sarum[1] mentioned the ring in marriage; which Dr Reynolds approved, and the King confessed that he was married withal, and added that he thought they would prove to be scarce well married who are not married with a ring....

And this was the substance and sum of that third general point....

In the fourth general head, touching discipline, Dr Reynolds first took exception to the committing of ecclesiastical censures unto lay chancellors.... Then he desireth that according to certain provincial constitutions they of the clergy might have meetings once every three weeks: first, in rural deaneries, and therein to have prophesying, according as the Reverend Father Archbishop Grindal and other bishops desired of her late Majesty[2]; secondly, that such things as could not be resolved upon there, might be referred to the archdeacon's visitation; and so thirdly, from thence to the episcopal synod, where the bishop with his presbytery should determine all such points as before could not be decided.

At which speech his Majesty was somewhat stirred, yet, which is admirable in him, without passion or show thereof; thinking that they aimed at a Scottish presbytery, which, saith he, as well agreeth with a monarchy as God and the Devil. Then Jack and Tom and Will and Dick shall meet, and at their pleasures censure me and my Council and all our proceedings. Then Will shall stand up and say, 'It must be thus'; then Dick shall reply and say, 'Nay, marry, but we will have it thus.' And therefore here I must once reiterate my former speech, *Le Roy s'avisera*. Stay, I pray you, for one seven years before you demand that of me, and if then you find me pursy and fat and my wind-pipes stuffed, I will perhaps hearken to you: for let that government be

[1] Dr John Gordon, who had just been appointed to the Deanery of Salisbury in succession to John Bridges, now Bishop of Oxford.

[2] See *Tudor Constitutional Documents*, pp. 182 ff.

once up, I am sure I shall be kept in breath; then shall we all of us have work enough, both our hands full...(pp. 76–81).

* * * * * *

Third Day[1]

* * * * * *

...And here his Majesty so soundly described the oath *ex officio*: first, for the ground thereof; secondly, the wisdom of the law therein; thirdly, the manner of proceeding thereby, and the necessary and profitable effect thereof, in such a compendious but absolute order that all the Lords and the rest of the present auditors stood amazed at it. The Archbishop of Canterbury[2] said that undoubtedly his Majesty spake by the special assistance of God's Spirit; the Bishop of London[3] upon his knee protested that his heart melted within him (and so he doubted not did the hearts of the whole company) with joy, and made haste to acknowledge unto Almighty God the singular mercy we have received at his hands in giving us such a King as since Christ his time the like he thought had not been; whereunto the Lords with one voice did yield a very affectionate acclamation. The civilians[4] present confessed that they could not in many hours' warning have so judicially, plainly, and accurately, and in such a brief[5] described it...(pp. 95–6).

* * * * * *

...And so his Majesty shut up all with a most pithy exhortation to both sides for unity, persuading diligence in each man's place, without violence on the one party or disobedience on the other, and willed them to deal with their friends abroad to that purpose: for his Majesty feared and had some experience that many of them were ticklish and humorous,—nor that only, but labourers to pervert others to their fancies; he now saw that the exceptions against the Communion Book were matters of weakness; therefore if the persons reluctant be discreet, they will be won betimes and by good persuasions; if undiscreet, better they were removed, for many by their factious behaviour were driven to be Papists. Now then of their fruits he shall judge them, obedience and humility being marks of honest and good men. Those he expected of them, and by their example and persuasion of all their sort abroad; for if hereafter, things being thus well

---

[1] 18 January.

[2] Archbishop Whitgift: he died 29 February, 1604.

[3] Richard Bancroft: Whitgift's successor as Archbishop of Canterbury.

[4] *I.e.* the Doctors of Civil Law.　　　　　[5] Abstract or summary.

ordered, they should be unquiet, neither his Majesty nor the State had any cause to think well of them. To which they gave all their unanimous assent, taking exception against nothing that was said or done, but promised to perform all duty to the Bishops as their Reverend Fathers, and to join with them against the common adversaries and for the quiet of the Church...(pp. 100–1).

* * * * * *

Finally, they jointly promised to be quiet and obedient now they knew it to be the King's mind to have it so. His Majesty's gracious conclusion was so piercing as that it fetched tears from some on both sides. My Lord of London ended all in the name of the whole company with a thanksgiving unto God for his Majesty and a prayer for the health and prosperity of his Highness, our gracious Queen, the young Prince, and all their royal issue.

His Majesty departed into the inner chamber: all the Lords presently[1] went to the Council Chamber to appoint Commissioners for the several matters before referred[2]...(pp. 105–6).

William Barlow, *The Sum and Substance of the Conference*...1604.

(4) Articles concerning Ministers, 1604

The following Articles were approved by the Commons on 5 May, 1604, and were ordered to be sent to the Lords with a view to a conference, but they met with little support in the Upper House. The Commons therefore subsequently prepared in their own House a Bill against pluralities and another for a learned ministry, but both Bills fell through in the House of Lords.

Certain Articles or Heads agreed upon by the Committees to be treated upon in the Conference with the Right Honourable the Lords

1. That the Articles only concerning the doctrine of Faith and of the Sacraments whereunto the ministers ought to subscribe by the Statute of the 13th year of the reign of the late Queen Elizabeth may be explained, perfected, and established by Parliament; and that no contrary doctrine may be taught within this realm; and that all masters of household[s] may be compelled to subscribe unto the same Articles as well as the ministers.

2. That from henceforth none other be admitted to be ministers of the Word and Sacrament[s] than such as are, at the time of their admittance, Bachelors of Art or of an higher Degree in Schools, having testimony from the University or College whereof he was, of his ability to preach and of his good life; or else such as are approved and allowed to be sufficient to preach and

---

[1] Immediately.

[2] Perhaps in the sense of reserved for subsequent consideration.

instruct the people, and to be of good life, by some testimonial of six preachers of the county where the party dwelleth.

3. That from henceforth no dispensation or toleration shall be allowed to any to have or retain two or more benefices with cure of souls or to be non-resident; and that such as now have double benefices or be non-resident shall give sufficient allowance yearly to maintain a preacher in their absence, and that for this purpose the incumbent shall be allotted to make his residency in one of his parsonages, to the intent that in the other church a certain and constant minister may be maintained and kept.

4. Also it is thought meet, where the living of the vicar or curate is under twenty pounds by the year, that for the better maintenance of the vicar or curate (being a preacher) there may be some increase made of his living as shall be thought convenient.

5. Also it is humbly desired that the Lords would confer with us touching a petition to be preferred to the King's Majesty that by his gracious favour such order be taken that no minister be forced to subscribe otherwise than to the Articles concerning only the doctrine of Faith and Sacraments whereunto by the said Statute made in the 13th year of the reign of the late Queen Elizabeth they are appointed to subscribe.

6. Also to confer with the Lords that such faithful ministers as dutifully carry themselves in their functions and callings, teaching the people diligently, may not be deprived, suspended, silenced, or imprisoned for not using of the cross in baptism or the surplice, which turneth to the punishment of the people.

Commons' Journals, i, 199–200.

(5) Proclamation enjoining Conformity, 1604

A proclamation [of 16 July 1604] enjoining conformity to the form of the Service of God established

The care which we have had and pains which we have taken to settle the affairs of this Church of England in an uniformity, as well of doctrine as of government, both of them agreeable to the Word of God, the doctrine of the primitive Church, and the laws heretofore established for those matters in this realm, may sufficiently appear by our former actions. For no sooner did the infection of the plague, reigning immediately after our entry into this kingdom, give us leave to have any assembly, but we held at our honour of Hampton Court for that purpose a Conference between some principal bishops and deans of this Church, and such other learned men as understood or favoured the opinions of those that seek alteration, before ourself and our Council. Of which Conference the issue was, that no well grounded matter appeared to us or our said Council why the state of the Church here by law established should in any material point be altered. Nor did those that before had seemed to affect such alteration, when they heard the contrary arguments, greatly insist upon it, but seemed to be satisfied themselves, and to undertake within reasonable time to satisfy all others, that were misled with opinion that there was any just cause of alteration. Whereupon we published by our proclamation what had been the issue of that Conference, hoping that when the same should be made known, all reasonable men would have rested satisfied with that which had been done, and not have moved further trouble or speech of matters whereof so solemn and advised determination had been made. Notwithstanding, at the late assembly of our Parliament there wanted not many that renewed with no little earnestness the questions before determined, and many more as well, about the Book of Common Prayer, as other matters of Church-government, and importuned us for our assent to many alterations therein; but yet with such success, as when they had heard both our own speeches made unto them at sundry times, shewing the reasons of our former proceedings in those matters, and likewise had had conference with some Bishops and other Lords of the Upper House about the same, they desisted from further prosecution thereof; finding that of all things that might any way tend to the furtherance of religion and establishment of a ministry fit for the same, we had before with the advice of our Council had such consideration as the present state of things would bear, and taken order how the same should be prosecuted by such means as might be used without any public disturbance or innovation: and so the end of all their motions and overtures falling out to be none other in substance than was before at the Conference at Hampton Court, that is, that no apparent or grounded reason was shewed why either the Book of Common Prayer or the Church discipline here by law established should be changed, which were unreasonable, considering that particular and personal abuses are remediable otherwise than by making general alterations; we have thought good once again to give notice thereof to all our subjects by public declaration, who we doubt not but will receive great satisfaction when they shall understand that after so much impugning, there appeareth no cause why the form of the Service of God wherein they have been nourished so many years should be changed; and consequently to admonish them all in general to conform themselves thereunto, without listening to the troublesome spirits of some persons who never receive contentment, either in civil or ecclesiastical matters, but in their own fantasies, especially of certain ministers who, under pretended zeal of reformation, are the chief authors of divisions and sects among our people. Of many of which we hope that now, when they shall see that such things as they have proposed for alteration prove upon trial so weakly grounded as deserve not admittance, they will out of their own judgment conform themselves to better advice, and not omit the principal and substantial parts of their duties for shadows and semblances of zeal, but rather bend their strength with our intent to join in one end, that is, the establishing of the Gospel and recovering of our people seduced out of the hands of the common adversaries of our religion, which shall never be well performed but by an uniformity of our endeavours therein. But if our hope herein fail us, we must advertise them that our duty towards God requireth at our hands, that what untractable men do not perform upon admonition they must be compelled unto by authority; whereof the supreme power resting in our hands by God's ordinance, we are bound to use the same in nothing more than in preservation of the Church's tranquillity, which by God's grace we are fully purposed to do. And yet by advice of our Council, and opinion of the Bishops, although our former proclamations, both before the Conference and since, ought to be a sufficient warning and admonition to all men who are within the danger of them, we have thought good to give time to all ministers disobedient to the orders of the Church and to ecclesiastical authority here by law established, and who for such disobedience, either in the days of the Queen our sister of famous memory deceased or since our reign, have incurred any censures of the Church or penalties of laws, until the last of November now next ensuing to bethink themselves of the course they will hold therein.

In which mean time both they may resolve either to conform themselves to the Church of England and obey the same, or else to dispose of themselves and their families some other ways, as to them shall seem meet, and the bishops and others whom it concerneth provide meet persons to be substitutes in the place of those who shall wilfully abandon their charges upon so slight causes; assuring them that after that day we shall not fail to do that which princely providence requireth at our hands, that is, to put in execution all ways and means that may take from among our people all grounds and occasions of sects, divisions, and unquietness: whereof as we wish there may never be occasion given us to make proof, but that this our admonition may have equal force in all men's hearts to work an universal conformity, so we do require all archbishops, bishops, and other ecclesiastical persons to do their uttermost endeavours by conferences, arguments, persuasions, and by all other ways of love and gentleness, to reclaim all that be in the ministry to the obedience of our Church laws: for which purpose only we have enlarged the time formerly prefixed for their remove or reformation, to the end that if it be possible that uniformity which we desire may be wrought by clemency and by weight of reason, and not by rigour of law. And the like advertisement do we give to all civil magistrates, gentlemen, and others of understanding, as well abroad in the counties as in cities and towns, requiring them also not in any sort to support, favour, or countenance any such factious ministers in their obstinacy; of whose endeavours we doubt not but so good success may follow, as this our admonition, with their endeavours, may prevent the use of any other means to retain our people in their due obedience to us, and in unity of mind to the service of Almighty God.

Given at our manor of Oatlands the 16th day of July, in the second year of our reign of England, France, and Ireland, and of Scotland the seven and thirtieth, Anno Domini MDCIV.

Cardwell, *Documentary Annals*, ii, 60–4.

(6) Proceedings against Clergy who refuse to conform, 1604

The Council's Letter for proceeding against the nonconformitans of the clergy [10 *December*, 1604]

...After our hearty commendations to your Lordship. Forasmuch as the time is now expired which by his Majesty's late proclamation, dated the sixteenth day of July last[1], was prescribed and limited to all those of the clergy for the conforming of themselves unto the laws and orders of the Church government established within this realm, that have heretofore, under a pretended zeal of reformation but indeed of a factious desire of innovation, refused to yield their obedience and conformity thereunto; by means whereof all such as persist in that wilful disobedience are subject to the penalty of deprivation from their benefices and other Church livings, of deposition from their ministry, and other censures of the Church which were, as well at all times heretofore as presently, in vigour and force; although his Majesty maketh

1 See p. 70 above.

no doubt but that your Lordship throughout your province, and the rest of the bishops, every one in his own diocese, will have regard to the execution of the said laws and constitutions in such sort as is meet and necessary for the uniformity of the Church discipline, nevertheless, such is the great care and zeal of his most excellent Majesty for a due proceeding to be had in a matter of so great consequence as this is, of redressing and reforming all offensive and scandalous divisions in the Church, as also to remove an ill-grounded opinion and conceit wherewith, as it seemeth, divers have nourished and flattered their own disobedience, presuming on a further enlargement of time and toleration than hath been granted or is intended by his Majesty, as we cannot omit both to assist your own readiness with our advice and concurrence of judgment, and that which is much more, to give you knowledge of the expectation his Majesty hath of your proceedings herein. For although it be much more agreeable to his most gracious mind and clemency to heal and cure such distemperatures by lenity and gentleness than by severity, as hath well appeared by the conferences that his Majesty heretofore hath ordained to be had in his own presence, by the course of advice and persuasion that he hath prescribed to be holden by those that are of chief place and authority in the Church, and lastly, by giving time and respite more than once unto such persons either misled or unresolved, to conform themselves upon better advisement; nevertheless his Majesty is well pleased to have it known that he is as far from alteration of his purpose to work an uniformity as they are importunate in their unjust desire of innovation, and expecteth that from henceforth without delay, where advice prevaileth not authority shall compel, and that the laws shall be put in execution where admonition taketh not effect; the penalty whereof they that will incur must impute it unto their own obstinacy, being guilty of disobedience to his Majesty, of uncharitableness unto any cure or charge that they have and in dutifulness might hold, and to themselves for any grievance or loss that they shall sustain; but as it is necessary where unity is to be effected there men of unquiet and factious spirit should not have place, so because by the removing and displacing of them opportunity and advantage may be taken by men of a corrupt mind and disposition (having the patronage and donation of some of the benefices so made void) to prefer ignorant and insufficient men into their places, his Majesty therefore hath commanded us in his name to require you all to take this especial charge upon you, that whosoever shall present any person to be admitted, not only in the rooms of any that shall be deprived but in all others, your Lordship shall duly inform yourself of the party's learning and integrity, and to be as well answerable for his sufficiency to instruct his people as to be conformable to his laws; a matter wherein the dependency upon the judgment of inferior officers hath brought great inconveniences, and whereof more especial care would now be had, seeing divers turbulent persons have mixed their complaints with this affirmation, that the names of good and understanding ministers shall now be supplied with idle drones and dumb images; which great enormity, as his Majesty himself should abhor more than any other, so he doubteth not but your Lordship and the rest will be most careful to extirpate all scandal and peril of any such effects of his religious care and wise directions, of which we need to use no further enlargement. What we have written in the premisses to your Lordship his Majesty requireth you forthwith to impart by your letters to all the bishops of your province, charging them, as they will answer the contrary at their perils, to omit no occasion, diligence, and care for the due execution of this charge and duty thus committed and commanded in his Majesty's name unto them: and so we bid your Lordship very heartily farewell. From Whitehall the tenth of December, MDCIV....

The Archbishop of Canterbury's directions to the same purpose [22 December, 1604]

Salutem in Christo. Your Lordship perceiving his Majesty's pleasure and constant resolution by the letter sent to me from the Lords, I have thought good to advertise you of such a course and uniform kind of proceeding with the disobedient and obstinate ministers as I think fit to be observed by myself, by your Lordship, and by the rest of my brethren, the bishops of this province.

Of such disobedient ministers some are already placed in the Church, some are not. Touching the second sort not placed, I doubt not but that you will strictly observe the xxxvith and xxxviith canons made the last Convocation, so as none of them be admitted hereafter to execute any ecclesiastical function without subscription, according to the tenor of the said canons. For the others already placed as aforesaid, they are of two kinds, and might both of them, having heretofore subscribed, be (as revolters from the same) by an ordinary course of justice deposed from the ministry: the one offereth and promiseth conformity, but is as yet unwilling again to subscribe; the other in his obstinacy will be induced to yield to neither. Touching such as will be contented to observe the orders and ceremonies prescribed in the Communion Book and fully to conform themselves accordingly to the use of their ministry, forasmuch as the near affinity between conformity and subscription doth give apparent hope that being men of sincerity, they will in a short time frame themselves to a more constant course, and subscribe to that again which they by their practice testify not to be repugnant to the Word of God, your Lordship may (an act being made to remain upon record of such their offer and promise) respite their subscription for some short time, advertising me of the names of every such person with all convenient speed, that thereupon such further order may be taken as shall be thought expedient in that behalf. Concerning those that utterly refuse both conformity and subscription, they are either curates, or stipendiary preachers, commonly called lecturers, or men beneficed. For the two first, the interest they have in their places is only by license from their Ordinary, and they are no longer to enjoy them *nisi quamdiu se bene gesserint*, so as upon such their refusal your Lordship is to suspend them *ab officio*, which is in effect a deprivation to them, and consequently by the law they are not to be restored until they shall both conform themselves and subscribe. As touching the third sort, for that it would not much trouble them nor work the conformity that is desired to put them to silence if they might enjoy their benefices, because I suppose they have been heretofore particularly admonished by your Lordship, but especially by his Majesty's proclamation, dated the 16th of July MDCIV[1], either to conform themselves to the Church and obey the same or else dispose of themselves and their families some other way, as being men unfit, for their obstinacy and contempt, to occupy such places, they are in another sort to be proceeded with; for in refusing to conform themselves to the use of the Communion Book, or in derogating or depraving any thing therein contained or any part thereof, they fall within the compass of divers laws, and particularly of the statute *primo Elizabethae* entituled 'An Act for Uniformity' etc. and so are subject to deprivation. I wish your Lordship diligently to peruse the said Act, being printed with the Communion Book, and for your better satisfaction herein do advertise you that the Lord Chief Justice and Mr Attorney-General being conferred with, are very resolute that you may lawfully by virtue thereof so proceed against such obstinate persons. The form which is to be used in their deprivation your chancellor very well knoweth; only let me put you in mind of the cxxii[d] canon, that your Lordship

---

[1] See p. 70 above.

in your own person pronounce the sentence; and if any by you so deprived shall appeal to me, I will be careful to execute the xcviii[th] constitution for stay thereof until the party shall subscribe: not doubting but that his Majesty, if there be cause, will take the like order for the Delegates[1]. Furthermore, if any of the said disordered persons shall willingly transgress any of the first twelve canons or of the three last, let the penalty therein mentioned be duly and respectively inflicted upon them. I have not hitherto greatly liked of any severe course; but perceiving by certain instructions lately cast abroad that the present opposition so lately prosecuted doth rather proceed from a combination of sundry factious, who in the pride of their mind are loath to be foiled (as they term it), than of any religious care or true conscience, I have thought it very necessary, for the repressing of such irregular designments, earnestly to commend to your Lordship the careful execution of these directions. And so with my very hearty commendations, I commit your Lordship unto the tuition of the Almighty. At Lambeth the 22 of December, MDCIV....

Cardwell, Documentary Annals, ii, 69–76.

(7) Petition concerning Religion, 1610

The exact date of this petition from the Commons is uncertain, but it was probably presented to the King along with the Petition of Grievances of 7 July, 1610 [p. 148 below].

Most gracious and dread Sovereign,

Since it hath pleased Almighty God of his unspeakable goodness and mercy towards us to call your Majesty to the government of this Kingdom, and hath crowned you with supreme power as well in the Church as in the commonwealth, for the advancement of his glory and the general benefit of all the subjects of this land,

We do in all humility present at the feet of your excellent Majesty ourselves and our desires, full of confidence in the assurances of your religious mind and princely disposition, that you will be graciously pleased to give life and effect to these our petitions, greatly tending (as undoubtedly we conceive) to the glory of God, the good of his Church, and safety of your most Royal Person, wherein we acknowledge our greatest happiness to consist.

I. Whereas good and provident laws have been made for the maintenance of God's true religion and safety of your Majesty's Royal Person, issue, and estate against Jesuits, seminary priests, and Popish recusants:

[1] On the Court of Delegates see *Tudor Constitutional Documents*, p. 40.

And although your Majesty by your godly, learned, and judicious writings have declared your Christian and princely zeal in the defence of the religion established, and have very lately (to the comfort of your best affected subjects) published to both Houses of Parliament your princely will and pleasure that recusants should not be concealed but detected and convicted:

Yet for that the laws are not executed against the priests, who are the corrupters of the people in religion and loyalty, and many recusants have already compounded, and (as it is to be feared) more and more (except your Majesty in your great wisdom prevent the same) will compound with those that beg their penalties[1], which maketh the laws altogether fruitless or of little or none effect, and the offenders to become bold, obdurate, and uncomfortable[2]:

Your Majesty therefore would be pleased, at the humble suit of your Commons in this present Parliament assembled, in the causes so highly concerning the glory of God, the preservation of true religion, of your Majesty and State, to suffer your Highness's natural clemency to retire itself and give place to justice, and to lay your royal command upon all your ministers of justice, both ecclesiastical and civil, to see the laws made against Jesuits, seminary priests, and recusants (of what kind and sort soever) to be duly and exactly executed without dread or delay And that your Majesty would be pleased likewise to take into your own hands the penalties due for recusancy, and that the same be not converted to the private gain of some, to your infinite loss, the emboldening of the Papists, and decay of true religion.

II. Whereas also divers painful and learned pastors that have long travailed in the work of the ministry with good fruit and blessing of their labours, who were ever ready to perform the legal subscription appointed by the Statute of the 13th of Elizabeth which only concerneth the confession of the true Christian Faith and doctrine of the Sacraments:

Yet for not conforming in points of ceremonies, and refusing the subscription directed by the late canons[3], have been removed from their ecclesiastical livings being their freehold, and debarred from all means of maintenance, to the great grief of sundry your Majesty's well-affected subjects:

Seeing the whole people that want instruction are by this

---

[1] *I.e.* the informers.   [2] In the sense of disquieting or uneasy.
[3] See p. 231.

means punished, and through ignorance lie open to the seduce-
ments of Popish and ill-affected persons:

We therefore most humbly beseech your Majesty would be
graciously pleased that such deprived and silenced ministers may
by licence or permission of the Reverend Fathers in their several
dioceses instruct and preach unto their people in such parishes
and places where they may be employed:

So as they apply themselves in their ministry to wholesome
doctrine and exhortation, and live quietly and peaceably in their
callings, and shall not by writing or preaching impugn things
established by public authority.

III. Whereas likewise, through plurality of benefices and
toleration of non-residency in many who possess not the meanest
of livings with cure of souls, the people in divers places want
instruction and are ignorant and easy to be seduced, whereby the
adversaries of our religion gain great advantage:

And although the pluralities and non-residents do frame
excuse of the smallness[1] of some livings and pretend the maintenance
of learning, yet we find by experience that they coupling many of
the greatest livings, do leave the least helpless, and the best as ill
served and supplied with preachers as the meanest:

And where pluralists heaping up many livings into one hand
do by that means keep divers learned men from maintenance, to
the discouragement of students and the hindrance of learning,

And the non-residents (forsaking or absenting themselves
from their pastoral charges) do leave the people as a prey to the
Popish seducers;

It might therefore please your most excellent Majesty, for
remedy of those evils in the Church, to provide that dispensations
for plurality of benefices with cure of souls may be prohibited,

And that the toleration of non-residency may be restrained.

So shall true religion be better upheld, and the people more
instructed in divine and civil duties.

IV. And forasmuch as excommunication is the heaviest censure for the most grievous offences which the Church doth retain,
yet exercised and inflicted upon an incredible number of the
common people by the subordinate officers of the jurisdiction
ecclesiastical, most commonly for very small causes grounded
upon the sole information of a base apparitor,

In which case the parties before they can be discharged are driven
to excessive expense for matters of very small moment, so that the

---

[1] The text reads 'smallest.'

richer break through more heinous offences and escape that censure by commutation of penance, to the great scandal of the Church government in the abuse of so high a censure, the contempt of the censure itself, and the grievance of your Majesty's poor subjects;

Wherefore your Majesty's most dutiful Commons most humbly beseech your Highness that some due and fit reformation may be had in the premisses.

Petyt, *Jus Parliamentarium*, pp. 318–21.

(8) Directions to Preachers, 1622

The King's letter to the Archbishop is dated 4 August, 1622.

The King's Letter to the Archbishop of Canterbury

Most Reverend Father in God, right trusty and entirely beloved Counsellor, we greet you well.

Forasmuch as the abuses and extravagances of preachers in the pulpit have been in all times suppressed in this realm by some Act of Council or State with the advice and resolution of grave and learned prelates; insomuch that the very licensing of preachers had the beginning by an order of Star Chamber the eighth day of July in the nineteenth year of the reign of King Henry the Eighth our noble predecessor: And whereas at this present divers young students, by reading of late writers and ungrounded divines, do broach many times unprofitable, unsound, seditious, and dangerous doctrines, to the scandal of the Church and disquiet of the State and present government, we upon humble representation unto us of these inconveniences by yourself and sundry other grave and reverend prelates of this Church, as also of our princely care and zeal for the extirpation of schism and dissension growing from these seeds, and for the settling of a religious and peaceable government both in Church and commonwealth, do by these our special letters straitly charge and command you to use all possible care and diligence that these limitations and cautions herewith sent unto you concerning preachers be duly and strictly from henceforth put in practice and observed by the several bishops within your jurisdiction. And to this end our pleasure is, that you send them forthwith copies of these directions, to be by them speedily sent and communicated unto every parson, vicar, curate, lecturer, and minister, in every cathedral or parish church within their several dioceses; and that you earnestly require them to employ their utmost endeavours in the performance of this so important a business, letting them know that we have a special eye unto their proceedings and expect a strict accompt thereof, both from you and every of them. And these our Letters shall be your sufficient warrant and discharge in that behalf....

Directions concerning Preachers sent with the Letter

I. That no preacher under the degree and calling of a Bishop or Dean of a cathedral or collegiate church (and they upon the King's days and set festivals) do take occasion, by the expounding of any text of Scripture whatsoever, to fall into any set discourse or common place[1], otherwise than by opening the coherence and division of the text, which shall not be comprehended and warranted, in essence, substance, effect, or natural inference, within some one of the Articles of Religion set forth one thousand five hundred sixty and two, or in some of the Homilies set forth by authority of the Church of England not only for a help for the non-preaching but withal for a pattern and boundary (as it were) for the preaching ministers. And for their further instructions for the performance hereof, that they forthwith read over and peruse diligently the said Book of Articles and the two Books of Homilies.

II. That no parson, vicar, curate, or lecturer shall preach any sermon or collation hereafter upon Sundays and holy days in the afternoon in any cathedral or parish church throughout the kingdom but upon some part of the Catechism or some text taken out of the Creed, Ten Commandments, or the Lord's Prayer (funeral sermons only excepted); and that those preachers be most encouraged and approved of who spend the afternoon's exercise in the examination of children in their Catechism, which is the most ancient and laudable custom of teaching in the Church of England.

III. That no preacher of what title so ever under the degree of a Bishop, or Dean at the least, do from henceforth presume to preach in any popular auditory the deep points of predestination, election, reprobation, or of the universality, efficacy, resistibility or irresistibility, of God's grace; but leave those themes rather to be handled by the learned men, and that moderately and modestly by way of use and application rather than by way of positive doctrines, being fitter for the Schools than for simple auditories.

IV. That no preacher of what title or denomination soever from henceforth shall presume in any auditory within this kingdom to declare, limit, or bound out by way of positive doctrine in any lecture or sermon the power, prerogative, and jurisdiction, authority, or duty of Sovereign Princes, or otherwise meddle

[1] *I.e.* the theme or topic of a sermon; the term was also applied to the text.

with matters of State and the differences between Princes and the people than as they are instructed and precedented[1] in the Homilies of Obedience and the rest of the Homilies and Articles of Religion set forth (as before is mentioned) by public authority, but rather confine themselves wholly to those two heads of faith and good life which are all the subject of the ancient sermons and homilies.

V. That no preacher of what title or denomination soever shall presume causelessly (or without invitation from the text) to fall into bitter invectives and undecent railing speeches against the persons of either Papists or Puritans, but modestly and gravely, when they are occasioned thereunto by the text of Scripture, free both the doctrine and the discipline of the Church of England from the aspersions of either adversary, especially where the auditory is suspected to be tainted with one or the other infection.

VI. Lastly, That the Archbishops and Bishops of the kingdom (whom his Majesty hath good cause to blame for their former remissness) be more wary and choice in their licensing of preachers, and revoke all grants made to any chancellor, official, or commissary to pass licences in this kind: And that all the lecturers throughout the Kingdom of England (a new body severed from the ancient clergy, as being neither parsons, vicars, nor curates) be licensed henceforward in the Court of Faculties by recommendation of the party from the Bishop of the diocese under his hand and seal, with a *fiat* from the Lord Archbishop of Canterbury [and] a confirmation under the Great Seal of England. And that such as do transgress any one of these directions be suspended by the Bishop of the diocese, or in his default by the Archbishop of the province, *ab officio et beneficio* for a year and a day, until his Majesty by the advice of the next Convocation shall prescribe some further punishment.

Rushworth, *Historical Collections*, i, 64–5.

§ 2. THE ROMAN CATHOLICS

If the King's attitude towards the Puritans roused the hostility of his Parliaments against him, still more did his attitude towards the Roman Catholics. Here he was betrayed by his very virtues. At his speech at the opening of his first Parliament in 1604 [p. 28] he said, 'My mind was ever so free from persecution, or thralling of my subjects in matters of conscience, as I hope that those of that profession within this kingdom have a proof since my coming, that I was so far from increasing their burdens with Rehoboam,

[1] Furnished with a precedent.

as I have, so much as either time, occasion, or law could permit, lightened them.' And this claim was justified, for although Parliament had passed an Act to confirm the penal laws of Elizabeth's reign [below], the pressure of them in practice was relaxed by lenient administration[1]. At this point, however, the cause of the many was prejudiced by the fanaticism of the few. First the Bye Treason, and then the Main Treason, set up a reaction in the mind of James, and brought to an untimely end the first attempt ever made by any English Government towards toleration for the Catholics. In February, 1605, the King announced a change of policy in the Council, 'protesting his utter detestation of' the 'superstitious religion' of the Papists, and that 'he was so far from favouring it, as if he thought his son and heir after him would give any toleration thereunto, he would wish him fairly buried before his eyes.'[2] The resolute enforcement of the penal laws which followed, led to Gunpowder Plot, and this in turn to the Acts of 1606 [p. 86], which represent the extreme limit of anti-Catholic legislation[3]. But as soon as the immediate danger was over, James was disposed once more to relax the severity of their administration; and this involved him in a fresh quarrel with his Parliaments. In 1610 he was urged by the Commons [p. 77] to cause to be executed, 'without dread or delay' the 'good and provident laws' against the priests, 'who are the corrupters of the people in religion and loyalty'; and similar demands appear in a petition of 1621 [p. 276].

(1) Act concerning Jesuits and Seminary Priests, 1604

An Act for the due execution of the Statutes against
Jesuits, Seminary Priests, Recusants, etc.

I. For the better and due execution of the Statutes heretofore made as well against Jesuits, seminary priests, and other such like priests as also against all manner of recusants: Be it ordained and enacted by authority of this present Parliament, That all and every the Statutes heretofore made in the reign of the late Queen of famous memory, Elizabeth, as well against Jesuits, seminary priests, and other priests, deacons, religious and ecclesiastical persons whatsoever, made, ordained, or professed, or to be made, ordained, or professed, by any authority or jurisdiction derived, challenged, or pretended from the See of Rome, as those which do in any wise concern the withdrawing of the King's subjects from their due obedience and the religion now professed, and the taking of the oath of obedience unto the King's Majesty his heirs and successors, together with all those made in the said late

---

[1] See also James I's views on priests and recusants in the speech to the judges in 1616 [p. 17 above].

[2] Henry Ellis, *Original Letters*, 2nd Series, iii, 216.

[3] But see also the Oaths Act of 1610 [p. 105], which contained clauses imposing penalties on recusant married women.

Queen's time against any manner of recusants, shall be put in due and exact execution.

*   *   *   *   *   *

IV. And be it further enacted..., That where any seizure shall be had of the two parts of any lands...for the not payment of the twenty pounds due and payable for each month, according to the Statute in that case lately made and provided[1], That in every such case every such two parts shall, according to the extent thereof, go towards the satisfaction and payment of the twenty pounds due and payable for each month and unpaid by any such recusant; And that the third part thereof shall not be extended[2] or seized by the King's Majesty his heirs or successors....And where any such seizure shall be had of the two parts of the lands... of any such recusant as is aforesaid and such recusant shall die (the debt or duty by reason of his recusancy not paid, satisfied, or discharged), that in every such case the same two parts shall continue in his Majesty's possession until the residue or remainder of the said debt or duty be thereby or otherwise paid, satisfied, or discharged; And that his Majesty his heirs or successors shall not seize or extend any third part descending to any such heirs, or any part thereof, either by reason of the recusancy of his or her ancestor or of the recusancy of any such heir.

V. And be it further enacted..., That all and every person and persons under the King's obedience which at any time...shall pass or go, or shall send or cause to be sent any child or other person under their or any of their government, into any the parts beyond the seas out of the King's obedience, to the intent to enter into...any college, seminary, or house of Jesuits, priests, or any other Popish order, profession, or calling whatsoever, or repair in or to any the same to be instructed, persuaded, or strengthened in the Popish religion, or in any sort so to profess the same, every such person...shall for every such offence forfeit to his Majesty... the sum of one hundred pounds; And every such person so passing or being sent beyond the seas to any such intent or purpose as is aforesaid, shall by authority of this present Act, as in respect of him or her self only and not to or in respect of any of his heirs or posterity, be disabled and made incapable to inherit, purchase, take, have, or enjoy any manors, lands, tenements, annuities, profits, commodities, hereditaments, goods, chattels, debts, duties, legacies, or sums of money within this Realm of England or any other his Majesty's Dominions; and that all and singular estates,

---

[1] 23 Eliz. c. 1: printed in *Tudor Constitutional Documents*, p. 152.
[2] Seized upon in satisfaction of a debt.

terms[1], and other interests whatsoever hereafter to be made, suffered, or done to or for the use or behoof of any such person or persons, or upon any trust or confidence mediately or immediately[2] to or for the benefit or relief of any such person or persons, shall be utterly void and of none effect to all intents, constructions, and purposes.

VI. And be it further enacted..., That if any person born within this Realm or any the King's Majesty's Dominions be at this present in any college, seminary, house, or place in any parts beyond the seas (to the end to be instructed or strengthened in the Popish religion) which shall not make return into this Realm or some of his Majesty's Dominions within one year next coming after the end of this session of Parliament and submit himself..., shall be, in respect of himself only and not to or in respect of any of his heirs or posterity, utterly disabled and uncapable to inherit, have, or enjoy any manors, [etc.].... Provided always, That if any such person or child so passing... shall after become conformable and obedient unto the laws and ordinances of the Church of England, and shall repair to the church and there remain and be as is aforesaid, and continue in such conformity according to the true intent and meaning of the said statutes and ordinances; that in every such case every such person and child, for and during such time as he or she shall so continue in such conformity and obedience, shall be freed and discharged of all and every such disability and incapacity as is before mentioned.

VII. And be it further enacted..., That no woman, nor any child under the age of one and twenty years (except sailors or ship-boys or the apprentice or factor of some merchant in trade of merchandise) shall be permitted to pass over the seas (except the same shall be by licence...) upon pain that the officers of the port that shall willingly or negligently suffer any such so to pass, or shall not enter the names of such passengers licensed, shall forfeit his office and all his goods and chattels; and upon pain that the owner of any ship or vessel that shall wittingly or willingly carry any such over the seas without licence as is aforesaid shall forfeit his ship or vessel and all the tackle; and every master or mariner of or in any ship or vessel offending as aforesaid shall forfeit all their goods and suffer imprisonment by the space of twelve months, without bail or mainprize.

1 & 2 Jac. I, c. 4: *Statutes of the Realm*, iv, 1020.

---

1 An estate or interest in land limited to a certain period.
2 Through an intermediary or directly.

(2) Penal Legislation of 1606

An Act for the better discovering and repressing of Popish Recusants

I. Forasmuch as it is found by daily experience that many his Majesty's subjects that adhere in their hearts to the Popish religion, by the infection drawn from thence, and by the wicked and devilish counsel of Jesuits, seminaries, and other like persons dangerous to the Church and State, are so far perverted in the point of their loyalties and due allegiance unto the King's Majesty and the Crown of England as they are ready to entertain and execute any treasonable conspiracies and practices, as evidently appears by that more than barbarous and horrible attempt to have blown up with gunpowder the King, Queen, Prince, Lords, and Commons in the House of Parliament assembled, tending to the utter subversion of the whole State, lately undertaken by the instigation of Jesuits and seminaries and in advancement of their religion by their scholars taught and instructed by them to that purpose, which attempt by the only goodness of Almighty God was discovered and defeated: And where divers persons Popishly affected do nevertheless, the better to cover and hide their false hearts and with the more safety to attend the opportunity to execute their mischievous designs, repair sometimes to church to escape the penalty of the laws in that behalf provided; For the better discovery therefore of such persons and their evil affections to the King's Majesty and the state of this his Realm, to the end that being known, their evil purposes may be the better prevented, be it enacted..., That every Popish recusant convicted or hereafter to be convicted, which heretofore hath conformed him or her self or which shall hereafter conform him or her self, and repair to the church and continue there during the time of Divine Service according to the laws and statutes in that behalf made and provided, shall within the first year next after the end of this session of Parliament (if he or she be conformed as aforesaid, before the end of this session of Parliament), or within the first year next after that he or she shall after this session of Parliament so conform him or her self and repair to church as aforesaid, and after the said first year shall once in every year following at the least receive the blessed Sacrament of the Lord's Supper in the church of that parish where he or she shall most usually abide or be within the said year wherein by the true meaning of this Statute he or she ought so to receive, and if there be no such parish church, then in the church next adjoining to the place of his or her such most usual abode: And if any recusant so conformed shall not receive the Sacrament of the Lord's Supper accordingly, he or she shall for such not receiving lose and forfeit for the first year twenty pounds and for the second year...forty pounds and for every year after...threescore pounds, until he or she shall have received the said Sacrament as is aforesaid....

II. And be it further enacted...that the churchwardens and constables of every town, parish, or chapel for the time being... shall once in every year present the monthly absence from church of all and all manner Popish recusants within such towns and parishes, and shall present the names of every of the children of the said recusants being of the age of nine years and upwards abiding with their said parents, and as near as they can the age of every of the said children, as also the names of the servants of such recusants, at the General or Quarter Sessions of that shire, limit, division, or liberty.

III. And be it further enacted..., That all such presentments shall be accepted, entered, and recorded in the said Sessions by the Clerk of the Peace or Town Clerk for the time being....

IV. And be it further enacted..., That the Justices of Assize and Gaol Delivery at their Assizes and the said Justices of Peace at any their said Sessions shall have power and authority by virtue of this Act to enquire, hear, and determine of all recusants and offences as well for not receiving the Sacrament aforesaid according to the meaning of this law as for not repairing to church according to the meaning of former laws, in such manner and form as the said Justices of Assize and Gaol Delivery do or may now do by former laws in the case of recusancy for not repairing to church: And also shall have power at their said Assizes and Gaol Delivery and at the Sessions (in which any indictment against any person either for not repairing to church according to former laws or not receiving the said Sacrament according to this law shall be taken) to make proclamation by which it shall be commanded that the body of every such offender shall be rendered to the sheriff of the same county or bailiff or other keeper of the gaol of the liberty before the next Assizes and general Gaol Delivery or before the next General or Quarter Sessions respectively to be holden for the said shire, division, limit, or liberty: And if at the said next Assizes and general Gaol Delivery or Sessions the same offender so proclaimed shall not make appearance of record, that then upon every such default recorded the same shall be as sufficient a conviction in law of the said offence whereof the party shall stand indicted as aforesaid as if upon the same indictment a trial by verdict thereupon had proceeded and been found against him or her and recorded.

V. And be it further enacted, That every offender in not repairing to Divine Service...that hereafter shall fortune to be thereof once convicted, shall...pay into the receipt of the Exchequer after the rate of twenty pounds for every month which shall be contained in the indictment whereupon such conviction shall be, and shall also for every month after such conviction, without any other indictment or conviction, forfeit twenty pounds ...except in such cases where the King shall and may by force of this Act refuse the same and take two parts of the lands, tenements, hereditaments, leases, and farms of such offender till the said party...shall conform himself and come to church.... And that every conviction recorded for any offence before mentioned shall from the Justices before whom the record of such conviction shall be remaining be certified into the King's Majesty's Court of Exchequer before the end of the term following such conviction, in such convenient certainty for the time and other circumstances as the Court of Exchequer may thereupon award out process for the seizure of the lands and goods of every such offender as the case shall require; and if default shall be made in any part of any payment aforesaid...that then and so often the King's Majesty...shall and may by process out of the said Exchequer take, seize, and enjoy all the goods and two parts as well of all the lands, tenements, and hereditaments, leases, and farms of such offender..., leaving the third part only of the same ...to and for the maintenance and relief of the same offender, his wife, children, and family.

VI. And whereas by an Act made...in the three and twentieth year of the reign of the late Queen Elizabeth[1], intituled an Act to retain the subjects of the said late Queen in their due obedience, it was...enacted..., That every person above the age of sixteen years which should not repair to some church, chapel, or usual place of common prayer but forbear the same, contrary to the tenor of a Statute made in the first year of the reign of the said late Queen for uniformity of common prayer[2], and being thereof lawfully convicted, should forfeit unto the said Queen for every month...which he or she should so forbear twenty pounds of lawful English money;...And whereas afterwards by another Act of Parliament of the said Queen[3] it was further enacted... how and when the said payments of the said twenty pounds

---

[1] 23 Eliz. c. 1: see *Tudor Constitutional Documents*, p. 152.
[2] 1 Eliz. c. 2: *ib.* p. 136.   [3] 29 Eliz. c. 6.

should be made, and that if default should be made...that then and so often the said Queen should and might, by process out of her Highness's Exchequer, take, seize, and enjoy all the goods, and two parts as well of all the lands [etc.]...of such offender..., leaving the third part only of the same...to and for the maintenance and relief of the same offender, his wife, children, and family....Now forasmuch as the said penalty of twenty pounds monthly is a greater burden unto men of small living than unto such as are of better ability and do refuse to come unto Divine Service as aforesaid, who rather than they will have two parts of their lands to be seized will be ready always to pay the said twenty pounds,...and yet retain the residue of their livings and inheritance in their own hands, being of great yearly value, which they do for the most part employ (as experience hath taught) to the maintenance of superstition and Popish religion and to the relief of Jesuits, seminaries, Popish priests, and other dangerous persons to the State: Therefore to the intent that hereafter the penalty for not repairing to Divine Service might be inflicted in better proportion upon men of great ability, Be it enacted..., That the King's Majesty...shall...have full power and liberty to refuse the penalty of twenty pounds a month, though it be tendered ready to be paid according to the law, and thereupon to seize and take to his own use...two parts in three parts to be divided as well of all the lands [etc.]...till every such offender shall conform him or her self respectively as aforesaid, in lieu and full recompense of the twenty pounds monthly that during his such seizure and retainer shall incur....

VII. Provided always...That the King's Majesty...shall not take into his two parts but leave to such offender his chief mansion house as part of his third part, and shall not demise, lease, nor put over[1] the said two parts nor any part thereof to any recusant....

VIII. And for the better trial how his Majesty's subjects stand affected in point of their loyalty and due obedience, Be it also enacted...that...it shall be lawful to and for any Bishop in his diocese, or any two Justices of the Peace whereof one of them to be of the Quorum,...to require any person of the age of eighteen years or above, being or which shall be convict or indicted of or for any recusancy, other than noblemen or noblewomen, for not repairing to Divine Service...or which shall not have received the said Sacrament twice within the year then next past, noblemen and noblewomen excepted or any person passing in or

---

[1] Transfer or make over.

through the county, shire, or liberty, and unknown except as is last before excepted, that being examined by them upon oath, shall confess or not deny himself or herself to be a recusant, or shall confess or not deny that he or she had not received the said Sacrament twice within the year then last past, to take the oath hereafter following upon the Holy Evangelist; which said Bishop or two Justices of the Peace shall certify in writing subscribed with his or their hands at the next General or Quarter Sessions for that shire, limit, division, or liberty within which the said oath shall be so taken, the Christian name, surname, and place of abode of every person which shall so take the said oath, which certificate shall be there recorded by the Clerk of the Peace or Town Clerk and kept amongst the records of the said Sessions.

IX. And be it further enacted, That if any such person or persons, other than noblemen or noblewomen, shall refuse to answer upon oath to such Bishop or Justices of Peace examining him or her as aforesaid, or to take the said oath so duly tendered unto him or her by such Bishop or two such Justices of Peace out of Sessions, That then the said Bishop or Justices of Peace shall and may commit the same person to the common gaol, there to remain without bail or mainprize until the next Assizes or General or Quarter Sessions...where the said oath shall be again in the said open Assizes or Sessions required of such person...; And if the said person or persons or any other person whatsoever, other than noblemen or noblewomen, of the age of eighteen years or above shall refuse to take the said oath being tendered...in... Assizes or...Quarter Sessions, every person so refusing shall incur the danger and penalty of Praemunire....

The tenor of which said oath hereafter followeth: I A.B. do truly and sincerely acknowledge, profess, testify, and declare in my conscience before God and the world, That our Sovereign Lord King James is lawful and rightful King of this Realm and of all other his Majesty's dominions and countries; and that the Pope, neither of himself, nor by any authority of the Church or See of Rome, or by any other means with any other, hath any power or authority to depose the King, or to dispose any of his Majesty's kingdoms or dominions, or to authorise any foreign prince to invade or annoy him or his countries, or to discharge any of his subjects of their allegiance and obedience to his Majesty, or to give licence or leave to any of them to bear arms, raise tumult, or to offer any violence or hurt to his Majesty's Royal Person, State, or Government, or to any of his Majesty's subjects within his Majesty's dominions. Also I do swear from my heart that

notwithstanding any declaration or sentence of excommunication
or deprivation made or granted, or to be made or granted, by the
Pope or his successors or by any authority derived or pretended to
be derived from him or his See against the said King his heirs or
successors, or any absolution of the said subjects from their
obedience, I will bear faith and true allegiance to his Majesty his
heirs and successors, and him or them will defend to the uttermost
of my power against all conspiracies and attempts whatsoever
which shall be made against his or their persons their crown and
dignity by reason or colour of any such sentence or declaration or
otherwise, and will do my best endeavour to disclose and make
known unto his Majesty his heirs and successors all treasons and
traitorous conspiracies which I shall know or hear of to be against
him or any of them: And I do further swear, That I do from my
heart abhor, detest, and abjure, as impious and heretical, this
damnable doctrine and position, that princes which be excommunicated or deprived by the Pope may be deposed or
murdered by their subjects or any other whosoever: And I do
believe and in my conscience am resolved that neither the Pope
nor any person whatsoever hath power to absolve me of this oath
or any part thereof, which I acknowledge by good and full
authority to be lawfully ministered unto me, and do renounce all
pardons and dispensations to the contrary: And all these things I
do plainly and sincerely acknowledge and swear, according to
these express words by me spoken, and according to the plain and
common sense and understanding of the same words, without any
equivocation or mental evasion or secret reservation whatsoever:
And I do make this recognition and acknowledgment heartily,
willingly, and truly, upon the true faith of a Christian, So help me
God. Unto which oath so taken the said person shall subscribe
his or her name or mark.

* * * * * *

XII. And forasmuch as it is found by late experience that
such as go voluntarily out of this realm of England to serve
foreign princes, states, or potentates are for the most part perverted in their religion and loyalty by Jesuits and fugitives with
whom they do there converse, Be it therefore enacted by the
authority aforesaid, That every subject of this realm that after the
tenth day of June next coming shall go or pass out of this realm to
serve any foreign prince, state, or potentate, or shall after the said
tenth day of June pass over the seas and there shall voluntarily
serve any such foreign prince, state, or potentate, not having

before his or their going or passing as aforesaid taken the oath aforesaid,...shall be a felon....

*   *   *   *   *   *

XIII. Provided always, That this last mentioned branch shall not extend to any person or persons which are already gone or shall go beyond the seas to serve any foreign prince, state, or potentate before the tenth day of June next coming, for his said going or passing before the said tenth day of June.

XIV. And further be it enacted..., That if any person or persons at any time after the said tenth day of June shall either upon the seas or beyond the seas or in any other place within the dominions of the King's Majesty...put in practice to absolve, persuade, or withdraw any of the subjects of the King's Majesty ...from their natural obedience..., or to reconcile them to the Pope or See of Rome, or to move them or any of them to promise obedience to any pretended authority of the See of Rome or to any other prince, state, or potentate, that then every such person, their procurers, counsellors, aiders, and maintainers knowing the same, shall be to all intents adjudged traitors, and being thereof lawfully convicted shall have judgment, suffer, and forfeit as in cases of High Treason: And if any such person as aforesaid at any time after the said tenth day of June shall be either upon the seas or beyond the seas or in any other place within the dominions of the King's Majesty...willingly absolved or withdrawn as aforesaid, or willingly reconciled, or shall promise obedience to any such pretended authority, prince, state, or potentate as aforesaid, that every such person and persons, their procurers and counsellors, aiders and maintainers knowing the same, shall be...adjudged traitors....

*   *   *   *   *   *

XVIII. And be it further enacted, That if any subject of this realm at any time after one month next after the end of this present session of Parliament shall not resort or repair every Sunday to some church, chapel, or some other usual place appointed for common prayer, and there hear Divine Service,... that then it shall and may be lawful to and for any one Justice of Peace of that limit, division, or liberty wherein the said party shall dwell, upon proof unto him made of such default by confession of the party or oath of witness, to call the said party before him, and if he or she shall not make a sufficient excuse and due proof thereof to the satisfaction of the said Justice of Peace, that it shall be lawful for the said Justice of Peace to give warrant to the churchwarden of the said parish wherein the said party shall dwell, under his hand and seal, to levy twelve pence for every such default by distress and sale of the goods of every such offender...; and that in default of such distress it shall and may be lawful for the said Justice of Peace to commit every such offender to some prison within the said shire...wherein such offender shall be inhabiting, until payment be made of the said sum or sums so to be forfeited; which forfeiture shall be employed to and for the use of the poor of that parish wherein the offender shall be resident....

XIX. This section repeals clauses 5 and 6 of 35 Eliz. c. 1[1], and substitutes the following: 'That every person which...shall willingly maintain...in his...house any servant, sojourner, or stranger who shall not go to...some church or chapel or usual place of common prayer to hear Divine Service...by the space of one month together not having a reasonable excuse,...shall forfeit ten pounds for every month that he...shall so...harbour any such servant [etc.]...and that every person which shall...keep in his...service, fee, or livery any person...which shall not go to ...some church...shall forfeit for every month...ten pounds....'

*   *   *   *   *   *

XXV. Provided always, That neither this Act nor anything therein contained shall extend to take away or abridge the authority or jurisdiction of the ecclesiastical censures for any cause or matter; but that the Commissioners of his Majesty his heirs and successors in Causes Ecclesiastical for the time being, and the Archbishops, Bishops, and other ecclesiastical judges may do and proceed as before the making of this Act they lawfully did or might have done; anything in this Act to the contrary in any wise notwithstanding.

XXVI. Provided always and be it enacted, That no person shall be charged or chargeable with any penalty or forfeiture by force of this Act which shall happen for his wife's offence in not receiving the said Sacrament during her marriage, nor that any woman shall be charged or chargeable with any penalty or forfeiture by force of this Act for any such offence of not receiving which shall happen during her marriage.

XXVII. Provided also and be it enacted by the authority of this Parliament, That in all cases where any Bishop or Justices of the Peace may by force of this Act require and take of any subject the oath above mentioned, that the Lords of the Privy Council for the time being or any six of them, whereof the Lord Chancellor, Lord Treasurer, or the Principal Secretary for the time to be one, shall have full power and authority by force of this Act at any time or times to require and take the said oaths before mentioned of any nobleman or noblewoman (then being above the age of

---

[1] These are printed in *Tudor Constitutional Documents*, p. 199.

eighteen years); And if any such nobleman or noblewoman (other than women married) shall refuse to take such oath or oaths, that in every such case such nobleman or noblewoman shall incur the pain and danger of a Praemunire.

XXVIII. Provided also and be it enacted..., That where any person...shall go or pass out of the Cinque Ports or any member thereof to any parts beyond the seas to serve any foreign prince, state, or potentate, that in every such case the Lord Warden of the Cinque Ports for the time being, or any person by him in that behalf appointed or to be appointed, shall have full power and authority by virtue hereof to take the bond and minister the oath to such passengers as is above mentioned.

3 & 4 Jac. I, c. 4: *Statutes of the Realm*, iv, 1071.

An Act to prevent and avoid dangers which may
grow by Popish Recusants

I. Whereas divers Jesuits, seminaries, and Popish priests daily do withdraw many of his Majesty's subjects from the true service of Almighty God and the religion established within this Realm to the Romish religion and from their loyal obedience to his Majesty, and have of late secretly persuaded divers recusants and Papists and encouraged and emboldened them to commit most damnable treasons, tending to the overthrow of God's true religion, the destruction of his Majesty and his royal issue, and the overthrow of the whole State and commonwealth, if God of his goodness and mercy had not within few hours before the intended time of the execution thereof revealed and disclosed the same: Wherefore to discover and prevent such secret damnable conspiracies and treasons as hereafter may be put in ure[1] by such evil disposed persons if remedy be not therefor provided, be it enacted..., That such person as shall first discover to any Justice of Peace any recusant or other person which shall entertain or relieve any Jesuit, seminary, or Popish priest, or shall discover any mass to have been said, and the persons that were present at such mass, and the priest that said the same, or any of them, within three days next after the offence committed, and that by reason of such discovery any of the said offenders be taken and convicted or attainted, that then the person which hath made such discovery shall not only be freed from the danger and penalty of any law for such offence if he be an offender therein, but also shall have the third part of the forfeiture of all such sums of money, goods, chattels, and debts which shall be forfeited by such offence (so

[1] Put in practice.

as the same total forfeiture exceed not the sum of one hundred and fifty pounds), and if it exceeds the sum of one hundred and fifty pounds, the said person so discovering the said offence shall have the sum of fifty pounds only for every such discovery....

II. And whereas the repair of such evil affected persons to the Court or to the City of London may be very dangerous to his Majesty's person, and may give them more liberty to meet, consult, and plot their treasons and practices against the State than if they should be restrained and confined unto their private houses in the country: For remedy hereof be it enacted..., That no Popish recusant convicted or to be convicted shall come into the Court or house where the King's Majesty or his Heir Apparent to the Crown of England shall be, unless he be commanded so to do by the King's Majesty his heirs or successors, or by warrant in writing from the Lords and others of the most honourable Privy Council,...upon pain to forfeit for every time so offending one hundred pounds, the one moiety to the King's Majesty..., the other moiety to him that will discover and sue for the same...: And that all Popish recusants indicted or convicted, and all other persons which have not repaired to some usual church or chapel and there heard Divine Service, but have forborne the same by the space of three months last past,...dwelling, abiding, or remaining within the City of London or the liberties thereof, or within ten miles of the said City, shall within three months next after the end of this session of Parliament depart from the said City of London and ten miles compass of the same, and also shall deliver up their names to the Lord Mayor of London in case such recusant do dwell or remain within the said City of London or the liberties thereof: And in case the said recusant shall dwell or remain in any other county within ten miles of the same City, then the said recusant shall deliver up his or her name to the next Justice of Peace within the such county where the said recusant shall so dwell or remain, within forty days after the end of this session of Parliament, upon pain that every person offending herein shall forfeit...the sum of one hundred pounds, the one moiety whereof shall be to the King's Majesty..., the other moiety to him or them that will sue for the same....And that all Popish recusants which shall hereafter come, dwell, or remain within the said City of London, ...or within ten miles of the said City, which now are or hereafter shall be indicted or convicted of such recusancy, or which shall at any time hereafter not repair unto some usual church or chapel and there hear Divine Service, but shall forbear the same by the

space of three months..., shall within ten days after such indictment or conviction depart from the said City of London and ten
miles compass of the same, and also shall deliver up their names
to the Lord Mayor of London...in case such recusant shall
dwell or remain within the said City...: And in case the said
recusant shall dwell or remain in any other county within ten
miles of the said City, then the said recusant shall deliver up
his or her name to the next Justice of Peace within such county
where the said recusant shall so dwell or remain, within the
said ten days,...upon pain that every person offending herein
shall likewise forfeit...the like sum of one hundred pounds,
the one moiety whereof shall be to the King's Majesty...and
the other to him or them that will sue for the same....

    III. Provided always, That such person or persons as now
use any trade, mystery, or manual occupation within the said
City of London or within ten miles of the same, and such as have
or shall have their only dwelling within the said City or ten miles
compass of the same, not having any other dwelling or place of
abode elsewhere, shall or may remain and continue in such place
within the said City or ten miles of the same as they have dwelled,
inhabited, or remained in by the space of three months next
before this present session of Parliament; anything herein contained to the contrary notwithstanding.

    IV. 35 Eliz. c. 2, § 7[1] repealed, which allowed recusants to obtain licences to
travel.

    V. Provided nevertheless and be it further enacted..., That
it shall and may be lawful for the King's most excellent Majesty
his heirs and successors or for three or more of his Majesty's most
honourable Privy Council...to give licence to every such recusant
to go and travel out of the compass of the said five miles[2] for such
time as in the said licence shall be contained for their travelling,
attending, and returning, and without any other cause to be
expressed within the said licence; And if any of the persons which
are so confined by virtue of the said Statute as is aforesaid shall
have necessary occasion or business to go and travel out of the
compass of the said five miles, that then and in every such case,
upon licence in writing in that behalf to be gotten under the
hands and seals of four of the Justices of Peace of the same
county, limit, division, or place next adjoining to the place of
abode of such recusant, with the privity and assent in writing of the
Bishop of the diocese or of the Lieutenant or of any Deputy

---

[1] Printed in *Tudor Constitutional Documents*, p. 163.
[2] The limit set by 35 Eliz. c. 2.

Lieutenant of the same county residing within the said county or liberty under their hands and seals;...it shall and may thereupon be lawful for every such person so licensed to go and travel about such their necessary business,...the said party so licensed first taking his corporal oath before the said four Justices of the Peace or any of them (who shall have authority by virtue of this Act to minister the same) that he hath truly informed them of the cause of this journey, and that he shall not make any causeless stays....And every person so confined which shall depart or go above five miles from the place whereunto he is or shall be confined not having such licence and not having such oath as aforesaid, shall incur the pain and penalty and forfeit as a recusant convicted and passing or going above five miles from the said place whereunto he is or shall be confined by the said Statute of tricesimo quinto Elizabeth should do.

VI. And be it further enacted by the authority aforesaid, That no recusant convict shall at any time after the end of this session of Parliament practise the Common Law of this Realm as a counsellor, clerk, attorney, or solicitor in the same, nor shall practise the Civil Law as advocate or proctor, nor practise physic, nor exercise or use the trade or art of an apothecary, nor shall be judge, minister, clerk, or steward of or in any Court or keep any Court, nor shall be Register or Town Clerk or other minister or officer in any Court, nor shall bear any office or charge as captain, lieutenant, corporal, sergeant, ancient-bearer[1], or other office in camp, troop, band, or company of soldiers, nor shall be captain, master, governor, or bear any office or charge of or in any ship, castle, or fortress of the King's Majesty's his heirs and successors, but be utterly disabled for the same; And every person offending herein shall also forfeit for every such offence one hundred pounds, the one moiety whereof shall be to the King's Majesty... and the other moiety to him that will sue for the same.....

VII. And be it also enacted by the authority aforesaid, That no Popish recusant convict, nor any having a wife being a Popish recusant convict,...shall exercise any public office or charge in the commonwealth, but shall be utterly disabled to exercise the same by himself or by his deputy, (except such husband himself, and his children which shall be above the age of nine years abiding with him, and his servants in household, shall once every month at the least, not having any reasonable excuse to the contrary, repair to some church or chapel usual for Divine Service and there hear Divine Service, and the said husband and such his

---

[1] Ensign- or standard-bearer.

children and servants as are of meet age receive the Sacrament of the Lord's Supper at such times as are limited by the laws of this Realm, and do bring up his said children in true religion).

VIII. And be it also enacted by the authority aforesaid, That every married woman being or that shall be a Popish recusant convicted (her husband not standing convicted of Popish recusancy) which shall not conform herself and remain conformed, but shall forbear to repair to some church or usual place of common prayer and there to hear Divine Service and sermon, if any then be, and within the said year receive the Sacrament of the Lord's Supper, according to the laws of this Realm, by the space of one whole year next before the death of her said husband, shall forfeit and lose to the King's Majesty his heirs and successors the issues and profits of two parts of her jointure and two parts of her dower in three parts, to be divided during her life of or out of any the lands, tenements, or hereditaments which are or were her said husband's, and also be disabled to be executrix or administratrix of her said husband, and to have or demand any part or portion of her said late husband's goods or chattels....

IX. And be it further enacted by the authority aforesaid, That every Popish recusant which is or shall be convicted of Popish recusancy shall stand and be reputed to all intents and purposes disabled as a person lawfully and duly excommunicated ...until he or she so disabled shall conform him or her self and come to church and hear Divine Service and receive the Sacrament of the Lord's Supper,...and also take the oath appointed and prescribed in [3 Jac. I, c. 4, § 9[1]]; And that every person or persons sued or to be sued by such person so disabled shall and may plead the same in disabling of such plaintiff as if he or she were excommunicated by sentence in the ecclesiastical court: Provided nevertheless, That it shall and may be lawful for any such person so disabled...to sue or prosecute any action or suit for or concerning only such of his or her lands, tenements, leases, rents, annuities, and hereditaments, or for the issues and profits thereof, which are not to be seized or taken into the King's hands...by force of any law for or concerning his or her recusancy....

X. And for that Popish recusants are not usually married nor their children christened nor themselves buried according to the law of the Church of England, but the same are done superstitiously by Popish persons in secret, whereby the days of their marriages, births, and burials cannot be certainly known: Be it

[1] See p. 90.

further enacted...That every man being or which shall be a Popish recusant convicted, or who shall be hereafter married otherwise than in some open church or chapel and otherwise than according to the orders of the Church of England by a minister lawfully authorised, shall be utterly disabled and excluded to have any estate of freehold into any the lands, tenements, and hereditaments of his wife as tenant by the courtesy of England[1]; and that every woman being or which shall be a Popish recusant convicted and who shall be hereafter married in other form than as aforesaid, shall be utterly excluded and disabled not only to claim any dower of the inheritance of her husband whereof she may be endowable, or any jointure of the lands and hereditaments of her husband or any of his ancestors, but also of her widow's estate and frank bank[2] in any customary lands whereof her husband died seised, and likewise be disabled and excluded to have or enjoy any part or portion of the goods of her said husband by virtue of any custom of any county, city, or place where the same shall lie or be: And if any such man shall be married with any woman contrary to the intent and true meaning of this Act, which woman hath or shall have no lands, tenements, or hereditaments whereof he may be intituled to be tenant by the courtesy, then such man so marrying as aforesaid shall forfeit and lose one hundred pounds, the one half thereof to be to the King's Majesty his heirs and successors, and the other moiety to such person or persons as shall sue for the same...: And that every Popish recusant which shall hereafter have any child born, shall within one month next after the birth thereof cause the same child to be baptized by a lawful minister...in the open church of the said parish where the child shall be born, or in some other church near adjoining or chapel where baptism is usually administered; or if by infirmity of the child it cannot be brought to such place, then the same shall within the time aforesaid be baptized by the lawful minister of any of the said parishes or places aforesaid, upon pain that the father of such child if he be living by the space of one month next after the birth of such child, or if he be dead within the said month then the mother of such child, shall for every such offence forfeit one hundred pounds of lawful money of England, one third part whereof to be to the King's Majesty his heirs and

---

[1] 'A tenure by which a husband, after his wife's death, holds certain kinds of property which she has inherited, the conditions varying with the nature of the property' (*Oxford Dictionary*).

[2] 'Frank bank' or 'free bench,' 'that estate in copyhold lands which the wife... hath after the death of her husband for her dower according to the custom of the manor' (Blount's *Law Dictionary*, 1670, quoted in the *Oxford Dictionary*).

successors, one other third part to the informer or him that will sue for the same, and the other third part to the poor of the said parish...: And if any Popish recusant man or woman not being excommunicate shall be buried in any place other than in the church or churchyard, or not according to the ecclesiastical laws of this Realm, that the executors or administrators of every such person so buried knowing the same, or the party that causeth him to be so buried, shall forfeit the sum of twenty pounds, the one third part whereof shall be to our Sovereign Lord the King, the other third part to the informer..., the other third to the poor of the parish where such person died....

XI. And be it further enacted by this present Parliament, That if the children of any subject within this Realm (the said children not being soldiers, mariners, merchants, or their apprentices or factors) to prevent their good education in England or for any other cause shall hereafter be sent or go beyond seas without licence of the King's Majesty or six of his honourable Privy Council (whereof the Principal Secretary to be one) under their hands and seals, that then all and every such child and children so sent or which shall so go beyond the seas shall take no benefit by any gift, conveyance, descent, devise, or otherwise, of or for any lands, tenements, hereditaments, leases, goods, or chattels, until he or they being of the age of eighteen years or above take the oath mentioned in [3 Jac. I, c. 4, § 9[1]] before some Justice of Peace of the county, liberty, or limit where such parents of such children as shall be so sent did or shall inhabit and dwell; And that in the mean time the next of his or her kin which shall be no Popish recusant shall have and enjoy the said lands, [etc.]... so given, conveyed, descended, or devised, until such time as the person so sent or gone beyond the seas shall conform him or her self and take the aforesaid oath and receive the Sacrament of the Lord's Supper; And after such oath taken and conforming of himself and receiving the Sacrament of the Supper of the Lord, he or they which have so received the profits of the said lands, [etc.]...shall make accompt of the profits so received, and in reasonable time make payment thereof, and restore the value of the said goods to such person as shall so conform his or her self as aforesaid: And that all such persons as shall send the said child or children over seas without licence as aforesaid, (unless the said child or children be merchants or their apprentices, or factors, mariners, or soldiers), shall forfeit one hundred pounds,... whereof the one third part shall be to the King..., the other

—————
[1] Printed on p. 90 above.

third part to such as shall sue for the same, and the other third part to the poor of such parish where such offender doth inhabit....

XII. And for that many subjects of this Realm, being neither merchants nor their factors nor apprentices, soldiers, nor mariners, are of late gone beyond the seas without licence and are not as yet returned; Be it further enacted. . . That if any of the said persons so gone beyond the seas without licence which are not yet returned shall not within six months next after their return into this Realm, then being of the age of eighteen years or more, take the oath above specified before some Justice of Peace of the county, liberty, or limit where such person shall inhabit or remain, that then every such offender shall take no benefit by any gift, [etc.]... until he or they, being of the said age of eighteen years or above, take the said oath; and that likewise in the mean time the next of kin to the person so offending which shall be no Popish recusant shall have and enjoy the said lands, [etc.]...until such time as the person so offending shall conform himself,...and after such conforming...he or they that shall have so received the profits of the said lands, [etc.]...shall make accompt....

XIII. And be it further enacted..., That every person or persons that is or shall be a Popish recusant convict, during the time that he shall be or remain a recusant, shall from and after the end of this present session of Parliament be utterly disabled to present to any benefice, with cure or without cure, prebend, or any other ecclesiastical living, or to collate or nominate to any Free School, Hospital, or donative whatsoever, and from the beginning of this present session of Parliament shall likewise be disabled to grant any avoidance to any benefice, prebend, or other ecclesiastical living; and that the Chancellor and Scholars of the University of Oxford, so often as any of them shall be void, shall have the presentation, nomination, collation, and donation of and to every such benefice, prebend, or ecclesiastical living, School, Hospital, and donative set, lying, and being in the counties of Oxford, Kent, Middlesex, Sussex, Surrey, Hampshire, Berkshire, Buckinghamshire, Gloucestershire, Worcestershire, Staffordshire, Warwickshire, Wiltshire, Somersetshire, Devonshire, Cornwall, Dorsetshire, Herefordshire, Northamptonshire, Pembrokeshire, Carmarthenshire, Brecknockshire, Monmouthshire, Cardiganshire, Montgomeryshire, the City of London, and in every city and town being a county of itself lying and being within any of the limits or precincts of any of the counties aforesaid or in or within any of them, as shall happen to be void during such time as the patron thereof shall be and remain a recusant convict as aforesaid;

And that the Chancellor and Scholars of the University of Cambridge shall have the presentation, nomination, collation, and donation of and to every such benefice, prebend, or ecclesiastical living, School, Hospital, and donative set, lying, and being in the counties of Essex, Hertfordshire, Bedfordshire, Cambridgeshire, Huntingdonshire, Suffolk, Norfolk, Lincolnshire, Rutlandshire, Leicestershire, Derbyshire, Nottinghamshire, Shropshire, Cheshire, Lancashire, Yorkshire, the County of Durham, Northumberland, Cumberland, Westmorland, Radnorshire, Denbighshire, Flintshire, Carnarvonshire, Angleseyshire, Merionethshire, Glamorganshire, and in every city and town being a county of itself lying within any of the limits or precincts of any of the counties last before mentioned or in or within any of them, as shall happen to be void during such time as the patron thereof shall be and remain a recusant convict as aforesaid: Provided that neither of the said Chancellors and Scholars of either the said Universities shall present or nominate to any benefice with cure, prebend, or other ecclesiastical living any such person as shall then have any other benefice with cure of souls; And if any such presentation or nomination shall be had or made of any such person so beneficed, the said presentation or nomination shall be utterly void....

XIV. Moreover because recusants convict are not thought meet to be executors or administrators to any person or persons whatsoever, nor to have the education of their own children, much less of the children of any other of the King's subjects, nor to have the marriage of them; Be it therefore enacted by the authority aforesaid, That such recusants convicted, or which shall be convicted at the time of the death of any testator, or at the time of the granting of any administration, shall be disabled to be executor or administrator by force of any testament hereafter to be made or letters of administration hereafter to be granted, nor shall have the custody of any child as guardian..., but shall be adjudged disabled to have any such wardship or custody of any such child or of their lands, [etc.]...: And that for the better education and preservation of the said children and of their estates, the next of the kin to such child or children to whom the said lands, [etc.]...of such child or children cannot lawfully descend...shall have the custody and education of the same child, and of his said lands and tenements being holden in knight's service, until the full age of the said ward of one and twenty years; And of his said lands, [etc.]...being holden in socage, as a guardian in socage; And of the said lands, [etc.]...holden by copy of court roll of any manor, so long as the custom of the said manor shall permit and allow the same, and in every of the said cases shall yield an accompt of the profits thereof to the said ward as the case shall require: And that if at any time hereafter any of the wards of the King's Majesty or of any other shall be granted or sold to any Popish recusant convict, such grant or sale shall be utterly void and of none effect.

XV. And be it further enacted..., That no person or persons shall bring from beyond the seas nor shall print, sell, or buy any Popish primers, Lady's psalters[1], manuals, rosaries, Popish catechisms, missals, breviaries, portals[2], legends and lives of saints, containing superstitious matter, printed or written in any language whatsoever, nor any other superstitious books printed or written in the English tongue, upon pain of forfeiture of forty shillings for every such book; One third part thereof to be to the King's Majesty..., one other third part to him that will sue for the same, and the other third part to the poor of the parish where such book or books shall be found,...and the said books to be burned: And that it shall be lawful for any two Justices of Peace within the limits of their jurisdiction or authority, and to all Mayors, Bailiffs, and chief officers of cities and towns corporate in their liberties, from time to time to search the houses and lodgings of every Popish recusant convict, or of every person whose wife is or shall be a Popish recusant convict, for Popish books and relics of Popery; And that if any altar, pyx, beads, pictures, or such like Popish relics, or any Popish book or books, shall be found in their or any of their custody as in the opinion of the said Justices, Mayor, Bailiff, or chief officer as aforesaid shall be thought unmeet for such recusant as aforesaid to have or use, the same shall be presently[3] defaced and burnt, if it be meet to be burned; And if it be a crucifix or other relic of any price, the same to be defaced at the General Quarter Sessions of the Peace in the county where the same shall be found, and the same so defaced to be restored to the owner again.

XVI. And be it also enacted..., That all such armour, gunpowder, and munition of whatsoever kinds as any Popish recusant convict within this Realm of England hath or shall have in his house or houses or elsewhere, or in the hands or possession of any other at his or their disposition, shall be taken from such Popish recusants, or others which have or shall have the same to the use of such Popish recusant, by warrant of four Justices of Peace at their General or Quarter Sessions to be holden in the

---

[1] *I.e.* copies of the Psalter of the Blessed Virgin.
[2] An erroneous form of 'portas,' a portable breviary.   [3] Immediately.

same county where such Popish recusant shall be resident, (other than such necessary weapons as shall be thought fit by the said four Justices of Peace to remain and be allowed for the defence of the person or persons of such recusants or for the defence of his, her, or their house or houses); And that the said armour and munition so taken shall be kept and maintained at the costs of such recusants in such places as the said four Justices of Peace at their said Sessions of the Peace shall set down and appoint.

XVII. And be it further enacted..., That if any such recusant having or which shall have any such armour, gunpowder, and munition, or any of them, or if any other person or persons which shall have any such armour, gunpowder, and munition, or any of them, to the use of any such recusant, shall refuse to declare or manifest unto the said Justices of Peace or any of them what armour he, she, or they have or shall have, or shall let, hinder, or disturb the delivery thereof to any of the said Justices or to any other person or persons authorised by their warrant to take and seize the same, then every such person so offending...shall forfeit and lose to the King's Majesty...his and their said armour, gunpowder, and munition, and shall also be imprisoned...by the space of three months....

XVIII. And yet nevertheless be it enacted..., That notwithstanding the taking away of such armour, gunpowder, and munition, the said Popish recusant shall and may be charged with the maintaining of the same, and with the buying, providing, and maintaining of horse and other armour and munition in such sort as other his Majesty's subjects from time to time shall be appointed and commanded, according to their several abilities and qualities; And that the said armour and munition at the charge of such Popish recusant for them and as their own provision of armour and munition, shall be shewed at every muster, show, or use of armour to be had or made within the said county.

XIX. Provided always, That neither this Act nor anything therein contained shall extend to take away or abridge the authority or jurisdiction of the ecclesiastical censures for any cause or matter; but that the Commissioners of his Majesty his heirs and successors in Causes Ecclesiastical for the time being, Archbishops, Bishops, and other ecclesiastical judges, may do and proceed as before the making of this Act they lawfully did or might have done....

3 & 4 Jac. I, c. 5: Statutes of the Realm, iv, 1077.

(3) The Oaths Act, 1610

An Act for administering the Oath of Allegiance, and reformation of Married Women Recusants

I. Whereas by a Statute made in the third year of your Majesty's reign intituled An Act for the better discovering and repressing of Popish Recusants[1] the form of an oath to be ministered and given to certain persons in the same Act mentioned is limited and prescribed, tending only to the declaration of such duty as every true and well affected subject, not only by bond of allegiance but also by the commandment of Almighty God, ought to bear to your Majesty your heirs and successors; which oath such as are infected with Popish superstition do oppugn[2] with many false and unsound arguments, the just defence whereof your Majesty hath heretofore undertaken and worthily performed to the great contentment of all your loving subjects notwithstanding the gainsayings of contentious adversaries; and to shew how greatly your loyal subjects do approve the said oath, they prostrate themselves at your Majesty's feet, beseeching your Majesty that the same oath may be administered to all your subjects, to which end we do with all humbleness beseech your Highness that it may be enacted, and be it enacted by the authority of this present Parliament, That all and every person and persons, as well ecclesiastical as temporal, of what estate, dignity, preeminence, sex, quality, or degree soever he, she, or they be or shall be, above the age of eighteen years, being hereafter in this Act mentioned and intended, shall make, take, and receive a corporal oath upon the Evangelists, according to the tenor and effect of the said oath set forth in the said fore-mentioned Statute, before such person or persons as hereafter in this Act is expressed, that is to say; All and every Archbishop and Bishop that now is or hereafter shall be, before the Lord Chancellor or Lord Keeper of the Great Seal for the time being; And all and every ecclesiastical judge, officer, and minister... before the Archbishop of the province or Bishop or other Ordinary of the diocese... wherein such ecclesiastical judge, officer, or minister ought to exercise his said office, place, or function; And all and every person and persons of or above the degree of a Baron of Parliament or Baroness of this your Highness's Realm of England, and of all your Highness's Privy Council residing in London or Westminster or within thirty miles thereof, and the Presidents of Wales and the North Parts, before any four of your Highness's Privy Council, whereof the Lord Chancellor, Lord Treasurer,

1 3 Jac. I, c. 4: printed on p. 86 above.   2 Oppose.

Lord Privy Seal, or Principal Secretary for the time being to be one; And if such person or persons live and reside in the country distant above thirty miles from London, then before the Lord Bishop of the diocese or such other person or persons as the Lord Chancellor or Lord Keeper...shall...authorise; And all and every the sworn servants, ordinary and extraordinary, of your Highness, the Queen's Grace, or of the Household of the Prince of Wales and of the rest of your Highness's children, before the Lord Steward, the Lord Chamberlains and Vice-Chamberlains to your Highness and the Queen, the Treasurer and Comptroller of your Highness's Household, the Master of your Highness's Horse, the Dean of the Chapel, and the Knight Marshal for the time being, the Officers of the Green Cloth, or any three of them; All and every temporal judge, justices of peace, sheriff[s], escheators[1], feodaries[2], and other officers and ministers of justice in this present Act not specially mentioned, and every other person or persons that doth or shall receive any fee of your Highness your heirs and successors, before the Lord Chancellor or Lord Keeper of the Great Seal, Lord Treasurer, Lord Admiral, Lord Warden of the Five Ports for the time being, or one of them, or before one of the Chief Justices either of your Majesty's Bench or of the Common Pleas, or before Justices of Assize of the same county where the parties reside, or other such persons as the Lord Chancellor or Keeper of the said Great Seal shall thereto authorise; And all Mayors, Bailiffs, or other chief officers of cities and towns corporate...before such person or persons as usually administer the oath to them at their first entrance into their said offices; And all and every the knights, citizens, burgesses, and Barons of the Five Ports, of the Commons' House of Parliament, at any Parliament or session of Parliament hereafter to be assembled, before he or they shall be permitted to enter into the said House, before the Lord Steward for the time being or his deputy or deputies; And the Master of the Ordnance, Lieutenant of the Tower of London and Mint-Master there, the four Principal Officers of your Navy under the Lord Admiral, before the Lord Chancellor or Lord Keeper of the Great Seal and the Lord Admiral for the time being, or any of them; And all the officers, ministers, servants, and others within your said Tower of London, before the Lieutenant of the Tower; And all the Vice-Admirals, captains, masters, officers, ministers, and soldiers in your Highness's ships or any of them, before the said four Principal Officers of your Navy

---

[1] An officer appointed in each county by the Lord Treasurer to certify escheats into the Exchequer.

[2] An officer of the Court of Wards appointed to collect the rents of wards' lands.

or any two of them; And all persons having charge of castles, fortresses, blockhouses, or garrisons, and all captains who shall have charge of soldiers within this your Highness's Realm, before the Justices of Assize of the same county or before two Justices of the Peace of the same county, city, or liberty where the same castles, fortresses, or blockhouses shall stand or the charge of soldiers shall be; All doctors, advocates, and proctors of the Civil Law and their clerks, before the Bishop of the diocese where they shall for the most part dwell or reside; And all and every person or persons temporal that hereafter shall sue livery or ouster-le-main[1] out of the hands of your Highness your heirs or successors, before his or their ouster-le-main sued forth and allowed, before the Master of the Wards and Liveries or before the Surveyor and Attorney of your Highness's said Court, in open court; All the serjeants-at-law, servants to the Judges in your Highness's Courts at Westminster, and all other in the Serjeants' Inns, before the Chief Justice of your Majesty's Bench, the Chief Justice of the Common Pleas, and the Chief Baron of your Exchequer, or some or one of them; All your Highness's subjects in the Inns of Court or that hereafter shall be admitted thereunto, and the Principals and Treasurers of every Inn of Chancery, before the Readers and Benchers of the several Houses whereto they belong, or four of them at the least, in their open Halls; All other your Majesty's subjects, as well ancients[2] as others, not being Principal or Treasurer, that now are or hereafter shall be admitted into any Inn of Chancery, before the Principal or Treasurer and ancients of the several Inns of Chancery, or four of them, in their open Halls; All prothonotaries[3], philizers[4], officers, ministers, attorneys, and clerks, that now are or hereafter shall be admitted to write or practise in any of your Highness's Courts at Westminster or in any other Court of Record, before the Judge or Judges of the same Court; All clerks of the Chancery and all their under-clerks and all other officers of the said Court of Chancery and their clerks, before the Master of the Rolls for the time being or before two of the Masters of the said Court of Chancery; All parsons, vicars, and curates, and all other persons ecclesiastical taking orders, and all and every schoolmaster or usher, before the Bishop of the diocese or other Ordinary in the same, sitting in open Court; The Vice-Chancellors of both the Universities for the time being, and the Presidents, Wardens, Provosts, Masters of Colleges

---

1 A livery of lands 'out of the hand' of the Sovereign.
2 The senior members who formed the governing bodies of the Inns of Court.
3 Usually the chief clerk or registrar of a Court.
4 A form of 'filacer,' an officer of the Courts at Westminster who filed original writs.

and Halls and all other Heads and Principals of Houses, Proctors, and Bedells of the Universities, publicly in the Convocation before the Senior Masters there present; And all and every other persons whatsoever that is or shall be promoted to any Degree in School, before the Vice-Chancellor of the said University for the time being in the Congregation House; All Fellows of Houses and all Scholars of Halls or Colleges that now are or hereafter shall be received into the same, being under the degree of a baron, before the President, Master, Provost, Warden, or other Head or chief governor of that College, Hall, or House whereinto he shall be received, and in the open Hall; And all Doctors of Physic, and all other who practise physic, that now are or hereafter shall be admitted into the College of Physicians in London, before the President of the same College for the time being; And all aldermen, sheriffs, and under-officers whatsoever of the cities and towns corporate, and all such as hereafter shall be made freemen of the said city or town corporate, before the Mayor, Bailiffs, or other chief officer of the said city or town, in the open Hall.

* * * * * *

III. And be it further enacted..., That it shall and may be lawful to and for any one of the Privy Council...and to and for every Bishop within his diocese to require any baron or baroness of the age of eighteen or above to take the said oath, and to and for any two Justices of Peace within any county, city, or town corporate, whereof one to be of the Quorum[1], to require any person or persons of the age of eighteen years or above under the degree of a baron or baroness to take the said oath; And if any person or persons of or above the said age and degree...be presented, indicted, or convicted for not coming to church or not receiving the Holy Communion...before the Ordinary,...then three of the Privy Council...whereof the Lord Chancellor, Lord Treasurer, Lord Privy Seal, or Principal Secretary to be one, upon knowledge thereof shall require such person or persons to take the said oath; And if any other person or persons whatsoever of and above the said age and under the said degree...be presented, indicted, or convicted for not coming to church or receiving the Holy Communion...before the Ordinary..., or if the minister, petty constable, and churchwardens, or any two of them, shall...complain to any Justice of Peace near adjoining to the place where any person complained of shall dwell, and the said Justices shall find cause of suspicion; That then any one Justice of Peace...shall upon notice thereof require such person or

[1] See *Tudor Constitutional Documents*, p. 454.

persons to take the said oath; And that if any person or persons being of the age of eighteen years or above shall refuse to take the said oath..., that then the persons authorised by this law to give the said oath shall and may commit the same offender to the common gaol, there to remain without bail or mainprize until the next Assizes or General Quarter Sessions to be holden for the said shire, division, limit, or liberty, where the said oath shall be again in the said open Sessions required of such person by the said Justices of Assize or Justices of the Peace then and there present, or the greater number of them: And if the said person or persons...shall refuse to take the said oath,...every person so refusing shall incur the danger and penalty of Praemunire... (except women covert, who shall be committed only to prison, there to remain without bail or mainprize till they will take the said oath).

IV. And be it further enacted, That every person refusing to take the said oath as above shall be disabled...to execute any public place of judicature or bear any other office (being no office of inheritance or ministerial function) within this your Highness's Realm of England, or to use or practise the Common Law or Civil Law, or the science of physic or surgery, or the art of an apothecary, or any liberal science for his or their gain within this Realm, until such time as the same person shall receive the same oath according to the intent of this Statute.

V. And be it further enacted, That if any married woman (being lawfully convicted as a Popish recusant for not coming to church) shall not within three months next after such conviction conform herself and repair to the church and receive the Sacrament of the Lord's Supper..., that then she shall be committed to prison by one of the Privy Council...or by the Bishop of the diocese if she be a baroness, or if she be under that degree, by two Justices of the Peace of the same county whereof one to be of the Quorum, there to remain without bail or mainprize until she shall conform herself and come to church and receive the Sacrament of the Lord's Supper, unless the husband of such wife shall pay to the King's Majesty his heirs or successors for the offence of his said wife for every month ten pounds of lawful money of England, or else the third part (in three parts to be divided) of all his lands and tenements, at the choice of the husband whose wife is so convicted as aforesaid, for and during so long time as she remaining a recusant convicted shall continue out of prison, during which time (and no longer) she may be at liberty.

7 & 8 Jac. I, c. 6: *Statutes of the Realm*, iv, 1162.

The Secretary of State[1]

In the reign of James I the older title of King's Secretary was replaced by its modern equivalent, Secretary of State. In its earlier form of Secretary of *Estate* this is used by Nicholas Faunt in a Discourse [p. 113] written about 1592; the modern form appears in the brief account of the office written by Robert Cecil, Earl of Salisbury [p. 124], and its general use may perhaps be dated from about the beginning of the century[2].

In this reign, as in the Tudor period, the Secretary was the keeper of the King's signet[3], the most private of the three official seals. The signet was employed in two different ways: (1) to authorise issues under the privy seal, and therefore as a stage through which formal documents passed on their way to the great seal[4]; and (2) to seal the King's personal correspondence and private commands. As has been pointed out[5], this is nothing less than the distinction between administration and politics. For the first of these purposes there existed a regular office, consisting of the four Clerks of the Signet who, though originally the Secretary's personal servants[6], were now appointed by letters patent and held office for life[7]. They ranked just below the four Clerks of the Privy Seal, with whom they worked in close association[8]. Their fixed salary was only £5 a year, and they depended for their remuneration mainly upon fees.

For the second purpose the Secretary commanded the services of another staff of clerks[9], who still ranked as his personal servants. Nicholas Faunt's account of the organisation of this branch of the Secretary's office [p. 113] must be regarded as an aspiration for the future rather than as a description of the present[10], but it sets forth an experienced official's conception of the way in which the ideal office would be organised and suggests the type to which, as time went on, it was likely to conform. Faunt also indicates the vast volume of the Secretary's work and the wide range of his activities. He was concerned with foreign policy as well as with domestic

---

1 On the office of Secretary in the seventeenth century, see Florence M. G. Evans, *The Principal Secretary of State, 1558–1680.*

2 Evans, p. 58.

3 At the accession of James I two new signets were prepared, 'one greater and one lesser,' shewing 'the union of the arms of both realms, England and Scotland' (Sir H. C. Maxwell-Lyte, *The Great Seal*, p. 137). In addition to these official signets, the King had a personal signet which was probably part of a ring (*ib.* p. 413).

4 In theory the privy seal was supposed to serve as a check upon the use of the signet, but at various times during the reign of Elizabeth the office of Lord Privy Seal was in abeyance, and the Queen's Secretary had the custody of both seals (Maxwell-Lyte, p. 25).

5 Evans, p. 195.   6 *Ib.* p. 6.

7 Maxwell-Lyte, p. 139.

8 In James I's reign the office of the privy seal was in the Palace of Whitehall 'separated only by a partition and passage from that of the signet' (*ib.* p. 38). The records of both offices suffered in the fire in the old Banqueting Hall there in 1619.

9 Evans, p. 6.   10 *Ib.* p. 152.

matters, and is therefore the common ancestor of the Home Secretary and the Secretary of State for Foreign Affairs. But it must be remembered that at the beginning of the seventeenth century the Secretary of State was still under the King's orders and was accountable to him alone [p. **126**]. The transition by which the Household officer was to become the head of a department of State, as the other custodians of the royal seals had already done, had not yet taken place.

By the reign of James I the arrangements of 1540 for two Secretaries keeping duplicate registers[1] had long broken down. On her accession Elizabeth had appointed only one Secretary, Sir William Cecil, afterwards Lord Burghley, and although Walsingham during his long tenure of office from 1573 to 1590 had worked with three colleagues in succession, Burghley's son Robert Cecil, afterwards Earl of Salisbury, was sole Secretary from 1596 until his death in 1612. In 1600 Cecil received the assistance of Dr John Herbert[2], a Master of Requests, but that he was only a subordinate appears from a contemporary reference to him as 'Mr Secretary Herbert, whom some call Mr Secondary Herbert in view of the wording of his patent.'[3] As from 1608 to 1612 Salisbury was Lord Treasurer as well as Secretary of State, help of this kind was very necessary, and even in spite of it a tendency was set up for business to pass into the hands of clerks, with the consequent domination of red tape and routine. Moreover, James took advantage of his Secretary's absorption in affairs to transfer the actual custody of the signet to the favourite Robert Carr, and to employ 'bed-chamber men' to conduct his private correspondence[4].

On Salisbury's death in 1612 the King might have found a successor of equal ability in Francis Bacon. If Bacon had been made Secretary, 'the process of separating the signet from the Secretary might have been completed; the secretariat, like the privy seal and the chancery before it, would no doubt have ceased to be a Household office and the Principal Secretary would have been recognised as a great officer of State, the representative of the Crown in Parliament and the minister chiefly responsible for the conduct of foreign affairs.'[5] But James appears to have been rather afraid of ability in a Secretary, and he tried an experiment instead. From 1612 to 1614 he did as Elizabeth had done from 1590 to 1596: he dispensed with a Secretary altogether, retaining the signet in the hands of Carr, now Earl of Rochester, and continuing to employ Dr John Herbert, who remained in office as assistant secretary until his death in 1617. The experiment was not a success, and in 1613 the Council petitioned that a Secretary might be appointed, as the affairs of the realm had 'suffered much for the want of a sufficient man that might ease and help to disburthen his Majesty in the care and pains of that place.'[6] The result was the appointment in 1614 of Sir Ralph Winwood, through whose hands the King's correspondence now passed. In 1616 Sir Thomas Lake was also made Secretary, and on Winwood's death in 1617 Sir Robert Naunton was appointed (Jan. 1618) to succeed him; thus, although the duplicate registers were not revived, the older plan of having two Secretaries of State was re-established, and from this time onward it became the rule. There is, however, a notable difference between the ability and standing of

---

[1] See *Tudor Constitutional Documents*, p. 203. [2] *Ib.* p. 212.
[3] Evans, p. 57.   [4] *Ib.* p. 64.   [5] *Ib.*   [6] *Ib.* p. 69.

the Tudor and Stuart Secretaries. Elizabeth had employed statesmen, like Burghley, Walsingham, and Robert Cecil; James appointed meritorious members of the bureaucracy, and these were overshadowed by favourites like Carr and Buckingham[1]. The Secretaries no longer had access to the King's mind; and even the private petitions which had formerly flowed in to them in great abundance were now diverted to the more powerful favourite[2], to the grievous loss of the regular officials in the matter of fees.

As soon as there were once more two Secretaries, one remained at Whitehall and the other followed the King; and the convenience of this arrangement contributed to its permanence[3]. The peripatetic habits of James I, who preferred Newmarket, Theobalds, Greenwich, and other places to London, made the Secretary at Whitehall the centre of government on its administrative side[4]. He was in close touch both with the Privy Council and with Parliament, and was therefore able to keep his finger upon the pulse of the machine. For an ambitious man this must have been some compensation for a certain loss of touch with the King and the Court.

When the system of two Secretaries was revived in 1616, James I embarked on another experiment; he made a tentative demarcation of their duties. It has been pointed out[5] that Winwood's political ideas were Puritan, and Naunton who succeeded him was also a staunch Protestant; while Lake was an Anglican who became a pensioner of Spain, and the religious sympathies of his successor Sir George Calvert led ultimately to his conversion to Rome. These selections, whether deliberate or not, and there may have been other reasons for making them, led to an arrangement by which the Puritan Secretary dealt with the relations with the Dutch and the Huguenots while the Anglican concerned himself mainly with France and Spain[6]. But although the Secretaries divided the foreign business and were often separated by the distance between Whitehall and the Court, either Secretary could handle any kind of business, both foreign and domestic; there were no watertight compartments or hard and fast divisions.

There are two other important aspects of the Secretary's office to be considered: his relation to the Privy Council and his relation to Parliament. The Secretary at Whitehall was the one member of the Council who attended with unfailing regularity[7]; under James, even more than under Elizabeth, he was coming to be the ordinary channel of communication between the Crown and the Council[8]; he often supervised the writing of the letters agreed on in Council[9]; and one of the Secretaries was usually a member of Council committees[10]. Thus the effective intervention of the Secretary in domestic affairs was made possible by his membership of the Privy Council just as his influence over foreign policy was due to his position as the writer of the King's letters and the keeper of his private seal[11]. In connexion with Parliament it should be observed that from 1540 to 1679 the Secretary received a writ of summons to the House of Lords along with the

[1] Evans, p. 180.   [2] *Ib.* p. 271.   [3] *Ib.* p. 76.
[4] *Ib.* p. 184.   [5] *Ib.* p. 71.
[6] In 1621 and 1622 Calvert was concerned in the negotiations over the Spanish match (Evans, pp. 75, 80).
[7] Evans, p. 225.   [8] *Ib.* p. 228.   [9] *Ib.* p. 225.
[10] *Ib.* pp. 230–1.   [11] *Ib.* p. 298.

Chief Justices and other legal advisers of the Crown[1], but his attendance there fell into disuse, for his proper sphere of Parliamentary activity was in the Commons. From the time of James I's third Parliament the duty of representing the Crown in the House seems to have passed definitely to the Secretaries[2], who explained the government policy there and, as far as was practicable, guided the debates.

At the beginning of the seventeenth century a Secretary of State still received only the traditional salary of £100 a year and a table at Court[3], but various fees and perquisites led to the office being valued in 1601 at nearly £3000 a year[4]. Under Elizabeth, Walsingham had sacrificed a large part of his private fortune in obtaining secret intelligence, but under James an allowance of £1200, afterwards raised to £1400, was made for this purpose; and when two Secretaries were appointed this was divided between them[5]. A retiring Secretary was also entitled by custom to make a bargain with his successor, and as much as £6000 or £7000, or even more, might be paid when the office changed hands[6].

The form of the oath required of a Secretary of State is printed below [p. 127].

(1) Nicholas Faunt on the Secretary's Office, c. 1592

Nicholas Faunt became clerk to Sir Francis Walsingham about 1580, and from 1603 he was a Clerk to the Signet. He died in 1609. He wrote his Discourse touching the Office of Principal Secretary in 1592, but the copy from which the following passages are taken is dated 1610.

Mr Faunt's Discourse touching the office of Principal Secretary of Estate, etc.

*   *   *   *   *   *

Now amongst all particular offices and places of charge in this State there is none of more necessary use, nor subject to more cumber and variableness, than is the office of Principal Secretary, by reason of the variety and uncertainty of his employment, and therefore with more difficulty to be prescribed by special method and order.

The examples of other nations yield us little or no good direction in this behoof.... So that if any good advice may be given for the settling of this office, it must come from ourselves, and from the experience that is gathered in former courses held therein at home. What may be the credit and dignity of this place, how many and how great matters are committed chiefly (and oftentimes only) to his trust, what free access he hath to the Prince, how he is the mouth of the Council of State, etc., it is not for me

---

[1] Evans, pp. 35, 250.   [2] Ib. p. 242.
[3] *Tudor Constitutional Documents*, p. 210.
[4] Evans, p. 211, note 3.
[5] Ib. p. 213.   [6] Ib. p. 216.

to enlarge, neither have I any such purpose; those things being somewhat accidentary, and always following the good conceipt and opinion had of the person in whom this credit and trust is to be reposed. Only I have thought it not amiss (as I could upon a sudden) to set down these few notes, which in my poor experience I think it not altogether unnecessary to be perused by him that shall enter into this place, touching the private ordering and distribution of the charge committed unto him, and that under the correction of far more ripe judgments; being not ignorant an that with the continuance of standing in this office there will daily grow new observations haply fitter for those times than these or any that can be now set down.

And first, I think this old maxim may be of some use touching this point, namely, that *frustra fit per plura quod fieri potest per pauciora.* For as to the Secretary himself, it shall be needful that he use as little as he may the advice and help of his equals or superiors in anything that toucheth the substance of his office and charge, a thing that would derogate from the credit of that place and his own sufficiency, neither yet by using any of the inferior officers to do such things as appertaineth not to them, and may be done by his own servants, give them likewise occasion to look into his doings, and as some are forward enough to take upon them to shew their own experience and skill for some further end, when both their advice and help may be well spared, so in the choice of his servants I am persuaded the said rule should especially hold; and by experience I can say that the multitude of servants in this kind is hurtful, and of late years hath bred much confusion, with want of secresy and dispatch in that place; for if in a principal servant to the Secretary secresy and faithfulness be chiefly required, what trust can there be reposed in many, and if many be employed in matters of secresy, who shall think himself principal in trust in those things which are hardly to be imparted to any, though the most faithful in the world, but that of necessity the Secretary must use one as his own pen, his mouth, his eye, his ear, and keeper of his most secret cabinet.

Again, when a servant shall know that such trust is reposed in him, then chiefly knoweth he his office and place, then is his credit sound, and he receiveth good encouragement to do his duty, especially that all things be done for his master's credit and honour, which in no case should be imparted or divided to any friend or favourite, howsoever otherwise near and dear to him.

Moreover, his servant must come to his place being called thereunto of a conscience to do good (as he may do much and that with his master's credit), and not to serve his own turn; but entering upon such conditions as shall be convenient for his maintenance in that place, he is wholly to yield himself to that calling and the business thereof, without seeking to make his profit of every suit, and other device that shall be put into his head, or to aspire to some higher place or change of employment, whereby both the service will be much hindered and neglected and himself become unable to perform that which is committed to his charge, being thus distracted with the care of his own estate (if at the first he be not sufficiently provided for) and to fall into the shifts which are now by servants in such places commonly used, to the hurt of the subjects, their own discredit, and the master's dishonour.

Lastly, the duty of a servant in this kind must proceed from a special love and affection he beareth towards his master, the same being grounded likewise upon some testimony of his master's good opinion and reciprocal love borne unto him. For if the servant take this charge in hand, he must give himself wholly to his master, *i.e.*, he must in a manner cast off the care of his private estate, to the end he may chiefly attend and intend this service, which assuredly will require a whole man, and therefore the master affecting and finding in him this extra-ordinary pains and care of his charge, cannot but regard his particular estate, and supply wherein he is wanting to himself upon some fit occasion offered to do him good, through which good harmony and content it is not to be doubted but that things will haply succeed to the good of the State in general and the particular comfort both of master and servant in so happy and weighty a calling as this is to be esteemed of those that have seriously cast their eyes upon it.

After these considerations had in the choice of the principal servant in whom the principal trust is to be reposed, it shall be also convenient to be provided of another for the dispatch of ordinary matters, and chiefly for continual attendance in the chamber where the papers are, whose particular charge may be to endorse them or give them their due titles, as they daily come in of all sorts, which (to reduce them into a few heads) are noted to be of three kinds, namely, Home Letters, which are the greatest multitude, Council Matters concerning any private or public cause, and Divers Matters which contain petitions to the Secretary, discourses, projects, relations, declarations or informations of private or public causes, etc., and every morning to set them in several bundles for the present use of them, and when they grow to be many, those that have been most dealt in and dispatched to be removed into some chest or place, lest confusion or loss of some of them grow through an exceeding and unnecessary multitude of papers, as hath been seen in that place. This servant, besides his charge of ordering the papers and clearing the table, so that there be no hindrance or confusedness in the searching of them when the Secretary shall sit down to do anything or answer many things, as he commonly must do in the morning as well as at other times, he may also be a remembrancer of all such matters as are of most necessary dispatch, and moved to him in the absence, or not in the presence, of his master, who cannot always remain in one place to take notice of all things required in that service, notwithstanding the use of the memorial book which is hereafter to be remembered, because the matters there are infinite and cannot be moved and brought in by order and method; and likewise make answer to all private home letters, dispatch all warrants, and do such other things as run daily in course touching the home service, which being faithfully performed will be a sufficient employment for one able person in that kind.

The other servant whom I first described would be chiefly charged with foreign matters, and others that may more nearly [concern] his Majesty and the State, both to keep his letters of negotiations that daily come in from foreign parts, and to answer them when need shall be; and yet not so but that he may at all times help the other upon urgent occasions, and likewise receive help from him in that he is able to do, and so mutually in some things one to help another when either of their hands shall be full of causes that require hasty dispatch. And this second servant may chiefly attend unto matters of intelligence, ciphers, and secret advertisements, to keep first in good order, to extract the substance of them for the present use, and to see them well digested into small books if they be material, and have any reference either to things past, present, or that be likely to fall out in action, as the most of that nature are, for that sometimes an old advertisement being well kept may serve to very good purpose, whenas the same being laid aside in the original paper or letter as it was sent, may sooner with grief in a general sort be heaped up or unperfectly remembered than recovered entirely as it was used with profit for the which it was carefully given at the first; and to this end it will be needful that he prepare certain cabinets or coffers fit to keep such things as he shall be accomptable for in particular. And though the Secretary have one more special to himself, of the freshest matters that occur, whereof he only reserveth the key to himself, yet oftentimes he must commit the secretest things to the trust of this servant, and be forced to send him to and fro from one cabinet to another himself cannot remove, or cause them to be removed to him; and therefore as those employments be of the highest trust, so must the servant trusted therewith be of special trust both for honesty and other good sufficiency, as hath been remembered before. For besides the known services he is to perform, it will fall out oftentimes that he shall be sent forth to deliver messages of great importance to ambassadors or other foreign ministers that are sent hither, to gentlemen of good quality being soundly and particularly affected to the Secretary, to other Councillors here, to confer with secret intelligencers both strangers and others, and generally do many things whereof no rule or prescription can be given, and that chiefly upon the credit and confidence that is reposed in him.

The Secretary being thus provided of his servants, he is to consider what other help of necessary collections made into books he should prepare for himself, and their better direction in that service. And first, he may divide and measure the day, so near as he can, according to the ordinary business thereof being of greatest weight and most needful dispatch. For a special help wherein he may have a general memorial book in paper lying before him, so soon as he riseth from his bed or whilst he lieth in his bed, if occasion so require, in which he may set down or cause to be set down all things presently occurring or that upon any occasion shall be remembered, and though for the multitude of them they cannot be dispatched in one day, yet daily to add new unto them, and to mark out with the pen so many as are dispatched or not to be dealt in at all, to the end that the multitude of affairs do not cause some important matter to be forgotten, but that still as he sitteth down before his papers this book may present unto him all things already remembered and give him occasion to remember and set down other things, though it be done in one word, or darkly in terms not easily to be understood of others if the matter be of secresy; and sometimes the reviewing of old remembrances howsoever blotted out, though a year or two past, may help for the observation of times, persons, places, and other circumstances that are wont to give great light to causes presently in question and handling.

Hereunto may be added the use of another paper book to be called a Journal, wherein is continually to be recorded the certain day of the month and the hours when any dispatch is made or received, for that thereupon may grow great question if negligence be used either in going or coming; or that when the letters (as oftentimes it falleth out) are missing, being in other hands, answer may be made by recital of the dates, a thing which may sometimes greatly import the matters in hand by this monthly observation of days and hours, besides that it will help sometimes in other consultations and discourses to know when such a dispatch was made and received, as also who brought it and carried it, which would be likewise noted in the said Journal, for that many times besides the letters there is much referred to the sufficiency and credit of the bearer; further, in this book should also be noted the arrival and dispatch of any ambassador or messenger sent abroad or coming hither, and of such gentlemen of note as accompany them, the landing of any personage[s] of honour that come to see this Court, the particular assemblies of the Council out of the Court and the occasion if it be remarkable, the times of conferences and private meetings of the Secretary and others in commission with him about the most important causes, the most notable accidents of all kinds in a few words, with many other things that in his description may fitly be observed for his help in so weighty a charge.

And further, it will be necessary to have sundry books of paper for the registering of all instructions and letters of charge committed to such as are to be sent abroad into foreign parts, into Ireland, or unto the sea; and the minutes of letters of further directions growing upon sundry accidents and new occasions sent unto them being material and concerning the several negotiations in hand; as likewise the answers and relations of their charges and commissions, with any other discourse or report concerning the same, are all, according to their dates so near as can be, to be inserted in order, after the said instructions or commissions, in several books, and so to be continued till the said negotiation be ended or broken off. Lastly, it shall not be amiss, but haply of good consequence, at the end of the said negotiation, message, commission, treaty, etc., to set down briefly the causes or occasions whereupon the same was discontinued, or how it end[ed], and what effect it brought forth, etc., which would serve instead of an history and apt introduction to other negotiations that are likely to follow of the same nature or not much different therefrom, but chiefly for the clearing of things in doubt, which hereby may be readily found out; whereas without this care both this necessary precedent will be ever wanting, and great inconveniences may grow through the loss of papers and unorderly keeping of them.

Books Peculiar for Foreign Services

The titles of such books as in my judgment will be of greatest use (though I know many others shall be profitably in time added hereunto) upon the diversity of employments in this service, may be these following, viz.

A Book of Treaties

Wherein a collection would be made of all the alliances that are between his Majesty and other princes, of the leagues and treaties presently in force, as also of the nature, quality, and term of the said leagues. Whether they be for offence or defence, for intercourse or trades, or in what other sort and mixture, etc.

A Book of the present negotiations. Or Books

And first, of the present negotiation and intelligence continued by Ambassadors resident in France, which will in short time make a great volume.

Then particularly another of the negotiation with the United Provinces, and (if occasion serve) with the governors, commissioners, deputies, or ministers of the other members of the Low Countries.

A book of the like for Scotland, where for the most part some one or other is employed by his Majesty; another for Germany, whither sometimes are also ministers sent the princes there about the levying of men, for the employment of moneys, etc.

Another touching the intercourse with Denmark, Sweden, Muscovia and Russia, Turkey, Barbary and the Levant, and especially with the Hanse Towns, that insist much upon ancient privileges and immunities, etc.

A particular volume for Ireland, which government requireth many and sundry directions by letters from his[1] Majesty and the Lords of the Council, and wherein it will be necessary to register the answers and relations of the charges and commissions sent unto them, for they are of weight, and daily questionable by reason of the variety of matters and sudden alteration and change of officers and offices, both touching the wars and course of justice, in the most peaceable [times].

[1] Here the MS. reads 'her Majesty,' but 'his' in many places elsewhere. As the date of the copy is 1610, the reference is evidently to James I.

Books for Home Service

For the home services divers kinds of books would be requisite, the rather for that there hath been found of late great confusion in the keeping of loose papers, though they be digested into bundles or otherwise kept in coffers. For the only lending of them forth, which must needs fall out sometimes, is very oftentimes the cause and means of their loss, which being of great use and not to be found thus registered, the service thereby is greatly hindered. These books may be thus intituled, viz.

A survey of the lands, with the commodities thereof

And the heads of this book may be those following, which being found out in this manner, it will be easy to recover the particulars from such persons as by reason of their proper offices and functions are best able to furnish the Secretary with the several notes according to the said heads, as namely, concerning the first head, to collect

The port towns, or creeks[1], with other landing-places in every county, as also the depths and dangers thereof.

The trades of the several ports, and whereupon their wealth doth consist.

The hundreds, rapes, wapentakes, and other divisions in every shire.

The market and corporate towns.

The gentlemen of name in every hundred.

The rivers, with the use and commodity of them.

The Borders against Scotland, with their length and breadth.

The strength of the said Borders, as hills, woods, heaths, straits, marshes, towns, and castles of defence.

What the commodities of this realm are; wherein the wealth of it doth consist.

What natural things it yieldeth.

What manufactures.

How they are carried out of the realm, by what persons, and into what countries.

What commodities of other countries we stand in need of for our necessary relief.

How they are brought in; by our own merchants, or by strangers.

Hereunto would be annexed certain notes of the serviceable men within the realm for direction in the wars, the names of such as are fit to be employed at home in the service of State, and others to be sent abroad as ambassadors or ministers, etc.

[1] This is only conjectural; the *E.H.R.* reads 'of Creetes.'

The names of the Doctors of the Civil Law, and which have ripest judgments, as also who be the best Common Lawyers, with other things of this nature, which being collected into some little book, may oftentimes be of great use.

The Sea Causes

The Navy Royal, wherein to understand the number of the ships, their burthen, the number of men required to furnish them with mariners, soldiers, and governors.

The quantities of powder, ordnance, and other munition, according to their several proportions.

The number of ships, their burthen and strength, in the several ports throughout the realm; the number of mariners and masters.

The number of guns fit for service, with their due proportion of victuals both for these and his[1] Majesty's ships, etc.

The Defence of the Realm within the land

Where is to be set down: First, the numbers of able men as they were mustered at the last general musters in the several counties.

The numbers of men furnished with weapons.

The number of trained men.

The qualities of the persons trained.

The order of training.

The times and days of training.

The charge of training.

The names of the captains.

The lieutenants and deputy-lieutenants.

The number of horsemen in the several counties: lances, light horse, petronels.

The order for repairing [to] the sea coast in case of invasion.

What are the selected bands, and how they are to be furnished, and drawn out of the inland counties to the aid of the maritime parts, if occasion so require.

The names of the castles and places fortified in the several counties.

The numbers of men contained in them.

The provision of ordnance, powder, and shot munition.

The Office of Ordnance, what is thereunto required.

The ordinary sort and provisions of ordnance of several kinds appointed to remain in a readiness.

[1] See note on p. 119 above.

The store of muskets, calivers, shot, powder, match, saltpetre, etc.

The store of armour in the Office of the Armoury.

The revenues of the land

First, his[1] Majesty's revenues in every kind:
The Crown land.
The Duchy land.
Lands accrued by forfeitures.
The impost of wines.
Tenths, fifteenths, and subsidies.
The Court of Wards.
The Courts of Justice.
Casualty and escheats.
The Firstfruits and Tenths.
The Customs, outwards and inwards.

The charges of the Crown

His[1] Majesty's charges, how it ariseth:
The charges of the Household.
The charges of Officers, and Courts as well of Justice as of Revenue.
The charges of keeping of forts, castles, and places of defence.
The charges of the Borders against Scotland.
The charges of the Navy.
The charges of Ireland.
Extraordinary charges of sundry natures: ambassadors, intelligencers, gifts.

The Courts of Justice

The manner of creating laws and executing of justice in the several Courts.
The orders observed in Parliaments.
The Court of King's Bench.
The Common Pleas.
The Court of Chancery.
The Exchequer.
The Court of Wards.
The Court of Requests.
The Duchy Court.
The Prerogative Court.
The Delegates, etc.

[1] See note on p. 119 above.

The proper office of every Court, and what is the use both to Prince and subject.

The chief office appertaining to the said Courts.

The manner of proceeding in the said Courts, as well in civil as criminal causes.

The order of the circuits, and manner of proceeding at assizes and sessions.

Many other books might be hereunto annexed, being also of very good use in their places: as books of coinage and Mint causes, of rates for victualling, of weights and measures, of orders touching his[1] Majesty's Household, of precedents of all matters that concern the service, of discoveries and new inventions, of descriptions most exactly taken of other countries, as well by maps and cards[2] as by discovering the present state of their government, their alliances, dependences, etc., with many other discourses, devices, plots, and projects of sundry natures, etc., all which sometimes may serve to very good purpose, and which will be daily delivered to the Secretary, especially if he be known to make accompt of virtuous employment, and of men that are liberally brought up and have their minds elevated through some in more inferior arts and faculties than other, seeing there will be nothing offered to a personage of his place that in their specie may not some way be profitable, being effected in the ripeness of their wits and with their greatest industry and travail, both which (as it hath been seen, I mean in those that profess any exactness or dexterity in their sciences) they will as freely bestow upon him as he shall be willing to accept the same at their hands, and employ it to the benefit and service of their Sovereign and country. And therefore these more necessary helps being first provided, the rest will be in convenient time supplied with ease.

Thus I have in some sort discovered my poor conceipt touching the necessary servants and books that the Secretary is to provide as instrumental means for the better discharging of his weighty office. Other things might yet further be added that more properly concern himself which he is to look unto without the help of these means above mentioned, being partly observations of some matters to be done by him and partly cautions to avoid the doing of other things, both by himself and others, which I may not well commit to writing, and yet all (as that which is already set down) of no great depth or matter that can immediately advance the credit and reputation of a Principal Secretary with

[1] See note on p. 119 above.   [2] In the sense of charts or plans.

his Sovereign and country (which is, notwithstanding, the mark whereat the greatest politics[1] in such places have ever seemed to aim), for that they are things that fall not within my reach and consideration, but only to the end I might lay down by way of discourse something of my own experience, to ground myself the rather in this opinion, which I have long since conceived, and now of late have seen how worthily it may have reference to other principles, namely, that circumstances in the observations of the smallest things, not only in places of charge but even in every man's particular calling and family, do greatly import both the credit and ability of him that undergoeth the burthen thereof; and so consequently, though not in so direct a manner yet by circumstance, that these few notes may likewise concern the substance, and in some good measure advance the credit and excellence, of this high office.

Printed in *English Historical Review*, xx, 499–508.

(2) Robert Cecil, Earl of Salisbury, on the Secretary's Office

Probably written some time after 1605, when Cecil was created Earl of Salisbury. It was printed in 1642.

The State and Dignity of a Secretary of State's place, with the care and peril thereof; written by the Right Honourable Robert, late Earl of Salisbury...

All officers and counsellors of princes have a prescribed authority by patent, by custom, or by oath, the Secretary only excepted; but to the Secretary, out of a confidence and singular affection, there is a liberty to negotiate at discretion at home and abroad, with friends and enemies, all matters of speech and intelligence.

All servants of princes deal upon strong and wary authority and warrant in disbursements as treasurers, in conference with enemies as generals, in commissions in executing offices by patents and instructions, and so in whatever else; only a Secretary hath no warrant or commission, no, not in matters of his own greatest particulars, but the virtue and word of his Sovereign.

For such is the multiplicity of actions, and variable motions and intents of foreign princes, and their daily practices, and in so many parts and places, as Secretaries can never have any commission so long and universal as to secure them.

So as a Secretary must either conceive the very thought of a King, which is only proper to God; or a King must exercise the

---

[1] *I.e.* politicians.

painful office of a Secretary, which is contrary to majesty and liberty; or else a prince must make choice of such a servant of such a prince as the prince's assurance must be his confidence in the Secretary and the Secretary's life his trust in the prince.

To deal now with the prince, *Tanquam infirmum futurum* cannot be a rule for a Secretary; for all that he hath to trust to is quite the contrary, which is, that his prince will be *semper idem*.

All strange princes hate secretaries, all aspirers, and all conspirers, because they either kill those monsters in their cradles, or else trace them out where no man can discern the print of their footing.

Furthermore this is manifest, that all men of war do malign them except they will be at their desires.

Their fellow-counsellors envy them because they have most easy and free access to princes; and wheresoever a prince hath cause to delay or deny to search or punish, none so soon bear so much burthen.

Kings are advised to observe these things in a Secretary: first, that he be created by himself, and of his own raising; secondly, that he match not in a factious family; and lastly, that he hath reasonable capacity and convenient ability.

On the other side, the place of Secretary is dreadful if he serve not a constant prince; for he that liveth by trust ought to serve truly; so he that lives at mercy ought to be careful in the choice of his master, that he is just *et de bonâ naturâ*.

If princes be not confident on those whom they have made choice of, they shall ill trust the work of a strange hand; and if the rule hath failed in some of those that have sinned in ingratitude to those princes, it is in those of the highest order, *Ero similis altissimo*.

But for those of private quality, who have no other consistence nor can ever look for equal blessedness, there the jealousy of a prince hath never beheld suspect, but mere contempt.

As long as any matter, of what weight soever, is handled only between the prince and the Secretary, those counsels are compared to the mutual affections of two lovers undiscovered to their friends.

When it cometh to be disputed in Council, it is like the conference of parents and solemnization of marriage; the first matter, the second order, and indeed the one the act, the other the publication.

If there be then a Secretary whose state can witness that he coveteth not for profit; and if his careful life and death shall record it that love is his object; if he deal less with other men's suits, whereby Secretaries gain, than ever any did; if he prefer his majesty and despise his own:

If such an one should find that his hope could not warrant him, no, not against the slanders of those wicked ones whom he must use only; then surely that Secretary must resolve that the first day of his entry is the first day of his misery, for if he be not worthy of trust he is less worthy of life, and a suspicion of a Secretary is both a trial and condemnation, and a judgment.

Harleian Miscellany (ed. Thomas Park, 1808–13), ii, 281.

The Court of King James, by Godfrey Goodman, Bishop of Gloucester, was probably written *c.* 1650 in defence of the King, but it was not printed until 1839.

...The King's Attorney is ever the rod and instrument to give the lash to those whom the King will cast down; Sir Robert Cecil did ever desire to be great with the King's Attorney. Sir Edward Coke, who was Attorney, did marry a Cecil, the Earl of Exeter's daughter, upon his preferment to be Chief Justice of the Common Pleas. The Earl of Salisbury being Master of the Wards, he had an inward familiarity with Sir Harry Hobart[1], who was then Attorney of the Court of Wards, and finding him to be a very wise and an honest man and his true friend, he was the means to prefer him to be the King's Attorney-General. And now upon this occasion he sent for him, and knowing that nothing would be alleged against him in point of the King's prerogative (which notwithstanding was the inward sore and the greatest exception,— for though he might fail in judgment therein, yet he was not punishable by law), he acquainted the Attorney thus far, that he was like a man tossed with the waves of the sea, who would fain come to shore but could not in regard of the dangers; so he himself having had great offices and overloaded with business, he would fain lay down his burden if he could with his own honour and safety. 'And now, Mr Attorney, let me crave your counsel. If a man be a Secretary to a prince, many things he must do upon the word of the prince: there are no witnesses to testify, nor doth the King set his hand and seal to all things; how far then shall that officer offend who hath no other commission but the King's word and command?' To whom the Attorney replied, that much must be ascribed to the honour and conscience of the prince; and if he should disclaim his own actions, that then the circumstances on both sides were to be examined, and if it should prove that

[1] Sir Henry Hobart was appointed Attorney of the Court of Wards and Liveries in 1605, and became Chief Justice of the Common Pleas in 1613.

the King's accusation should be without probabilities, surely he should utterly disenable himself; for that the rest of his servants would decline his employment, and then in effect he should only speak by his seal, and as much trouble should be in every slight trivial business as in the greatest actions of State, for no man would do anything without sufficient warrant under hand and seal. Then the Earl requested him that if ever there should be any proceedings against him, that the Attorney would do him what good honest office he could; which the Attorney promised to do.

Neither did the Earl of Salisbury here rest, but he had the promise of many Privy Councillors, and, as I take it, under their hands, that if the Earl were committed or should fall into troubles, that then they would all become suitors and use their uttermost endeavours that he might come to a speedy trial, and know his accusers and what should be objected against him;....

Goodman, The Court of King James, p. 42.

(3) The Secretary's Oath, c. 1613

This closely resembles the Privy Councillor's oath printed on p. 132 below.

The Oath of the Secretaries of State

You shall swear to be a true and faithful servant unto the King's Majesty as one of the Principal Secretaries of State to his Majesty: you shall not know or understand any manner thing to be attempted, done, or spoken against his Majesty's person, honour, crown, or dignity royal; but you shall let and withstand the same to the uttermost of your power, and either do or cause to be revealed either to his Majesty himself or to his Privy Council. You shall keep secret all matters revealed and committed unto you, or that shall be secretly treated in Council. And if any of the said treaties[1] or counsels shall touch any of the Councillors, you shall not reveal the same unto him, but shall keep the same until such time as by the consent of his Majesty or the Council publication shall be made thereof. You shall to your uttermost bear faith and allegiance to the King's Majesty his heirs and lawful successors, and shall assist and defend all jurisdictions, preeminences, and authorities granted to his Majesty and annexed to his Crown, against all foreign princes, persons, prelates, or potentates, etc., by Act of Parliament or otherwise. And generally in all things you shall do as a true and faithful servant and subject ought to do to his Majesty. So help you God and the holy contents of this book.

Acts of the Privy Council, 1613–1614, p. 5.

[1] *I.e.* things treated of.

The Privy Council[1]

By the end of the reign of Elizabeth the great nobles who had formerly dominated the Privy Council had disappeared, and it had come to consist of twelve members, all of whom were great Officers of State or of the Household[2]. This is the Council described by Scaramelli the Venetian when he visited Richmond on 7 April, 1603, a fortnight after the accession of James [p. 131]. At first the new King was content to introduce into the Council the Duke of Lennox, the Earl of Mar, and other Scotchmen, and these were sworn in on 4 May[3]; but this was only the beginning of that enlargement of the Council which is the most striking feature of its development under James I[4]. On 10 May, 1603, it was resolved that the number of members should be limited to twenty-four; and, although in 1607 the Venetian Ambassador reported that the Council contained twenty-five, four of whom were Scots, between 1605 and 1615 the numbers appear to have varied from sixteen to twenty-two[5]. In 1617 they rose to twenty-eight, and in 1623 they stood at thirty-five[6]. Although this involved a dilution of the official element, the officials continued to be the backbone of the Council, and the regularity of their attendances gave them practical control. Thus, in 1616 the Archbishop of Canterbury attended eighty-four meetings out of eighty-seven; and in 1622 at most of the seventy-five meetings the chief Officers of State were present[7]. At the beginning of the reign the Secretaries of State did not come much to the Council, but as they became more important they attended oftener; in 1617 the Councillors asked that one of the Secretaries might come to them, as without him they 'will not willingly assemble,'[8] and in 1619 the presence of a Secretary at all meetings was assumed as a matter of course[9]. The King himself sometimes presided at the Council when important business was being transacted, and he occasionally came in to its meetings, but James I did not like the trouble of coming and there were long periods during which he absented himself altogether. Thus, in 1616 he only attended four meetings out of eighty-seven; in 1622 two out of seventy-five[10].

The Privy Council usually met at Whitehall: in 1616 out of eighty-seven meetings sixty-seven were held there, and in 1622 no less than sixty-five out of seventy-five[11]. The other meetings took place wherever the King was holding his Court: at Windsor, Greenwich, Hampton Court, Oatlands, Theobalds, or Nonesuch; we also hear of them upon occasion at Newmarket, Salisbury, and Lambeth[12], and the Council when in London sometimes sat in the Star Chamber at Westminster[13]. When the King was away

---

[1] See *The Privy Council of England, 1603–1784*, by Professor E. R. Turner.

[2] See the list of 30 July, 1598, referred to in E. I. Carlyle, 'Committees of Council under the Earlier Stuarts,' in *English Historical Review*, xxi, 673.

[3] Dasent, *Acts of the Privy Council*, xxxii, 496.

[4] Turner, i, 71–2.   [5] *Ib.* i, 72.

[6] *Ib.* i, 73.   [7] *Ib.* i, 98–9.

[8] *Ib.* i, 105.   [9] *Ib.* i, 97.

[10] *Ib.* i, 101–2.   [11] *Ib.* i, 87.

[12] *Ib.* i, 87–9.   [13] *Ib.* i, 90.

from his capital, a part of the Council did not follow him but remained in London for the transaction of routine business, as had been the case under the Tudors[1], and this body often resorted to the private houses of particular Councillors, as for instance York House, Suffolk House, the Lord Treasurer's lodgings, or even the house of the Lord Mayor for the time being[2].

An important result of the increase in the numbers of the Privy Council was a tendency for business to be transacted in committees. Under James I these were for the most part of a temporary character, appointed to investigate a particular question and to report on the results. Of such a kind was the committee of six appointed on 4 May, 1603, 'to take knowledge and consider of all monopolies and grants that are offensive to the subjects of this land and to inform his Majesty of the same, that such order may be taken for the calling in of those that are grievous and burdensome to the subject as his Majesty in his princely wisdom shall think fit and convenient.'[3] In 1613 there were as many as twelve temporary committees, and these included committees for the Navy, the Household, the Wardrobe, and the state of Ireland[4]. In 1617 a new departure was taken which was destined to be of some constitutional importance. The ordinary proceedings of the Council were supposed to be secret, and the Privy Councillor's oath [p. 132] pledged every member to have regard to this. A Council order of 21 October, 1614 [p. 132], concerning the presentation of petitions makes careful provision for the exclusion of unauthorised persons from the Council Chamber, and cases are on record of punishments inflicted by the Star Chamber for spreading reports of what went on there; but it was found very difficult in practice to prevent information leaking out[5]. Thus, when in 1617 it became of urgent importance that secrecy should be maintained with regard to the negotiations with Spain, a new kind of committee was appointed the activities of which lay outside the ordinary business of the Council. Originating in a suggestion made by Sir John Digby, afterwards Earl of Bristol, the English Ambassador to Madrid, a committee for foreign affairs came into being which, although at first concerned only with the Spanish Match, continued to exist for dealing with diplomatic relations throughout the rest of the reign of James I. Its origin in the affairs of Spain gave it the Spanish name of the Junta, and it was this body that was the predecessor of the permanent Committee for Foreign Affairs of the reign of Charles I[6]. In his essay *Of Counsel* [p. 133] Bacon approves what he calls 'standing commissions' and in a letter of 1620 addressed to King James [p. 136] he develops the idea; but he appears to be contemplating independent bodies nominated by the Crown rather than committees of the Council appointed by itself. It is not very far from Bacon's plan to the modern departments of State.

In its relation to the administration of justice the general position taken up by the Jacobean Council was that it would not interfere with the ordinary course of the law; but in spite of this, petitions for redress of grievances came

---

[1] *Tudor Constitutional Documents*, p. 217.   [2] Turner, i, 89–90.

[3] Dasent, *Acts of the Privy Council*, xxxii, 497.

[4] *English Historical Review*, xxi, 674.

[5] Turner, i, 118–21.

[6] *E.H.R.* xxi, 674–7. See also the chapter on 'Standing Committees of the Privy Council' in Turner, ii, 210–30.

in to it in great numbers and it dealt freely with private suits. On 30 May, 1603, Tuesday afternoons were set apart 'to consider and give answer to suitors that shall prefer petitions,' six of the Lords at least meeting for that purpose, 'provided that they shall entertain no suit whereby any cause depending in a Court of Justice may be interrupted, unless upon extraordinary occasion the same be referred unto them from his Majesty.'[1] Nevertheless, on 7 August, 1603, the Council threatened to imprison two litigants unless they dropped proceedings in the courts to overthrow a monopoly for sealing cards, probably because these patents were regarded as belonging to the prerogative of the Crown[2]. Other cases occur in which the intervention of the Council could be justified on similar grounds, but they suggest that its jurisdiction as ordinarily exercised covered a wide field. On 20 October, 1612, on a question raised at the Cambridgeshire Quarter Sessions whether proctorial jurisdiction extended to the village of Chesterton, the Council, on a petition from the University, ordered the Attorney-General to stay proceedings against the proctors, as they were satisfied that under its charter the University jurisdiction extended for a radius of one mile[3]. On the same day the Council heard a complaint from the University 'that one Thomas Smart, late Mayor of the Town of Cambridge, did at a Quarter Sessions lately holden at the Guildhall of the said town where both he and Mr Dr Goche[4], then Vice-Chancellor, were to sit as Justices of the Peace, contend with the said Vice-Chancellor for precedency of place, notwithstanding the example of almost two hundred years to the contrary, and a judgment given by the late Earl of Essex, Earl Marshal, now of record, and also his Majesty's express pleasure signified unto the Lord Chancellor that as well in all commissions as at any meetings the said Vice-Chancellor should take place before the Mayor of the said town.'[5] The Council accordingly 'declared and ordered that the said Vice-Chancellor ought and is to take chief place and precedency of the Mayor at all times and in all places whatsoever.'

It was part of the work of the Privy Council to stimulate into due activity the sheriffs, justices of the peace, and other lethargic local authorities. An illustration of this, in the form of a Council letter of 24 March, 1614, to the Justices of the County of Middlesex, is printed below [p. 138].

As in the reign of Elizabeth, the Privy Councillors in virtue of their office occupied an important position in Parliament. They were strongly represented on committees of the House of Commons, and Bills were sometimes referred to 'all the Privy Council of the House.'[6] The ultimate control of foreign policy was in the hands of James and the favourites, and especially of Buckingham while he lived, but the Council had a share in advising the King[7]; and that was why it was worth the while of the King of Spain to do what Louis XIV did later, and to influence its more venal members by means of bribes and pensions, although the statement in a Venetian report of 1618 is probably an exaggeration: 'The Spanish Ambassador usually bribes a great part of the Privy Council.'[8]

[1] Dasent, xxxii, 499.   [2] Ib. p. 501.
[3] Acts of the Privy Council, 1613–1614, p. 84.
[4] Barnabas Goche, Master of Magdalene 1604–1626.
[5] Ib. p. 86.   [6] Turner, i, 202.
[7] Ib. i, 141–6.   [8] Ib. i, 85–6.

As James I was frequently in financial difficulties, the Council had an important part to play in connexion with the various expedients devised for raising a revenue independently of Parliamentary grants. The Council decided upon impositions, loans, and later on upon ship-money, and they were responsible for working out the schemes of retrenchment associated with the Treasurership of Lionel Cranfield[1]. The right of the Council to imprison without shewing cause had not yet been called in question; and in 1622 a case occurs which appears to anticipate in a manner the proceedings of 1629 in connexion with the Forced Loan: Lord Saye and Sele was committed to the Fleet prison by the Council Table 'for hindering the contribution or benevolence in his quarters.'[2]

The office of Lord President of the Council was in abeyance under James I until the appointment of Viscount Mandeville in 1621[3]. In 1613 there were three Clerks of the Council, but in that year two others were appointed to be Clerks of the Council Extraordinary; and in 1617 there were four regular Clerks[4]. There was a separate Privy Council for Scotland.

(1) A Venetian's Description of the Council, 1603

Giovanni Carlo Scaramelli, Venetian Secretary in England, to the Doge and Senate [7 *April*, 1603]

...I accordingly went down to Richmond, although it was Easter Day, and found all the Palace, outside and in, full of an extraordinary crowd almost in uproar and on the tip-toe of expectation. I was immediately introduced into the Council Chamber. There I found sitting on long benches on each side of a table the Lord Chancellor, the Treasurer, the High Admiral, the Equerry (*Scudiero*), the Lord Chief Justice of England, the Treasurer and the Comptroller of the Royal Household, the Chancellor of the Exchequer, and others not Peers but Knights. They numbered eleven in all, and no one was missing except the Archbishop of Canterbury, who is Primate of England and President of the Council as well. I was received with every mark of respect for your Serenity, although, as I have already reported, these Lords of the Council behave like so many kings. They compelled me to sit down on a brocaded chair at the head of the table, and listened to me with gracious and friendly mien....

Calendar of State Papers (Venetian), 1592–1603, p. 567.

---

[1] Turner, i, 154: see also, p. 356 below.
[2] *Ib.* i, 188.   [3] *Ib.* i, 105.
[4] *Ib.* i, 121–2. A curious result of the clerical character of these officials is that whereas warrants of arrest issued by the Council went for execution to Messengers of the King's Chamber, warrants to search for papers were issued separately to one of the Clerks of the Council (*Acts of the Privy Council*, 1613–1614, pp. 25, 27).

(2) Oath of a Privy Councillor, c. 1613

Compare the Secretary's oath printed on p. 127 above.

The Oath of a Privy Councillor

You shall swear to be a true and faithful servant unto the King's Majesty as one of his Privy Council: You shall not know or understand of any manner thing to be attempted, done, or spoken against his Majesty's person, honour, crown, or dignity royal, but you shall let and withstand the same to the uttermost of your power, and either cause it to be revealed to his Majesty himself or to such of his Privy Council as shall advertise his Highness of the same. You shall in all things to be moved, treated, and debated in Council faithfully and truly declare your mind and opinion according to your heart and conscience, and shall keep secret all matters committed and revealed unto you, or that shall be treated of secretly in Council. And if any of the said treaties[1] or counsel shall touch any of the Councillors, you shall not reveal it unto him, but shall keep the same unto such time as by the consent of his Majesty or of the Council publication shall be moved thereof. You shall to your uttermost bear faith and true allegiance to the King's Majesty his heirs and lawful successors, and shall assist and defend all jurisdictions, preeminences, and authorities granted unto his Majesty and annexed to his Crown, against all foreign princes, persons, prelates, or potentates, etc., by Act of Parliament or otherwise. And generally in all things you shall do as a faithful and true servant and subject ought to do to his Majesty, so help you God and the holy contents of this book.

Acts of the Privy Council, 1613–1614, p. 4.

(3) Secrecy of Council Proceedings, 1614

This passage also indicates the nature of the procedure with regard to petitions.

At Whitehall, the 21 of October, 1614....It is this day ordered by the Board (according to his Majesty's express pleasure and commandment given unto their Lordships) [that] the Clerks of the Council shall from henceforth take care that none be present in the Council Chamber (the Council sitting) but only such as be of the Privy Council; and for all other persons of what quality soever that are to attend their Lordships for public service, be it by direction from the Board or otherwise, they are not to presume to

---

[1] *I.e.* things treated of.

enter into the Council Chamber (the Council sitting) until they be called in, and the business for which they are called being dispatched, immediately to depart.

It is also ordered that all suitors shall deliver their petitions at the Board as soon as the Lords are set in Council, which the Clerk of the Council attendant is presently [*i.e.* immediately] to take into his keeping, and to attend Mr Secretary with them at his next convenient leisure, who having perused the same may, according to the nature of each petition, as he shall think meet, give directions to the said Clerk of the Council then attendant to make a dispatch and offer it to the Board to be signed; or, if it be a matter of importance, then to acquaint the Board with it at their next sitting.

Acts of the Privy Council, 1613–1614, pp. 599–600.

(4) Bacon on Counsel

The first edition of Bacon's *Essays* was published in 1597, but only ten essays were included in it. The edition of 1612 contained many more, but the most complete collection, containing 58 essays, appeared in 1625.

Of Counsel[1]

*   *   *   *   *   *

The ancient times do set forth in figure both the incorporation and inseparable conjunction of counsel with kings, and the wise and politic use of counsel by kings: the one, in that they say Jupiter did marry Metis, which signifieth counsel; whereby they intend that Sovereignty is married to Counsel: the other in that which followeth, which was thus: They say, after Jupiter was married to Metis, she conceived by him and was with child, but Jupiter suffered her not to stay till she brought forth, but eat her up; whereby he became himself with child, and was delivered of Pallas armed, out of his head. Which monstrous fable containeth a secret of empire; how kings are to make use of their Council of State. That first they ought to refer matters unto them, which is the first begetting or impregnation; but when they are elaborate, moulded, and shaped in the womb of their Council, and grow ripe and ready to be brought forth, that then they suffer not their Council to go through with the resolution and direction, as if it depended on them; but take the matter back into their own hands, and make it appear to the world that the decrees and final directions (which, because they come forth with prudence

1 Bacon uses 'counsel' in the sense of 'Council' as well as 'advice,' so this word is not always printed here exactly as it stands in the original text of the Essay.

and power, are resembled to Pallas armed) proceeded from themselves; and not only from their authority, but (the more to add reputation to themselves) from their head and device.

Let us now speak of the inconveniences of counsel, and of the remedies. The inconveniences that have been noted in calling and using counsel, are three. First, the revealing of affairs, whereby they become less secret. Secondly, the weakening of the authority of princes, as if they were less of themselves. Thirdly, the danger of being unfaithfully counselled, and more for the good of them that counsel than of him that is counselled. For which inconveniences, the doctrine of Italy, and practice of France, in some kings' times, hath introduced *cabinet* councils; a remedy worse than the disease.

As to secrecy: princes are not bound to communicate all matters with all counsellors; but may extract and select. Neither is it necessary that he that consulteth what he should do, should declare what he will do. But let princes beware that the unsecreting of their affairs comes not from themselves. And as for cabinet councils, it may be their motto, *plenus rimarum sum* [they are full of leaks]: one futile person that maketh it his glory to tell, will do more hurt than many that know it their duty to conceal. It is true there be some affairs which require extreme secrecy, which will hardly go beyond one or two persons besides the king: neither are those councils unprosperous; for, besides the secrecy, they commonly go on constantly in one spirit of direction, without distraction. But then it must be a prudent king, such as is able to grind with a hand-mill; and those inward counsellors had need also be wise men, and especially true and trusty to the king's ends; as it was with King Henry the Seventh of England, who in his greatest business imparted himself to none, except it were to Morton and Fox.

For weakening of authority: the fable[1] sheweth the remedy. Nay, the majesty of kings is rather exalted than diminished when they are in the chair of counsel; neither was there ever prince bereaved of his dependences by his Council; except where there hath been either an over-greatness in one Councillor or an over-strict combination in divers; which are things soon found and holpen.

For the last inconvenience, that men will counsel with an eye to themselves: certainly *non inveniet fidem super terram* [he will not find faith on the earth] is meant of the nature of times, and not of all particular persons. There be that are in nature faithful,

---

[1] Of Jupiter and Metis.

and sincere, and plain, and direct; not crafty and involved; let princes, above all, draw to themselves such natures. Besides, counsellors are not commonly so united but that one counsellor keepeth sentinel over another; so that if any do counsel out of faction or private ends, it commonly comes to the king's ear. But the best remedy is, if princes know their counsellors as well as their counsellors know them:

Principis est virtus maxima nosse suos.

And on the other side, counsellors should not be too speculative into their sovereign's person. The true composition of a counsellor is rather to be skilful in their master's business than in his nature; for then he is like to advise him, and not feed his humour. It is of singular use to princes if they take the opinions of their Council both separately and together. For private opinion is more free; but opinion before others is more reverent. In private, men are more bold in their own humours; and in consort, men are more obnoxious to others' humours; therefore it is good to take both; and of the inferior sort rather in private, to preserve freedom; of the greater rather in consort, to preserve respect. It is in vain for princes to take counsel concerning matters, if they take no counsel likewise concerning persons; for all matters are as dead images; and the life of the execution of affairs resteth in the good choice of persons. Neither is it enough to consult concerning persons *secundum genera,* as in an idea or mathematical description what the kind and character of the person should be; for the greatest errors are committed and the most judgment is shewn in the choice of individuals. It was truly said, *optimi consiliarii mortui* [the best counsellors are the dead]: books will speak plain when counsellors blanch. Therefore it is good to be conversant in them, specially the books of such as themselves have been actors upon the stage.

The councils at this day in most places are but familiar meetings, where matters are rather talked on than debated. And they run too swift to the Order or Act of Council. It were better that in causes of weight the matter were propounded one day and not spoken to till the next day; *in nocte consilium* [night is the season for counsel]. So was it done in the Commission of Union between England and Scotland; which was a grave and orderly assembly. I commend set days for petitions; for both it gives the suitors more certainty for their attendance, and it frees the meetings for matters of estate, that they may *hoc agere.* In choice of committees for ripening business for the Council, it is better to choose

indifferent persons than to make an indifference by putting in
those that are strong on both sides. I commend also standing
commissions; as for trade, for treasure, for war, for suits, for some
provinces; for where there be divers particular councils and but
one Council of Estate (as it is in Spain), they are, in effect, no
more than standing commissions: save that they have greater
authority. Let such as are to inform councils out of their
particular professions, (as lawyers, seamen, mint-men, and the
like,) be first heard before committees; and then, as occasion
serves, before the Council. And let them not come in multitudes,
or in a tribunitious manner; for that is to clamour councils, not
to inform them. A long table and a square table, or seats about
the walls, seem things of form, but are things of substance; for at
a long table a few at the upper end, in effect, sway all the business;
but in the other form there is more use of the Councillors' opinions
that sit lower. A king, when he presides in Council, let him
beware how he opens his own inclination too much in that which
he propoundeth; for else Councillors will but take the wind of
him, and instead of giving free counsel, sing him a song of *placebo*.

Bacon, *Works* (ed. J. Spedding), vi, 424–7.

(5) Bacon on Standing Commissions, 1620

This letter from Bacon to James I was written *c*. 1 January, 1620. In addition to
the scheme for standing commissions, it refers to the desirability of the King's paying
occasional visits to the Star Chamber.

Amongst the counsels which (since the time I had the honour
to be first of your learned and after of your privy council)[1] I have
given your Majesty faithfully, according to my small ability, I do
take comfort in none more than that I was the first that advised
you to come in person into the Star Chamber; knowing very well
that those virtues of your Majesty's which I saw near hand,
would out of that throne, both as out of a sphere illustrate your
own honour and as out of a fountain water and refresh your whole
land; and because your Majesty in that you have already done
hath so well effected that which I foresaw and desired, even
beyond my expectation, it is no marvel if I resort still to the
branches of that counsel that hath borne so good fruit.

The Star Chamber in the institution thereof hath two uses:
the one as a supreme Court of Judicature; the other as an open

---

[1] Bacon had become one of Queen Elizabeth's learned counsel in 1596, and
James I had confirmed him in office on his accession. He was made a Privy Councillor
in 1616.

Council. In the first kind your Majesty hath sat there now twice: the first time in a cause of force concerning the duels; the second time in a cause of fraud concerning the forgeries and conspiracies against the Lady of Exeter[1]; which two natures of crimes, force and fraud, are the proper objects of that Court.

In the second kind your Majesty came the first time of all, when you did set in frame and fabric the several jurisdictions of your Courts. There wants a fourth part of the square to make all complete, which is, if your Majesty will be pleased to publish certain commonwealth commissions; which, as your Majesty hath well begun to do in some things and to speak of in some others, so if your Majesty will be pleased to make a solemn declaration of them in that place, this will follow:

First, that your Majesty shall do yourself an infinite honour, and win the hearts of your people to acknowledge you as well the most politic King as the most just. Secondly, it will oblige your Commissioners to a more strict account when they shall be engaged by such a public charge and commandment. And thirdly, it will invite and direct any man that finds himself to know anything concerning those commissions to bring in their informations. So as I am persuaded it will eternise your name and merit, and that King James his commissions will be spoken [of] and put in ure[2] as long as Britain lasts; at the least in the reign of all good Kings.

For the particulars, besides the two Commissions of the Navy and the buildings about London...I wish these following to be added.

Commissions for advancing the clothing of England, as well the old drapery as the new, and all the incidents thereunto.

Commission for staying treasure within the realm, and the reiglement[3] of moneys.

Commission for the provision of the realm with corn and grain, and the government of the exportation and importation thereof; and directing of public granaries, if cause be.

Commission for introducing and nourishing manufactures within the realm, for the setting people a-work, and the considering of all grants and privileges of that nature.

Commission to prevent the depopulation of towns and houses of husbandry, and for nuisances and highways.

Commission for the recovery of drowned lands.

Commission for the suppressing of the grievances of informers.

---

[1] See p. 141.   [2] *I.e.* put in practice.   [3] Regulation or control.

Commission for the better proceedings in the plantations of Ireland.

Commission for the provision of the realm with all kinds of warlike defence: ordnance, powder, munition, and armour.

Of these you may take and leave as it shall please you: and I wish the articles concerning every one of them (first allowed by your Council) to be read openly, and the Commissioners' names.

For the good that comes of particular and select committees and commissions I need not commonplace, for your Majesty hath found the good of them; but nothing to that that will be when such things are published, because it will vindicate them from neglect and make many good spirits that we little think of co-operate in them.

I know very well that the world, that commonly is apt to think that the care of the commonwealth is but a pretext in matters of State, will perhaps conceive that this is but a preparative to a Parliament. But let not that hinder your Majesty's magnanimity, *in opere operato* that is so good; and besides, that opinion for many respects will do no hurt to your affairs.

Bacon's Letters and Life (ed. J. Spedding), vii, 70.

(6) The Council and the Justices of the Peace, 1614

A letter to the Justices of Peace in the county of Middlesex:
24 March, 1614

So general a complaint is brought unto us of the many robberies and burglaries ordinarily of late committed in that county of Middlesex (and especially in the skirts and confines of the City of London), as we cannot but suspect it chiefly to proceed from some neglect in you the Justices of Peace, unto whose care and duty do properly belong the prevention of such like mischiefs by diligent apprehending and punishing such loose and vagrant persons as are now observed to abound within your jurisdictions, and the due observance and execution of such laws and statutes as are provided on that behalf. And for that the remedy hereof is of so great consequence as it not only concerns the honour of the government in general but even the safety of every man in his own particular, we have hereby thought fit to require you, in his Majesty's name, that from henceforth such orders be taken in your assemblies as the like liberty be no more left unto those loose and idle persons (by whom these robberies are committed), but such good and due courses settled for their punishment as the necessity of the cause requireth. And, whereas your night watches and privy searches have heretofore been kept and observed, as the principal means to restrain and apprehend those idle and vagrant persons, we have also thought fit to recommend unto you the due observance of those courses, and that the said privy searches be often made and at uncertain times. And lastly, whereas by law authority is given unto the Justices of Peace to erect houses of correction within their several counties or cities, the neglect is doubtless without all excuse that hitherto no such provision hath been made within that county of Middlesex, notwithstanding the want thereof hath been as great as in any one place within this kingdom: we do therefore hereby will and require you to consider of the statute, and to proceed without further delay in the providing and erecting of a house or houses of correction within that county according to the true meaning and intent of that law, which is conceived to be the only remedy for the preventing of such mischiefs as by default thereof doth fall upon his Majesty's subjects.

Acts of the Privy Council, 1613–1614, pp. 392–3.

The Star Chamber[1]

By the reign of James I the Star Chamber had acquired a fixed and regular procedure as the Courts at Westminster had done long before, and the history of its development had therefore come to an end. The problem of the seventeenth century is how to account for the fact that a Court hitherto useful and even popular perished in a storm of execration in 1641. The explanation is to be found in the intervention of the Star Chamber in cases that were religious or political in character and so involved the Court in the great controversies of the time. Politically, it came to be regarded as an 'efficient engine of prerogative government'[2]; in the sphere of religion, it worked in close concert with the High Commission to punish the rebels against the Laudian administration of the Church[3]. Thus 'the Parliamentary statesman saw the expediency of abolishing the most efficient means of prerogative government; the common lawyer saw a means of at length triumphing over a rival judicature; the Puritan saw the fall of a Court by which he had been persecuted.'[4]

But during the life of James I the decline in the popularity of the Star Chamber had scarcely begun. 'Before the reign of Charles I,' writes Spedding[5], 'I doubt whether any man whose opinion carries weight would have condemned it.' The Court was still occupied in its original crusade against force and fraud[6], and in particular in the vindication of authority—not now against 'over-mighty lords' but against local feeling which deflected the course of justice by influencing over-pliable justices of the peace[7]. It

---

[1] On the Star Chamber in Wales, see *A Catalogue of Star Chamber Proceedings relating to Wales*, compiled by I. ab O. Edwards (1929).

[2] Sir W. S. Holdsworth, *A History of English Law* (3rd edition), i, 479.

[3] 'The Court of High Commission stood to the Church and to the ordinary ecclesiastical courts somewhat in the same relation as the Council and Star Chamber stood to the State and the ordinary courts of the State, central and local. It is no wonder therefore that throughout its history its relations to the Council and Star Chamber were close. Both were semi-political, semi-judicial courts engaged in carrying out in their several spheres a common policy.' (*ib.* i, 608.)

[4] *Ib.* i, 514.

[5] Bacon, *Letters and Life*, vii, 92.

[6] 'Which two natures of crimes, force and fraud, are the proper objects of that Court' (Bacon, see p. 137 above).

[7] A later case, *Attorney-General* v. *Moody*, 1632, is a good illustration of this aspect of the Star Chamber's activities. When Sir Cornelius Vermuyden was engaged in the work of draining the Fens his operations were interfered with by certain persons who claimed rights of common over the lands that were being drained. They 'beat the workmen, set up a pair of gallows for to terrify the workmen, threw some of them into the water and held them under a while'; and when a writ came down from the Star Chamber to summon them to answer for a riot, they set the messenger who carried it in the stocks. One Mr Hawthorne was then 'throwen into the river and kept in with poles a great while'; and 'some of the rioters poured water in at the necks of some of the workmen.' But in the end the Star Chamber was too strong for the indignant locality, and some of the parties were fined £1000 apiece. It was urged in

still punished breaches of proclamations[1]; it issued orders and decrees; and on occasion it interfered in private affairs[2]; but its powers were as a rule exercised with discretion, and they existed for the public benefit. Nor, until the Court was drawn into the fatal current of later politics, does it appear to have concerned itself in any very provocative way with matters of religion.

James I occasionally visited the Star Chamber and made speeches there, acting upon the advice of Bacon, who regarded these solemn public appearances as in the interest of the monarchy [p. 17 and p. 136]. On 12 February, 1617, the King delivered himself on the subject of duelling in the case of 'two very young gentlemen' who were convicted and fined £1000 by the Court; but he afterwards remitted the fines[3]. Again, in February 1619 he sat for five days at the trial of Sir Thomas Lake for defaming the Countess of Exeter, and himself pronounced the sentence of fine and imprisonment inflicted by the Court [p. 142].

On 25 September, 1623, the King issued a proclamation [p. 143] for the better enforcement of the Star Chamber Decree of 1586 concerning printers[4]. This brings together the Star Chamber and the High Commission as both of them proper authorities for the punishment of press offences.

(1) Bacon on the Star Chamber, 1621

This letter, addressed by Bacon to the King, was written in June, 1621.

May it please your Majesty,

For that your Majesty is pleased to call for my opinion concerning the sacred intention you have, to go on with the reformation of your Courts of Justice and relieving the grievances of your people which your Parliament hath entered into, I shall never be a recusant[5] (though I be confined) to do your service.

Your Majesty's Star Chamber, next your Court of Parliament, is your highest chair. You never came upon that mount but your garments did shine before you went off. It is the supreme

---

[1] 'Indeed the world is now much terrified with the Star Chamber, there being not so little an offence against any proclamation but is liable and subject to the censure of that Court' (Chamberlain to Carleton, 8 July, 1620, quoted in Scofield, p. 49).

[2] In the case of the *Attorney-General* v. *Comber*, 13 Jac. I, the Court served a writ *ne exeat regno* upon the defendant 'for that he swore he would depart the kingdom rather than he would marry' (J. S. Burn, *The Star Chamber* (1870), p. 83).

[3] *Ib.* p. 84.

[4] Printed in *Tudor Constitutional Documents*, p. 279.

[5] In addition to its technical ecclesiastical meaning, this word could be applied to anyone refusing to do something commanded or desired. On 3 May, 1621, Bacon had been sentenced to imprisonment during the King's pleasure, but he was only in the Tower for a few days. In June he was, however, still excluded from the Court.

defence of one Amazon, who appears in the record as 'the widow Smith,' that she had 'since married with a minister, a grave divine'; but the Court fined her £500, which presumably the minister had to pay (*Reports of cases in the Star Chamber and High Commission*, ed. S. R. Gardiner; Camden Society, 1886, p. 59).

court of judicature ordinary; it is an open council. Nothing I would think can be more seasonable (if your appointments permit it) than if your Majesty will be pleased to come thither in person the morrow of this term (which is the time anniversary before the circuits and the Long Vacation) and there make an open declaration that you purpose to pursue the reformation which the Parliament hath begun.

*   *   *   *   *   *

Bacon's Letters and Life (ed. J. Spedding), vii, 289.

(2) William Hudson on the Star Chamber, *c.* 1633

On the origin of the name of the Court see *Tudor Constitutional Documents*, p. 219. Hudson's courtly explanation given below can scarcely be taken seriously.

And so I doubt not but *Camera Stellata* (for so I find it called in our ancient year-books) is most aptly named; not because the Star Chamber where the Court is kept is so adorned with stars gilded, as some would have it, for surely the chamber is so adorned because it is the seal of that Court, *et denominatio* being *a praestantiori magis dignum trahit ad se minus*; and it was so fitly called because the stars have no light but what is cast upon them from the sun by reflection, being his representative body, and as his Majesty himself was pleased to say when he sat there in his royal person, representation must needs cease when the person is present. So in the presence of his great majesty, the which is the sun of honour and glory, the shining of those stars is put out, they not having any power to pronounce any sentence in this Court, for the judgment is the King's only, but by way of advice they deliver their opinions, which his wisdom alloweth or dis-alloweth, increaseth or moderateth, at his royal pleasure. Which was performed by his most excellent Majesty with more than Solomon's wisdom in the great cause of the Countess of Exeter against Sir Thomas Lake; where his Majesty during the dignity of that Court sat five continual days in a chair of state elevated above the table about which his Lords sat; and after that long and patient hearing, and the opinions particularly given of his great Council, he pronounced a sentence more accurately eloquent, judiciously grave, and honourably just, to the satisfaction of all the hearers and of all the lovers of justice, than all the records extant in this Kingdom can declare to have been at any former time done by any of his royal progenitors.

William Hudson, *A Treatise of the Court of Star Chamber* (printed in *Collectanea Juridica*, 1792, ii, 1– 240), p. 8.

(3) Proclamation concerning Printers, 1623

Dated 25 September, 1623. The Star Chamber Decree of 1586 referred to in the preamble is printed in *Tudor Constitutional Documents*, pp. 279–84.

A Proclamation against the disorderly printing, uttering, and dispersing of Books, Pamphlets, etc.

Whereas the three and twentieth day of June in the eight and twentieth year of the reign of our late dear sister Queen Elizabeth, for the repressing of sundry intolerable offences, troubles, and disturbances, as well in the Church as in the civil government of the State and common weal, occasioned by the disorderly printing and selling of books, a decree was made in the High Court of Star Chamber containing many just and provident ordinances for preventing of those inconveniencies, and amongst the rest that no person or persons should imprint or cause to be imprinted any book, work, or copy against the form and meaning of any restraint or ordinance contained or to be contained in any statute or laws of this realm, or in any injunction made or set forth by her Majesty or her Privy Council, or against the true intent and meaning of any letters patents, commissions, or prohibitions under the Great Seal of England, or contrary to any allowed ordinance set down for the good governance of the Company of Stationers within the City of London, upon pain of imprisonment by the space of six months without bail or mainprize, and such further punishment as in the said decree is set down: And that every person that should wittingly sell, utter, put to sale, bind, stitch, or sew, or wittingly cause to be sold, uttered, put to sale, bound, stitched, or sewed, any books or copies whatsoever printed contrary to the intent and true meaning of the ordinances or articles aforesaid, should suffer three months imprisonment for his or their offence; the true intent and meaning of which said decree hath been cautelously[1] abused and eluded by printing in the parts beyond the sea and elsewhere as well sundry seditious, schismatical, and scandalous books and pamphlets as also such allowed books, works, and writings as have been imprinted within the realm by such to whom the sole printing thereof by letters patents or lawful ordinance or authority doth appertain according to the true intent of the said decree, and by importing the same into this our realm.

[1] Craftily, deceitfully.

We, willing not only to tread in the steps of our said dear sister but to add such further strength as shall be meet to those provident and good orders made in her time, have thought fit to publish and declare unto all our subjects that it is our express will and commandment that the said decree be from henceforth strictly observed and put in execution; and to meet with the malice and craft of such as by sleight or cunning shall attempt or go about to undermine or avoid[1] all or any part of the said decree, we do straitly prohibit and forbid that no person or persons whatsoever, either our natural born subjects, denizen, or stranger, do at any time hereafter, either within our own dominions or without, imprint or cause to be imprinted, or bring in or cause to be brought in, into this our realm, or sew, stitch, bind, sell, put to sale, or disperse any seditious, schismatical, or other scandalous books or pamphlets whatsoever, or any other book or books, though lawful or allowed to be printed by such to whom the printing thereof doth belong, which shall be printed contrary to the true intent of the said decree, or shall be printed out of this realm of purpose to avoid the said decree or any prohibition or restraint contained in any letters patents, privilege, or lawful ordinance, upon pain of our indignation and heavy displeasure, and of the pains, punishments, and imprisonments contained in the said decree, and such further censures as by our Court of Star Chamber and High Commission respectively shall be thought meet to be inflicted on them for such their offences.

And we do straitly charge, authorise, and command the Master and Keepers or Wardens of the mystery or art of Stationers of the City of London and their successors and their deputies, that they from time to time, taking with them such officers as in or by their charters or the said decree are appointed, do make careful and diligent search for all such scandalous and offensive books or pamphlets as are or shall be imported into this realm or here imprinted contrary to this our royal commandment, and seize the same, and do their uttermost endeavours as well for suppressing thereof as for bringing the offenders unto justice, as they the said Master, Wardens, and their deputies and every of them will answer their neglect at their perils.

Willing and hereby straitly charging and commanding all and every our justices of peace, mayors, sheriffs, bailiffs, constables, and headboroughs, and all customers[2], comptrollers, searchers, waiters[3], and all other our officers, ministers, and subjects what-

---

[1] Make void.
[2] Custom-house officers.
[3] An alternative term for 'customers.'

soever, as they tender our favour and will avoid our indignation and displeasure, from time to time to their uttermost powers to see this our royal pleasure duly executed, and to be aiding and assisting to the persons before mentioned in the due execution of this our commandment.

Given at our manor of Hampton Court the five and twentieth day of September in the one and twentieth year of our reign of Great Britain, France, and Ireland.

Rymer, *Foedera* (edition of 1704–35), xvii, 522–3.

The High Commission Court

In 1591, in Cawdrey's case[1], the Elizabethan judges had recognised the High Commission as a legal ecclesiastical court, but this did not prevent James I's judges, led by Coke, from launching an attack upon its procedure and authority. In 1606 they held that the Court had no power to imprison any man because this was not expressly conferred on it by the Act of Supremacy; and since the Common Law did not recognise imprisonment by the spiritual courts neither did the Court possess it at Common Law [p. 147]. Later on, in 1611, this view was developed at length by Coke in the *Fourth Institute* [p. 156]; and practical effect was given to it by the Courts at Westminster in cases in which they set at liberty on writs of *habeas corpus* persons imprisoned by the High Commission Court. Moreover, in 1606 the Judges, when appealed to by the Privy Council concerning the legality of the *ex officio* oath[2], gave an opinion that its use, except in causes testamentary or matrimonial, where it was justified by long custom, was contrary to the principles of English law.

This high authority for questioning the legality of the proceedings of the Court led the Commons in 1610 to include a protest against it in a petition of grievances [p. 148], complaining, among other things, that it fined and imprisoned without proper authority; that petty offences came under its cognisance, 'whereby the least offenders, not committing anything of any enormous or high nature, may be drawn from the most remote places of the kingdom to London or York, which is very grievous and inconvenient'; that 'their pursuivants and other ministers employed in the apprehension of suspected offenders in anything spiritual and in the searching for any supposed scandalous books, use to break open men's houses, closets, and desks, rifling all corners and secret custodies, as in cases of high treason or suspicion thereof'; and that there was no appeal from the decisions of the Court. Objection was also taken to the use of the *ex officio* oath, by which a man might be forced 'to accuse himself of any offence.' The King promised to give favourable consideration to the petition, and in the new Commission issued in 1611 after the death of Archbishop Bancroft, two minor concessions were made: 1. 'That no sentence definitive of any cause or matter determinable by virtue of this Commission shall hereafter be given without the personal presence, hearing, and full assent' of five Commissioners at the least; and 2. That 'it shall be lawful for any persons that shall hereafter be sentenced...by virtue of this...Commission which shall find themselves grieved by reason of any such sentence, to become suitors unto us by way of supplication as of our grace to have a commission of re-view to be granted by us for the re-examination of their cause.' The *ex officio* oath was, however, retained, and the High Commission was further empowered to suppress unlawful conventicles on the one hand, and to carry out the penal laws against the Roman Catholics on the other[3]. Thus under James I the authority

---

[1] *Tudor Constitutional Documents*, pp. 362, 372.

[2] See *ib.* p. 193, note 1; also p. 164 below.

[3] The Letters Patent of 1611 are of special importance, as in them 'the procedure and organisation of the Commission as a court received their first official sanction'

of the Crown is as insurmountable an obstacle in the way of the desires of the Commons as it had ever been under Elizabeth, or even under Henry VIII. The proceedings of the High Commission also contributed to the growing unpopularity of the Bishops, upon whom the responsibility for the grievances of its victims was thrown.

In 1611 the position which the Judges had taken up was defended by Coke against Archbishop Abbot, at first before the Council and afterwards in the King's own presence[1], and an attempt was made to get round his opposition by placing him and six other Judges upon the new Commission then being drafted. Coke at once asked to see the Commission, and when it was read to him he pointed out so many illegalities in it that the Judges declined to serve, and 'rejoiced that they did not sit by force of it' [p. 163].

It has been pointed out that matrimonial cases are the most numerous of those coming before the Court; moral offences, of both clergy and laity, come next; and simony, plurality, drunkenness, and other clerical irregularities, take the third place. Heresy and schism occur less often than might be expected, and these terms as interpreted by the Court do not bear quite the popular meaning. 'Just as any misdeed is at common law a tort, and any entrance upon another's land is a trespass, so the quarrelling of two old women in church was schism, witchcraft was heresy, and the failure of the parson to read prayers on a Wednesday because he was reaping his harvest for fear of a storm, was nonconformity.'[2]

(1) Opinion of the Judges, 1606

If High Commissioners have power to imprison

...There was moved a question amongst the Judges and Serjeants at Serjeants' Inn, if the High Commissioners in Ecclesiastical Causes may by force of their commission imprison any man or no?

First of all it was resolved by all, that before the Statute of 1 El. cap. 1 the King might have granted a commission to hear and determine ecclesiastical causes: but then, notwithstanding any clause in their commission, the Commissioners ought to proceed according to the ecclesiastical law allowed within this realm, for he cannot alter neither his temporal nor his ecclesiastical laws within this realm by his grant or commission: *vide* Cawdrey's case, Fifth Report. And they could not in any case have punished any delinquent by fine or imprisonment unless they had authority so to do by Act of Parliament. Then all the question rests upon the Act of 1 El., which as to this purpose rests upon three branches.

(R. G. Usher, *The Rise and Fall of the High Commission*, p. 236). They are printed, with a few omissions, in Prothero, pp. 424–35, where the subsequent alterations and additions made in 1613 and 1625 are also noted. See also the discussion of James I's Commissions in the Introduction (pp. xliii–v).

[1] Usher, pp. 212–19.   [2] *Ib.* p. 257.

1. Such Commissioners have power to exercise, use, occupy, execute, all jurisdiction spiritual and ecclesiastical.

2. Such Commissioners by force of letters patent have power to visit, reform, etc., all heresies, etc., which by any manner of spiritual or ecclesiastical power, etc., can or lawfully may be reformed, etc., so that these branches limit the jurisdiction, and what offences shall be within the jurisdiction of such Commissioners, by force of letters patent of the King; and this is all, and only such offences may lawfully be reformed by the ecclesiastical law.

3. The third branch is, that such Commissioners after such commission delivered to them so authorised, shall have power and lawful authority by virtue of this Act and the said letters patent, to exercise, use, and execute all the premisses according to the tenor and effect of the said letters patent. This branch gives them power to execute their commission. But it was objected that this branch doth not give the Queen power by her letters patent to alter the proceedings of the ecclesiastical law, or gave to the Queen absolute power by her letters patent to prescribe what manner of proceedings or punishment concerning the lands, goods, or bodies of the subject....

These are the tenor and effect of the letters patent before remembered; and if any other construction shall be made,

1. It shall be against the express letters, *scilicet*, said letters patent;

2. It shall be full of great peril and inconvenience, for then not only imprisonment of body but confiscation of lands, goods, etc. And some corporal punishment may be imposed for heresy, schism, incontinence, etc.; also power may be given to them to burn any man for heresy: which would be against the Common Law of the land.

Coke, Twelfth Report (edition of 1777).

(2) Petition of Grievances, 1610

This petition was presented to the King on 7 July, 1610. It deals at length with the Court of High Commission, but also refers to impositions, proclamations, and the Council of Wales.

To the King's most Excellent Majesty

Most gracious Sovereign, Your Majesty's most humble Commons assembled in Parliament, being moved as well out of their duty and zeal to your Majesty as out of the sense of just grief wherewith your loving subjects are generally through the whole realm at this time possessed because they perceive their common and ancient right and liberty to be much declined and infringed in these late years, do with all duty and humility present these our just complaints thereof to your gracious view, most instantly craving justice therein and due redress.

And although it be true that many of the particulars whereof we now complain were of some use[1] in the late Queen's time, and then not much impugned, because the usage of them being then more moderate gave not so great occasion of offence, and consequently not so much cause to enquire into the right and validity of them; yet the right being now more thoroughly scanned by reason of the great mischiefs and inconveniencies which the subjects have thereby sustained, we are very confident that your Majesty will be so far from thinking it a point of honour or greatness to continue any grievance upon your people because you found them begun in your predecessor's times, as you will rather hold it a work of great glory to reform them, since your Majesty knoweth well that neither continuance of time nor errors of men can or ought to prejudice truth or justice, and that nothing can be more worthy of so worthy a King, nor more answerable to the great wisdom and goodness which abound in you, than to understand the griefs and redress the wrongs of so loyal and well deserving people.

In this confidence, dread Sovereign, we offer these grievances (the particulars whereof are hereunder set down) to your gracious consideration; and we offer them out of the greatest loyalty and duty that subjects can bear to their Prince: most humbly and instantly beseeching your Majesty, as well for Justice sake (more than which, as we conceive, in these petitions we do not seek) as also for the better assurance of the State, and general repose of your faithful and loving subjects, and for testimony of your gracious acceptation of their full affections, declared as well by their joyful receiving of your Majesty at your happy entrance into these kingdoms, which you have been often pleased with favour to remember, as also by their extraordinary contributions granted since unto you, such as have been never yielded to any former Prince upon the like terms and occasions, that we may receive to these our complaints your most gracious answer; which we cannot doubt but will be such as may be worthy of your princely self and will give satisfaction and great comfort to all your loyal and most dutiful loving subjects, who do and will pray for the happy preservation of your most royal Majesty.

[1] *I.e.* were in use to a certain extent.

The policy and constitution of this your kingdom appropriates unto the Kings of this realm, with the assent of the Parliament, as well the sovereign power of making laws as that of taxing or imposing upon the subjects' goods or merchandises, wherein they have justly such a propriety as may not without their consent be altered or changed. This is the cause that the people of this kingdom, as they ever shewed themselves faithful and loving to their Kings and ready to aid them in all their just occasions with voluntary contributions, so have they been ever careful to preserve their own liberties and rights when anything hath been done to prejudice or impeach the same. And therefore when their Princes, occasioned either by their wars or their over-great bounty or by any other necessity, have without consent of Parliament set impositions either within the land or upon commodities either exported or imported by the merchants, they have in open Parliament complained of it in that it was done without their consents, and thereupon never failed to obtain a speedy and full redress, without any claim made by the Kings of any power or prerogative in that point. And though the law of propriety[1] be originally and carefully preserved by the common laws of this realm, which are as ancient as the kingdom itself, yet these famous Kings, for the better contentment and assurance of their loving subjects, agreed that this old fundamental right should be farther declared and established by Act of Parliament, wherein it is provided that no such charges should ever be laid upon the people without their common consent, as may appear by sundry records of former times.

We therefore, your Majesty's most humble Commons assembled in Parliament, following the example of this worthy care of our ancestors and out of a duty to those for whom we serve, finding that your Majesty, without advice or consent of Parliament, hath lately in time of peace set both greater impositions and far more in number than any your noble ancestors did ever in time of war, have with all humility presumed to present this most just and necessary petition unto your Majesty, That all impositions set without the assent of Parliament may be quite abolished and taken away, and that your Majesty, in imitation likewise of your noble progenitors, will be pleased that a law may be made during this session of Parliament to declare that all impositions set or to be set upon your people their goods or merchandises, save only by common assent in Parliament, are and shall be void: Wherein your Majesty shall not only give your subjects good satisfaction in

---

[1] Property

point of their right, but also bring exceeding joy and comfort to them which now suffer, partly through the abating the price of native commodities and partly through the raising of all foreign, to the overthrow of merchants and shipping, the causing of a general dearth and decay of wealth among your people, who will be hereby no less discouraged than disabled to supply your Majesty when occasion shall require it.

Whereas by the Statute 1 Eliz. cap. 1, intituled *An Act restoring to the Crown the Ancient Jurisdiction over the State Ecclesiastical, etc.,* power was given to the Queen and her successors to continue and make a Commission in Causes Ecclesiastical, the said Act is found to be inconvenient and of dangerous extent in divers respects:

First, For that it enableth the making of such a Commission as well to any one subject born as to more.

Secondly, For that whereas by the intention and words of the Statute ecclesiastical jurisdiction is restored to the Crown, and your Highness by that Statute enabled to give only such power ecclesiastical to the said Commissioners, yet under colour of some words in that Statute where the Commissioners are authorised to execute their Commission according to the tenor and effect of your Highness's letters patents and by letters patents grounded thereupon, the said Commissioners do fine and imprison and exercise other authority not belonging to the ecclesiastical jurisdiction restored by that Statute, which we conceive to be a great wrong to the subject: And that those Commissioners might as well by colour of those words, if they were so authorised by your Highness's letters patents, fine without stint and imprison without limitation of time: As also, according to will and discretion, without any rules of law, spiritual or temporal, adjudge and impose utter confiscation of goods, forfeiture of lands, yea, and the taking away of a limb, and of life itself: And this for any matter whatsoever pertaining to spiritual jurisdiction, which never was nor could be meant by the makers of that law.

Thirdly, For that by the Statute the King and his successors (however your Majesty hath been pleased out of your gracious disposition otherwise to order) make and direct such Commission into all the counties and dioceses, yea, into every parish of England; and thereby all causes may be taken from jurisdiction of bishops, chancellors, and archdeacons, and laymen solely to be enabled to excommunicate and exercise all other censures spiritual.

Fourthly, That every petty offence pertaining to spiritual

jurisdiction is by colour of the said words, and letters patents grounded thereupon, made subject to excommunication and punishment by that strange and exorbitant power and commission, whereby the least offenders, not committing anything of any enormous or high nature, may be drawn from the most remote places of the kingdom to London or York, which is very grievous and inconvenient.

Fifthly, For that limit touching causes subject to this Commission being only with these words, viz. 'Such as pertain to spiritual or ecclesiastical jurisdiction,' it is very hard to know what matters or offences are included in that number; and the rather because it is unknown what ancient canons or laws spiritual are in force and what not: From hence ariseth great inconveniency and occasion of contention.

And whereas upon the same Statute a Commission Ecclesiastical is made, therein is grievance apprehended thus:

First, For that thereby the same men have both spiritual and temporal jurisdiction, and may both force the party by oath to accuse himself of any offence and also enquire thereof by a jury; and lastly, may inflict for the same offence at the same time and by one and the same sentence both a spiritual and a temporal punishment[1].

Secondly, Whereas upon sentences of deprivation or other spiritual censures given by force of ordinary jurisdiction an appeal lieth for the party aggrieved, that is here excluded by express words of the Commission: Also here is to be a trial by jury yet no remedy by traverse nor attaint[2]; neither can a man have any writ of error, though a judgment or sentence be given against him, amounting to the taking away of all his goods and imprisoning of him during life, yea, to the adjudging him in case of *praemunire*, whereby his lands are forfeited and he out of the protection of the law.

Thirdly, That whereas penal laws and offences against the same cannot be determined in other Courts or by other persons than by those trusted by Parliament with the execution thereof, yet the execution of many such Statutes (divers whereof were made since the first of Eliz.) are commended and committed to these Commissioners Ecclesiastical, who are either to inflict the punishment contained in the Statute, being *praemunire* and of other high nature, and so enforce a man upon his own oath to accuse and expose himself to those punishments, or else to inflict

---

[1] The text reads 'jurisdiction,' but this is evidently a mistake.

[2] 'Traverse' is formal denial at law; 'attaint' was 'a legal process instituted for reversing a false verdict and convicting the jurors' (*Oxford Dictionary*).

other temporal punishments at their pleasure. And yet besides and after that done, the party shall be subject, in the Courts mentioned in the Acts, to punishment by the same Acts appointed and inflicted: which we think very unreasonable.

Fourthly, That the Commission giveth authority to enforce men called into question to enter into recognizance, not only for appearance from time to time but also for performance of whatsoever shall be by the Commissioners ordered. And also that it giveth power to enjoin parties defendant or accused to pay such fees to the ministers of the Court as by the Commissioners shall be thought fit.

And touching the execution of the Commission, it is found grievous these ways among other:

First, For that laymen are by the Commissioners punished for speaking (otherwise than in judicial places and courses) of the simony and other misdemeanours of the spiritual men, though the thing spoken be true and the speech tending to the inducing of some condign punishment.

Secondly, In that these Commissioners usually appoint and allot to women discontented at and unwilling to live with their husbands such portion and allowance for present maintenance as to them shall seem meet; to the great encouragement to wives to be disobedient and contemptuous against their husbands.

Thirdly, In that their pursuivants and other ministers employed in the apprehension of suspected offenders in anything spiritual and in the searching for any supposed scandalous books, use to break open men's houses, closets, and desks, rifling all corners and secret custodies, as in cases of high treason or suspicion thereof.

All which premisses amongst other things considered, your Majesty's most loyal and dutiful Commons in all humbleness beseech you that, for the easing of them as well from the present grievance as from the fear and possibility of greater in times future, your Highness would vouchsafe your royal assent and allowance to and for the ratifying of the said Statute, and the reducing thereof, and consequently of the said Commission, to reasonable and convenient limits, by some Act to be passed in the present session of Parliament.

Amongst many other points of happiness and freedom which your Majesty's subjects of this kingdom have enjoyed under your royal progenitors, Kings and Queens of this Realm, there is none which they have accounted more dear and precious than this, to be guided and governed by certain rule of law, which giveth both to the Head and members that which of right belongeth to them, and not by any uncertain or arbitrary form of government. Which, as it hath proceeded from the original and constitution and temperature of this Estate, so hath it been the principal means of upholding the same in such sort as that their Kings have been just, beloved, happy, and glorious, and the kingdom itself peaceable, flourishing, and durable so many ages. And the effect as well of the contentment that the subjects of this kingdom have taken in this form of government as also of the love, respect, and duty which they have by reason of the same rendered unto their Princes may appear in this, That they have, as occasion hath required, yielded more extraordinary and voluntary contributions to assist their Kings than the subjects of any other known kingdom whatsoever. Out of this root hath grown the indubitable right of the people of this kingdom not to be made subject to any punishment that shall extend to their lives, lands, bodies, or goods, other than such as are ordained by the common laws of this land or the Statutes made by their common consent in Parliament.

Nevertheless it is apparent both that proclamations have been of late years much more frequent than heretofore, and that they are extended not only to the liberty but also to the goods, inheritances, and livelihood of men: some of them tending to alter some points of the law and make them new; other some made shortly after a session of Parliament for matter directly rejected in the same session; others appointing punishments to be inflicted before lawful trial and conviction; some containing penalties in form of penal statutes; some referring the punishment of offenders to the Courts of arbitrary discretion, which have laid heavy and grievous censures upon the delinquents; some, as the proclamation for search, accompanied with letters commanding enquiry to be made against the transgressors at the Quarter Sessions; and some vouching former proclamations to countenance and warrant the latter: as by a catalogue hereunder written more particularly appeareth.

By reason whereof there is a general fear conceived and spread amongst your Majesty's people that proclamations will by degrees grow up and increase to the strength and nature of laws; whereby not only that ancient happiness, freedom, will be as much blemished (if not quite taken away) which their ancestors have so long enjoyed, but the same may also (in process of time) bring a new form of arbitrary government upon the realm. And this our fear is the more increased by occasion as well of certain books lately published, which ascribe a greater power to proclamations than heretofore hath been conceived to belong unto them, as also of the care taken to reduce all the proclamations made since your Majesty's reign into one volume, and to print them in such form as Acts of Parliament formerly have been and still are used to be, which seemeth to imply a purpose to give them more reputation and more establishment than heretofore they have had.

We therefore, your Majesty's humble subjects the Commons in this Parliament assembled, taking these matters into our consideration and weighing how much it doth concern your Majesty both in honour and safety that such impressions should not be enforced to settle in your subjects' minds, have thought it to appertain to our duties, as well towards your Majesty as to those that have trusted and sent us to their service, to present unto your Majesty's view these fears and griefs of your people, and to become humble suitors unto your Majesty that thenceforth no fine or forfeiture of goods or other pecuniary or corporal punishment may be inflicted upon your subjects (other than restraint of liberty, which we also humbly beseech may be but upon urgent necessity, and to continue but till other order may be taken by course of law) unless they shall offend against some law or statute of this realm in force at the time of their offence committed. And for the greater assurance and comfort of your people, that it will please your Majesty to declare your royal pleasure to that purpose, either by some law to be made in this session of Parliament or by some such other course (whereof your people may take knowledge) as to your princely wisdom shall seem most convenient.

＊　　＊　　＊　　＊　　＊　　＊

Forasmuch as the exercise of authority over the counties of Gloucester, Hereford, Wigorn, and Salop[1] by the President and Council of Wales by way of instructions upon a pretext of a Statute made in the thirty-fourth year of the reign of King Henry the Eighth[2] is conceived not to be warranted by that or any other law of this realm of England,...It is therefore the most humble petition of the Commons in this present Parliament assembled that your most excellent Majesty will also be pleased to command that the Judges may deliver their opinion...concerning the right of the aforesaid jurisdiction over these four counties by force of that Statute:...And that if the said jurisdiction over these four counties shall appear to your Majesty by the opinion of the Judges or otherwise not to be warranted by law, that then your

---

[1] Worcestershire and Shropshire.   [2] See *Tudor Constitutional Documents*, p. 335.

Majesty will be pleased, out of your most princely and gracious favour towards all your loyal dutiful subjects, to order the ceasing of the said jurisdiction over those counties....

*   *   *   *   *   *

Petyt, *Jus Parliamentarium*, pp. 321–31.

(3) Coke on the High Commission, 1611

Of the High Commission in Causes Ecclesiastical

Two questions have been made concerning the jurisdiction of these Commissioners: First, what causes do belong to the High Commissioners by force of the Act of 1 El. cap. 1, and of the letters patents thereupon grounded; Secondly, in what cases the High Commissioners by the said Act...may impose fine and imprisonment, and in what not.

It is said, by force of the Statute of 1 El. For that before this Act it is agreed that all ordinaries and ecclesiastical judges whatsoever ought in all ecclesiastical causes to have proceeded according to the censures of the Church, and could not in any case have punished any delinquent by fine or imprisonment unless they had authority so to do by Act of Parliament. And the Papal authority (as hath been confessed) did never fine or imprison in any case, but ever proceeded only by ecclesiastical censures. Seeing then the state of the question concerning fine and imprisonment dependeth wholly upon the Statute of 1 Eliz. and is of greatest consequence, and openeth the way to the other question, for it is confessed that by letters patents only (without an Act of Parliament) such power to fine and imprison in ecclesiastical causes cannot be granted, the point of fine and imprisonment shall be first handled. And for that every Act of Parliament doth consist of the letter, and of the meaning of the makers of the Act, the Act of 1 Eliz. doth neither by meaning nor letter give any power to the High Commissioners to fine or imprison any but in certain particular causes, as shall manifestly out of the Act itself appear hereafter. And seeing every Act of Parliament, upon consideration had of all the parts thereof together, is the best expositor of itself, the parts of this Act of 1 Eliz. do necessarily fall into consideration.

....The nature of the Act doth appear to be an Act of restitution....From whence this reason is drawn, that seeing the express letter and meaning is to restore to the Crown the ancient jurisdiction ecclesiastical, and no Commissioner by force of that ancient ecclesiastical jurisdiction could impose fine and imprisonment, that these Commissioners having their force from this Act of restitution cannot punish any party by fine or imprisonment otherwise than shall be hereafter expressed.

* * * * * *

The...clause...concerning the visitation of the ecclesiastical state and persons...was enacted out of necessity, for that all the Bishops and most of the clergy of England being then Popish, it was necessary to raise a Commission to deprive them, that would not deprive themselves, and in case of restitution of religion to have a more summary proceeding than by the ordinary and prolix course of law is required. This branch concerns only ecclesiastical persons: so as, as necessity did cause this Commission, so it should be exercised but upon necessity, for it was never intended that it should be a continual standing Commission, for that should prejudice all the Bishops of England in their ecclesiastical jurisdiction, and be grievous to the subject to be drawn up from all the remote parts of the realm where before their own diocesan they might receive justice at their own doors.

* * * * * *

The jurisdiction being restored to Queen Eliz. her heirs and successors, next and immediately doth the Act, etc., give her power to assign and authorise Commissioners to execute this jurisdiction restored and united to her....Out of this clause of assignation it is to be observed that the substance of the commission of assignation or deputation is described and portrayed out both for manner and matter by this clause. (1) That it ought to be under the Great Seal. (2) The Commissioners to be assigned ought to be natural born subjects of Queen Eliz. her heirs or successors. (3) Their authority, viz. To exercise, use, occupy, and execute under your Highness your heirs and successors all manner of jurisdiction, etc., and to visit and reform all such errors, heresies, schisms, abuses, offences, etc., which by any manner of ecclesiastical or spiritual power can or lawfully may be reformed, corrected, etc. (4) The local limits and bounds of their Commission, viz., within the realm of England, etc. So as by this clause there is no question but the Commissioners for such causes as are committed to them by force of this Act may, if the Commissioners be competent, proceed to deprivation of the Popish clergy, which was the main object of the Act, or to punish them by ecclesiastical censures, and by no words or meaning hitherto can punish by fine or imprisonment, for that no ecclesiastical power could reform and correct (as the Statute speaketh) in that manner. And without question, if the Commissioners be competent, that is, if they be spiritual men, they may proceed to sentence of excommunication;...and upon certificate made of the excommunication according to law, a *significavit* or *cap. excom.* shall be awarded out of the Chancery for the taking and imprisoning of the bodies of such excommunicate persons.

Now after the letters patents of the Commission are described and limited, followeth a clause of direction for the Commissioners to keep themselves within their Commission in these words: And that such persons so to be named, etc., after the said letters patents to them delivered, shall have full power and authority by virtue of this Act and the said letters patents....to exercise, use, and execute all the premisses according to the tenor and effect of the said letters patents, any matter or cause to the contrary in any wise notwithstanding. This is a clause of reference merely to the former parts of the Act, and yet by colour of this clause the High Commissioners do pretend to fine and imprison. That this clause referreth wholly to the former parts of the Act it is apparent by the very words thereof....And therefore we marvel how in a case of so great consequence, and so visible to every eye that looks into the Act of 1 Eliz., the very words thereof are (for the advantage of the High Commissioners) in the very binding clause altered and changed. For there it is alleged that the Statute of 1 Eliz. saith that the High Commissioners shall execute the premisses by virtue of this Act according to their Commission indefinitely, without reference or restraint, whereas the words of the Act be, 'according to the said letters patents,' the effect whereof was limited and expressed before. And by the authority that is claimed by the Commissioners who seeth not but that confiscation of lands, forfeiture of goods and chattels, etc., as well may be imposed as fine and imprisonment? But were it not a violent interpretation, directly against the letter and meaning of the Act, and full of great inconvenience, to make of these latter words this construction, viz., that the High Commissioners should correct and punish all the errors, heresies, schisms, offences, abuses, contempts, and enormities, etc., under such pains, forfeiture, and penalty as Queen Elizabeth her heirs and successors by any letters patents should impose or appoint; and that consequently by force of the generality of this construction she did impose and appoint fine and imprisonment? Which construction should be, first, directly against the words and meaning of the Act, for the causes aforesaid. Secondly, that by the same reason by the generality of such a construction Queen Elizabeth might have imposed forfeiture of lands, confiscation of goods, nay, corporal punishment, loss of member, and of life also, for incontinency, solicitation of chastity, working on a holiday, or any inferior offence punishable by the ecclesiastical law, and yet the sentence of the Commissioners in such cases should be both fatal and final, and uncontrollable by any ordinary means, either by appeal, error, *moderata misericordia*[1], or otherwise. Thirdly, that this violent construction, under mystical and cloudy words, should extend to fine and imprisonment, etc., [of] all persons, as well laymen of what estate, degree, or sex soever in cases ecclesiastical (where they were not to be fined and imprisoned before) as to ecclesiastical persons who were the proper objects of this Act. And then by the construction that hath been made of the other side in cases where an executor detaineth a legacy, or a parishioner payeth not his tithes, or the like concerning *meum* and *tuum*, the Queen, etc., might have inflicted (as hath been said) what punishment she would, and the High Commissioners fine and imprisonment (as it standeth at this day), without limitation of time, be it never so great, or time of imprisonment, be it never so long, and without controlment by any ordinary remedy, be the sentence never so unjust or erroneous; than which nothing could be more absurd and inconvenient.... And seeing it hath been granted that the Papal authority or any other having ecclesiastical jurisdiction could not fine and imprison before this Act of 1 Eliz., and that it is expressly said in the preamble of this Act that where in the reign of King H. 8 divers good laws were made as well for the extinguishment of foreign authority as for restoring to the Crown the ancient jurisdictions, etc., by reason whereof the subjects were kept in order, and 'disburdened of great and intolerable charges and exactions' (which good laws being repealed by Queen Mary the said Act doth revive and restore); it followeth *a concessis* and by the letter of this Act that it was never the meaning of the makers thereof to extend the said clause to fine and imprison the subject for ecclesiastical causes and to make him subject to greater confiscations, forfeitures, and punishments, where his body before this Act was not subject to imprisonment but upon the King's writ *de excom. capiendo*, nor his body, lands, and goods to fines or other penalties or punishments by them to be imposed, etc., for this were not by this Act of restitution 'to ease them of former intolerable charges' (as the Statute speaketh), but by this Act to make them subject to greater and more heavy pains, punishments, and charges than ever they were before.... We must therefore retire ourselves to the text of the Act of 1 Eliz., the only ground of this question, and thereupon the conclusion is, that no letters

---

[1] 'A writ founded on Magna Charta, which lies for him who is amerced in a court not of record, for any transgression beyond the quality or quantity of the offence; it is directed to the lord of the court or his bailiff, commanding him to take a moderate amerciament of the parties' (T. E. Tomlin, *Law Dictionary*; 4th edn. 1835).

patents can by virtue of this Act of 1 Eliz. give any power to the Commissioners to imprison, except it be in certain particular cases which now fall into consideration. For example, the Statute of 1 H. 7. cap. 4 doth give power to Bishops, etc., to commit priests convicted of any incontinency to prison, and that no Bishop, etc., shall be chargeable therefor in an action of false imprisonment. Now seeing that such jurisdiction ecclesiastical (that is, to hear, determine, and punish, etc.) as by any spiritual or ecclesiastical power or authority before the said Act of 1 Eliz. had been or might lawfully have been exercised or used for the visitation of the ecclesiastical state and persons, and for reformation and correction of the same, and of all manner of errors, heresies, schisms, etc., and that every Bishop, etc., might punish such offenders by imprisonment according to the said Act, that such power (and the like in any other case by Act of Parliament, if any be) is united to the Crown, and may be committed over to the High Commissioners as before the said Act by any spiritual or ecclesiastical power had been or lawfully might be used; which be the words of the Act itself.

*   *   *   *   *   *

Every statute ought to be expouned according to the intent of them that made it, where the words thereof are doubtful and uncertain, and according to the rehearsal of the statute....

*   *   *   *   *   *

But if the meaning of the makers of the Act had been to have inflicted newly upon the subject not only fine and imprisonment but by the same reason confiscation of goods, forfeiture of lands, nay, any corporal punishment, etc., they would not under such cloudy and dark words have inflicted those greater punishments for lesser offences without some limitation, as they did for the greatest offences of all, and not to have left lesser offences to the absolute and uncontrollable power of the High Commissioners by any ordinary mean.

If the High Commissioners might have fined and imprisoned men for offences against the ecclesiastical laws, to what end were the Statutes of 23 Eliz., 28 Eliz., etc., made against men for abstaining and not coming to Divine Service, etc., and why did those Acts inflict a penalty of 20*l.* the month and imprisonment, etc., with a discharge of the penalty, etc., upon submission, if the High Commissioners might have fined and imprisoned them absolutely, without certainty of any sum, or limitation of any time of imprisonment, and without any ability or power by submission or conformity to ease themselves? And yet absence from Divine

Service is a mere ecclesiastical cause, and the like may be said of divers other Acts of Parliament of like nature.

Thus hath this Statute been plainly expounded by the parts of the same according to the natural and genuine sense, and the original institution of the High Commission by force of the said Act truly expressed.

And concerning the form of commissions and practice by the High Commissioners in the reign of the late Queen Eliz. by fining and imprisoning for adultery, fornication, simony, usury, defamation, etc., it may be that such fines have been imposed, but, as we be informed, not one of them levied in all the reign of Queen Eliz. by any judicial process out of the Exchequer....

In Atmer's case, the whole Court of Exchequer in the late Queen's reign judicially resolved, being the King's proper Court, that the High Commissioners could not punish any man for working on a holy day, albeit it be a matter of ecclesiastical conusance[1], but ought by the true meaning of the Statute of 1 Eliz. to be punished by the diocesan, which is to be seen of record.

Also in the reign of Queen Eliz. William Taylor, clerk, parson of Springfield in Essex, did implead William Massy, gent., before the High Commissioners for giving unreverent speeches to the minister, etc., for carrying his corn on holy days, for not suffering the parson and parishioners to come through his yard in Rogation week in the perambulation[2], and not giving them a repast as usually he had done; that he whistled and knocked on the parson's barn-door and said he did it to make him music for his daughter's marriage, and many other articles of like nature: and it was ruled upon open motion and often debating by the whole Court of Common Pleas that the High Commissioners could not deal with such inferior offences but are to be left to the proper diocesan, who is to reform the same with less charge and travail in the proper diocese. And thereupon a prohibition was granted by the Court of Common Pleas, whereby it appeareth that they cannot hold plea of all ecclesiastical causes.

The like prohibition was granted out of the Common Pleas in the said late Queen's reign between Robert Pool, clerk, parson of Winchelsey, and Thomas Gray to the High Commissioners for that they held plea for assaulting and laying violent hands on the said Robert Pool being a parson, upon open motion and argument by the whole Court....

[1] Cognizance.
[2] In many parishes the bounds were beaten in Rogation week—the week in which Ascension Day falls.

And concerning fine and imprisonment, anno 9 Reginae Eliz., which was about eight years after the Statute of 1 Eliz., ...Thomas Lee, an attorney of the Common Pleas, being convented before the High Commissioners for hearing of a mass, was by them in their proceedings committed to prison, which matter being returned by *habeas corpus*, he was upon great consideration had by the Lord Dyer and the whole Court of Common Pleas discharged of his imprisonment, for that the High Commission had no power to imprison him in that case.

* * * * * *

Coke, *Fourth Institute*, ch. 74.

(4) Coke's refusal to serve on the Commission, 1611

Mich. 9 Jacobi Regis

Memorandum, That upon Thursday in this term a High Commission in Causes Ecclesiastical was published in the Great Chamber of the Archbishop at Lambeth, in which I with the Chief Justice, Chief Baron, Justice Williams, Justice Crook, Baron Altham, and Baron Bromley were named Commissioners amongst all the Lords of the Council, divers Bishops, Attorney and Solicitor, and divers Deans and Doctors of the Canon and Civil Laws; and I was commanded to sit by force of the said Commission, which I refused for these causes:

1. For this, that I, nor any of my brethren of the Common Pleas were acquainted with the Commission, but the Judges of the King's Bench were.

2. That I did not know what was contained in the new Commission, and no Judge can execute any commission with a good conscience without knowledge; and that always the gravity of the Judges hath been to know their commission, for *tantum sibi est permissum quantum commissum*: and if the Commission be against law, they ought not to sit by virtue of it.

3. That there was not any necessity that I should sit who understood nothing of it, so long as the other Judges were there the advice of whom had been had in this new Commission.

4. That I have endeavoured to inform myself of it, and have sent to the Rolls to have a copy of it, but it was not enrolled.

5. None can sit by force of any commission until he hath took the oath of supremacy according to the Statute of 1 Eliz. And for this, if they will read the Commission so that we may hear it, and have a copy to advise upon it, then I will either sit or shew cause to the contrary. But the Lord Treasurer would for divers reasons persuade me to sit, which I utterly denied.

And to this the Chief Justice, Chief Baron, and some other of the Judges seemed to incline, upon which the Lord Treasurer conferred in private with the Archbishop, Bancroft, who said to him that he had appointed divers causes of heresy, incest, and enormous crimes to be heard upon this day, and for that he would proceed; but at last he was content that the Commission should be solemnly read, and so it was, which contained three great skins of parchment, and contained divers points against the laws and statutes of England: and when this was read, all the Judges rejoiced that they did not sit by force of it. And then the Lords of the Council, viz., the Archbishop, the Lord Treasurer, the Lord Privy Seal, the Lord Admiral, the Lord Chamberlain, the Earl of Shrewsbury, the Earl of Worcester, with the Bishops, took the oath of supremacy and allegiance, and then we as Commissioners were required to take the oath, which I refused until I had considered of it; but as the subject of the King I, and the other Judges also, took the oaths of supremacy and allegiance.

Then the Lord Archbishop made an oration in commendation of the care and providence of the King for the peace and quiet of the Church, also he commended the Commissioners, also the necessity of the Commission to proceed summarily, in these days wherein sins of a detestable nature and factions and schisms did abound, and protested to proceed sincerely by force of it, and then he caused to be called a most blasphemous heretic, and after him another, who was brought hither by his appointment to shew to the Lords and the auditory the necessity of that Commission.

And after, the Archbishop came to the Chief Justice and to me and promised us that we should have a copy of the Commission, and then I should observe the diversity between the old Commission[1] and this; and all the time that the long Commission was in reading, the oath in taking, and the oration made, I stood, and would not sit as I was requested by the Archbishop and the Lords, and so by my example did all the rest of the Justices.

And the Archbishop said that the King had commanded him to sit by virtue of this new Commission in some open place and at certain days; and for that cause he appointed the Great Chamber at Lambeth in winter and the Hall in the summer; and every Thursday in the term time at two of the clock in the afternoon, and in the forenoon he would have a sermon, for the better informing the Commissioners of their duty....

Coke, *Twelfth Report* (edition of 1777).

[1] The Commission of 1608. This, like James I's Commission of 1605, differs little from Elizabeth's Commission of 1601 (Prothero, p. xliii).

(5) The Ex Officio Oath

The nature of the proceedings under the oath *ex officio* is illustrated by the following interrogatories dated May, 1584. These elicited Burghley's famous protest of 1 July, and to this Archbishop Whitgift replied with a reasoned defence of the procedure, dated 15 July, 1584.

Apud Lambeth, May 1584

Articuli sive Interrogatoria objecta et ministrata. Ex officio mero C.D. Rectori, etc., coram Reverendissimo Patre Johanne Cantuar., Archiepiscop., C.M., D.G., etc., Commissariis et Delegatis Regiae Majestatis ad Causas Ecclesiasticas per literas patentis Magno Sigillo Angliae rite et legitime fultis, ad omnia infrascripta, etc.

1. *Inprimis objicimus, ponimus, et articulamur,* That you are a deacon or minister and priest admitted: declare by whom and what time you were ordered, and likewise that your ordering was according to the Book in that behalf by law of this land provided. *Et objicimus conjunctim de omni et divisim de quolibet.*

2. *Item objicimus, ponimus, et articulamur,* That you deem and judge such your ordering, admission, and calling into the ministry to be lawful, and not repugnant to the Word of God. *Et objicimus ut supra.*

3. *Item objicimus, ponimus, et articulamur,* That you have sworn as well at the time of your ordering as institution, duty and allegiance to the Queen's Majesty, and canonical obedience to your Ordinary and his successor, and to the Metropolitan and his successors, or to some of them. *Et objicimus ut supra.*

4. *Item objicimus, etc.,* That by a Statute...made in the first year of the Queen's Majesty's reign that now is, one virtuous and godly Book intituled The Book of Common Prayer...was authorised and established...and so yet remaineth. *Et objicimus ut supra.*

5. *Item objicimus, etc.,* That by the said Statute all and singular ministers...have been and are bound to say and use a certain form of...prayer...and none other.....*Et objicimus ut supra.*

6. *Item objicimus, etc.,* That in the said Statute her Majesty, the Lords Temporal, and all the Commons in that Parliament assembled, do in God's name earnestly charge and require all the Archbishops, Bishops, and other Ordinaries that they shall endeavour themselves to the uttermost of their knowledge that the due and true execution of the said Act might be had throughout their diocese[s] and charges, as they would answer before Almighty God, etc. *Et objicimus ut supra.*

7. *Item objicimus, ponimus, et articulamur,* That you deem and

judge the said whole Book to be a godly and a virtuous book, agreeable, or at the least not repugnant to the Word of God; if not, we require and command you to declare wherein and in what points. *Et objicimus ut supra.*

8. *Item objicimus, etc.,* That for the space of these three years, two years, one year, half a year, three, two, or one month last past, you have at the time of the Communion and at all or some other times in your ministration used and worn only your ordinary apparel, and not the surplice as is required; declare how long, how often, and for what cause, consideration, or intent you have so done or refused so to do. *Et objicimus ut supra.*

9. *Item objicimus, etc.,* That within the time aforesaid you have baptised divers, or at the least one infant, and have refused to use or not used the sign of the Cross in the forehead, with the words in the said Book of Common Prayer there prescribed to be used; declare how many you have so baptised, and for what cause, consideration, and intent. *Et objicimus ut supra.*

10. *Item objicimus, etc.,* That within the time aforesaid you have been sent unto and required divers times, or at the least once, to baptise children, or some one child, being very weak, and have refused, neglected, or at the least so long deferred the same, till such children or child died without the Sacrament of Baptism; declare whose child, when, and for what consideration. *Et objicimus ut supra.*

11. *Item objicimus, etc.,* That you have within the time aforesaid celebrated matrimony otherwise than is by the said Book prescribed and without a ring, and have refused at such times to call for the ring and to use such words in that behalf as the said Book doth appoint...; declare the circumstances of time, person, and place, and for what cause, intent, and consideration. *Et objicimus ut supra.*

12. *Item objicimus, etc.,* That you have within the time aforesaid neglected or refused to use the form of thanksgiving for women, or some one woman, after child, both according to the said Book; declare the like circumstances thereof, and for what intent, cause, or consideration you have so done or refused so to do. *Et objicimus ut supra.*

13. *Item* we have objected, etc., That you...baptised divers infants, or at the least one,...and not used the interrogatories to the godfathers and godmothers....

14. *Item...,* That you have...used any other form of Litany ..., or that you have often, or once, wholly refused to use the said Litany....

15. *Item . . .*, That you have . . . refused and omitted to read divers Lessons prescribed by the said Book, and have divers times either not read any Lessons at all or read others in their places. . . .

16. *Item . . .*, That . . . you have either not used at all or else used another manner of . . . service at Burial from that which the said Book prescribeth. . . .

17. *Item objicimus, etc.*, That within the time aforesaid you have advisedly and of set purpose not only omitted and refused to use the foresaid parts, or some of them, of the said Book, but also some other parts of the said Book of Common Prayer, as being persuaded that in such points it is repugnant to the Word of God; declare what other parts of the said Book you have refused to use, for what intent, cause, and consideration. *Et objicimus ut supra.*

18. *Item objicimus, etc.*, That within the time aforesaid you have at the Communion, and in other parts of your ministration, advisedly added unto, diminished, and taken from, altered, and transposed manifoldly, at your own pleasure, sundry parts of the said Book of Common Prayer; declare the circumstances of time and place, and for what intent, cause, and consideration. *Et objicimus ut supra.*

19. *Item objicimus, etc.*, That within the time aforesaid you have advisedly and of set purpose preached, taught, declared, set down, or published by writing, public or private speech, matter against the said Book of Common Prayer, or of something therein contained, as being repugnant to the Word of God or not convenient to be used in the Church, or something have written or uttered tending to the depraving, despising, or defacing of something contained in the said Book. Declare what, and the like circumstances thereof, and for what cause or consideration you have so done. *Et objicimus ut supra.*

20. *Item objicimus, etc.*, That you at this present do continue all or some of your former opinions against the said Book, and have a settled purpose to continue hereafter such additions, diminutions, alterations, and transpositions, or some of them, as you heretofore unlawfully have used in your public ministration; and that you have used private conferences and assembled or been present at conventicles, for the maintenance of your doings herein and for the animating and encouraging of others to continue in the like disposition in this behalf that you are of. Declare the like circumstances, and for what intent, cause, and consideration. *Et objicimus ut supra.*

21. *Item objicimus*, etc., That you have been heretofore noted, defamed, presented, or detected publicly to have been faulty in all and singular the premisses and of every or some of them; and that you have been divers and sundry times, or once at the least, admonished by your Ordinary or other ecclesiastical magistrate to reform the same and to observe the form and order of the Book of Common Prayer, which you have refused or defer to do. Declare the like circumstances thereof. *Et objicimus ut supra.*

22. *Item*, That for the testification hereafter of your unity with the Church of England and your conformity to laws established, you have been required simply and absolutely to subscribe with your hand:

That her Majesty, under God, hath and ought to have the sovereignty and rule over all manner of persons born within her realm, dominions, and countries, of what state, either ecclesiastical or temporal, soever they be, and that none other foreign power, prelate, state, or potentate hath or ought to have any jurisdiction, power, superiority, preeminence, or authority, ecclesiastical or spiritual, within her Majesty's said realms, dominions, or countries.

That the Book of Common Prayer, and of ordering Bishops, Priests, and Deacons, containeth in it nothing contrary to the Word of God, and that the same may lawfully be used; and that you who do subscribe will use the form in the said Book prescribed in public prayer and administration of the Sacraments, and none other.

That you allow the Book of Articles of Religion agreed upon by the Archbishops and Bishops of both Provinces and the whole clergy in the Convocation holden at London in the year of our Lord God 1562 and set forth by her Majesty's authority; and do believe all the Articles therein contained to be agreeable to the Word of God.

Declare by whom and how often; which hitherto you have advisedly refused to perform, and so yet do persist. *Et objicimus, etc.*

23. *Item*, That you have taken upon you to preach, read, or expound the Scriptures as well in public places as in private houses, not being licensed by your Ordinary nor any other magistrate having authority by the laws of this land so to license you; declare the like circumstances hereof. *Et objicimus ut supra.*

24. *Item, Quod premissa omnia et singula*, etc.

Strype, *Life of Whitgift* (ed. of 1718), Appendix, Book III, No. 4.

The Lord Treasurer Burghley to the Archbishop of Canterbury: disliking his four and twenty Articles of Enquiry into ministers' conformity

* * * * * *

But now, my good Lord, by chance I am come to the sight of an instrument of 24 Articles of great length and curiosity, found in a Romish style, to examine all manner of ministers in this time, without distinction of persons. Which Articles are intituled, *Apud Lambeth, May* 1584, *to be executed ex officio mero, etc.* And upon this occasion I have seen them. I did recommend unto your Grace's favour two ministers, curates of Cambridgeshire, to be favourably heard; and your Grace wrote to me they were contentious, seditious, and persons vagrant....But now they coming to me and I asking them how your Grace had proceeded with them, they say they are commanded to be examined by the Register[1] at London. And I asked them, Whereof? They said, of a great number of Articles, but they could have no copies of them. I answered, then they might answer according to the truth. They said they were so many in number and so divers as they were afraid to answer to them, for fear of captious interpretation. Upon this I sent for the Register, who brought me the Articles. Which I have read, and find so curiously penned, so full of branches and circumstances, as I think the Inquisitors of Spain use not so many questions to comprehend and to trap their preys.

I know your canonists can defend these with all their particles, but surely, under your Grace's correction, this judicial and canonical sifting of poor ministers is not to edify or reform. And in charity I think they ought not to answer to all these nice points, except they were very notorious offenders in Papistry or heresy. Now, my good Lord, bear with my scribbling. I write with a testimony of a good conscience. I desire the peace of the Church. I desire concord and unity in the exercise of our religion. I favour no sensual and wilful recusants. But I conclude that, according to my simple judgment, this kind of proceeding is too much savouring of the Romish Inquisition, and is rather a device to seek for offenders than to reform any. This is not the charitable instruction that I thought was intended. If those poor ministers should in some few points have any scrupulous conceptions meet to be removed, this is not a charitable way to send them to answer to

---

[1] Or Registrar.

your common Register upon so many Articles at one instant, without any commodity of instruction by your Register, whose office is only to receive their answers. By which the parties are first subject to condemnation before they be taught their error.

It may be, as I said, the canonists may maintain this proceeding by rules of their laws, but though *omnia licent* yet *omnia non expediunt.* I pray your Grace bear that one (perchance a) fault, that I have willed them not to answer these Articles except their conscience may suffer them. And yet I have sharply admonished them that if they be disturbers in their churches they must be corrected. And yet upon your Grace's answer I will leave them to your authority as becometh me. *Ne sutor ultra crepidam.* Neither will I put *falcem in alterius messem.* My paper teacheth me to end. *Primo Julii,* 1584.

Strype, *Life of Whitgift* (ed. of 1718), Appendix, Book III, No. 9.

Reasons why it is convenient that those which are culpable in the Articles ministered generally by the Archbishop of Canterbury and others her Majesty's Commissioners for Causes Ecclesiastical should be examined of the same Articles upon their oaths

I. That by the ecclesiastical laws remaining in force such Articles may be ministered, it is so clear by law that it was never hitherto called into doubt.

II. This manner of proceeding hath been used against such as were vehemently suspected, presented, or detected by their neighbours; or where faults were notorious (as by open preaching) since there hath been any law ecclesiastical in this realm.

III. For the discovery of any Popery, it hath been used in King Edward's time in the deprivation of sundry Bishops at that time, as it may appear by the processes; although withal, for the proof of those things that they denied, witnesses were also used.

IV. In her Majesty's most happy reign, even from the beginning, this manner of proceeding hath been used against the one extreme and the other; as generally against all Papists, and against those that would not follow the Book of Common Prayer established by authority....

V. It is meet also to be done *ex officio mero* because upon the conviction of such offenders no pecuniary penalty is set down whereby the informer (as in other temporal Courts) may be considered for his charges and pains: so that such faults should else be wholly unreformed.

[VI.] This course is not against charity, for it is warranted by law, necessary for reforming of offenders and disturbers of the unity of the Church, and for avoiding delays and frivolous exceptions against such as otherwise should inform, denounce, accuse, or detect them; and because none are in this manner to be proceeded against but whom their own speeches or acts, the public fame, and some of credit, as their Ordinary and such like, shall denounce and signify to be such as are to be reformed in this behalf.

VII. That the form of such proceeding by articles *ex officio mero* is usual, it may appear by all records in ecclesiastical courts from the beginning, in all ecclesiastical commissions,...and from the beginning of her Majesty's reign in the Ecclesiastical Commission till this hour: and therefore warranted by statute.

VIII. If it be said that it is against law, reason, and charity for a man to accuse himself, *quia nemo tenetur seipsum prodere, aut propriam turpitudinem revelare,* I answer that by law, charity, and reason *proditus per denuntiationem alterius, sive per famam, tenetur seipsum ostendere, ad evitandum scandalum, et seipsum purgandum. Praeterea, Praelatus potest inquirere sine praevia fama; a fortiori ergo Delegati per Principem possunt. Ad haec, in istis articulis turpitudo non inquiritur aut flagitium, sed excessus et errata clericorum circa publicam functionem ministerii, de quibus Ordinario rationem reddere coguntur.*

IX. Touching the substance of the Articles, first is deduced their being deacons or ministers, with the lawfulness of that manner of ordering: secondly, the establishing of the Book of Common Prayer by statute, and the charge given to the Bishops and Ordinaries for seeing the execution of the said statute: thirdly, the goodness of the Book by the same words whereby the Statute 8 Eliz. calleth and termeth it: fourthly, several branches of breaches of the Book, being *de propriis factis*: fifthly, is deduced detections against them and such monitions as have been given them, to testify their conformity hereafter; and whether they will willingly still continue such breaches of law in their ministration: sixthly, their assembling of conventicles for the maintenance of their factious dealings.

X. For the second, fourth, and sixth points, no man will think it unmeet they should be examined of, if they would have them touched for any breach of the Book.

XI. The Article for examination whether they be deacons or ministers ordered according to the laws of this land is most necessary: first, for the grounding of the proceeding, lest the breach of the Book be objected to them who are not bound to observe it: secondly, to meet with such schismatics (whereof there is sufficient experience) which either thrust themselves into the ministry without any lawful calling at all, or else take orders at Antwerp or elsewhere beyond the seas.

XII. The Article for their opinion of the lawfulness of their admission into the ministry is to meet with such hypocrites as to be enabled for a living will be content to be ordered at a Bishop's hand, and yet for satisfaction of their factious humour will afterwards have a calling of certain brethren ministers, with laying on of hands in a private house and in a conventicle, to the manifest slander of this Church of England and to the nourishing of a flat schism. Secondly, for the detecting of such as, not only privately but by public speeches and written pamphlets spread abroad, do deprave the whole order ecclesiastical of this Church and the lawfulness of calling therein; avouching no calling lawful but where their fancied monstrous Seignory, with the assent of the people, do admit into the ministry.

XIII. The sequel that should follow of these Articles being confessed or proved is not so much as deprivation from ecclesiastical living, if there be not obstinate persisting or iterating the same offence. A matter far different from the bloody Inquisition in time of Popery, or of the Six Articles, where death was the sequel against the culpable.

XIV. It is to be considered what encouragement and probable appearance it would breed to the dangerous Papistical recusant if place be given by the chief magistrates ecclesiastical to persons that tend of singularity, to the disturbance of the good peace of the Church and to the discredit of that for disallowing whereof the obstinate Papist is worthily punished.

XV. The number of these singular persons, in comparison of the quiet and conformable, are few, and their qualities, as also for excellence of gift in learning, discretion, and considerate zeal, far inferior to those other that yield their conformity.....

Inconveniences of not proceeding ex officio mero *unto examination upon Articles* super fama aut denuntiatione alterius *but only upon Presentment and Conviction by Witnesses*

I. It will give a precedent for the obstinate Papists, the Brownists, the Family men[1], and all other sectaries to look for the like measure, and to be convinced[2] only by witnesses upon presentment; whereas they spread their poison in secret and among their favourers, and therefore can hardly be so convinced or brought to reformation, though it be never so well known what kind of men they be.

---

[1] The Family of Love.   [2] Convicted.

II. It will come also to the same point as afore, because the detected by presentment is not hereby convinced, but is by law to be put to his clearing by answering articles upon his oath, together with compurgators if they be enjoined, whereas no witnesses are to be had for proof of it.

III. This course cannot be taken, by reason of the number of those that are to be reformed and the distances of the place.

IV. Also because if the chief gentleman in the parish or most of the parish be so affected, nothing will be presented, as experience teacheth.

V. Further, the great trouble in writing out so many commissions for the giving of charge and examining of witnesses must be considered.

VI. The trouble likewise in procuring the commissioners and witnesses below in the country, and the charges of them both, and the registrers, in writing and transmitting the depositions up, which is not meet to be upon the party's charges, especially being not yet known whether there be cause to remove him or not.

VII. Again, if Archbishops and Bishops should be driven to use process by witnesses, and excluded from other means warranted by law (as by the answer of the party notoriously defamed or presented), the execution of the law, which ought in equality to be ministered according to the proper nature of a law (which ought to be common and general to all sorts and to have an equal and uniform execution) should be unequal, by having use against all other persons and by restraining the use and execution in this point against some persons.

VIII. The Archbishops and Bishops should be overpressed with charges if they should be compelled to procure and produce witnesses for every disorder of this nature.

Strype, *Life of Whitgift* (ed. of 1718), Book III, ch. 8, p. 160.

The Crown and the Judges

The year 1605 and subsequent years saw the failure of an attempt of the ecclesiastical courts to maintain their judicial independence. The conflict between them and the courts of common law was no new thing; it was only that in the reign of James I it came to a head. The temporal courts had been accustomed to enforce their monopoly of temporal jurisdiction by sending out 'writs of prohibition' forbidding the spiritual courts to proceed further in particular cases which might come before them until the judges had satisfied themselves that the case raised a spiritual question and did not fall within temporal jurisdiction. Thus the courts of common law claimed an unqualified superiority, for they asserted their right to decide what the limits of ecclesiastical jurisdiction were. The action of the judges was resisted by the Archbishop, who in 1605 presented a formal protest to the King which was named by Coke *Articuli Cleri* [p. 177], after the articles of grievances presented to Henry III by Archbishop Boniface on behalf of the clergy in 1267. The interest of this protest for present purposes lies in the fact that the arguments used on both sides foreshadow, in relation to this smaller question, the Royalist and Parliamentarian positions in the greater controversy which was soon to arise. It was necessary for the argument of the clergy that they should exalt the authority of the Crown. All jurisdiction, they said, 'flowed originally from the King,' and it flowed in two separate streams. The King possessed in his own person all spiritual and all temporal jurisdiction; the one he delegated to the bishops and the other to the judges. Thus if there was any dispute as to what was and what was not matter for the spiritual courts, the proper arbiter was the King. The task of answering Bancroft fell upon Coke, who had just been made Chief Justice of the Common Pleas, and he brought to it vast legal learning, an exaggerated respect for technicalities, a strong professional feeling, and lying somewhere behind all this, a genuine sense of the danger of this attempt to extend the royal and ecclesiastical authority[1]. The technicalities of his argument would not interest and do not concern us: the important point is that he took occasion to assert, in language of remarkable breadth and simplicity, the legislative supremacy of Parliament. The right of issuing prohibitions, he said in effect, is an ancient and established custom; it is therefore part of the law of the realm; as such, the King cannot touch it, for he is not above the Law. 'The law of the realm cannot be changed but by Parliament.'

In 1607 the question of prohibitions was raised again by Bancroft in rather a different form [p. 186]. He carried his previous argument a step further, and represented to James that as he was the source of all jurisdiction, spiritual as well as temporal, it was within his power to withdraw spiritual causes from the jurisdiction of the bishops and temporal causes from the jurisdiction of the judges, and to hear and determine them himself as the supreme judge of the realm. It must be remembered that in the seventeenth century the judges of the courts of common law were the recognised legal advisers of the Crown,

[1] *D.N.B.* xi, 231.

and it was to these experts—as to the Attorney-General or Solicitor-General by modern usage—that all political questions involving points of law would naturally be referred. Bancroft's suggestion attracted James and, in accordance with the practice of the day, he referred it to the judges, only to encounter the uncompromising resistance of Coke. 'Nothing can be more pedantic,' says Dicey[1], 'nothing more artificial, nothing more unhistorical, than the reasoning by which Coke induced or compelled James to forego the attempt to withdraw cases from the courts for his Majesty's personal determination. But no achievement of sound argument, no stroke of enlightened statesmanship, ever established a rule more essential to the very existence of the constitution than the principle enforced by the obstinacy and the fallacies of the great Chief Justice.' In the concluding passage of Coke's argument [p. 187] we find, as it were caught up and entangled in what is mainly technical, the two opposing principles of the Stuart controversy; and in defiance of the unanimous opinion of his judges—for his colleagues followed Coke—James did not again allow himself to be allured by the vision of an English King Solomon sitting upon the lion throne to judge causes in person.

Certain other decisions in the courts of law during the reign of James raise and settle constitutional questions of the utmost importance, and at the same time exhibit Coke and his colleagues as pursuing a definite policy, the object of which was to establish the Bench as an independent authority arbitrating between the Crown and the subject.

(1) The extra-judicial opinion of 1610 by which Coke defined the legal limits of the use of Proclamations. The repeal of Henry VIII's statute giving proclamations the force of law[2] had not done away with proclamations; it had only deprived them of statutory authority, leaving them such weight as they possessed at common law. During the early part of the reign of James I proclamations had, as a matter of fact, been issued far more frequently than under Elizabeth, and the matter attracted the attention of Parliament. In their petition of July 7, 1610 [p. 148], the Commons complained that proclamations had been issued creating new offences unknown to the law; imposing penalties for known offences greater than those authorised by law; and requiring accused persons to be brought before tribunals which were not legally authorised to try their offence. In his answer to the petition the King undertook to consult the judges, and he submitted to Coke and his colleagues test questions which covered the whole ground in dispute. The reply of the judges [p. 187] is one of the minor charters of English liberty. 'Here are set forth in a few words,' says Sir William Anson[3], 'some salient features of our constitution, and this at a time when a clear statement of the points at issue between Crown and Parliament was greatly needed, and when the first step to be taken towards a settlement of constitutional difficulties was that the nature of those difficulties should be understood.'

(2) A case of 1615, known as *Peacham's Case* [p. 188], is constitutionally important as an instance of an attempt on the part of the Crown to influence the judges privately. Edmond Peacham, the Rector of Hinton St George in Somerset, having written some intemperate accusations against

---

[1] *The Law of the Constitution*, p. 18.
[2] 31 Henr. VIII, c. 8: printed in *Tudor Constitutional Documents*, p. 532.
[3] *The Law and Custom of the Constitution* (4th edition), i, 323.

his bishop, was tried for libel in the High Commission Court in 1614 and sentenced to be deprived of his orders[1]. During his imprisonment his house was searched, and notes for a treasonable sermon were discovered which brought him under the eye of the Council. He hinted that the King would one day be smitten with a death as sudden as that which overtook Ananias or Nabal [p. 188], and James, we are told, was so impressed that he slept every night behind a barricade of feather-beds; so the Council was more anxious than usual to procure a conviction. Yet as the sermon had not been printed or published, it was uncertain whether it could be regarded as an 'overt act' proving the traitorous imagination of compassing the King's death. In this difficulty the Council according to custom consulted the judges, and enquired of them whether the course proposed was legally unassailable, and if the evidence was sufficient to procure a conviction. Hallam's suggestion that the judges were being 'tampered with'[2] is entirely without foundation. It was not an innovation to consult the judges in such a case; the innovation came when the King, fearing lest in debate among themselves the hostile Coke should carry his colleagues with him, gave instructions that the judges should not, as heretofore, be consulted collectively, but separately and individually. To this course of action Coke offered an uncompromising resistance. His chief idea in politics was the maintenance of the independence and authority of the judicial bench, and he saw quite clearly that the Crown might apply pressure successfully to individuals which would have been resisted by the judges acting collectively. 'Such particular and auricular taking of opinions,' he told Bacon [p. 189], 'is not according to the custom of this realm,'[3] and at first he refused to answer. In the end he surrendered and gave his opinion, but it was hostile to the Crown.

(3) The case of *Commendams*[4] in 1616 [p. 192] raised a similar question. The interest of it lies in Coke's determined but unsuccessful resistance to an attempt on the part of the Crown to delay proceedings in a case where the royal prerogative was concerned. While Bishop Neile held the see of Lichfield, he had received from the King the grant of a living to be held *in commendam*—with his bishopric; but two other persons claimed that the presentation was theirs and not the King's, and in the course of the proceedings before the Exchequer Chamber they questioned the King's right to make presentations *in commendam* at all. At this point the King intervened in defence of his prerogative, and directed Attorney-General Bacon to write to Chief Justice Coke requesting that the judges would delay their decision until the King had spoken with them. But in this also, Coke saw impending an attack upon the independence of the judicial office. If the judges were to be called into the King's presence to debate with him the merits of a pending action, would not the courtier displace the judge and the independence of the Bench be gone? At first he carried his colleagues with him, and a joint letter was sent to the King saying that their oath forbade them to delay justice, and Bacon's letter was against law. But the King called the judges into his presence, and a scene took place in which comedy and tragedy were combined

---

[1] Gardiner, *History of England* 1603–1642, ii, 272.
[2] *The Constitutional History of England* (edition of 1876), i, 343.
[3] Bacon, *Letters* (ed. Spedding), v, 100.
[4] A full account of the case is given in Gardiner, iii, 13–19.

in something like equal proportions. After hearing in respectful silence a lecture from James in which he pointed out with some reason that in cases which concerned his prerogative he was virtually a party, and therefore entitled to be heard, all the twelve judges threw themselves simultaneously upon their knees and implored pardon, Coke alone venturing while in that posture to argue with the King. They were then asked one by one 'whether if at any time in a case depending before the judges which his Majesty conceived to concern him either in power or profit, and thereupon required to consult with them, and that they should stay proceedings in the meantime—they ought not to stay accordingly?' Eleven of the judges answered in the affirmative; Coke alone replied that 'when that case should be, he would do that should be fit for a judge to do.' The case of *Commendams* was fatal to Coke, and he was soon afterwards deprived for his 'perpetual turbulent carriage' towards the Church, the prerogative, and the courts of law[1]. 'The common speech is,' wrote Chamberlain to Carleton on 14 November, 1616, 'that four P's have overthrown and put him down—that is, pride, prohibitions, praemunire, and prerogative.'[2] The first dismissal of a judge for reasons that were in the main political, is a landmark in constitutional history.

A word should be said here about the remarkable and lifelong antagonism between Coke and Bacon[3]. As early as 1593 they had both been candidates for the post of Attorney-General, and Coke had been appointed; while in 1598 Coke had made the wealthy Lady Elizabeth Hatton his second wife, to whom Bacon had been paying assiduous court. And now Coke's disgrace coincided with Bacon's rise; and in the long conflict between King James and his Chief Justice it was Bacon who had had the planning of the King's campaign. But the antagonism between the two men was not accidental or personal only; they represent opposing tendencies in thought and action. Bacon was by far the greater man, for in him the philosopher included both the lawyer and the statesman; and thinking after the manner of a philosopher he advocated a large reform of English law. Coke on the other hand, with a mind fanatically narrow, was possessed with a profound veneration for the law as it stood—for its technicalities as well as its substance—and he was convinced that it was not by change and reform but by the following of precedents that the liberties of England were to be defended. Thus upon one of the great test questions in the politics of the time—the nature and limits of the royal prerogative—Bacon half suggested, half accepted the mystical views of James; while Coke resolutely opposed the inferences which the King drew from the principles which he laid down, and entrenched himself in precedents, and verbal interpretations of statute law. Coke's idea was that the Bench should be independent of the Crown and should act as arbiter of the Constitution to decide all disputed questions. Bacon, on the other hand, referred all disputed questions to the King, saying, with his mind running upon the ivory throne on which King Solomon sat to give judgment, that

1 Bacon, *Letters* (ed. Spedding), vi, 95.
2 *D.N.B.* xi, 235.
3 This question is discussed by Sir W. S. Holdsworth in Vol. v of his *History of English Law* (3rd edition).

the judges 'must be lions, but yet lions *under* the throne.'[1] Thus Coke represented a rigid conservatism—the conservatism of constitutional liberties as they were; Bacon represented reform—but reform carried out by a philosopher-king wielding a sovereignty unlimited and half-divine. We come upon the same antagonism again, a generation later, in the persons of Pym and Strafford.

But that State is rare in which the kings are philosophers or the philosophers kings. Bacon was not a king, and James was not really a philosopher. The philosopher had fallen on evil days, for the kings were Stuarts; and what was really needed was the conservation of existing liberties against encroachment, and not the efficient paternal government which Bacon and Strafford dreamed of but which James and Charles could never hope to attain.

In the eyes of his contemporaries Coke's legal fame overtopped his other claims to greatness. In 1631, when his death was expected, Charles I gave orders that his papers should be secured, lest anything against the prerogative should be found among them and published, 'for he is held too great an oracle among the people, and they may be misled by anything that carries such an authority as all things do which he either speaks or writes.' 'His parts,' says Fuller, 'were admirable; he had a deep judgment, faithful memory, active fancy; and the jewel of his mind was put into a fair case. . . . His learned and laborious works on the laws will last to be admired by the judicious posterity whilst Fame has a trumpet left her and any breath to blow therein.'[2]

The important part played by the Judges in the general political scheme is indicated in a speech made to them by Coke's great antagonist as Lord Keeper, before they went on circuit in the summer of 1617 [p. 198].

(1) Articuli Cleri, 1605

Certain Articles of Abuses which are desired to be reformed in granting of Prohibitions, and the Answers thereunto

Upon mature deliberation and consideration...by all the Judges of England and the Barons of the Exchequer, with one unanimous consent under their hands (resolutions of highest authorities in law), which were delivered to the Lords of the Council....

1. His Majesty hath power to reform abuses in prohibitions.

Objection. The clergy well hoped that they had taken a good course in seeking some redress at his Majesty's hands concerning sundry abuses offered to his ecclesiastical jurisdiction by the over frequent and undue granting of prohibitions; for both they and

---

[1] 'And therefore it is proper for you by all means with your wisdom and fortitude to maintain the laws of the realm. Wherein, nevertheless, I would not have you headstrong, but heart-strong; and to weigh and remember with yourself that the twelve Judges of the realm are as the twelve lions under Salomon's throne: they must be lions, but yet lions under the throne: they must shew their stoutness in elevating and bearing up the throne' (Speech to Justice Hutton, *Letters and Life*, ed. J. Spedding, vi, 201).

[2] *Worthies* (ed. Nuttall), 1840, ii, 452.

we supposed (all jurisdiction, both ecclesiastical and temporal, being annexed to the Imperial Crown of this realm) that his Highness had been held to have had sufficient authority in himself, with the assistance of his Council, to judge what is amiss in either of his said jurisdictions, and to have reformed the same accordingly; otherwise a wrong course is taken by us if nothing may be reformed that is now complained of but what the temporal Judges shall of themselves willingly yield unto. This is therefore the first point which upon occasion lately offered before your Lordships by some of the Judges we desire may be cleared, because we are strongly persuaded as touching the validity of his Majesty's said authority, and do hope that we shall be able to justify the same notwithstanding anything that the Judges or any other can allege to the contrary.

Answer of the Judges. No man maketh any question but that both the jurisdictions are lawfully and justly in his Majesty, and that if any abuses be, they ought to be reformed; but what the law doth warrant in cases of prohibitions to keep every jurisdiction in his true limits, is not to be said an abuse, nor can be altered but by Parliament.

2. The forms of prohibitions prejudicial to his Majesty's authority in causes ecclesiastical.

Objection. Concerning the form of prohibitions, forasmuch as both the ecclesiastical and temporal jurisdictions be now united in his Majesty which were heretofore *de facto*, though not *de jure*, derived from several heads, we desire to be satisfied by the Judges whether, as the case now standeth, the former manner of prohibitions heretofore used, importing an ecclesiastical court to be *aliud forum a foro regio*, and the ecclesiastical law not to be *legem terrae*, and the proceedings in those courts to be *contra coronam et dignitatem regiam*, may now without offence and derogation to the King's ecclesiastical prerogative be continued, as though either the said jurisdictions remained now so distinguished and severed as they were before, or that the laws ecclesiastical which we put in execution were not the King's and realm's ecclesiastical laws as well as the temporal laws.

Answer. It is true that both the jurisdictions were ever *de jure* in the Crown, though the one sometimes usurped by the See of Rome; but neither in the one time nor in the other hath ever the form of prohibitions been altered, nor can be but by Parliament. And it is *contra coronam et dignitatem regiam* for any to usurp to deal in that which they have not lawful warrant from the Crown to deal in, or to take from the temporal jurisdiction that which belonged to it. The prohibitions do not import that the ecclesiastical courts are *aliud* than the King's or not the King's courts, but do import that the cause is drawn into *aliud examen* than it ought to be; and therefore it is always said in the propositions (be the court temporal or ecclesiastical to which it is awarded) if they deal in any case which they have not power to hold plea of, that the cause is drawn *ad aliud examen* than it ought to be, and therefore *contra coronam et dignitatem regiam.*

3. A fit time to be assigned for the defendant if he will seek a prohibition.

Objection. As touching the time when prohibitions are granted, it seemeth strange to us that they are not only granted at the suit of the defendant in the ecclesiastical court after his answer (whereby he affirmeth the jurisdiction of the said court, and submitteth himself unto the same), but also after all allegations and proofs made on both sides, when the cause is fully instructed and furnished for sentence; yea, after sentence, yea, after two or three sentences given, and after execution of the said sentence or sentences, and when the party for his long continued disobedience is laid in prison upon the writ of *excommunicato capiendo,* which courses, forasmuch as they are against the rules of the Common Law in like cases, as we take it, and do tend so greatly to the delay of justice, vexation and charge of the subject, and the disgrace and discredit of his Majesty's jurisdiction ecclesiastical, the Judges, as we suppose, notwithstanding their great learning in the laws, will be hardly able in defence of them to satisfy your Lordships.

Answer. Prohibitions by law are to be granted at any time to restrain a court to intermeddle with or execute anything which by law they ought not to hold plea of, and they are much mistaken that maintain the contrary. And it is the folly of such as will proceed in the ecclesiastical court for that whereof that court hath not jurisdiction, or in that whereof the King's temporal courts should have the jurisdiction. And so themselves by their extraordinary dealing are the cause of such extraordinary charges, and not the law; for their proceedings in such case are *coram non judice.* And the King's courts that may award prohibitions, being informed either by the parties themselves or by any stranger that any court, temporal or ecclesiastical, doth hold plea of that whereof they have not jurisdiction, may lawfully prohibit the same, as well after judgment and execution as before.

*   *   *   *   *   *

10. No prohibition to be granted at his suit who is plaintiff in the spiritual court.

Objection. We suppose it to be no warrantable nor reasonable course that prohibitions are granted at the suit of the plaintiff in the ecclesiastical court who, having made choice thereof, and brought his adversary there into trial, doth by all intendment of law and reason, and by the usage of all other judicial places, conclude himself in that behalf; and although he cannot be presumed to hope for help in any other court by way of prohibition, yet it is very usual for every such person so proceeding, only of mere malice, for vexation of the party and to the great delay and hindrance of justice, to find favour for the obtaining of prohibitions, sometimes after two or three sentences, thereby taking advantage (as he must plead) of his own wrong, and receiving aid from that court which by his own confession he before did contemn; touching the equity whereof we will expect the answer of the Judges.

Answer. None may pursue in the ecclesiastical court for that which the King's courts ought to hold plea of, but upon information thereof given to the King's courts, either by the plaintiff or by any mere stranger, they are to be prohibited, because they deal in that which appertaineth not to their jurisdiction, where if they would be careful not to hold plea of that which appertaineth not to them this needed not; and if they will proceed in the King's courts against such as pursue in the ecclesiastical courts for matter temporal, that is to be inflicted upon them which the quality of their offence requireth, and how many sentences soever are given, yet prohibitions thereupon are not of favour but of justice to be granted.

*　　*　　*　　*　　*　　*

12. No prohibition to be granted under pretence that one witness cannot be received in the ecclesiastical court to ground a judgment upon.

Objection. There is a new devised suggestion in the temporal courts commonly received and allowed, whereby they may at their will and pleasure draw any cause whatsoever from the ecclesiastical court: for example, many prohibitions have lately come forth upon this suggestion, that the laws ecclesiastical do require two witnesses where the Common Law accepteth of one, and therefore it is *contra legem terrae* for the ecclesiastical judge to insist upon two witnesses to prove his cause; upon which suggestion, although many consultations[1] have been granted (the same being no way as yet able to warrant and maintain a prohibition), yet because we are not sure but that, either by reason of the use of it or of some future construction, it may have given to it more

[1] See p. 186, note 2.

strength than is convenient, the same tending to the utter over-throw of all ecclesiastical jurisdiction, we most humbly desire that by your Lordships' good means the same may be ordered to be no more used.

Answer. If the question be upon payment or setting out of tithes, or upon the proof of a legacy, or marriage, or such like incidence, we are to leave it to the trial of their law though the party have but one witness; but where the matter is not determin-able in the ecclesiastical court, there lieth a prohibition either upon or without such a surmise.

13. No good suggestion for a prohibition that the cause is neither testamentary nor matrimonial.

Objection. As the former device last mentioned endeavoureth to strike away at one blow the whole ecclesiastical jurisdiction, so there is another as usual or rather more frequent than the former, which is content to spare us two kinds of causes to deal in, viz., testamentary and matrimonial: and this device insulteth mightily in many prohibitions, commanding the ecclesiastical judge that be the cause never so apparently of ecclesiastical cognizance yet he shall surcease, for that is neither a cause testamentary nor matrimonial: which suggestion, as it grew at the first upon mistaking, and omitting the words *de bonis et catallis*, etc., as may appear by divers ancient prohibitions in the Register, so it will not be denied but that, besides these two, divers and sundry other causes are notoriously known to be of ecclesiastical cognizance, and that consultations are as usually awarded, if suit in that behalf be prosecuted notwithstanding the said suggestion, as their prohibitions are easily granted; which, as an injury marching with the rest to wound poor men, protract suits, and prejudice the courts ecclesiastical, we desire that the Judges will be pleased to redress.

Answer. If they observe well the answer to the former objections, they may be thereby satisfied that we prohibit not so generally as they pretend, nor do in any wise deal further than we ought to do, to the prejudice of that which appertaineth to that jurisdiction; but when they will deal with matters of temporal contracts, coloured with pretended ecclesiastical matter, we ought to prohibit them with that form of prohibitions, mentioning that it concerneth not matter of marriage nor testamentary, and they shall not find that we have granted any but by form warranted both by the Register and by law: and when suggestions carrying matter sufficient appear to us judicially to be untrue and insuffi-cient, we are as ready to grant consultations as prohibitions; and we may not alter the form of our prohibitions upon the conceits of ecclesiastical judges, and prohibitions granted in the form set down in the article are of that form which by law they ought to be, and cannot be altered but by Parliament.

14. No prohibition upon surmise only to be granted either out of the King's Bench or Common Pleas, but out of the Chancery only.

Objection. Amongst the causes whereby the ecclesiastical jurisdiction is oppressed with multitude of prohibitions upon surmises only, this hath a chief place, in that through encroachment (as we suppose) there are so many several courts and Judges in them that take upon them to grant the same, as in the King's Bench five and in the Common Pleas as many, the one court oftentimes crossing the proceedings of the other, whereas we are persuaded that all such kinds of prohibitions, being original writs, ought only to issue out of the Chancery, and neither out of the King's Bench nor Common Pleas. And that this hath been the ancient practice in that behalf appeareth by some statutes of the realm and sundry judgments at the Common Law, the renewing of which practice carrieth with it an apparent show of great benefit and conveniency, both to the Church and to the subject: for if prohibitions were to issue only out of one court, and from one man of such integrity, judgment, sincerity, and wisdom as we are to imagine the Lord Chancellor of England to be endued with, it is not likely that he would ever be induced to prejudice and pester the ecclesiastical courts with so many needless prohibitions, or after a consultation to send out in one cause, and upon one and the same libel not altered, prohibition upon prohibition, his own act remaining upon record before him to the contrary. The further consideration whereof, when upon the Judges' answer thereunto it shall be more thoroughly debated, we must refer to your Lordships' honourable direction and wisdom.

Answer. A strange presumption in the ecclesiastical judges to require that the King's courts should not do that which by law they ought to do, and always have done, and which by oath they are bound to do! And if this shall be holden inconvenient, and they can in discharge of us obtain some Act of Parliament to take it from all other courts than the Chancery, they shall do unto us a great ease: but the law of the realm cannot be changed but by Parliament, and what relief or ease such an Act may work to the subject, wise men will soon find out and discern; but by these articles thus dispersed abroad there is a general unbeseeming aspersion of that upon the Judges which ought to have been forborne.

* * * * *

21. That persons imprisoned upon the writ of *de excommunicato capiendo* are unduly delivered and prohibitions unduly awarded for their greater security.

Objection. Forasmuch as imprisonment upon the writ of *excommunicato capiendo* is the chiefest temporal strength of ecclesiastical jurisdiction, and that by the laws of the realm none so committed for their contempt in matters of ecclesiastical cognizance ought to be delivered until the ecclesiastical courts were satisfied or caution given in that behalf, we would gladly be resolved by what authority the temporal judges do cause the sheriffs to bring the said parties into their courts, and by their own discretions set them at liberty, without notice thereof first given to the ecclesiastical judges, or any satisfaction made either to the parties at whose suit he was imprisoned or the ecclesiastical court where certain lawful fees are due; and after all this, why do they likewise send out their prohibitions to the said court commanding that all censures against the said parties shall be remitted, and that they be no more proceeded with for the same causes in those courts. Of this desire we hope your Lordships do see sufficient cause, and will therefore procure us from the Judges some reasonable answer.

Answer. We affirm, if the party excommunicated be imprisoned, we ought upon complaint to send the King's writ for the body and the cause, and if in the return no cause, or no sufficient cause, appear, then we do (as we ought) set him at liberty; otherwise, if upon removing the body the matter appear to be of ecclesiastical cognizance, then we remit him again; and this we ought to do in both cases, for the temporal courts must always have an eye that the ecclesiastical jurisdiction usurp not upon the temporal.

22. The King's authority in ecclesiastical causes is greatly impugned by prohibitions.

Objection. We are not a little perplexed touching the authority of his Majesty in causes ecclesiastical, in that we find the same to be so impeached by prohibitions that it is in effect thereby almost extinguished; for it seemeth that the innovating humour is grown so rank, and that some of the temporal judges are come to be of the opinion that the Commissioners appointed by his Majesty for his Causes Ecclesiastical, having committed unto them the execution of all ecclesiastical jurisdiction annexed to his Majesty's Imperial Crown, by virtue of an Act of Parliament made in that behalf and according to the tenor and effect of his Majesty's letters patents, wherein they are authorised to imprison and impose fines as they shall see cause, cannot otherwise proceed, the said Act and letters patents notwithstanding, than by ecclesiastical censures only; and thereupon of latter days, whereas certain lewd persons (two, for example sake), one for notorious adultery and other intolerable contempts, and another for abusing of a bishop of this kingdom with threatening speeches and sundry railing terms no way to be endured, were thereupon fined and imprisoned by the said Commissioners till they should enter into bonds to perform further orders of the said court, the one was delivered by an *habeas corpus* out of the King's Bench and the other by a like writ out of the Common Pleas: and sundry other prohibitions have been likewise awarded to his Majesty's said Commissioners upon these suggestions, viz., that they had no authority either to fine or imprison any man; which innovating conceit being added to this that followeth, That the writ of *de excommunicato capiendo* cannot lawfully be awarded upon any certificate or *significavit* made by the said Commissioners, we find his Majesty's said supreme authority in causes ecclesiastical, so largely amplified in sundry statutes, to be altogether destitute in effect of any means to uphold it if the said proceedings by temporal judges shall be by them maintained and justified; and therefore we most humbly desire your Lordships that they may declare themselves herein, and be restrained hereafter, if there be cause found, from using the King's name in their prohibitions to so great prejudice of his Majesty's said authority, as in debating the same before your Lordships will hereafter more fully appear.

Answer. We do not, neither will we in any wise impugn the ecclesiastical authority in anything that appertaineth unto it; but if any by the ecclesiastical authority commit any man to prison, upon complaint to us that he is imprisoned without just cause we are to send to have the body and to be certified of the cause; and if they will not certify unto us the particular cause, but generally, without expressing any particular cause, whereby it may appear unto us to be a matter of the ecclesiastical cognizance, and his imprisonment be just, then we do and ought to deliver him: and this is their fault, and not ours. And although some of us have dealt with them to make some such particular certificate to us whereby we may be able to judge upon it, as by law they ought to do, yet they will by no means do it; and therefore their error is the cause of this, and no fault in us, for if we see not a just cause of the party's imprisonment by them, then we ought and are bound by oath to deliver him.

* * * * * *

24. That temporal judges are sworn to defend the ecclesiastical jurisdiction.

Objection. We may not omit to signify unto your Lordships that, as we take it, the temporal judges are not only bound by their ancient oath that they shall do nothing to the disherison of the Crown, but also by a later oath unto the King's Supremacy wherein they do swear that to their power they will assist and defend all jurisdictions, privileges, preeminences, and authorities united and annexed to the Imperial Crown of this realm; in which words the ecclesiastical jurisdiction is specially aimed at: so that whereas they do oftentimes insist upon for their oath for doing of justice in temporal causes and do seldom make mention of the second oath taken by them for the defence of the ecclesiastical jurisdiction, with the rights and immunities belonging to the Church, we think that they ought to weigh their said oaths better together, and not so far to extend the one as that it should in any sort prejudice the other: the due consideration whereof (which we most instantly desire) would put them in mind, any suggestion to the contrary notwithstanding, to be as careful not to do anything that may prejudice the lawful proceedings of the ecclesiastical judges in ecclesiastical causes as they are circumspect not to suffer any impeachment or blemish of their own jurisdictions and proceedings in causes temporal.

Answer. We are assured that none can justly charge any of us with violating our oaths, and it is a strange part to tax judges in this manner, and to lay so great an imputation upon us; and what scandal it will be to the justice of the realm to have so great levity and so foul an imputation laid upon the Judges as is done in this, is too manifest. And we are assured it cannot be shewed that the like hath been done in any former age; and for less scandals than this of the justice of the realm divers have been severely punished.

25. That excommunication is as lawful as prohibition, for the mutual preservation of both his Majesty's supreme jurisdictions.

Objection. To conclude, whereas for the better preserving of his Majesty's two supreme jurisdictions before mentioned, viz., the ecclesiastical and the temporal, that the one might not usurp upon the other, two means heretofore have of ancient time been ordained, that is to say, the censure of excommunication and the writ of prohibition, the one to restrain the encroachment of the temporal jurisdiction upon the ecclesiastical, the other of the ecclesiastical upon the temporal, we most humbly desire your Lordships that by your means the Judges may be induced to resolve us why excommunications may not as freely be put in ure[1] for the preservation of the jurisdiction ecclesiastical as prohibitions are under pretence to defend the temporal, especially against such contentious persons as do wittingly and willingly, upon false and frivolous suggestions, to the delay of justice, vexation of the subject, and great scandal of ecclesiastical jurisdictions daily procure, without fear either of God or men, such undue prohibitions as we have heretofore mentioned.

Answer. The excommunication cannot be gainsaid, neither may the prohibition be denied upon the surmise made, that the matter pursued in the ecclesiastical court is of temporal cognizance, but as soon as that shall appear unto us judicially to be false, we grant the consultation[2].

For the better satisfaction of his Majesty and your Lordships touching the objections delivered against prohibitions, we have thought good to set down (as may be perceived by that which hath been said) the ordinary proceeding in his Majesty's courts therein, whereby it may appear both what the Judges do and ought to do in those causes; and the ecclesiastical judges may do well to consider what issue the course they herein hold can have in the end: and they shall find it can be no other but to cast a scandal upon the justice of the realm; for the Judges doing but what they ought and by their oaths are bound to do, it is not to be called in question, and if it fall out that they err in judgment, it cannot otherwise be reformed but judicially in a superior court or by Parliament.—Subscribed by all the Judges of England and the Barons of the Exchequer, Pasch. 4 Jacobi, and delivered to the Lord Chancellor of England.

Which answers and resolutions, although they were not enacted by authority of Parliament as our Statute of *Articuli Cleri* in 9 E. 2 was, yet being resolved unanimously by all the Judges of England and Barons of the Exchequer, are for matters in law of highest authority next unto the Court of Parliament.

State Trials, ii, 131–59.

(2) Prohibitions, 1607
Prohibitions del Roy

...Upon Sunday the 10th of November[3]...the King, upon complaint made to him by Bancroft, Archbishop of Canterbury,

---

[1] *I.e.* put in practice.

[2] 'Consultation' is the converse of 'prohibition'—a writ returning to the ecclesiastical court a cause removed into the temporal court.

[3] In 1607 10 November fell on a Tuesday, so the probable date is 8 November (Gardiner, ii, 39).

concerning prohibitions, the King was informed that when the question was made of what matters the ecclesiastical judges have cognizance, either upon the exposition of the statutes concerning tithes or any other thing ecclesiastical, or upon the Statute 1 El. concerning the High Commission, or in any other case in which there is not express authority in law, the King himself may decide it in his royal person; and that the Judges are but the delegates of the King, and that the King may take what causes he shall please to determine from the determination of the Judges and may determine them himself. And the Archbishop said that this was clear in Divinity, that such authority belongs to the King by the Word of God in the Scripture. To which it was answered by me, in the presence and with the clear consent of all the Judges of England and Barons of the Exchequer, that the King in his own person cannot adjudge any case, either criminal, as treason, felony, etc., or betwixt party and party, concerning his inheritance, chattels, or goods, etc., but this ought to be determined and adjudged in some court of justice according to the law and custom of England....

*   *   *   *   *   *

...Then the King said that he thought the law was founded upon reason, and that he and others had reason as well as the Judges. To which it was answered by me, that true it was that God had endowed his Majesty with excellent science and great endowments of nature, but his Majesty was not learned in the laws of his realm of England; and causes which concern the life or inheritance or goods or fortunes of his subjects are not to be decided by natural reason but by the artificial reason and judgment of law, which law is an act which requires long study and experience before that a man can attain to the cognizance of it; and that the law was the golden metwand and measure to try the causes of the subjects, and which protected his Majesty in safety and peace. With which the King was greatly offended, and said that then he should be under the law, which was treason to affirm, as he said; to which I said that Bracton saith, *quod Rex non debet esse sub homine sed sub Deo et lege.*

Coke, Twelfth Report (edition of 1777).

(3) Proclamations, 1610

*   *   *   *   *   *

...It was resolved by the two Chief Justices, Chief Baron, and Baron Altham, upon conference betwixt the Lords of the

Privy Council and them, that the King by his proclamation cannot create any offence which was not an offence before, for then he may alter the law of the land by his proclamation in a high point; for if he may create an offence where none is, upon that ensues fine and imprisonment: also the law of England is divided into three parts, common law, statute law, and custom, but the King's proclamation is none of them: also *malum aut est malum in se aut prohibitum*; that which is against common law is *malum in se*; *malum prohibitum* is such an offence as is prohibited by Act of Parliament and not by proclamation.

Also it was resolved, that the King hath no prerogative but that which the law of the land allows him.

But the King, for prevention of offences, may by proclamation admonish his subjects that they keep the laws and do not offend them; upon punishment to be inflicted by the law, etc.

Lastly, if the offence be not punishable in the Star Chamber, the prohibition of it by proclamation cannot make it punishable there; and after this resolution no proclamation imposing fine and imprisonment was afterwards made, etc.

Coke, *Twelfth Report* (edition of 1777).

(4) Peacham's Case, 1615

Interrogatories whereupon Peacham is to be examined

Questions in general

1. Who procured you, moved you, or advised you to put in writing these traitorous slanders which you have set down against his Majesty's person and government, or any of them?

*   *   *   *   *   *

4. What use mean you to make of the said writings? Was it by preaching them in sermon or by publishing them in treatise? If in sermon, at what time and in what place meant you to have preached them? If by treatise, to whom did you intend to dedicate or exhibit or deliver such treatise?

5. What was the reason and to what end did you first set down in scattered papers, and after knit up in form of a treatise or sermon, such a mass of treasonable slanders against the King, his posterity, and the whole State?

6. What moved you to write the King might be stricken with death on the sudden, or within eight days, as Ananias or Nabal? Do you know of any conspiracy or danger to his person, or have you heard of any such attempt?

7. You have confessed that these things were applied to the King, and that after the example of preachers and chronicles, kings' infirmities are to be laid open. This sheweth plainly your use must be to publish them. Shew to whom and in what manner.

*   *   *   *   *   *

Upon these [twelve] interrogatories Peacham this day was examined before torture, in torture, between torture, and after torture; notwithstanding, nothing could be drawn from him, he still persisting in his obstinate and insensible denials and former answers....January the 19th, 1614[–15].

*   *   *   *   *   *

[Sir Francis Bacon to the King, 27 January, 1615]

...For the course your Majesty directeth and commandeth for the feeling of the Judges of the King's Bench their several opinions by distributing ourselves and enjoining secrecy, we did first find an encounter in the opinion of my Lord Coke, who seemed to affirm that such particular and, as he called it, auricular taking of opinions was not according to the custom of this realm, and seemed to divine that his brethren would never do it.....I took my fellows aside and advised that they should presently[1] speak with the three Judges before I could speak with my Lord Coke, for doubt of infusion[2], and that they should not in any case make any doubt to the Judges, as if they mistrusted they would not deliver any opinion apart, but speak resolutely unto them, and only make their coming to be to know what time they would appoint to be attended with the papers. This sorted not amiss, for Mr Solicitor came to me this evening and related to me that he had found Judge Dodderidge very ready to give opinion in secret; and fell upon the same reason which upon your Majesty's first letter I had used to my Lord Coke at the Council Table, which was that every Judge was bound expressly by his oath to give your Majesty counsel when he was called, and whether he should do it jointly or severally, that rested in your Majesty's good pleasure as you would require it. And though the ordinary course was to assemble them, yet there might intervene cases wherein the other course was more convenient. The like answer made Justice Crooke. Justice Houghton, who is a soft man, seemed desirous first to confer, alleging that the other three Judges had all served the Crown before they were Judges, but that he had not been much acquainted with business of this nature.

---

[1] Immediately.
[2] Insidious suggestion, insinuation.

We purpose therefore forthwith they shall be made acquainted with the papers; and if that could be done as suddenly as this was, I should make small doubt of their opinions, and howsoever, I hope force of law and precedent will bind them to the truth; neither am I wholly out of hope that my Lord Coke himself, when I have in some dark manner put him in doubt that he shall be left alone, will not continue singular....

[The same to the same, 31 January, 1615]

...For Peacham's case, I have since my last letter been with my Lord Coke twice,...at the former of which times I delivered him Peacham's papers, and at this latter the precedents which I had with care gathered and selected....At the former I told him that he knew my errand, which stood upon two points: the one to inform him of the particular case of Peacham's treasons..., the other to receive his opinion to myself and in secret, according to my commission from your Majesty. At the former time he fell upon the same allegation which he had begun at the Council Table,—that judges were not to give opinion by fractions, but entirely according to the vote whereupon they should settle upon conference; and that this auricular taking of opinions, single and apart, was new and dangerous; and other words more vehement than I repeat. I replied in civil and plain terms, that I wished his Lordship in my love to him to think better of it, for that this that his Lordship was pleased to put into great words seemed to me and my fellows, when we spake of it amongst ourselves, a reasonable and familiar matter for a King to consult with his Judges either assembled or selected or one by one. And then to give him a little outlet to save his first opinion, wherewith he is most commonly in love, I added that Judges sometimes might make a suit to be spared for their opinion till they had spoken with their brethren, but if the King upon his own princely judgment, for reason of estate, should think it fit to have it otherwise and should so demand it, there was no declining; nay, that it touched upon a violation of their oath, which was to counsel the King without distinction whether it were jointly or severally.

* * * * * *

The true state of the question whether Peacham's case be treason or not. In the handwriting of King James

...That his writing of this libel is an overt act, the Judges themselves do confess; that it was made fit for publication, the form of it bewrays the self; that he kept not these papers in a secret and safe fashion but in an open house and lidless cask[1], both himself and the messenger do confess....Nay, he confesses that in the end he meant to preach it....

The only question that remains then is, whether it may be verified and proved that by the publishing of this sermon, or rather libel of his, he compassed or imagined the King's death; which I prove he did by this reason. Had he compiled a sermon upon any other ground, or stuffed the bulk of it with any other matter, and only powdered it here and there with some passages of reprehension of the King; or had he never so bitterly railed against the King, and upbraided him of any two or three though monstrous vices, it might yet have been some way excusable; or yet had he spued forth all the venom that is in this libel of his in a railing speech, either in drunkenness, or upon the occasion of any sudden passion or discontentment, it might likewise have been excused in some sort; but upon the one part, to heap up all the injuries that the hearts of men or malice of the Devil can invent against the King, to disable him utterly not to be a King, not to be a Christian, not to be a man or a reasonable creature, not worthy of breath here nor salvation hereafter: and upon the other part, not to do this hastily or rashly but after long premeditation, first having made collections in scattered papers, and then reduced it to a method in a formal treatise, a text chosen for the purpose, a prayer premitted[2], applying all his wits to bring out of that text what he could *in malem partem* against the King—this I say is a plain proof that he intended to compass or imagine by this means the King's death. For will ye look upon the person or quality of the man, it was the far likeliest means he could use to bring his wicked intention to pass: his person an old, unable, and unwieldy man; his quality a minister, a preacher, and that in so remote a part of the country as he had no more means of access to the King's person than he had ability of body or resolution of spirit to act such a desperate attempt with his own hands upon him; and therefore, as every creature is ablest in their own element either to defend themselves or annoy their adversaries, as birds in the air, fishes in the water, and so forth, what so ready and natural means had he whereby to annoy the King as by publishing such a seditious libel, and so under the specious pretext of conscience to inflame the hearts of the people against him? Now here is no illation[3] nor inference made upon

---

[1] *I.e.* casket.
[2] *I.e.* introduced by way of preface.
[3] Inference or deduction.

the statute, it stands *in puris naturalibus*, but only a just inference and probation of the guilty intention of this party. So the only thing the Judges can doubt of is of the delinquent's intention; and then the question will be, whether if these reasons be stronger to enforce the guiltiness of his intention, or his bare denial to clear him, since nature teaches every man to defend his life as long as he may; and whether, in case there were a doubt herein, the Judges should not rather incline to that side wherein all probability lies. But if judges will needs trust better the bare negative of an infamous delinquent, without expressing what other end he could probably have, than all the probabilities or rather infallible consequences upon the other part, caring more for the safety of such a monster than the preservation of a Crown in all ages following, whereupon depend the lives of many millions, happy then are all desperate and seditious knaves, but the fortune of this Crown is more than miserable. *Quod Deus avertat.*

State Trials, ii, 869–80.

(5) Case of Commendams, 1616

At Whitehall the sixth of June, Anno 1616

* * * * * *

His Majesty having this day given order for a meeting of the Council, and that all the Judges (being twelve in number) should be sent for to be present, when the Lords were set and the Judges ready attending, his Majesty came himself in person to Council and opened to them the cause of that assembly, which was: That he had called them together concerning a question that had relation to no private person but concerned God and the King, the power of the Crown, and the state of his Church whereof he was protector, and that there was no fitter place to handle it than at the head of his Council-table: That there had been a question pleaded and argued concerning Commendams the proceedings wherein had either been mishandled or misreported, for his Majesty a year since had received advertisements concerning that case in two extremes: by some, that it did trench far into his prerogative royal in the general power of granting Commendams; and by others, that the doubt rested only upon a special nature of a Commendam, such as in respect of the incongruity and exorbitant form thereof might be questioned without impeaching or weakening the general power at all.

* * * * * *

His Majesty, apprehending the matter to be of so high a

nature, commanded his Attorney-General to signify his Majesty's pleasure to the Lord Chief Justice that in regard of his Majesty's other most weighty occasions, and for that his Majesty held it necessary...that his Majesty be first consulted with before the Judges proceeded to argument, therefore the day appointed for the Judges' argument should be put off till they might speak with his Majesty.

*   *   *   *   *   *

That upon this letter received, the Lord Chief Justice returned word to his Majesty's said Attorney by his servant that it was fit the rest of his brethren should understand his Majesty's pleasure immediately by letters from his said Attorney to the Judges of the several benches, and accordingly it was done. Whereupon all the said Judges assembled, and by their letter under their hands certified his Majesty that they held those letters...to be contrary to law, and such as they could not yield to the same by their oath; and that thereupon they had proceeded at the day, and did now certify his Majesty thereof. Which letter of the Judges his Majesty also commanded to be openly read; the tenor whereof followeth *in haec verba*.

Most dread and most gracious Sovereign,
...We are and ever will be ready with all faithful and true hearts, according to our bounden duties, to serve and obey your Majesty, and think ourselves most happy to spend our lives and abilities to do your Majesty true and faithful service. In this present case...what information hath been made unto you...we know not. This we know, that the true substance of the case summarily is this. It consisteth principally upon the construction of two Acts of Parliament, the one of the twenty-fifth year of K. Edw. III, and the other of the twenty-fifth of K. Hen. VIII, whereof your Majesty's Judges upon their oaths, and according to their best knowledge and learning, are bound to deliver the true understanding faithfully and uprightly. And the case is between subjects for private interest and inheritance, earnestly called on for justice and expedition. We hold it our duties to inform your Majesty that our oath is in these express words: That in case any letters come unto us contrary to law, that we do nothing by such letters but certify your Majesty thereof, and go forth to do the law notwithstanding the same letters. We have advisedly considered of the said letter of Mr Attorney, and with one consent do hold the same to be contrary to law, and such as we could not yield to the same by our oath; assuredly persuading

TECD   13 ourselves that your Majesty being truly informed, that it standeth not with your royal and just pleasure to give way to them. And therefore, knowing your Majesty's zeal to justice, and to be most renowned therefor, we have, according to our oaths and duties, (at the day openly prefixed the last term), proceeded, and thereof certified your Majesty; and shall ever pray to the Almighty for your Majesty in all honour, health, and happiness long to reign over us...(27 April).

His Majesty having considered of this letter, by his princely letters returned answer,...which letter also by his Majesty's commandment was publicly read, and followeth *in haec verba*:

...We perceive by your letter that you conceive the commandment given you by our Attorney-General in our name to have proceeded upon wrong information; but if ye list to remember what princely care we have ever had, since our coming to this crown, to see justice administered to our subjects with all possible expedition, and how far we have ever been from urging the delay thereof in any sort, ye may easily persuade yourselves that it was no small reason that moved us to send you that direction. Ye might very well have spared your labour in informing us of the nature of your oath. For although we never studied the Common Law of England, yet are we not ignorant of any points which belong to a King to know: We are therefore to inform you hereby that we are far from crossing or delaying anything which may belong to the interest of any private parties in this case; but we cannot be contented to suffer the prerogative royal of our Crown to be wounded through the sides of a private person. We have no care at all which of the parties shall win his process in this case, so that right prevail and that justice be truly administered; but on the other part, we have reason to foresee that nothing be done in this case which may wound our prerogative in general. And therefore so that we may be sure that nothing shall be debated amongst you which may concern our general power of giving Commendams, we desire not the parties to have an hour's delay of justice; but that our prerogative should not be wounded in that regard for all times hereafter upon pretext of a private party's interest, we sent you that direction, which we account to be wounded as well if it be publicly disputed upon as if any sentence were given against it. We are therefore to admonish you, that since the prerogative of our Crown hath been more boldly dealt withal in Westminster Hall during the time of our reign than ever it was before in the reigns of divers princes immediately preceding us, that we will no longer endure that popular and unlawful liberty; and therefore were we justly moved to send you that direction to forbear to meddle in a case of so tender a nature till we had further thought upon it. We have cause indeed to rejoice of your zeal for the speedy execution of justice. But we would be glad that all our good subjects might so find the fruits thereof as that no pleas before you were of older dates than this is. But as to your argument which you found upon your oath, you give our predecessors who first founded that oath a very uncharitable meeting in perverting their intention and zeal to justice to make a weapon of it to use against their successors. For although your oath be, that you shall not delay justice betwixt any private parties, yet was it not meant that the King should thereby receive harm before he be forewarned thereof; neither can ye deny but that every term ye will out of your own discretions, for reasons known unto you, put off either the hearing or determining of an ordinary cause betwixt private persons till the next term following. Our pleasure therefore is, who are head and fountain of justice under God in our dominions, and we out of our absolute power and authority royal do command you, that you forbear to meddle any further in this plea till our coming to town, and that out of our own mouth you may hear our pleasure in this business; which we do out of the care we have that our prerogative may not receive an unwitting and indirect blow, and not to hinder justice to be administered to any private parties, which no importunity shall persuade us to move you in, like as only for avoiding the unreasonable importunity of suitors in their own particular that oath was by our predecessors ordained to be ministered unto you. So we heartily wish you well to fare....

This letter being read, his Majesty resorted to take into his consideration the parts of the Judges' letter and other their proceedings in that cause, and the errors therein committed and contained; which errors his Majesty did set forth....

* * * * * *

After this his Majesty's declaration, all the Judges fell down upon their knees and acknowledged their error for matter of form, humbly craving his Majesty's gracious favour and pardon for the same.

But for the matter of the letter, the Lord Chief Justice of the King's Bench entered into a defence thereof, the effect whereof was that the stay required by his Majesty was a delay of justice, and therefore contrary to law and the Judges' oath; and that the Judges knew well amongst themselves that the case (as they meant to handle it) did not concern his Majesty's prerogative of grant of Commendams; and that if the day had not held by the not coming of the Judges, the suit had been discontinued, which had been a failing in justice, and that they could not adjourn it because Mr Attorney's letter mentioned no day certain, and that an adjournment must always be to a day certain.

Unto which answer of the Chief Justice his Majesty did reply, that for the last conceit, it was mere sophistry, for that they might in their discretions have prefixed a convenient day such as there might have been time for them to consult with his Majesty before the same, and that his Majesty left that point of form to themselves. And for that other point, that they should take upon them peremptorily to discern whether the cause concerned the King's prerogative without consulting with his Majesty first and informing his princely judgment, was a thing preposterous; for that they ought first to have made that appear to his Majesty, and so to have given him assurance thereof upon consultation with him.

And for the main matter, that it should be against the law and against their oath, his Majesty said he had said enough before; unto which the Lord Chief Justice in effect had made no answer, but only insisted upon the former opinion; and therefore the King required the Lord Chancellor to deliver his opinion upon that point, Whether the stay that had been required by his Majesty were contrary to law or against the Judges' oath?

* * * * * *

After this the Lord Chancellor delivered his opinion clearly and plainly, that the stay that had been by his Majesty required was not against law or any breach of a Judge's oath, and required that the oath itself might be read out of the statute; which was done by the King's Solicitor, and all the words thereof weighed and considered.

Thereupon his Majesty and the Lords thought good to ask the Judges severally their opinion, the question being put in this manner: Whether, if at any time in a case depending before the Judges which his Majesty conceived to concern him either in power or profit, and thereupon required to consult with them and that they should stay proceedings in the mean time, they ought not to stay accordingly? They all (the Lord Chief Justice only except) yielded that they would, and acknowledged it to be their duty so to do; only the Lord Chief Justice of the King's Bench said for answer, that when that case should be, he would do that should be fit for a Judge to do. And the Lord Chief Justice of the Common Pleas (who had assented with the rest) added that he would ever trust the justness of his Majesty's commandment.

After this was put to a point, his Majesty thought fit, in respect of the further day of argument appointed the Saturday following for the Commendams, to know from his Judges what he might expect from them concerning the same. Whereupon the Lord of Canterbury breaking the case into some questions, his Majesty did require his Judges to deal plainly with him, whether they meant in their argument to touch the general power of granting Commendams, yea or no. Whereupon all his said Judges did promise and assure his Majesty that in the argument of the said case of Commendams they would speak nothing which should weaken or draw into doubt his Majesty's prerogative for the granting of them; but intended particularly to insist upon the point of the *lapse* and other individual points of this case, which they conceive to be of a form differing from all other Commendams which have been practised.

The Judges also went further, and did promise his Majesty that they would not only abstain from speaking anything to weaken his Majesty's prerogative of Commendams but would directly and in plain terms affirm the same, and correct the erroneous and bold speeches which had been used at the bar in derogation thereof.

Also all the Judges did in general acknowledge and profess with great forwardness that it was their duty, if any counsellor at the bar presumed at any time to call in question his Majesty's high prerogatives and regalities, that they ought to reprehend them and silence them; and all promised so to do hereafter.

*   *   *   *   *   *

The Judges having thus far submitted and declared themselves, his Majesty admonished them to keep the bounds and limits of their several Courts, and not to suffer his prerogative to be wounded by rash and unadvised pleading before them, or by new inventions of law; for as he well knew that the true and ancient Common Law is the most favourable for kings of any law in the world, so he advised them to apply themselves to the study and practice of that ancient and best law, and not to extend the power of any of their Courts beyond their due limits, following the precedent of the best ancient judges in the times of best government; and then they might assure themselves that he for his part, in the protection of them and expediting of justice, would walk in the steps of the ancient and best kings: and thereupon gave them leave to proceed in their argument.

When the Judges were removed, his Majesty, that had forborne to ask the votes and opinion of his Council before the Judges, because he would not prejudicate the freedom of the Judges' opinions, concerning the point whether the stay of proceedings that had been by his Majesty required could by any construction be thought to be within the compass of the Judges' oath which they had heard read unto them, did then put the question to his Council; who all with one consent did give opinion that it was far from any colour or shadow of such interpretation, and that it was against common sense to think the contrary, especially since there is no mention made in their oath of the delay of justice, but only that they shall not deny justice, nor be moved by any of the King's letters to do anything contrary to law or justice....

Bacon's Letters and Life (ed. J. Spedding), v, 357–69.

(6) Bacon's Speech to the Judges, 1617

The Speech which was used by the Lord Keeper of the Great Seal in the Star Chamber before the Summer Circuits, the King being then in Scotland, 1617

The King, by his perfect declaration published in this place concerning Judges and Justices, hath made the speech of his Chancellor accustomed before the circuits rather of ceremony than of use.... Yet nevertheless somewhat must be said to fulfil an old observance....

First, you that are the Judges of Circuits are as it were the planets of the Kingdom (I do you no dishonour in giving you that name), and no doubt you have a great stroke in the frame of this government, as the other have in the great frame of the world. Do therefore as they do: move always and be carried with the motion of your first mover, which is your Sovereign. A popular Judge is a deformed thing, and *plaudite's* are fitter for players than for magistrates. Do good to the people, love them, and give them justice. Let it be, as the Psalm saith, *nihil inde expectantes*: looking for nothing, neither praise nor profit.

Yet my meaning is not, when I wish you to take heed of popularity, that you should be imperious and strange to the gentlemen of the country. You are above them in power but your rank is not much unequal; and learn this, that power is ever of greatest strength when it is civilly carried.

Secondly, you must remember that, besides your ordinary administration of justice, you do carry the two glasses or mirrors of the State; for it is your duty in these your visitations to represent to the people the graces and care of the King, and again, upon your return, to present to the King the distastes and griefs of the people.

    *   *   *   *   *   *

As for the other glass I told you of, of representing to the King the griefs of his people, without doubt it is properly your part; for the King ought to be informed of anything amiss in the state of his countries from the observations and relations of the Judges (that know indeed the pulse of the country) rather than from discourse. But for this glass (thanks be to God) I do hear from you all that there was never greater peace, obedience, and contentment in the country, though the best governments be always like the fairest crystals, wherein every little icicle or grain is seen which in a fouler stone is never perceived.

    *   *   *   *   *   *

And you the Justices of Peace in particular, let me say this to you: Never King of this realm did you so much honour as the King hath done you in his speech, by being your immediate director, and by sorting you and your service with the service of ambassadors, and of his nearest attendants. Nay more, it seems his Majesty is willing to do the state of Justice of Peace honour actively also, by bringing in with time the like form of commission into the government of Scotland as that glorious King, Edward the Third, did plant this commission here in this kingdom. And therefore you are not fit to be copies except you be fair written, without blots or blurs or anything unworthy your authority. And so I will trouble you no longer for this time.

Bacon, Letters and Life (ed. J. Spedding), vi, 211–14.

Parliament

Parliament in the reign of James I was not the same deferential assembly which had been bullied and browbeaten by Henry VIII. One of the great achievements of the Tudor period on the constitutional side was the consolidation of Parliamentary institutions. The very fact that the Tudor kings had found Parliaments subservient and had therefore used them, had given Parliaments a great place in the State. It might have been possible for Henry VIII to have ignored the authority which Parliament claimed over legislation and taxation; to have accomplished the Reformation by royal Injunction instead of by Act of Parliament; to have recruited his finances by royal writs instead of subsidies; to have discontinued by degrees the practice of summoning the Estates. But the fact that he did not do so mightily strengthened the position of Parliament. The Tudors allowed Parliamentary influence to be confirmed by a whole century of precedents, and thus the road which for the first Tudor had been only an ill-marked track had become to the feet of the first Stuart the beaten way of the Constitution. 'Parliament,' says Prothero[1], 'had in fact confirmed its position as an indispensable element in the State. Without the training, the prestige, and the sense of self-importance conferred on it by a century of Tudor legislation, it could never have been styled by Pym, the soul of the body politic.' And in Parliament, the House of Commons was no longer relatively unimportant. The Tudors, seeking a counterpoise to the baronage, had done their best to elevate the country gentry and the commercial classes into political importance; and during the sixteenth century these classes had steadily improved their position. The gentry had been enriched by the practice of enclosure and the spoils of the monasteries, while the commercial classes had profited by the growth of trade and the merchant ventures in the New World at the expense of Spain; and the best of the energy and enterprise of these classes was concentrated in the House of Commons.

The House which had succeeded to the powers of the Tudor absolutism had not inherited the Tudor political genius. All the Tudors had been dignified and effective personalities, and Henry VIII and Elizabeth had been great statesmen. The Stuarts, coming to power at a time when statesmanship was more important than ever to the Crown, displayed qualities of only the ordinary type. They were for the most part conscientious and meritorious, but the dynasty only produced one statesman, and he was neither conscientious nor meritorious—Charles II. The contrast between the Houses may be measured by comparing Queen Anne with Queen Elizabeth and Charles I with Henry VIII. Set side by side with this decline of statesmanship on the part of the Crown, the advance of Parliament to its new position. If the policy of the Stuart dynasty should seem to be dangerous, if it should appear to threaten the public weal as the country gentry and the commercial classes conceived it, Parliament was now qualified to come forward as a critic of the Government, or even as a rival to the Crown, if

[1] *Statutes and Constitutional Documents*, 1558–1625, p. xxiv.

any powerful motives should arise to induce it to take up an attitude of independence.

§ 1. PARLIAMENT AND ELECTIONS

Near the beginning of James's first Parliament a secular question arose which was to disturb the cordiality of the relations between the Commons and the Crown. Before the election, James issued a proclamation,[1] in which he described in general terms the persons to be chosen, and required in particular 'that an express care be had that there be not chosen any persons bankrupts or outlawed, but men of known good behaviour and sufficient livelihood, and such as are not only taxed to the payment of subsidies and other like charges but also have ordinarily paid and satisfied the same.' Returns of the persons elected were to be made to Chancery, and warning was given in the proclamation that 'if any shall be found to be made contrary to this proclamation, the same is to be rejected as unlawful and insufficient, and the city or borough to be fined for the same.' The electors for the County of Bucks returned Sir Francis Goodwin, an outlaw, but his election was declared null and void in Chancery, in accordance with the terms of the proclamation, and a second writ was issued, under which Sir John Fortescue was chosen. As soon as Parliament met, the whole question was raised in the House of Commons [p. 202], and Goodwin was declared to have been lawfully elected, on the ground that he had been wrongly described as an outlaw at the time of the election, and even if he had been an outlaw, there were precedents for outlaws sitting in the House. The King replied with the statement that the Commons derived all their privileges from him, and they ought not to meddle with the returns; as to whether an outlaw was eligible or not, he advised them to consult the judges. The Commons drew up a memorial defending their action, and asked the Lords to lay it before the King, but they refused to confer with the judges. James, now thoroughly angry, demanded a conference between the judges and a Committee of the House in the presence of the Council, and when the Commons hesitated, he took—not exactly the Elizabethan tone, but the tone which Elizabeth might have taken if she had expressed herself in terms of the Stuart doctrine of prerogative,—he 'desired and commanded' it 'as an absolute King.' 'Upon this unexpected message there grew some amazement, and silence: but at last one[2] stood up and said, "The Prince's command is like a thunderbolt; his command upon our allegiance like the roaring of a lion; to his command there is no contradiction"' [p. 213]. The House, not yet grown to its full stature, surrendered to this argument, and the conference took place. The result was a compromise, for at the personal request of the King both elections were annulled and a new writ was issued for the County of Bucks. But on 11 April it was reported to the House that the King had acknowledged that the House of Commons was a court of record, and a proper, though not the exclusive, judge of the returns; and as a matter of fact the right of the House was not again called in question.

Their differences with the King led the Commons to draw up in June, 1604, the first of the striking constitutional documents of the Stuart period—*The Form of Apology and Satisfaction to be presented to his Majesty*

[1] The substance of this is printed in Prothero, pp. 280–1.   [2] Yelverton.

[p. **217**], already referred to above[1]. This document, in which the Commons 'with great thankfulness to God acknowledge that he hath given us a King of such understanding and wisdom as is rare to find in any prince in the world,' is profoundly respectful in form, but in substance it is a lecture to a foreign King on the constitutional customs of the realm which he had come to govern, but which he so imperfectly understood.

(1) The Bucks Election, 1604

The following extracts from the *Commons' Journals* will serve to explain the proceedings in the House over this important case.

[22 March, 1604.]...The first motion was made by Sir William Fleetwood, one of the knights returned for the County of Bucks, on the behalf of Sir Francis Goodwin knight, who upon the first writ of summons directed to the Sheriff of Bucks was elected the first knight for that shire; but the return of his election being made, it was refused by the Clerk of the Crown *quia utlagatus*: And because Sir John Fortescue, upon a second writ, was elected and entered in that place, his desire was that this return might be examined and Sir Francis Goodwin received as a member of the House. The House gave way to the motion and, for a more deliberate and judicial proceeding in a case of privilege so important to the House, ordered that the Serjeant (the proper officer of the House) should give warning to the Clerk of the Crown to appear at the Bar at eight a clock the next morning, and to bring with him all the writs of summons, indentures, and returns of elections for the County of Bucks made and returned for this Parliament: And to give warning also to Sir Francis Goodwin to attend in person, whom their pleasure was to hear, *ore tenus*, deliver the state of his own cause, and the manner and reasons of the proceeding in the election of the knights of the shire for that county...(p. 149).

[23 March, 1604]...Mr Speaker stood up and informed the House that if any burgess were returned for two places, or any member of the House deceased during the time of the session of any Parliament, the ancient course had been for the Speaker in the name of the House to direct a warrant under his hand to the Clerk of the Crown to make forth a writ for a new election; and since the like had happened in this session and might daily happen, he therein prayed to know the pleasure of the House. The voice of the House, in affirmation of the ancient order, gave general warrant to Mr Speaker to hold the same course during the time of this session.

[1] Pp. 51–2.

Sir George Coppin, knight, Clerk of the Crown in the Chancery, this day (according to former order), being attended by the Serjeant of the House with his mace, appeared at the Bar, and produced all the writs of summons, indentures, and returns made of the knights for Buckinghamshire for this Parliament, which were severally read by the Clerk of the House and then the Clerk of the Crown commanded to retire to the door: And after, Sir Francis Goodwin himself, whom it specially concerned, attending to know the pleasure of the House, was called in to deliver the state of his own cause *ore tenus*; wherein he was heard at large, and commanded again to retire until the House had determined what to do.

In the mean time the whole case was at large opened and argued, *pro et contra*, by sundry learned and grave members of the House, and after much dispute the question was agreed upon and made: Whether Sir F. Goodwin were lawfully elected and returned one of the knights for Bucks, and ought to be admitted and received as a member of this House? Upon this question it was resolved in the affirmative, That he was lawfully elected and returned, and *de jure* ought to be received. Hereupon the Clerk of the Crown was commanded to file the first indenture of return, and order was given that Sir Francis should presently take the oath of supremacy usual and his place in the House; which he did accordingly...(p. 151).

[27 March, 1604]...Sir Edward Coke his Majesty's Attorney-General, and Mr Doctor Hone, bring a message from the Lords...They desire...that the former committees[1] may, in a second conference to be had, have authority to treat touching the case of Sir Francis Goodwin....Upon this message it was argued by some, That in no sort they should give account to the Lords of their proceeding in the House, but that Mr Speaker should, from the House, be a suitor to his Majesty to have access, and as their common mouth give his Highness satisfaction by direction from the House. That now the judgment of Sir Francis Goodwin's case having passed the House, it could not nor ought not to be reversed by them. A precedent *Anno* 27 Eliz. cited, where a bill brought down from the Lords upon the first reading was rejected. The Lords sent messengers to demand a reason of their judgment. It was denied to yield any reason.

This argument brought forth this question, which Mr Speaker

---

[1] The persons to whom the case had been committed, *i.e.* the committee. The singular and plural forms both occur on p. 207 below.

was ordered by the House presently to make, viz.: Whether they should confer with the Lords touching the case of Sir Francis Goodwin the knight for Buckinghamshire? And resolved, That they should not. It was then considered as fit to return some answer to the message from the Lords, and Mr Secretary Herbert, with some other of the committees, were appointed to deliver to their Lordships from the House, That they did conceive it did not stand with the honour and order of the House to give account of any of their proceedings....

Sir Edward Coke his Majesty's Attorney-General, Mr D[octor] Carew, Mr D[octor] Hone, and Mr Tyndall delivered from the Lords, That their Lordships taking notice in particular of the return of the Sheriff of Bucks and acquainting his Majesty with it, his Highness conceived himself engaged and touched in honour that there might be some conference of it between the two Houses; and to that end signified his pleasure unto them, and by them to this House.

Upon this message, so extraordinary and unexpected, the House entered into some consideration what were fit to be done; and resolved, That his Majesty might be moved for access the next day...(p. 156).

[29 March, 1604]...Mr Speaker relateth what he had delivered to the King by warrant from the House the day before touching their proceeding in Sir Francis Goodwin's case, and his Majesty's answer;...His Majesty answered, he was loth he should be forced to alter his tune; and that he should now change it into matter of grief by way of contestation. He did sample[1] it to the murmur and contradiction of the people of Israel.

He did not attribute the cause of his grief to any purpose in the House to offend him, but only to a mistaking of the law. For matters of fact, he answered them all particularly. That for his part, he was indifferent which of them were chosen, Sir John or Sir Francis: That they could suspect no special affection[2] in him, because this was a counsellor not brought in by himself.

That he had no purpose to impeach their privilege; but since they derived all matters of privilege from him and by his grant, he expected they should not be turned against him. That there was no precedent did suit this case fully: precedents in the times of minors, of tyrants, of women, of simple kings, not to be credited, because for some private ends. By the law this House ought not to meddle with returns, being all made into the Chancery, and are

---

[1] Compare.   [2] Bias, partiality.

to be corrected or reformed by that Court only into which they are returned. 35 H. VI it was the resolution of all the Judges that matter of outlawry was a sufficient cause of dismission of any member out of the House. That the Judges have now resolved that Sir Francis Goodwin standeth outlawed according to the laws of this land.

In conclusion, it was his Majesty's special charge unto us that (1) The course already taken should be truly reported. (2) That we should debate the matter, and resolve amongst ourselves. (3) That we should admit of conference with the Judges. (4) That we should make report of all the proceedings unto the Council.

This relation being made, the House did not enter into any further consideration of the matter at that time, but resolved and ordered that it should be the first matter moved the next morning...(p. 158).

[30 March, 1604]...Moved and urged by one touching the difference now on foot between the King and the House, That there is just fear of some great abuse in the late election: That, in his conscience, the King hath been much misinformed, and that he had too many misinformers; which he prayed God might be removed, or lessened in their number: That now the case of Sir John Fortescue and Sir Francis Goodwin was become the case of the whole kingdom: That old lawyers forget, and commonly interpret the law according to the time: That by this course the free election of the country is taken away, and none shall be chosen but such as shall please the King and Council. Let us therefore with fortitude, understanding, and sincerity seek to maintain our privilege, which cannot be taken or construed any contempt in us, but merely a maintenance of our common right, which our ancestors have left us and is just and fit for us to transfer to our posterity.

Another:—For a law to be made that never any man outlawed should shew his face here again. The difference, he observed, was some unrespective[1] carriage towards his Majesty in this matter; and therefore let our proceeding be dutiful and careful towards him in advising of some speedy course to give his Majesty satisfaction.... Not now the case of Sir John and Sir Francis, but a case of great difference between the King and us, wherein we are deeply to consider the consequence if this pique be bruited in the country abroad or beyond the seas. It is fit we let the King see how much we take to heart this matter....

A third:—That we ought not to contest with the King: That

[1] Disrespectful.

it is fit to have a conference: That by it we shall lose no privilege but rather gain, for the matters of the conference will be two; satisfaction of the King and putting in certainty our privilege. All is not yet said that may be said. We are not to dispute with one that is governor of thirty legions; *Confitendum est, ne frustra interrogasset.* Let us deal plainly and freely with the Lords, and let them know all the reasons. They are jealous of the honour of a Privy Councillor, we of the freedom of election. It is fit great men maintain their prerogative; so is it fit that we maintain our privileges. This is a Court of Record; therefore ought we by all means seek to preserve the honour and dignity of it. If a burgess be chosen for two places, the burgess makes his choice for which he will serve; and a warrant shall be directed from Mr Speaker in the name of the House to the Clerk of the Crown to send forth a writ for a new election for the other place left; which is a direct proof that it is a Court of power and of Record. We have a Clerk and a Register: all matters that pass here are entered of record and preserved....

Some others were strong in opinion that we ought not to confer nor to commit, saying that Majesty had conferred with Justice, yet Majesty had left the stopping of the wound to us. We should taint ourselves with three great blemishes if we should alter our judgment,—levity, cruelty, and cowardice. There be three degrees of upright judgment,—motion, examination, judgment: all these have passed us. No Court can reform their own judgment. Every day a term here. Every act that passeth this House is an act of Parliament. Shall Justice float up and down? Shall he be a member to-day, and shall we tear him off to-morrow? If the member be sound, it is violence. If the hand tear the rest, it is cruelty. No part torn but it may bleed, to the ruin of the whole. Let Sir Francis Goodwin stand as he is. Duty and courage may stand together. Let not the House be inveigled by suggestions. This may be called a *quo warranto*, to seize our liberties.

There hath been three main objections:

1. The King's exception: we could shew no precedent in this kind.

Answer. The King could shew no such writ before. Our hands were never sought to be closed before, nor we prevented. It opens a gap to thrust us all into the Petty Bag. A Chancellor may call a Parliament of what persons he will by this course: any suggestion by any person may be cause of sending a new writ.

2. By the Lord Chief Justice: By the law we had nothing to do to examine returns.

Answer. Judges cannot take notice of private customs or privileges; but we have a privilege which stands with the law. The Judges informed the King of the law, but not of a case of privilege. It is true 35 H. VI all the Judges resolved that no outlawed man ought to be admitted, but that was controlled by Parliament. It is the same opinion now: let us control it as then. We have done no offence to the State: let us therefore be constant in our own judgments...(p. 159).

      *   *   *   *   *   *

Question. Whether we ought to satisfy the King in his commandment? The King's message was, that we should consider within ourselves and resolve of ourselves; then no need to confer with the Judges. If we cannot, then it is fit to be resolved by the Judges. The Judges have judged and we have judged; what need then of conference? Let there be no spark of that grace taken from us which we have had already from his Majesty. Let our reasons be put into articles, and delivered in all humbleness unto him.

Upon the conclusion of this debate, in this manner the House proceeded to Question: And the first was,

1 *Q.* Whether the House was resolved in the matter? And the Question was answered by general voice, That the whole House was resolved.

2 *Q.* Whether the reasons of their proceeding shall be set down in writing?

Resolved, That they shall be set down in writing: And ordered further, That a committee should be named for that purpose, and appointed first, to set them down in writing; and to bring them to the House there to be published and to receive their allowance ...(p. 160).

[2 April, 1604]...It was then moved that committees might be named to take the examination of the Sheriff of Buckinghamshire, who was by former order sent for and now come....The examination was presently[1] taken by these committees, and returned in this form:

Interr. 1. Why he removed the county[2] from Aylesbury to Brickhill?

He saith it was by reason of the plague being at Aylesbury, the county being the 25th of January, at which time three were dead of the plague there: This was the only motive of removing his county.

---

[1] *I.e.* immediately.

[2] A meeting summoned by the sheriff, such as an election, would be called 'the county'.

Interr. 2. Whether he were present at the first election?

Saith he was present; and was as faithful to wish the second place to Sir Francis Goodwin as the first to Sir John Fortescue. Sent Sir Francis Goodwin word before the election he should not need to bring any freeholders, for the election he thought would be without scruple for them both: first to Sir John; 2 to Sir Francis. About eight of the clock he came to Brickhill; was then told by Sir George Throckmorton and others that the first voice would be given for Sir Francis: He answered, he hoped it would not be so; and desired every gentleman to deal with his free-holders. After eight of the clock went to the election, a great number there being children, never at the county. After the writ read, he first intimated the points of the proclamation; then jointly propounded Sir John Fortescue and Sir Francis Goodwin. The freeholders cried first, 'A Goodwin! a Goodwin!' Every Justice of Peace on the bench said, 'A Fortescue! a Fortescue!' and came down from the bench before they named any for a second place; and desired the freeholders to name Sir John Fortescue for the first. Sir Francis Goodwin, being in a chamber near, was sent for by the Sheriff and Justices; and he came down and earnestly persuaded with the freeholders, saying Sir John was his good friend; had been his father's; and that they would not do Sir John that injury. Notwithstanding, the freeholders would not desist, but still cried, 'A Goodwin! a Goodwin!' some crying, 'A Fortescue!' to the number of sixty or thereabouts; the other, for Sir Francis Goodwin, being about two or three hundred. And Sir Francis Goodwin, to his thinking, dealt very plainly and earnestly in this matter for Sir John Fortescue, for that Sir Francis Goodwin did so earnestly protest it unto him....

* * * * * *

Sir Charles Cornwallis moveth in excuse of Sir Francis Goodwin's absence from the House; and prayeth that they would as well in their own judgment pardon it, as witness and affirm his care and modesty upon all occasions to the King, in that he hath forborne, during all the time of this question, to come into the House.... * * * * * *

Mr Speaker remembereth the matter of conference with the Judges, and offereth to repeat and put again the questions that were formerly made (being before uncertainly and unperfectly left, he said) in the case of Buckinghamshire: viz. 1. Whether the House were resolved in the matter? (2) Whether they should confer with the Judges? And at length induced the House to entertain the latter question, and being made, was carried by general voice in the negative:—No conference. Upon this passage it was urged for a rule, That a question being once made, and carried in the affirmative or negative, cannot be questioned again, but must stand as a judgment of the House.

It was thought fit that Mr Speaker should attend the committee for penning the reasons in Sir Francis Goodwin's case; not by commandment, but voluntary of himself...(pp. 161–2).

[3 April, 1604]...The reasons of the proceeding of the House in Sir Francis Goodwin's case, penned by the committee, were (according to former order) brought in by Mr Francis Moore and read by the Clerk, directed in form of a Petition:

To the King's most excellent Majesty

The humble answer of the Commons' House of Parliament to his Majesty's objections in Sir Francis Goodwin's case

Most gracious, our dear, and dread Sovereign: Relation being made to us by our Speaker of your Majesty's royal clemency and patience in hearing us, and of your princely prudence in discerning, shewing affectionate desire rather to receive satisfaction to clear us than cause to pardon us, we do in all humbleness render our most bounden thanks for the same; protesting by the bond of our allegiance that we never had thought to offend your Majesty, at whose feet we shall ever lie prostrate with loyal hearts to sacrifice ourselves and all we have for your Majesty's service: And in this particular we could find no quiet in our minds that would suffer us to entertain other thoughts until we had addressed our answer to your most excellent Majesty; for which, nevertheless, we have presumed of the longer time in respect we have prepared some precedents, requiring search, to yield your Majesty better satisfaction.

There were objected against us by your Majesty and your reverend Judges four things to impeach our proceedings in receiving Francis Goodwin, knight, into our House.

Objectio 1. The first, that we assumed to ourselves power of examining of the elections and returns of knights and burgesses, which belonged to your Majesty's Chancery and not to us; for that all returns of writs were examinable in the Courts wherein they are returnable, and the Parliament writs being returnable into the Chancery, the returns of them must needs be there examined and not with us.

Our humble answer is, That until the seventh year of King Henry IV all Parliament writs were returnable into the Parliament, as appeareth by many precedents of record ready to be shewed, and consequently the returns there examinable; in which year a Statute was made that thenceforth every Parliament writ containing the day and place where the Parliament shall be holden should have this clause, viz. *Et electionem tuam in pleno comitatu factum, distincte et aperte, sub sigillo tuo et sigillis eorum qui electioni illi interfuerint, nobis in Cancellariam nostram, ad diem et locum in brevi contentos certifices indilate.*

By this, although the form of the writ be somewhat altered, yet the power of the Parliament to examine and determine of elections remaineth, for so the Statute hath been always expounded ever since by use to this day: And for that purpose both the Clerk of the Crown hath always used, all the Parliament-time, to attend upon the Commons' House with the writs and returns, and also the Commons, in the beginning of every Parliament, have ever used to appoint special committees all the Parliament-time for examining controversies concerning elections and returns of knights and burgesses, during which time the writs and indentures remain with the Clerk of the Crown; and after the Parliament ended and not before, are delivered to the Clerk of the Petty Bag in Chancery to be kept there. Which is warranted by reason and precedents: reason, for that it is fit that the returns should be in that place examined where the appearance and service of the writ is appointed; the appearance and service is in Parliament, therefore the return examinable in Parliament. Precedents: one in the twenty-ninth year of the reign of the late Queen Elizabeth where, after one writ awarded into Norfolk for choice of knights, and election made and returned, a second was, before the Parliament day, awarded by the Lord Chancellor, and thereupon another election and return made; and the Commons, being attended with both writs and returns by the Clerk of the Crown, examined the cause, allowed the first, and rejected the second. So *Anno* 23 *Elizabethae Reginae* a burgess was returned dead, and a new chosen, and returned by a new writ: the party returned dead appeared; the Commons, notwithstanding the Sheriff's return, admitted the first chosen and rejected the second. Also the said three-and-twentieth year a burgess chose for Hull was returned lunatic, and a new chosen upon a second writ. The first claimed his place; the Commons examined the cause, and finding the return of lunacy to be true, they refused him, but if it had been false they would have received him....

All which together, viz. use, reason, and precedents, do concur to prove the Chancery to be a place appointed to receive the returns, as to keep them for the Parliament; but not to judge of them. And the inconvenience might be great if the Chancery might, upon suggestions or Sheriffs' returns, send for new elections, and those not subject to examination in Parliament: For so, when fit men were chosen by the counties and boroughs, the Lord Chancellor or the Sheriffs might displace them and send out new writs until some were chosen to their liking, a thing dangerous in precedents for the time to come, howsoever we rest securely from it at this present by the now Lord Chancellor's integrity.

Objectio 2. That we dealt in the cause with too much precipitation, not seemly for a council of gravity, and without respect to your most excellent Majesty our Sovereign who had directed the writ to be made; and being but half a body, and no Court of Record alone, refused conference with the Lords, the other half, notwithstanding they prayed it of us.

Our humble answer is to the precipitation, that we entered into this cause as in other Parliaments of like cases hath been accustomed, calling to us the Clerk of the Crown and viewing both the writs and both the returns, which...hath been warrant by continual usage amongst us: and there, upon well finding that the later writ was awarded and sealed before the Chancery was repossessed of the former (which the Clerk of the Crown and the Sheriff of the county did both testify, and well held to be a clear fault in law), proceeded to sentence with the less respect of the latter election. For our lack of respect to your Majesty, we confess with grief of our hearts we are right sorry it shall be so conceived; protesting that it was no way made known unto us before that time that your Majesty had taken to yourself any special notice, or directed any course in that cause, other than the ordinary awarding writs by your Highness's officers in that behalf. But if we had known as much (as some will have) by your Majesty's royal mouth, we would not without your Majesty's privity have proceeded in that manner. And further it may please your Majesty to give us leave to inform you that in the examination of the cause the Sheriff avouched unto us that Goodwin agreed to yield the first place of the two knights to Sir John Fortescue, and in his own person at the time of election, with extraordinary earnestness, entreated the electors it might so be, and caused the indentures to be made up to that purpose; but the electors utterly refused to seal them.

Concerning our refusing conference with the Lords, there was none desired until after our sentence passed; and then we thought that in a matter private to our own House, which by rules of order might not be by us revoked, we might without any imputation refuse to confer: Yet understanding...that your Majesty had been informed against us, we made haste (as in all duty we were bound) to lay open to your Majesty, our good and gracious Sovereign, the whole manner of our proceeding, not doubting, though we were but part of a body as to make new laws, yet for any matter of privileges of our House we are and ever have been a Court of ourselves of sufficient power to discern and determine without their Lordships, as their Lordships have used always to do for theirs without us.

Objectio 3. That we have by our sentence of receiving Goodwin admitted that outlaws may be makers of laws; which is contrary to all laws.

Our humble answer is, That notwithstanding the precedents which we truly delivered of admitting and retaining outlaws in personal actions in the Commons' House, and none remitted for that cause, yet we received so great satisfaction, delivered from your royal Majesty's own mouth with such excellent strength and light of reason, more than before in that point we heard or did conceive, as we forthwith prepared an Act to pass our House that all outlaws henceforth shall stand disabled to serve in Parliament: But as concerning Goodwin's particular, it could not appear unto us, having thoroughly examined all parts of the proceedings against him, that he stood an outlaw by the laws of England at the time of the election made of him by the county....

Objectio 4. That we proceeded to examine the truth of the fact of outlawry and gave our sentence upon that, whereas we ought to have been bound by the Sheriff's return of the outlawry from further examining whether the party were outlawed or not.

Our humble answer is, That the precedents cited before in our answer to the first objection do prove the use of the Commons' House to examine *veritatem facti* in elections and returns, and have not been tied peremptorily to allow the return; as if a knight or burgess be untruly returned dead or lunatic, yet when he appeareth to the House to be living and sound they have, contrary to the return, received him into the House, preferring the truth manifested, before the return: By which discreet proceeding there is avoided that great inconvenience above mentioned of giving liberty to Sheriffs by untrue returns to make and remove whom they list to and from the Parliament service, how meet soever the parties be in the judgment of the county or borough that elected them.

Thus in all humility we have presented to your most excellent Majesty the grounds and reasons of our late action; led with no affections but guided by truth, warranted in our consciences, imitating precedents, maintaining our ancient privileges, honouring your excellent Majesty in all our services, to which in all loyalty and devotion we bind us and ours for ever; praying daily on the knees of our hearts to the Majesty of the Almighty that your Majesty and your posterity may in all felicity reign over us and ours to the end of the world.

These reasons so set down and published to the House, Mr Secretary Herbert was sent with message to the Lords, That the House had resolved of their answer to his Majesty in Sir Francis Goodwin's case and had set it down in writing; and that it should be sent to their Lordships before four of the clock in the afternoon: Who immediately returned their Lordships' answer, That they would be ready at that time in the Council Chamber at Whitehall with thirty of the Lords to receive what then should be delivered. Then were named threescore to attend the delivery of the said reasons at the time and place aforesaid...(pp. 162–4).

[5 April, 1604]...Mr Speaker excuseth his absence by reason he was commanded to attend upon his Majesty, and bringeth message from his Majesty to this effect: That the King had received a parchment from the House; whether it were an absolute resolution, or reason to give him satisfaction, he knew not: He thought it was rather intended for his satisfaction. His Majesty protested, by that love he bare to the House as his loving and loyal subjects and by the faith he did ever owe to God, he had as great a desire to maintain their privileges as ever any prince had, or as they themselves. He had seen and considered of the manner and the matter; he had heard his Judges and Council; and that he was now distracted in judgment: Therefore for his further satisfaction he desired and commanded as an absolute King that there might be a conference between the House and the Judges; and that for that purpose there might be a select committee of grave and learned persons out of the House; that his Council might be present, not as umpires to determine, but to report indifferently on both sides.

Upon this unexpected message there grew some amazement, and silence: but at last one stood up and said, The Prince's command is like a thunderbolt; his command upon our allegiance like the roaring of a lion; to his command there is no contradiction; but how or in what manner we should now proceed to perform obedience, that will be the question.

Another answered, Let us petition to his Majesty that he

will be pleased to be present, to hear, moderate, and judge the case himself.

Whereupon Mr Speaker proceeded to this Question: Whether to confer with the Judges in the presence of the King and Council? Which was resolved in the affirmative, and a select committee presently named for the conference....

It was further resolved and ordered by the House..., That the fore-said committees should insist upon the fortification and explaining of the reasons and answers delivered unto his Majesty, and not proceed to any other argument or answer, what occasion soever moved in the time of that debate...(p. 166).

[11 April, 1604]...Sir Francis Bacon after the meeting of the committees in the Court of Wards reporteth what had passed in conference in the presence of his Majesty and his Council.

The King said he would be president himself. This attendance renewed the remembrance of the last, when we departed with such admiration. It was the voice of God in man, the good spirit of God in the mouth of man: I do not say the voice of God and not of man: I am not one of Herod's flatterers: A curse fell upon him that said it, a curse on him that suffered it. We might say, as was said to Solomon, We are glad, O King, that we give account to you, because you discern what is spoken. We let pass no moment of time until we had resolved and set down an answer in writing, which we now had ready: That since, we received a message from his Majesty by Mr Speaker of two parts, the one paternal, the other royal: 1. That we were as dear unto him as the safety of his person or the preservation of his posterity; 2. Royal; that we should confer with his Judges, and that in the presence of himself and his Council: That we did more now to King James than ever was done since the Conquest in giving account of our judgments: That we had no intent in all our proceedings to encounter his Majesty or to impeach his honour or prerogative.

This was spoken by way of preamble by him you employed.

How to report his Majesty's speeches he knew not; the eloquence of a King was inimitable.

The King addressed himself to him, as deputed by the House, and said he would make three parts of what he had to say: The cause of the meeting was to draw to an end the difference in Sir Francis Goodwin's case.

If they required his absence he was ready, because he feared he might be thought interested, and so breed an inequality on their part.

He said that he would not hold his prerogative or honour, or receive anything of any or all his subjects; this was his magnanimity.

That he would confirm and ratify all just privileges; this his bounty and amity; as a King royally, as King James sweetly and kindly, out of his good-nature.

One point was, whether we were a Court of Record, and had power to judge of returns. As our Court had power, so had the Chancery; and that the Court that first had passed their judgment should not be controlled.

Upon a surmise, and upon the Sheriff's return, there grew a difference.

That there [are] two powers, one permanent, the other transitory: That the Chancery was a confidentiary Court to the use of the Parliament during the time.

Whatsoever the Sheriff inserts beyond the authority of his mandate, a nugation[1].

The Parliaments of England not to be bound by a Sheriff's return.

That our privileges were not in question: That it was private jealousies, without any kernel or substance. He granted it was a Court of Record and a judge of returns. He moved that neither Sir John Fortescue nor Sir Francis Goodwin might have place. Sir John losing place, his Majesty did meet us half-way: That when there did arise a schism in the Church between a Pope and an Anti-pope, there could be no end of the difference until they were both put down.

Upon this report a motion was made that it might be done by way of warrant; and therein to be inferred that it was done at the request of the King: And was further said (as anciently it hath been said) that we lose more at a Parliament than we gain at a battle: That the authority of the committee was only to fortify what was agreed on by the House for answer, and that they had no authority to consent.

It was further moved by another, That we should proceed to take away our dissension and to preserve our liberties, and said that in this we had exceeded our commission, and that we had drawn upon us a note of inconstancy and levity. But the acclamation of the House was, that it was a testimony of our duty, and no levity.

So as the Question was presently made: Whether Sir John Fortescue and Sir Francis Goodwin shall both be secluded, and a

---

[1] Trifling, of no importance.

warrant for a new writ directed? And upon the Question resolved, that a writ should issue for a new choice; and a warrant directed accordingly.

A motion made, That thanks should be presented by Mr Speaker to his Majesty for his presence and direction in this matter: And thereupon ordered that his Majesty's pleasure should be known by Sir Roger Aston for their attendance accordingly.

Because it had been conceived by some that Sir Francis Goodwin being the member specially interested, it were fit he should give testimony of his liking and obedience in this course; being dealt withal to that end, he writ his letter to Mr Speaker which, before this Question made (for better satisfaction of the House) was read in these words:

Sir, I am heartily sorry to have been the least occasion either of question between his Majesty and that honourable House or interruption to those worthy and weighty causes which by this time in all likelihood had been in very good forwardness. Wherefore, understanding very credibly that it pleased his Majesty when the committees last attended him to take course with them for a third writ and election for the knightship of the county of Bucks, I am so far from giving any impediment thereunto that, contrariwise, I humbly desire his Majesty's direction in that behalf to be accomplished and performed...(p. 168).

[13 April, 1604]...Mr Speaker returneth to the House the effect of his message of thanks delivered the last day in the name of the House to his Majesty; as also of his Majesty's answer, viz:

That he related to his Highness the humble and dutiful acceptation of what his Majesty had done, together with the humble thanks of the House for his zealous and paternal delivery of his grace unto us by his own mouth: what wonder they conceived in his judgment; what joy in his grace; what comfort they had in his justice; what approbation they made of his prudence; and what obedience they yielded to his power and pleasure.

That his direction gave all men satisfaction; that they were determined to pursue the course he had prescribed; that now they were become suitors, he would be pleased to receive a representation of the humble thanks and service of the House.

His Majesty answered, That upon this second access he was forced to reiterate what he had said before: That this question was unhappily cast upon him, for he carried as great a respect to our privileges as ever any prince did: He was no ground-searcher: He was of the mind that our privileges was his strength: That he thought the ground of our proceeding was our not understanding that he had intermeddled before we had decided: That he thought also we had no wilful purpose to derogate anything from him, for our answer was a grave, dutiful, and obedient answer.

But as the Devil had unhappily cast this question between them, so he saw God had turned it to two good ends and purposes:

1. One, that he knew and had approved our loyalty:

2. Another, that he had so good an occasion to make testimony of his bounty and grace.

That as we came to give him thanks, so did he redouble his thanks to us: That he had rather be a King of such subjects than to be a King of many kingdoms....

* * * * * *

The warrant for a new election of a knight for Bucks read, and allowed in this form:

Whereas the Right Honourable Sir John Fortescue, knight, Chancellor of his Majesty's Duchy of Lancaster, and Sir Francis Goodwin, knight, have been severally elected and returned knights of the shire for the county of Bucks to serve in this present Parliament; upon deliberate consultation, and for some special causes moving the Commons' House of Parliament, it is this day ordered and required by the said House that a writ be forthwith awarded for a new election of another knight for the said shire. And this shall be your warrant. Directed: To my very loving friend Sir George Coppin, knight, Clerk of the Crown in his Majesty's High Court of Chancery...(p. 171).

Commons' Journals, i, 149–171.

(2) Form of Apology and Satisfaction, 1604

This is dated 20 June, 1604.

To the King's most excellent Majesty: From the House of Commons assembled in Parliament

Most gracious Sovereign, We cannot but with much joy and thankfulness of mind acknowledge your Majesty's great graciousness in declaring lately unto us by the mouth of our Speaker that you rested now satisfied with our doings.

Which satisfaction notwithstanding, though most desired and dear unto us, yet proceeding merely from your Majesty's most gracious disposition and not from any justification which on our behalf hath been made, we found this joy intermingled with no small grief, and could not, dread Sovereign, in our dutiful love to your Majesty and in our ardent desire of the continuance of your

favour towards us, but tender in humble sort this farther satisfaction, being careful to stand right not only in the eye of your
Majesty's Grace but also (and that much more) in the balance of
your princely judgment, on which all assuredness of love and grace
is founded. Into which course of proceedings we have not been
rashly carried by vain humour of curiosity, of contradiction, of
presumption, or of love of our own devices or doings,—unworthy
affections in a Council of Parliament, and more unworthy in
subjects towards their Lord and Sovereign.

But, as the searcher and judge of all hearts doth know, for
these and for no other undue ends in the world: to increase and
nourish your Majesty's gracious affection towards your loyal and
most loving people; to assure and knit all your subjects' hearts
most firmly to your Majesty; to take away all cause of jealousy on
either part, and diffidence for times ensuing; and to prevent and
control all sinister reports which might be unreasonably spread,
either at home or abroad, with prejudice to your Majesty or the
good state of your kingdom.

With these minds, dread Sovereign, your Commons of
England, represented in us their knights, citizens, and burgesses,
do come with this humble declaration to your Highness, and in
great affiance of your most gracious disposition, that your Majesty,
with benignity of mind correspondent to our dutifulness, will be
pleased to peruse it.

We know, and with great thankfulness to God acknowledge,
that he hath given us a King of such understanding and wisdom
as is rare to find in any prince in the world.

Howbeit, seeing no human wisdom, how great soever, can
pierce into the particularities of the rights and customs of people
or of the sayings and doings of particular persons but by tract
of experience and faithful report of such as know them (which it
hath pleased your Majesty's princely mouth to deliver), what
grief, what anguish of mind hath it been unto us at some time in
presence to hear, and so in other things to find and feel by effect,
your gracious Majesty (to the extreme prejudice of all your
subjects of England, and in particular of this House of the
Commons thereof) so greatly wronged by misinformation as well
touching the estate of the one as the privileges of the other, and
their several proceedings during this Parliament: Which misinformations, though apparent in themselves and to your subjects
most injurious, yet have we in some humble and dutiful respect
rather hitherto complained of amongst ourselves than presumed
to discover and oppose against your Majesty.

But now, no other help or redress appearing, and finding those misinformations to have been the first, yea, the chief and almost the sole cause of all the discontentful and troublesome proceedings so much blamed in this Parliament,

And that they might be again the cause of like or greater discontents and troubles hereafter (which the Almighty Lord forbid), we have been constrained, as well in duty to your royal Majesty whom with faithful hearts we serve as to our dear native country for which we serve in this Parliament, to break our silence, and freely to disclose unto your Majesty the truth of such matters concerning your subjects the Commons as hitherto by misinformation hath been suppressed or perverted: Wherein that we may more plainly proceed (which next unto truth we affect in this discourse), we shall reduce these misinformations to three principal heads.

First, Touching the cause of the joyful receiving of your Majesty into this your kingdom.

Secondly, Concerning the rights and liberties of your subjects of England, and the privileges of this House.

Thirdly, Touching the several actions and speeches passed in the House, it has been told us to our faces by some of no small place (and the same spoken also in the presence of your Majesty) that on the 24th of March was a twelvemonth[1] we stood in so great fear that we would have given half we were worth for the security wherein we now stand.

Whereby some misunderstanders of things might perhaps conjecture that fear of our own misery had more prevailed with us in the duty which on that day was performed, than love of your Majesty's virtues and hope of your goodness towards us.

We contrariwise most truly protest the contrary, that we stood not at that time, nor of many a day before, in any doubt or fear at all.

We all professing true religion by law established (being by manifold degrees the greater, the stronger, and more respective[2] part of this your Majesty's realm), standing clear in our consciences touching your Majesty's right, were both resolute with our lives and all other our abilities to have maintained the same against all the world, and vigilant also in all parts to have suppressed such tumult as, but in regard of our poor united minds and readiness, by the malcontented and turbulent might have been attempted.

---

[1] March 24, 1603, was the date of the death of Queen Elizabeth and the proclamation of James I.   [2] Worthy of consideration.

But the true cause of our extraordinary great cheerfulness and joy in performing that day's duty, was the great and extraordinary love which we bear towards your Majesty's most royal and renowned person, and a longing thirst to enjoy the happy fruits of your Majesty's most wise, religious, just, virtuous, and gracious heart; whereof not rumour but your Majesty's own writings had given us a strong and undoubted assurance.

For from hence, dread Sovereign, a general hope was raised in the minds of all your people that under your Majesty's reign religion, peace, justice, and all virtue should renew again and flourish; that the better sort should be cherished, the bad reformed or repressed, and some moderate ease should be given us of those burdens and sore oppressions under which the whole land did groan.

This hope being so generally and so firmly settled in the minds of all your most loyal and most loving people, recounting what great alienation of men's hearts the defeating of great hopes doth usually breed, we could not in duty as well unto your Majesty as to our country, cities, and boroughs, who hath sent us hither not ignorant or uninstructed of their griefs, of their desires, and hopes, but, according to the ancient use and liberty of Parliaments, present our several humble petitions to your Majesty of different nature, some for right and some for grace, to the easing and relieving of us of some just burdens and of other some unjust oppressions, wherein what due care and what respect we have had that your Majesty's honour and profit should be enjoyed with the content and satisfaction of your people, shall afterwards in their several due places appear.

Now concerning the ancient rights of the subjects of this realm, chiefly consisting in the privileges of this House of Parliament, the misinformation openly delivered to your Majesty hath been in three things:

First, That we held not privileges of right, but of grace only, renewed every Parliament by way of donature upon petition, and so to be limited.

Secondly, That we are no Court of Record, nor yet a Court that can command view of records, but that our proceedings here are only to acts and memorials, and that the attendance with the records is courtesy, not duty.

Thirdly and lastly, That the examination of the return of writs for knights and burgesses is without our compass, and due to the Chancery.

Against which assertions, most gracious Sovereign, tending

directly and apparently to the utter overthrow of the very fundamental privileges of our House, and therein of the rights and
liberties of the whole Commons of your realm of England which
they and their ancestors from time immemorable have undoubtedly
enjoyed under your Majesty's most noble progenitors, we, the
knights, citizens, and burgesses of the House of Commons
assembled in Parliament, and in the name of the whole commons
of the realm of England, with uniform consent for ourselves and
our posterity, do expressly protest, as being derogatory in the
highest degree to the true dignity, liberty, and authority of your
Majesty's High Court of Parliament, and consequently to the
rights of all your Majesty's said subjects and the whole body of
this your kingdom: And desire that this our protestation may be
recorded to all posterity.

And contrariwise, with all humble and due respect to your
Majesty our Sovereign Lord and Head, against those misinformations we most truly avouch,

First, That our privileges and liberties are our right and due
inheritance, no less than our very lands and goods.

Secondly, That they cannot be withheld from us, denied, or
impaired, but with apparent wrong to the whole state of the realm.

Thirdly, And that our making of request in the entrance of
Parliament to enjoy our privilege is an act only of manners, and
doth weaken our right no more than our suing to the King for
our lands by petition....

Fourthly, We avouch also, That our House is a Court of
Record, and so ever esteemed.

Fifthly, That there is not the highest standing Court in this
land that ought to enter into competency[1], either for dignity or
authority, with this High Court of Parliament, which with your
Majesty's royal assent gives laws to other Courts but from other
Courts receives neither laws nor orders.

Sixthly and lastly, We avouch that the House of Commons
is the sole proper judge of return of all such writs and of the
election of all such members as belong to it, without which the
freedom of election were not entire: And that the Chancery, though
a standing Court under your Majesty, be to send out those writs
and receive the returns and to preserve them, yet the same is
done only for the use of the Parliament, over which neither the
Chancery nor any other Court ever had or ought to have any
manner of jurisdiction.

From these misinformed positions, most gracious Sovereign,

---

[1] Competition.

the greatest part of our troubles, distrusts, and jealousies have risen; having apparently found that in the first Parliament of the happy reign of your Majesty the privileges of our House, and therein the liberties and stability of the whole kingdom, have been more universally and dangerously impugned than ever (as we suppose) since the beginnings of Parliaments.

Besides that in regard of her sex and age which we had great cause to tender, and much more upon care to avoid all trouble which by wicked practice might have been drawn to impeach the quiet of your Majesty's right in the succession, those actions were then passed over which we hoped, in succeeding times of freer access to your Highness of renowned grace and justice, to redress, restore, and rectify. Whereas contrariwise in this Parliament, which your Majesty in great grace (as we nothing doubt) intended to be a precedent for all Parliaments that should succeed, clean contrary to your Majesty's so gracious desire, by reason of these misinformations not privileges but the whole freedom of the Parliament and realm have from time to time upon all occasions been mainly hewed at. As

First, The freedom of persons in our election hath been impeached.

Secondly, The freedom of our speech prejudiced by often reproofs.

Thirdly, Particular persons noted with taunt and disgrace who have spoken their consciences in matters proposed to the House, but with all due respect and reverence to your Majesty.

Whereby we have been in the end subject to so extreme contempt as a gaoler durst so obstinately withstand the decrees of our House[1]. Some of the higher clergy to write a book against us, even sitting the Parliament[2]. The inferior clergy to inveigh against us in pulpits, yea, to publish their protestations, tending to the impeachment of our most ancient and undoubted rights in treating of matters for the peace and good order of the Church.

What cause we your poor Commons have to watch over our privileges is manifest in itself to all men. The prerogatives of princes may easily and do daily grow; the privileges of the subject are for the most part at an everlasting stand. They may be by good providence and care preserved, but being once lost are not recovered but with much disquiet. If good kings were immortal as well as kingdoms, to strive so for privilege were but vanity

[1] See Shirley's case: pp. 302, 303 below.
[2] See note on the Bishop of Bristol: pp. 224, 225 below.

perhaps and folly; but seeing the same God who in his great mercy hath given us a wise King and religious doth also sometimes permit hypocrites and tyrants in his displeasure and for the sins of the people, from hence hath the desire of rights, liberties, and privileges, both for nobles and commons, had its just original, by which an harmonical and stable State is framed, each member under the Head enjoying that right and performing that duty which for the honour of the Head and happiness of the whole is requisite.

Thus much touching the wrong done to your Majesty by misinformation touching our privileges. The last kind of mis-information made to your Majesty hath been touching the actions and speeches of particular persons used in the House. Which imputation notwithstanding, seeing it reacheth the whole House in general, who neither ought, neither have, at any time suffered any speech touching your Majesty other than respective[1], dutiful, and as become loyal subjects of a King so gracious; and forasmuch as it is very clear unto us by the effect that divers things spoken in the House have been perverted and very untruly reported to your Majesty, if it might seem so fit in your Majesty's wisdom and were seemingly[2] for us to crave, we should be most glad if, for our better justification and for your further satisfaction which we principally desire, the accusers and the accused might be con-fronted.

And now, most gracious Sovereign, these necessary grounds of our causes and defences being truly laid, and presented sin-cerely to your Majesty's grace and wisdom, the justification of such particulars wherein your Highness seemed doubtful of our dutiful carriage (though not so much for the matter as for the manner of our proceedings) we trust will be plain; and to expedite which particulars we find them to have been of three different natures:

The first sort, concerning the dignity and privileges of our House.

The second, the good estate of the realm and Church.

The third was for ease of certain grievances and oppressions.

*   *   *   *   *   *

The rights of the liberties of the Commons of England consisteth chiefly in these three things:

First, That the shires, cities, and boroughs of England, by representation to be present, have free choice of such persons as they shall put in trust to represent them.

---

[1] This word, used in a different sense on p. 219 above, here means respectful.
[2] Fittingly, becomingly.

Secondly, That the persons chosen, during the time of the Parliament as also of their access and recess, be free from restraint, arrest, and imprisonment.

Thirdly, That in Parliament they may speak freely their consciences without check and controlment, doing the same with due reverence to the Sovereign Court of Parliament, that is, to your Majesty and both the Houses, who all in this case make but one politic body whereof your Highness is the Head.

These three several branches of the ancient inheritance of our liberty were in three matters ensuing apparently injured: the freedom of election in the case of Sir Francis Goodwin; the freedom of the persons elected in Sir Thomas Shirley's imprisonment; the freedom of our speech, as by divers other reproofs, so also in some sort by the Bishop of Bristol's invective[1].

For the matter of Sir Francis Goodwin, the knight chosen for Buckinghamshire, we were and still are of a clear opinion that the freedom of election was in that action extremely injured; that by the same right it might be at all times in a Lord Chancellor's power to reverse, defeat, to evert[2] and substitute[3], all the elections and persons elected over all the realm. Neither thought we that the Judges' opinion, which yet in due place we greatly reverence, being delivered what the Common Law was, which extends only to inferior and standing Courts, ought to bring any prejudice to this High Court of Parliament, whose power being above the law is not founded on the Common Law but have their rights and privileges peculiar to themselves.

For the manner of our proceeding, which your Majesty seemed to blame in that, the second writ going out in your Majesty's name, we presumed to censure it without first craving access to acquaint your Highness with our reasons therein, we trust our defence shall appear just and reasonable. It is the form of the Court of Chancery, as of divers other Courts, that writs going out in your Majesty's name are returned also as to your Majesty in that Court from whence they issue; howbeit therefore no man ever repaireth to your Majesty's person, but proceeds according to law notwithstanding the writ. This being the universal custom of this kingdom, it was not nor could be admitted into our conceits that the difference was between your Majesty and us (for God forbid that between so gracious a Sovereign and so dutiful and loving subjects any difference should arise); but it always was and still is conceived that the controversy was between the Court of Chancery and our Court, an usual controversy between Courts

---

[1] See also pp. 222, 225.   [2] Upset, overthrow.   [3] Replace.

about their preeminences and privileges: And that the question was, whether the Chancery or our House of the Commons were judge of the members returned for it. Wherein though we supposed the wrong done to be most apparent, and extremely prejudicial for the rights and liberties of this realm, yet such and so great was our willingness to please your Majesty as to yield to a middle course proposed by your Highness, preserving only our privileges by voluntary cessions of the lawful right. And this course as it were of deceiving of ourselves and yielding in our apparent right (wheresoever we could but invent such ways of escape as that the precedent might not be hurtful) we have held, dread Sovereign, more than once this Parliament, upon desire to avoid that which in your Majesty by misinformation, whereof we have had cause always to stand in doubt, might be distasteful or not approvable, so dear hath your Majesty's gracious favour been unto us.

In the delivery of Sir Thomas Shirley our proceedings were long; our defence of them shall be brief. We had to do with a man, the Warden of the Fleet, so intractable and of so resolved obstinacy as that nothing we could do, no, not your Majesty's royal word for confirmation thereof, could satisfy him for his own security. This was the cause of the length of that business: our privileges were so shaken before, and so extremely vilified, as that we held it not fit in so unreasonable a time and against so mean a subject to seek our right by any other course of law or by any strength than by our own.

The Bishop of Bristol's book[1] was injurious and grievous to us, being written expressly with contempt of the Parliament and of both the Houses in the highest degree; undertaking to deface[2] the reasons proposed by the Commons, approved by the honourable Lords, confirmed by the Judges, and finally by your royal Majesty not disassented to. And to increase the wrong, with strange untruths he had perverted those reasons in their main drift and scope, pretending that they were devised to impugn the Union itself; whereas both by their title and by themselves it was clear and evident that they were only used against alteration of name, and that not simply, but before the Union of both realms in substance were perfected. This book being thus written and published to the world, containing moreover sundry slanderous passages and tending to murmurs, distraction, and sedition, we could not do less against the writer thereof than to complain of

---

[1] *A Discourse plainly proving the evident Utility and urgent Necessity of the desired happy Union of England and Scotland* (1604): by John Thornborough, Bishop of Bristol. See *Commons' Journals*, i, 226.   [2] Discredit.

the injury to the Lords of the Higher House, whereof he had now attained to be a member.

These wrongs were to the dignity of our House and privileges. Touching the causes appertaining to State and Church, true it is we were long in treating and debating the matter of Union. The propositions were new, the importance great, the consequences far reaching and not discoverable but by long disputes; our numbers also as large, and each hath liberty to speak. But the doubts and difficulties once cleared or removed, how far we are from opposing to the just desires of your Majesty, as some evil-disposed minds would perhaps insinuate who live by division and prosper by disgrace of other men, the great expedition, alacrity, and unanimity which was used and shewed in passing the Bill may sufficiently testify.

For matter of religion, it will appear by examination of truth and right that your Majesty should be misinformed if any man should deliver that the Kings of England have any absolute power in themselves either to alter Religion (which God defend should be in the power of any mortal man whatsoever), or to make any laws concerning the same otherwise than as in temporal causes, by consent of Parliament. We have and shall at all times by our oaths acknowledge that your Majesty is Sovereign Lord and Supreme Governor in both. Touching our own desires and proceedings therein, they have not been a little misconceived and misreported. We have not come in any Puritan or Brownist spirit, to introduce their parity[1] or to work the subversion of the state ecclesiastical as now it standeth; things so far and so clearly from our meaning as that with uniform consent in the beginning of this Parliament we committed to the Tower a man who out of that humour in a petition exhibited to our House had slandered the Bishops. But according to the tenor of your Majesty's writ of summons directed to the counties from whence we came, and according to the ancient and long continued use of Parliaments as by many records from time to time appeareth, we come with another spirit, even with the spirit of peace. We disputed not of matters of faith and doctrine; our desire was peace only and our device of unity, how this lamentable and long-lasting dissension amongst the ministers, from which both atheism, sects, and all ill life have received such encouragement and so dangerous increase, might at length, before help come too late, be extinguished. And for the ways of this peace, we are not all addicted to our own inventions but ready to embrace any fit way that may be offered;

---

[1] The text reads 'party,' but see p. 27 above.

neither desire we so much that any man in regard of weakness of conscience may be exempted after Parliament from obedience unto laws established, as that in this Parliament such laws may be enacted as by the relinquishment of some few ceremonies of small importance, or by any way better, a perpetual uniformity may be enjoined and observed.

Our desire hath also been to reform certain abuses crept into the ecclesiastical state even as into the temporal. And lastly, that the land might be furnished with a learned, religious, and godly ministry; for the maintenance of whom we would have granted no small contributions, if in these as we trust just and religious desires we had found that correspondency from others which was expected. These minds and hearts we in secret present to that Sovereign Lord who gave them, and in public profess to your gracious Majesty who we trust will so esteem them.

There remains the matters of oppression or grievance in the Bill of Assarts[1]. Your Majesty's counsel was heard, namely, your Solicitor and Sir Francis Bacon; it was also desired by the House that other of your Council would have been present. We knew that our passing the Bill could not bind your Majesty; howbeit for sundry equitable considerations (as to us they seemed) we thought good to give so much passage to the Bill in hope your Majesty might either be pleased to remit in some sort unto this equity that right which the rigour of law had given, or otherwise intreated by this kind of solicitation, to let them fall into your Majesty's hands full of piety and mercy, and not into the jaws of devouring promoters. And this do we understand to be your gracious intent, wherewith we rest joyfully content and satisfied. The grievance was not unjust in rigour of law, and was particular. But a general, extreme, unjust, and crying oppression is in cart-takers and purveyors, who have rummaged and ransacked since your Majesty's coming-in far more than under any of your royal progenitors: there hath been no prince since Henry III except Queen Elizabeth who hath not made some one law or other to repress or limit them. They have no prescription, no custom to plead; for there hath not been any Parliament wherein complaint hath not been made and claim of our rights, which doth interrupt prescription. We have not in this present Parliament sought anything against them but execution of those laws which are in force already. We demand but that justice which our princes are sworn neither to deny, delay, nor sell.

That we sought into the accounts of your Majesty's expense

---

[1] 'Assart' was the rooting up of trees on forest land in order to turn it into arable.

was not our presumption, but upon motion from the Lords of your Majesty's Council, and after from your officers of your Highness's Household, and that upon a demand of a perpetual yearly revenue in lieu of the taking away of those oppressions; unto which composition neither know we well how to yield, being only for justice and due right, which is unsaleable. Neither yet durst we impose it by law upon the people without first acquainting them and having their consents unto it. But if your Majesty might be pleased in your gracious favour to treat of composition with us for some grievance which is by law and just, how ready we should be to take that occasion and colour to supply your Majesty's desire concerning these also which we hold for unjust, should appear, we nothing doubt, to your Majesty's full satisfaction.

And therefore we come, lastly, to the matter of wards and such other burdens (for so we acknowledge them) as to the tenures of *capite* and knight's service are incident. We cannot forget (for how were it possible?) how your Majesty in a former most gracious speech in your Gallery at Whitehall advised us for unjust burdens to proceed against them by Bill, but for such as were just, if we desired any ease that we should come to yourself by way of petition, with tender of such countervailable composition in profit as for the supporting of your royal estate was requisite. According unto which your Majesty's most favourable grant and direction, we prepared a petition to your most excellent Majesty for leave to treat with your Highness touching a perpetual composition to be raised by yearly revenue out of the lands of your subjects for wardships and other burdens depending upon them or springing with them; wherein we first entered into this dutiful consideration, that this prerogative of the Crown which we desire to compound for was matter of mere profit, and not of any honour at all or princely dignity. For it could not then, neither yet can, by any means sink into our understandings that these economical matters of education and marrying of children, which are common also to subjects, should bring any renown or reputation to a potent monarch whose honour is settled on a higher and stronger foundation. Faithful and loving subjects, valiant soldiers, an honourable nobility, wise counsellors, a learned and religious clergy, and a contented and a happy people are the true honour of a King; and contrariwise, that it would be an exceeding great honour and of memorable renown to your Majesty with all posterity, and in present an assured bond of the hearts of all your people, to remit unto them this burden under which our children are born.

This prerogative then appearing to be a mere matter of great profit, we entered into a second degree of consideration: with how great grievance and damage of the subject, to the decay of many houses and disabling of them to serve their Prince and country; with how great mischief also by occasion of many forced and ill-suited marriages; and lastly, with how great contempt and reproach of our nation in foreign countries; how small a commodity now was raised to the Crown in respect of that which with great love and joy and thankfulness, for the restitution of this original right in disposing of our children, we would be content and glad to assure unto your Majesty.

We fell also from hence into a third degree of consideration: that it might be that in regard that the original of these wardships was serving of the King in his wars against Scotland, which cause we hope now to be at an everlasting end, and in regard, moreover, of that general hope which at your Majesty's first entry by the whole land was embraced (a thing known unto all men), that they should be now for ever eased of this burden, your Majesty, out of your most noble and gracious disposition and desire to overcome our expectation with your goodness, may be pleased to accept the offer of a perpetual and certain revenue, not only proportionable to the uttermost benefit that any of your progenitors ever reaped thereby but also with such an overplus and large addition as in great part to supply your Majesty's other occasions, that our ease might breed you plenty with their humble minds.

With these dutiful respects we intended to crave access unto your Majesty. But that ever it was said in our House by any man that it was a slavery under your Majesty more than under our former princes, hath come from an untrue and calumnious report. Our sayings have always been that this burden was just, that the remitting thereof must come from your Majesty's grace, and that the denying our suit was no wrong.

And thus, most gracious Sovereign, with dutiful minds and sincere hearts towards your Majesty, have we truly disclosed our secret intents and delivered our outward actions in all these so much traduced and blamed matters; and from henceforward shall remain in great affiance that your Majesty resteth satisfied both in your grace and in your judgment, which above all worldly things we desire to effect before the dissolving of this Parliament, where in so long time, with so much pains and endurance of so great sorrow, scarce anything hath been done for their good and content who sent us hither and whom we left full of hope and joyful expectation.

There remaineth, dread Sovereign, yet one part of our duty at this present which faithfulness of heart, not presumption, doth press. We stand not in place to speak or do things pleasing; our care is and must be to confirm the love and tie the hearts of your subjects the commons most firmly to your Majesty. Herein lieth the means of our well deserving of both. There was never prince entered with greater love, with greater joy and applause of all his people. This love, this joy, let it flourish in their hearts for ever. Let no suspicion have access to their fearful thoughts that their privileges, which they think by your Majesty should be protected, should now by sinister informations or counsel be violated or impaired, or that those which with dutiful respects to your Majesty speak freely for the right and good of their country shall be oppressed or disgraced. Let your Majesty be pleased to receive public information from your Commons in Parliament as to the civil estate and government, for private informations pass often by practice: the voice of the people, in the things of their knowledge, is said to be as the voice of God. And if your Majesty shall vouchsafe, at your best pleasure and leisure, to enter into your gracious consideration of our petition for the ease of these burdens under which your whole people have of long time mourned, hoping for relief by your Majesty, then may you be assured to be possessed of their hearts, and if of their hearts, of all they can do or have.

And so we your Majesty's most humble and loyal subjects, whose ancestors have with great loyalty, readiness, and joyfulness served your famous progenitors, Kings and Queens of this Realm, shall with like loyalty and joy, both we and our posterity, serve your Majesty and your most royal issue for ever, with our lives, lands, and goods, and all other our abilities, and by all means endeavour to procure your Majesty honour, with all plenty, tranquillity, content, joy, and felicity.

Petyt, *Jus Parliamentarium* (1739), pp. 227–43.

§ 2. PARLIAMENT AND THE CANONS

In 1604 an attempt was made by the clergy to recover the legislative power of which the Reformation had deprived them by issuing a code of 141 canons [p. 231], compiled by the Archbishop, passed in Convocation, and approved by the King. The question was raised again in 1606, when fresh canons were approved by Convocation, but the Commons viewed with peculiar jealousy anything which trenched upon their legislative province, and early in 1607 a bill passed their House 'to restrain the execution of canons ecclesiastical not confirmed by Parliament,'[1] although the influence

[1] *Commons' Journals*, i, 326, 348.

of the bishops secured its rejection in the Lords. This is the basis of subsequent legal opinion that ecclesiastical canons are not binding on the laity unless confirmed by Parliament, and it thus inflicted a serious blow upon the authority of Convocation, and prepared the way for 'the divorce which later history was to pronounce between the corporate life of the nation and the corporate life of the Church.'

The Canons of 1604

Constitutions and Canons Ecclesiastical, treated upon by the Bishop of London, President of the Convocation for the Province of Canterbury, and the rest of the Bishops and Clergy of the said Province; and agreed upon with the King's Majesty's License, in their Synod begun at London, Anno Domini 1603, and in the Year of the Reign of our Sovereign Lord James, by the Grace of God King of England, France, and Ireland the First, and of Scotland the Thirty-seventh.

OF THE CHURCH OF ENGLAND

I. *The King's Supremacy over the Church of England in Causes Ecclesiastical to be maintained*

As our duty to the King's most excellent Majesty requireth, we first decree and ordain, That the Archbishop of Canterbury (from time to time), all bishops of this province, all deans, archdeacons, parsons, vicars, and all other ecclesiastical persons, shall faithfully keep and observe, and (as much as in them lieth) shall cause to be observed and kept of others, all and singular laws and statutes made for restoring to the Crown of this kingdom the ancient jurisdiction over the state ecclesiastical, and abolishing of all foreign power repugnant to the same. Furthermore, all ecclesiastical persons having cure of souls, and all other preachers and readers of divinity lectures, shall, to the uttermost of their wit, knowledge, and learning, purely and sincerely (without any colour or dissimulation) teach, manifest, open, and declare, four times every year (at the least), in their sermons and other collations and lectures, that all usurped and foreign power (forasmuch as the same hath no establishment nor ground by the law of God) is for most just causes taken away and abolished; and that therefore no manner of obedience or subjection within his Majesty's realms and dominions is due unto any such foreign power, but that the King's power within his realms of England, Scotland, and Ireland, and all other his dominions and countries, is the highest power under God; to whom all men, as well inhabitants as born within the same, do by God's laws owe most loyalty and obedience, afore and above all other powers and potentates in earth.

II. *Impugners of the King's Supremacy censured*

Whosoever shall hereafter affirm, That the King's Majesty hath not the same authority in causes ecclesiastical that the godly kings had amongst the Jews and Christian emperors in the primitive Church; or impeach in any part his regal supremacy in the said causes restored to the Crown, and by the laws of this realm therein established; let him be excommunicated *ipso facto*, and not restored but only by the archbishop, after his repentance and public revocation of those his wicked errors.

III. *The Church of England a true and Apostolical Church*

Whosoever shall hereafter affirm, That the Church of England by law established under the King's Majesty is not a true and an apostolical Church, teaching and maintaining the doctrine of the Apostles; let him be excommunicated *ipso facto*, and not restored but only by the archbishop, after his repentance and public revocation of this his wicked error.

IV. *Impugners of the public Worship of God established in the Church of England censured*

Whosoever shall hereafter affirm, That the form of God's worship in the Church of England established by law and contained in the Book of Common Prayer and Administration of Sacraments, is a corrupt, superstitious, or unlawful worship of God, or containeth anything in it that is repugnant to the Scriptures; let him be excommunicated *ipso facto*, and not restored but by the bishop of the place or archbishop, after his repentance and public revocation of such his wicked errors.

V. *Impugners of the Articles of Religion established in the Church of England censured*

Whosoever shall hereafter affirm, That any of the nine and thirty Articles agreed upon by the archbishops and bishops of both provinces and the whole clergy in the Convocation holden at London in the year of our Lord God one thousand five hundred sixty-two, for avoiding diversities of opinions and for the establishing of consent touching true religion, are in any part superstitious or erroneous, or such as he may not with a good conscience subscribe unto; let him be excommunicated *ipso facto*, and not restored but only by the archbishop, after his repentance and public revocation of such his wicked errors.

VI. *Impugners of the Rites and Ceremonies established in the Church of England censured*

Whosoever shall hereafter affirm, That the rites and ceremonies of the Church of England by law established are wicked, anti-christian, or superstitious, or such as, being commanded by lawful authority, men who are zealously and godly affected may not with any good conscience approve them, use them, or, as occasion requireth, subscribe unto them; let him be excommunicated *ipso facto*, and not restored until he repent, and publicly revoke such his wicked errors.

VII. *Impugners of the Government of the Church of England by Archbishops, Bishops, &c., censured*

Whosoever shall hereafter affirm, That the government of the Church of England under his Majesty by archbishops, bishops, deans, archdeacons, and the rest that bear office in the same, is anti-christian or repugnant to the Word of God; let him be excommunicated *ipso facto*, and so continue until he repent, and publicly revoke such his wicked errors.

VIII. *Impugners of the form of Consecrating and Ordering Archbishops, Bishops, &c., in the Church of England censured*

Whosoever shall hereafter affirm or teach, That the form and manner of making and consecrating bishops, priests, or deacons, containeth anything in it that is repugnant to the Word of God, or that they who are made bishops, priests, or deacons in that form are not lawfully made, nor ought to be accounted, either by themselves or by others, to be truly either bishops, priests, or deacons until they have some other calling to those divine offices; let him be excommunicated *ipso facto*, not to be restored until he repent, and publicly revoke such his wicked errors.

IX. *Authors of Schism in the Church of England censured*

Whosoever shall hereafter separate themselves from the communion of saints, as it is approved by the Apostles' rules, in the Church of England, and combine themselves together in a new brotherhood, accounting the Christians who are conformable to the doctrine, government, rites, and ceremonies of the Church of England to be profane, and unmeet for them to join with in Christian profession; let them be excommunicated *ipso facto*, and not restored but by the archbishop, after their repentance and public revocation of such their wicked errors.

X. *Maintainers of Schismatics in the Church of England censured*

Whosoever shall hereafter affirm, That such ministers as refuse to subscribe to the form and manner of God's worship in the Church of England prescribed in the Communion Book, and their adherents, may truly take unto them the name of another Church not established by law, and dare presume to publish it, That this their pretended Church hath of long time groaned under the burden of certain grievances imposed upon it, and upon the members thereof before mentioned, by the Church of England, and the orders and constitutions therein by law established; let them be excommunicated, and not restored until they repent, and publicly revoke such their wicked errors.

XI. *Maintainers of Conventicles censured*

Whosoever shall hereafter affirm or maintain, That there are within this realm other meetings, assemblies, or congregations of the King's born subjects than such as by the laws of this land are held and allowed, which may rightly challenge to themselves the name of true and lawful Churches; let him be excommunicated, and not restored but by the archbishop, after his repentance and public revocation of such his wicked errors.

XII. *Maintainers of Constitutions made in Conventicles censured*

Whosoever shall hereafter affirm, That it is lawful for any sort of ministers and lay persons, or either of them, to join together, and make rules, orders, or constitutions in causes ecclesiastical without the King's authority, and shall submit themselves to be ruled and governed by them; let them be excommunicated *ipso facto*, and not be restored until they repent, and publicly revoke those their wicked and anabaptistical errors.

OF DIVINE SERVICE AND ADMINISTRATION OF THE SACRAMENTS

XIII. *Due Celebration of Sundays and Holy-days*

All manner of persons within the Church of England shall from henceforth celebrate and keep the Lord's Day, commonly called Sunday, and other holy-days, according to God's holy will and pleasure and the orders of the Church of England prescribed in that behalf; that is, in hearing the Word of God read and taught; in private and public prayers; in acknowledging their offences to God, and amendment of the same; in reconciling themselves charitably to their neighbours, where displeasure hath been; in oftentimes receiving the Communion of the Body and Blood of

Christ; in visiting of the poor and sick; using all godly and sober conversation.

XIV. *The prescript form of Divine Service to be used on Sundays and Holy-days*

The common prayer shall be said or sung distinctly and reverently upon such days as are appointed to be kept holy by the Book of Common Prayer, and their eves, and at convenient and usual times of those days, and in such place of every church as the bishop of the diocese, or ecclesiastical ordinary of the place, shall think meet for the largeness or straitness of the same, so as the people may be most edified. All ministers likewise shall observe the orders, rites, and ceremonies prescribed in the Book of Common Prayer, as well in reading the Holy Scriptures and saying of prayers as in administration of the Sacraments, without either diminishing in regard of preaching, or in any other respect, or adding anything in the matter or form thereof.

XV. *The Litany to be read on Wednesdays and Fridays*

The Litany shall be said or sung when and as it is set down in the Book of Common Prayer, by the parsons, vicars, ministers, or curates, in all cathedral, collegiate, parish churches and chapels, in some convenient place, according to the discretion of the bishop of the diocese or ecclesiastical ordinary of the place. And that we may speak more particularly, upon Wednesdays and Fridays weekly, though they be not holy-days, the minister, at the accustomed hours of service, shall resort to the church and chapel, and, warning being given to the people by tolling of a bell, shall say the Litany prescribed in the Book of Common Prayer: whereunto we wish every householder dwelling within half a mile of the church to come, or send one at the least of his household fit to join with the minister in prayers.

XVI. *Colleges to use the prescript form of Divine Service*

In the whole Divine Service and administration of the Holy Communion in all colleges and halls in both universities, the order, form, and ceremonies shall be duly observed as they are set down and prescribed in the Book of Common Prayer, without any omission or alteration.

XVII. *Students in Colleges to wear Surplices in time of Divine Service*

All masters and fellows of colleges or halls, and all the scholars and students in either of the universities, shall in their churches and chapels, upon all Sundays, holy-days, and their eves, at the time of Divine Service, wear surplices, according to the order of the Church of England: and such as are graduates shall agreeably wear with their surplices such hoods as do severally appertain to their degrees.

XVIII. *A reverence and attention to be used within the Church in time of Divine Service*

In the time of Divine Service, and of every part thereof, all due reverence is to be used; for it is according to the Apostle's rule, *Let all things be done decently and according to order*; answerable to which decency and order, we judge these our directions following: No man shall cover his head in the church or chapel in the time of Divine Service except he have some infirmity; in which case let him wear a nightcap or coif. All manner of persons then present shall reverently kneel upon their knees when the general Confession, Litany, and other prayers are read; and shall stand up at the saying of the Belief, according to the rules in that behalf prescribed in the Book of Common Prayer: and likewise when in time of Divine Service the Lord Jesus shall be mentioned, due and lowly reverence shall be done by all persons present, as it hath been accustomed, testifying by these outward ceremonies and gestures their inward humility, Christian resolution, and due acknowledgment that the Lord Jesus Christ, the true and eternal Son of God, is the only Saviour of the world, in whom alone all the mercies, graces, and promises of God to mankind, for this life and the life to come, are fully and wholly comprised. None, either man, woman, or child, of what calling soever, shall be otherwise at such times busied in the church than in quiet attendance to hear, mark, and understand that which is read, preached, or ministered; saying in their due places audibly with the minister the Confession, the Lord's Prayer, and the Creed; and making such other answers to the public prayers as are appointed in the Book of Common Prayer: neither shall they disturb the service or sermon by walking or talking, or any other way; nor depart out of the church during the time of service and sermon without some urgent or reasonable cause.

XIX. *Loiterers not to be suffered near the Church in time of Divine Service*

The churchwardens or questmen and their assistants shall not suffer any idle persons to abide either in the churchyard or church-porch during the time of Divine Service or preaching; but shall cause them either to come in, or to depart.

XX. *Bread and Wine to be provided against every Communion*

The churchwardens of every parish, against the time of every Communion, shall at the charge of the parish, with the advice and direction of the minister, provide a sufficient quantity of fine white bread and of good and wholesome wine for the number of communicants that shall from time to time receive there: which wine we require to be brought to the communion-table in a clean and sweet standing pot or stoup of pewter, if not of purer metal.

XXI. *The Communion to be thrice a Year received*

In every parish church and chapel where Sacraments are to be administered within this realm, the Holy Communion shall be ministered by the parson, vicar, or minister, so often and at such times as every parishioner may communicate at the least thrice in the year (whereof the feast of Easter to be one), according as they are appointed by the Book of Common Prayer. Provided, That every minister, as oft as he administereth the Communion, shall first receive the Sacrament himself. Furthermore, no bread or wine newly brought shall be used; but first the words of institution shall be rehearsed, when the said bread and wine be present upon the communion-table. Likewise the minister shall deliver both the bread and the wine to every communicant severally.

XXII. *Warning to be given beforehand for the Communion*

Whereas every lay person is bound to receive the Holy Communion thrice every year, and many notwithstanding do not receive that Sacrament once in a year, we do require every minister to give warning to his parishioners publicly in the church at morning prayer, the Sunday before every time of his administering that Holy Sacrament, for their better preparation of themselves; which said warning we enjoin the said parishioners to accept and obey, under the penalty and danger of the law.

XXIII. *Students in Colleges to receive the Communion four times a Year*

In all colleges and halls within both the universities, the masters and fellows, such especially as have any pupils, shall be careful that all their said pupils, and the rest that remain amongst them, be well brought up, and throughly instructed in points of religion, and that they do diligently frequent public service and sermons, and receive the Holy Communion; which we ordain to be administered in all such colleges and halls the first or second Sunday of every month, requiring all the said masters, fellows, and scholars, and all the rest of the students, officers, and all other the servants there, so to be ordered that every one of them shall communicate four times in the year at the least, kneeling reverently and decently upon their knees, according to the order of the Communion-book prescribed in that behalf.

XXIV. *Copes to be worn in Cathedral Churches by those that administer the Communion*

In all cathedral and collegiate churches the Holy Communion shall be administered upon principal feast-days, sometimes by the bishop, if he be present, and sometimes by the dean, and at some times by a canon or prebendary, the principal minister using a decent cope, and being assisted with the gospeller and epistler agreeably, according to the advertisements published anno 7 Eliz. The said Communion to be administered at such times, and with such limitation, as is specified in the Book of Common Prayer. Provided, That no such limitation by any construction shall be allowed of, but that all deans, wardens, masters or heads of cathedral and collegiate churches, prebendaries, canons, vicars, petty canons, singing men, and all others of the foundation, shall receive the Communion four times yearly at the least.

XXV. *Surplices and Hoods to be worn in Cathedral Churches, when there is no Communion*

In the time of Divine Service and prayers, in all cathedral and collegiate churches when there is no Communion, it shall be sufficient to wear surplices; saving that all deans, masters and heads of collegiate churches, canons, and prebendaries, being graduates, shall daily, at the times both of prayer and preaching, wear with their surplices such hoods as are agreeable to their degrees.

*   *   *   *   *   *

LV. *The Form of a Prayer to be used by all Preachers before their Sermons*

Before all sermons, lectures, and homilies, the preachers and ministers shall move the people to join with them in prayer in this form, or to this effect, as briefly as conveniently they may: Ye shall pray for Christ's Holy Catholic Church, that is, for the whole congregation of Christian people dispersed throughout the whole world, and especially for the Churches of England, Scotland, and Ireland: and herein I require you most especially to pray for the king's most excellent Majesty, our Sovereign Lord JAMES, King of England, Scotland, France, and Ireland, Defender of the Faith, and Supreme Governor in these his realms and all other his dominions and countries, over all persons, in all causes, as well ecclesiastical as temporal: Ye shall also pray for our gracious Queen ANNE, the noble Prince HENRY, and the rest of the King and Queen's royal issue: Ye shall also pray for the ministers of God's Holy Word and Sacraments, as well archbishops and bishops as other pastors and curates: Ye shall also pray for the King's most honourable Council, and for all the nobility and magistrates of this realm; that all and every of these, in their several callings, may serve truly and painfully to the glory of God and the edifying and well governing of his people, remembering the account that they must make: Also ye shall pray for the whole commons of this realm, that they may live in true faith and fear of God, in humble obedience to the King, and brotherly charity one to another. Finally, let us praise God for all those which are departed out of this life in the faith of Christ, and pray unto God that we may have grace to direct our lives after their good example; that, this life ended, we may be made partakers with them of the glorious resurrection in the Life Everlasting; always concluding with the Lord's Prayer.

LVI. *Preachers and Lecturers to read Divine Service and administer the Sacraments twice a Year at the least*

Every minister being possessed of a benefice that hath cure and charge of souls, although he chiefly attend to preaching, and hath a curate under him to execute the other duties which are to be performed for him in the church, and likewise every other stipendiary preacher that readeth any lecture, or catechizeth, or preacheth in any church or chapel, shall twice at the least every year read himself the Divine Service upon two several Sundays publicly, and at the usual times, both in the forenoon and after-noon, in the church which he so possesseth, or where he readeth, catechizeth, or preacheth, as is aforesaid; and shall likewise as often in every year administer the sacraments of Baptism (if there be any to be baptized) and of the Lord's Supper, in such manner and form, and with the observation of all such rites and ceremonies, as are prescribed by the Book of Common Prayer in that behalf; which if he do not accordingly perform, then shall he that is possessed of a benefice (as before) be suspended; and he that is but a reader, preacher, or catechizer, be removed from his place by the bishop of the diocese, until he or they shall submit themselves to perform all the said duties in such manner and sort as before is prescribed.

* * * * * *

LVIII. *Ministers reading Divine Service and administering the Sacraments to wear Surplices, and Graduates therewithal Hoods*

Every minister saying the public prayers, or ministering the Sacraments, or other rites of the Church, shall wear a decent and comely surplice with sleeves, to be provided at the charge of the parish. And if any question arise touching the matter, decency, or comeliness thereof, the same shall be decided by the discretion of the Ordinary. Furthermore, such ministers as are graduates shall wear upon their surplices at such times, such hoods as by the orders of the universities are agreeable to their degrees, which no minister shall wear (being no graduate) under pain of suspension. Notwithstanding, it shall be lawful for such ministers as are not graduates to wear upon their surplices, instead of hoods, some decent tippet of black, so it be not silk.

* * * * * *

LXXIII. *Ministers not to hold private Conventicles*

Forasmuch as all conventicles and secret meetings of priests and ministers have been ever justly accounted very hurtful to the state of the Church wherein they live; we do now ordain and constitute, That no priests, or ministers of the Word of God, or any other persons, shall meet together in any private house or elsewhere, to consult upon any matter or course to be taken by them, or upon their motion or direction by any other, which may any way tend to the impeaching or depraving of the doctrine of the Church of England, or of the Book of Common Prayer, or of any part of the government and discipline now established in the Church of England, under pain of excommunication *ipso facto*.

LXXIV. *Decency in Apparel enjoined to Ministers*

The true, ancient, and flourishing Churches of Christ, being ever desirous that their prelacy and clergy might be had as well in outward reverence as otherwise regarded for the worthiness of their ministry, did think it fit, by a prescript form of decent and comely apparel, to have them known to the people, and thereby to receive the honour and estimation due to the special messengers and ministers of Almighty God: we therefore following their grave judgment and the ancient custom of the Church of England, and hoping that in time newfangleness of apparel in some factious persons will die of itself, do constitute and appoint, That the archbishops and bishops shall not intermit to use the accustomed apparel of their degrees. Likewise all deans, masters of colleges, archdeacons, and prebendaries, in cathedral and collegiate churches (being priests or deacons), doctors in divinity, law, and physic, bachelors in divinity, masters of arts, and bachelors of law, having any ecclesiastical living, shall usually wear gowns with standing collars and sleeves strait at the hands, or wide sleeves as is used in the universities, with hoods or tippets of silk or sarcenet, and square caps. And that all other ministers admitted or to be admitted into that function shall also usually wear the like apparel as is aforesaid, except tippets only. We do further in like manner ordain, That all the said ecclesiastical persons above mentioned shall usually wear in their journeys cloaks with sleeves, commonly called priests' cloaks, without guards, welts[1], long buttons, or cuts. And no ecclesiastical person shall wear any coif or wrought nightcap, but only plain nightcaps of black silk, satin, or velvet. In all which particulars concerning the apparel here prescribed, our meaning is not to attribute any holiness or special worthiness to the said garments, but for decency, gravity, and order, as is before specified. In private houses, and in their studies, the said persons ecclesiastical may use any comely and scholarlike apparel, provided that it be not cut or pinkt[2]; and that in public they go not in their doublet and hose, without coats or cassocks; and also that they wear not any light-coloured stockings. Likewise poor beneficed men and curates (not being able to provide themselves long gowns) may go in short gowns of the fashion aforesaid.

LXXV. *Sober Conversation required in Ministers*

No ecclesiastical person shall at any time, other than for their honest necessities, resort to any taverns or alehouses, neither shall they board or lodge in any such places. Furthermore, they shall not give themselves to any base or servile labour, or to drinking or riot, spending their time idly by day or by night playing at dice, cards, or tables, or any other unlawful game: but at all times convenient they shall hear or read somewhat of the Holy Scriptures, or shall occupy themselves with some other honest study or exercise, always doing the things which shall appertain to honesty, and endeavouring to profit the Church of God; having always in

---

[1] *I.e.* without trimming or ornamentation.   [2] *I.e.* slashed or ornamented.

mind that they ought to excel all others in purity of life, and should be examples to the people to live well and christianly, under pain of ecclesiastical censures, to be inflicted with severity, according to the qualities of their offences.

*   *   *   *   *   *

CXXXIII. *Proctors not to be clamorous in Court*

Forasmuch as it is found by experience that the loud and confused cries and clamours of proctors in the courts of the archbishop are not only troublesome and offensive to the judges and advocates, but also give occasion to the standers-by of contempt and calumny toward the court itself; that more respect may be had to the dignity of the judge than heretofore, and that causes may more easily and commodiously be handled and despatched, we charge and enjoin, That all proctors in the said courts do especially intend[1] that the acts be faithfully entered and set down by the registrar, according to the advice and direction of the advocate; that the said proctors refrain loud speech and brabbling[2], and behave themselves quietly and modestly: and that, when either the judges or advocates, or any of them, shall happen to speak, they presently[3] be silent, upon pain of silencing for two whole terms then immediately following every such offence of theirs. And if any of them shall the second time offend herein, and after due monition shall not reform himself, let him be for ever removed from his practice.

*   *   *   *   *   *

WE of our princely inclination and royal care for the maintenance of the present estate and government of the Church of England, by the laws of this our realm now settled and established, having diligently, with great contentment and comfort, read and considered of all these their said Canons, Orders, Ordinances, and Constitutions, agreed upon as is before expressed; and finding the same such as we are persuaded will be very profitable, not only to our clergy but to the whole Church of this our kingdom and to all the true members of it (if they be well observed), have therefore for us, our heirs, and lawful successors, of our especial grace, certain knowledge, and mere motion, given, and by these presents do give our royal assent, according to the form of the said Statute or Act of Parliament aforesaid, to all and every of the said Canons, Orders, Ordinances, and Constitutions, and to all and every thing in them contained, as they are before written.

And furthermore, we do not only by our said prerogative

---

[1] Endeavour.   [2] Brawling or squabbling.   [3] Immediately.

royal, and supreme authority in causes ecclesiastical, ratify, confirm, and establish, by these our letters patents, the said Canons, Orders, Ordinances, and Constitutions, and all and every thing in them contained, as is aforesaid; but do likewise propound, publish, and straightway enjoin and command by our said authority, and by these our letters patents, the same to be diligently observed, executed, and equally kept by all our loving subjects of this our kingdom, both within the province of Canterbury and York, in all points wherein they do or may concern every or any of them, according to this our will and pleasure hereby signified and expressed; and that likewise, for the better observation of them, every minister, by what name or title soever he be called, shall in the parish church or chapel where he hath charge, read all the said Canons, Orders, Ordinances, and Constitutions once every year, upon some Sundays or holy-days, in the afternoon, before Divine Service, dividing the same in such sort as that the one half may be read one day and the other another day: the book of the said Canons to be provided at the charge of the parish betwixt this and the Feast of the Nativity of our Lord God next ensuing: straitly charging and commanding all archbishops, bishops, and all other that exercise any ecclesiastical jurisdiction within this realm, every man in his place, to see and procure (so much as in them lieth) all and every of the same Canons, Orders, Ordinances, and Constitutions to be in all points duly observed; not sparing to execute the penalties in them severally mentioned upon any that shall wittingly or wilfully break or neglect to observe the same, as they tender the honour of God, the peace of the Church, the tranquillity of the kingdom, and their duties and service to us their King and Sovereign.

In witness, &c.

Cardwell, *Synodalia*, i, 248–329.

§ 3. PARLIAMENT AND IMPOSITIONS

The imposition was an additional custom levied at the ports on certain goods,—not primarily to raise a revenue but in order to regulate trade. The history of the ordinary custom may be regarded as a series of bargains between the Crown and Parliament, by which the Crown relinquished its power to tax at will one commodity after another, and undertook to tax them only at a fixed and known rate. The first arrangement was that of 1275, when Edward I agreed to levy only the *Antiqua Custuma* upon the staple commodities of wool, woolfells, and leather, and also upon lead and tin; and by degrees all commodities were brought under the fixed bargain, until the Stuart customs of tonnage and poundage, levied at a fixed rate, covered the whole ground as far as native trade was concerned. But one right the King had never relinquished—the right to close the gates of the sea to stranger merchants. With them he had made no bargain, and he could admit them to trade on such terms as he might see fit. This immemorial prerogative of taxing aliens had for a long time been very widely interpreted as allowing the Crown an unlimited discretion to tax for the regulation of trade in such a way as to protect native trade against foreign merchants. In 1535 Henry VIII had fortified himself with a statute[1] which left the regulation of trade entirely in the King's hands; and although the statute was limited to his life, both Mary and Elizabeth carried on the same policy after his death, and laid impositions upon merchandise by proclamation in order to protect English trade[2]. Thus James and Cecil had no reason to doubt that they possessed the legal power to levy impositions: the innovation lay in this—that they now proceeded to increase impositions above what the necessities of a protective policy required, expressly in order to increase the revenue of the Crown.

Moreover, the decision in Bate's case [p. 338] in 1606 had provided a firm legal foundation for Cecil's new policy. 'No exportation or importation,' said Chief Baron Fleming in the judgment given in the Court of Exchequer, 'can be but at the King's ports. They are the gates of the King, and he hath absolute power by them to include or exclude whom he shall please.' Thus in 1608 a revised Book of Rates was issued, by which the rates were slightly and cautiously increased so as to bring in a revenue of about £70,000 more than heretofore. But not content with getting the money, James could not resist the temptation to philosophise about the authority by which he obtained it. 'This special power and prerogative,' he said, in the commission of 28 July, 1608[3] which authorised the levying of impositions, 'hath both by men of understanding in all ages, and by the laws of all nations, been yielded and acknowledged to be proper and inherent in the persons of princes, that they may, according to their several occasions, raise to themselves...fit and competent means by levying of customs and impositions.'

The discontent of the merchants and the language used by the King brought the new policy under the consideration of Parliament, which was called to the session of 1610 mainly in order to deal with the King's necessities, now represented, in spite of the increase in impositions, by a deficit of about £300,000[4]. The Commons were not disposed to accept the decision in Bate's case, but as the revenue from impositions was not part of the King's parliamentary revenue, James had a case when on 11 May he sent a message through the Speaker 'to command the House not to dispute of the King's power and prerogative in imposing upon merchandises exported or imported.' Against this prohibition the Commons pleaded their ancient privilege of freedom of speech, which was now beginning to take a new shape. In a petition of May 23 [p. 245] they claimed it as 'an ancient, general, and undoubted right of Parliament to debate freely all matters which do properly concern the subject and his right or state; which freedom of debate being once foreclosed, the essence of the liberty of Parliament is withal dissolved.'

---

[1] 26 Henr. VIII, c. 10.

[2] In a recent article Professor F. C. Dietz has called attention to Elizabeth's imposition of 19 September 1673 on sweet wines from Spain and the Levant, which 'apparently escaped the precedent hunters of the early seventeenth century' ('Elizabethan Customs Administration' in E.H.R. xlv, 44).

[3] Printed in Prothero, p. 353.   [4] Gardiner, ii, 65.

The King did not persist, and a great debate on impositions took place which marks a stage in the progress of constitutional ideas. Hakewill's speech [p. 247] comes very near to being an anticipation of the modern doctrine of supply. Indefinite taxes, like indefinite penalties, are alien to the whole spirit of the law of England. There are only two ways in which impositions can be legally levied: either under statute law or under common law. A survey of the King's functions shews that from these two sources is drawn a revenue certain in amount, and sufficient to meet all necessary expenses of government. Each liability is met by a corresponding source of revenue, and the object of this is, to secure certainty for the subject as to the amount of his burdens. If the moneys thus provided are insufficient, let the King come to Parliament for more. This neat and logical account of the sources of the royal revenue left no room for supreme sovereignty or absolute power; and if Hakewill thus eliminated it by implication, Whitelocke, in a scarcely less important speech [p. 259], openly attacked it. The supreme and ultimate power in the State, he says in effect, rests not in the King alone but in Parliament. 'It will not be denied that the power of imposing hath so great a trust in it...that it hath ever been ranked among those rights of sovereign power. Then is there no further question to be made but to examine where the sovereign power is in this kingdom, for there is the right of imposition. The sovereign power is agreed to be in the King; but in the King is a twofold power—the one in Parliament, as he is assisted with the consent of the whole State; the other out of Parliament, as he is sole and singular, guided merely by his own will. And if of these two powers in the King, one is greater than the other and can direct and control the other, that is *suprema potestas*, the sovereign power, and the other is *subordinata*. It will then be easily proved that the power of the King in Parliament is greater than his power out of Parliament, and doth rule and control it.' Such arguments as these are remote from the facts and ideas of the Tudor past, but they shew how the future was beginning to shape.

The outcome of the debate of 1610 was an arrangement with the King. James undertook to remit the most burdensome of the impositions, and the Commons agreed to grant him the remainder on condition that it should be declared illegal by statute to levy impositions in the future without consent of Parliament; but before the bargain was completed fresh disputes arose over other matters, and on 9 February, 1611, James dissolved his first Parliament, after it had sat, although with long intervals between the sessions, for nearly seven years.

The opinions of Coke and Raleigh on impositions are indicated by the extracts printed below [p. 264].

(1) Petition of Right of 1610

This Petition, dated 23 May, 1610, was drawn up in answer to the King's Speech of 21 May in defence of his right to levy impositions.

To the King's most Excellent Majesty

Most gracious Sovereign, Whereas your Majesty's most humble subjects the Commons assembled in Parliament have received, first by message and since by speech from your Majesty, a commandment of restraint from debating in Parliament your Majesty's right of imposing upon your subjects' goods exported or imported out of or into this realm, yet allowing us to examine the grievance of those impositions in regard of quantity, time, and other circumstances of disproportion thereto incident; we your said humble subjects, nothing doubting but that your Majesty had no intent by that commandment to infringe the ancient and fundamental right of the liberty of the Parliament in point of exact discussing of all matters concerning them and their possessions, goods, and rights whatsoever (which yet we cannot but conceive to be done in effect by this commandment), do with all humble duty make this remonstrance to your Majesty.

First, we hold it an ancient, general, and undoubted right of Parliament to debate freely all matters which do properly concern the subject and his right or state; which freedom of debate being once foreclosed, the essence of the liberty of Parliament is withal dissolved.

And whereas in this case the subjects' right on the one side and your Majesty's prerogative on the other cannot possibly be severed in debate of either, we allege that your Majesty's prerogatives of that kind concerning directly the subject's right and interest are daily handled and discussed in all Courts at Westminster, and have been ever freely debated upon all fit occasions, both in this and all former Parliaments, without restraint: Which being forbidden, it is impossible for the subject either to know or to maintain his right and property to his own lands and goods, though never so just and manifest.

It may farther please your most excellent Majesty to understand that we have no mind to impugn, but a desire to inform ourselves of, your Highness's prerogative in that point, which, if ever, is now most necessary to be known; and though it were to no other purpose, yet to satisfy the generality of your Majesty's subjects, who finding themselves much grieved by these new impositions do languish in much sorrow and discomfort.

These reasons, dread Sovereign, being the proper reasons of Parliament, do plead for the upholding of this our ancient right and liberty. Howbeit, seeing it hath pleased your Majesty to insist upon that judgment in the Exchequer as being direction sufficient for us without farther examination, upon great desire of leaving your Majesty unsatisfied in no one point of our intents and proceedings, we profess touching that judgment that we neither do nor will take upon us to reverse it; but our desire is, to know the reasons whereupon the same was grounded, and the rather for that a general conceit is had that the reasons of that judgment may be extended much farther, even to the utter ruin of the ancient liberty of this kingdom and of your subjects' right of propriety of their lands and goods.

Then for the judgment itself, being the first and last that ever was given in that kind, for aught appearing unto us, and being only in one case and against one man, it can bind in law no other but that person, and is also reversible by writ of error granted heretofore by Act of Parliament, and neither he nor any other subject is debarred by it from trying his right in the same or like case in any of your Majesty's Courts of Record at Westminster.

Lastly, we nothing doubt but our intended proceeding in a full examination of the right, nature, and measure of these new impositions (if this restraint had not come between) should have been so orderly and moderately carried, and so applied to the manifold necessity of these times, and given your Majesty so true a view of the state and right of your subjects, that it would have been much to your Majesty's content and satisfaction (which we most desire), and removed all cause of fears and jealousies from the loyal hearts of your subjects, which is (as it ought to be) our careful endeavour; whereas, contrariwise, in that other way directed by your Majesty we cannot safely proceed without concluding[1] for ever the right of the subject, which without due examination thereof we may not do.

We therefore, your Highness's loyal and dutiful Commons, not swerving from the approved steps of our ancestors, most humbly and instantly beseech your gracious Majesty that without offence to the same we may, according to the undoubted right and liberty of Parliament, proceed in our intended course of a full examination of these new impositions; that so we may cheerfully pass on to your Majesty's business, from which this stop hath by diversion so long withheld us. And we your Majesty's most humble, faithful, and loyal subjects shall ever (according to our bounden duty) pray for your Majesty's long and happy reign over us.

Commons' Journals, i, 431–2.

(2) The Debate on Impositions, 1610

This debate began on 23 June, 1610, and was spread over four days, ending on 3 July.

Mr Hakewill's Argument

Mr Speaker, The question now in debate amongst us is, whether his Majesty may by his prerogative royal, without assent of Parliament, at his own will and pleasure, lay a new charge or

---

[1] *I.e.* putting an end to,—and so extinguishing.

imposition upon merchandises to be brought into or out of this kingdom of England, and enforce merchants to pay the same?

I must confess that when this point was first stirred amongst us...I was very sorry.....For, Sir, when the case of Bates... was argued in the Exchequer...I was then present at all the arguments both at the bar and at the bench; and I do confess that by the weighty and unanswerable reasons, as I then conceived them, of those grave and reverend Judges sitting in their seat of justice I was much persuaded.....But though I were then, and when the question was first moved in this House, very confident, yet, as you shall perceive anon, I was not very constant in that opinion; for being, amongst others, employed by this House to make search in the Exchequer for records which by the practice of former ages might guide our judgments in this weighty point, and having diligently collected the arguments made in the Exchequer, and not only so, but compared my own collections with reports thereof made by divers other of my friends, and finding that some of the records urged in those arguments were untruly vouched and many misapplied, I then began to stagger in my opinion, and presently fell to examine the weight of the reasons which had been alleged, which in my poor censure I found not of strength sufficient, without the full concurrence of clear precedents of former times, to maintain the judgment given or my opinion grounded thereupon. And therefore, Sir, in love to the truth I did forsake my former opinion as erroneous and do now embrace the contrary, that is, That his Majesty hath no right to impose; and so am now become a convert. Those reasons that moved me thus to change, and the weakness which I discovered in the reasons alleged against the opinion which I now hold, I will with your patience open unto you, and will therein follow the commandment of Christ to Peter,—being converted, seek to convert my brethren....

That I may the better convey myself through my argument and be the better conceived of you that are to hear me, I will divide that which I have to say into certain parts, which I will prosecute in order.

First, I hold it necessary to consider whether custom were due to the King by the Common Law.

Secondly, admitting it to be due by the Common Law, whether it were a sum certain, not to be increased at the King's pleasure or otherwise.

Thirdly, supposing that by the Common Law the King might, by way of imposition, have increased his custom at his own will by his absolute power without assent in Parliament, whether or no he be not bound to the contrary by Acts of Parliament....

Lastly, I will discover unto you the weakness of such reasons as have been made in maintenance of the King's right to impose....

That custom is due by the Common Law I collect first by the name thereof, for though at this day it be...called in our law Latin *custuma*, yet in ancient time it had no other name here amongst us...than *consuetudo*,...which implies an approved continuance without a known beginning.... To this may be added that Magna Charta...termeth this not only *consuetudo*, which as I have said implies antiquity beyond all remembrance of a beginning, but *antiqua consuetudo*, not only custom but old and ancient custom.....But that which most of all moveth me to believe that this duty was and is due by the Common Law is this, that in all cases where the Common Law putteth the King to sustain charge for the protection of the subject, it always yieldeth him out of the thing protected some gain towards the maintenance of the charge: as for the protection of wards, lunatics, and idiots, the profits of their lands; for the maintenance of the courts of justice it giveth him fines.....This observation, which might be further proved by divers other instances in things of other nature, maketh me to think that because the Common Law expecteth that the King should protect merchants in their trades by maintaining, repairing, and fortifying the havens at home; by clearing the sea of pirates and enemies in their passage; and by maintaining ambassadors abroad to treat with foreign princes upon all such occasions; that it also giveth him out of merchandises exported and imported some profit for the sustentation of this public charge. Otherwise were the law very unreasonable and unjust....

...I will therefore proceed to my second consideration.... That this duty given by the Common Law...unto the King was and is a duty certain, not to be enhanced by the King at his own pleasure without assent in Parliament, I hope I shall be able clearly to prove unto you.....And first, I lay this as a ground which will not be denied me by any man, that the Common Law of England, as also all other wise laws in the world, delight in certainty and abandon incertainty, as the mother of all debate and confusion, than which nothing is more odious in law.....And if in any case between the King and his subject more than other this certainty be required, most of all it is requisite in cases where the Common Law giveth the King a perpetual profit or revenue to be raised out of the interest and property of his poor subject's

estate, either in lands or goods. If in all other things the law, as
I have said, and wherein I suppose you have yielded to me, do
require certainty and limitation, and only in this case where it is
most requisite it hath omitted and neglected it, we must conclude
the law to be most unreasonable, improvident, and contrary to
itself; which is to say, were to conclude it to be no law. Out of these
grounds I may then in my opinion safely and with some confidence
deduce and maintain this position: That the Common Law of
England giveth to the King...no perpetual revenue or matter
of profit out of the interest or property of the subject but it either
limiteth a certainty therein at the first, or otherwise hath so provided that if it be uncertain in itself it is reduceable to a certainty
only by a legal course, that is to say, either by Parliament, by judges,
or jury; and not by the King's own absolute will and pleasure.....
You see in general how the law, by requiring certainty in matter
of profit between the King and the subject, preventeth many
mischiefs which would fall out if the law were otherwise; and
therefore, without more saying, I might here conclude that custom,
being due by the Common Law, was and is a sum certain, not to
be increased at the King's pleasure by way of imposition. But
because there are many other revenues due to the King by the Common Law as well as custom, if they all, or as many as we can call
to mind, shall fall out to be, as I have said, sums certain, and not
subject to be increased at the King's will, this will be a forcible
argument that custom is likewise certain, and not to be enhanced
at the King's pleasure.... The Common Law giveth the King a
fine for the purchase of an original writ. Is it certain? It is, and
ever hath been. If the debt or damages demanded amount to above
40*l*., the fine is and ever hath been 6*s*. 8*d*. and no more; if to 100*l*.,
then 10*s*. and no more. May the King increase this fine at his
pleasure? There is no man that will say he may. There is a fine due
by the Common Law *pro licentia concordandi*. Is it not certainly
known, and so hath always been, to be the tenth part of the land
comprised in the writ of covenant?...And can the King demand
any more of the subject?.... Nay, there is one duty well known to us
all which the Common Law giveth to the King, and is in his
nature a custom (our very case), in which the King is bound to a
certainty which he cannot exceed; and that is *prisage*, a duty given
by the Common Law to the King upon every shiploading of wine
brought into the kingdom by English merchants, and is one tun
of wine before the mast and another behind. I am unwilling to
trouble you with any more particulars of this kind. But let any
man shew me one particular to the contrary, and I will then yield

that my position, being false in one, may be in more; but till my position hath been in this point infringed, this general concordance of the law in all these particulars is argument enough for me, without having alleged other reasons, to conclude that custom being, as all these are, a revenue due to the King by the Common Law arising out of the property and interest of the subject, is, as all these are, limited and bounded by the Common Law to a certainty, which the King hath not power to increase....

*　　*　　*　　*　　*　　*

...And so leaving the judgment of the whole to your wisdoms who can best discern whether the argument be of weight, I proceed to my second reason, which is drawn from the policy and frame of this commonwealth and the providence of the Common Law; the which, as it requires at the subjects' hands loyalty and obedience to their Sovereign, so doth it likewise require at the hands of the Sovereign protection and defence of the subject against all wrongs and injuries whatsoever offered, either by one subject to another or by the common enemy to them all or any of them. This protection the law considereth cannot be without a great charge to the King; and because, as Christ saith, 'no man goeth to war upon his own charge,'[1] the Common Law therefore hath not only given the King great prerogatives and favours touching his own patrimony, more (I believe) than any other prince in the world hath, but also hath, for the sustentation of his great and necessary expenses in the protection of his subjects, given him out of the interest and property of the subject an ample and very honourable revenue in very many particular cases, some of which I will call to your remembrance. He receiveth out of the subject's purse for wardships and the dependences thereupon, as we have of late accounted, about 45,000*l.* by the year. This is a revenue which no other king of the world hath; and as it appears by the Statute of 14 E. 3. c. 1., 'It ought to be employed in maintenance of the wars.' And so doubtless was the first institution of the Common Law, for the lord hath the profit of the ward's lands to no other end than to maintain a man in the war during the infancy of him who otherwise should serve in person. He hath likewise all forfeitures upon treason and outlawry, and upon penal laws, fines and amerciaments, profits of courts, treasure

---

[1] Perhaps a confused recollection of Luke xiv, 31: 'Or what king, going to make war against another king, sitteth not down first, and consulteth whether he be able with ten thousand to meet him that cometh against him with twenty thousand?' The speaker seems to have read into this the previous verse about counting the cost of building a tower, and then to have misrepresented the result.

trove, prisage, butlerage, wreck, and so many more as the very enumeration of the particulars would take up long time. To what other end hath the Common Law thus provided for the maintenance of the King's charge by all these ways and means of raising profit out of the interest and property of the subject's estate in lands and goods but only to this end, that after these duties paid, the poor subject might hold and enjoy the rest of his estate to his own use, free and clear from all other burdens whatsoever? To what end hath the law given a part to the King and left the rest to the subject, if that which is left be also at the King's will, to make his profit thereof as he pleaseth? To give a small portion to him that may at his pleasure take more or all, is a vain and an idle act which shall never be imputed to a wise law. But it may be objected that as the revenues are ordinary, so are they by the law provided only for the sustaining of the King's ordinary charge; and that if the law have not taken further consideration, and limited some certain course how upon sudden and extraordinary occasions the King's charge may be sustained, there is yet no reason shewed to the contrary why the King may not upon such occasion take some extraordinary course for the raising of money, as by the laying of impositions upon merchandises, or by a tax within the realm, rather than the commonwealth for want thereof should perish or be endangered.

And hereupon by the knight that last spake[1] it was held that upon occasion of a sudden and unexpected war the King may not only lay impositions but levy a tax within the realm without assent of Parliament; which position in my opinion is very dangerous, for to admit this were by consequence to bring us into bondage. You say that upon occasion of sudden war the King may levy a tax. Who shall be judge between the King and his people of the occasion? Can it be tried by any legal course in our law? It cannot. If then the King himself must be the sole judge in this case, will it not follow that the King may levy a tax at his own pleasure, seeing his pleasure cannot be bounded by law? You see into what a mischief the admittance of one error hath drawn you. But for a full answer to the objection, I say that the providence of the Common Law is such and so excellent as that for the defraying of the King's charge upon any occasions of a sudden war it hath, over and above all the ordinary revenues which it giveth the King, which in the time of war cannot indeed but fall short, made an excellent provision; for, Sir, the war must needs be either offensive or defensive. Offensive must either be

---

[1] Sir Robert Hitcham.

upon some nation beyond the seas, or against the Scots or Welsh or other borderers within the island. If it be an offensive war upon some nation beyond the seas, it cannot be a sudden accident; for it is the King's own act, and he may, and it is fitting he should, take deliberation; and if it be a just and necessary war, he may crave and easily obtain assistance of his subjects by grant of aid in Parliament. If an offensive war upon some of his neighbours within the continent of this island, as the Scots or the Welsh, which also cannot be sudden or unexpected to the King, being his own act, you know how politicly the Kings of this realm have provided by reserving tenures by which many of their subjects are bound to serve them in those wars in person at their own charge. Only a defensive war, by invasion of foreign enemies, may be sudden; in which case the law hath not left the King to war upon his own expense or to rely upon his ordinary revenue, but hath notably provided that every subject within the land, high and low, whether he hold of the King or not, in case of foreign invasion may be compelled at his own charge to serve the King in person.... The reason of which in my opinion was to no other end than that the King might have no pretence whatsoever for the raising of money upon his subjects at his own pleasure without their common assent in Parliament. I do then conclude this argument, that seeing the Common Law for maintenance of the King's ordinary charge hath given him such an ample revenue out of the interest and property of the subject, and provided also for sudden occasions, in so doing it hath secluded and secured the rest of the subject's estate from the King's power and pleasure; and consequently that the King hath not power upon any occasion at his pleasure to charge the estate of his subjects by all impositions, tallages, or taxes, for I hold them in one degree, or any other burden whatsoever, without the subject's free and voluntary assent, and that in Parliament. If it were otherwise, you see how it were to the utter dissolution and destruction of that politic frame and constitution of this commonwealth which I have opened unto you, and of that excellent wise providence of the Common Law for the preserving of property and the avoidance of oppression. These two arguments used by me, that of certainty and this of the provision made by the Common Law, are in my poor opinion arguments of direct proof that the King cannot impose. I will now...urge an argument or two of inference and presumption.... They are drawn either from the actions or forbearances of the Kings of this realm, or from the actions and forbearances of the people.

First, in the actions and forbearances of the Kings I observe that all the Kings of this realm since Hen. 3 have sought and obtained an increase of custom, more or less, by the name of subsidy, of the gift of their subjects in Parliament.... Is it likely that if any or all of these Kings had thought they had had in them any lawful power by just prerogative to have laid impositions at their pleasure, they would not rather have made use of that than have taken this course by Act of Parliament, so full of delay, so prejudicial to their right, so subject to the pleasure of their people, who never undergo burdens but with murmuring and much unwillingness? Can there be anything more hateful to the high spirit of a King than to subject himself to the pleasure of his people, especially for matter of relief, and that by way of prayer, having lawful power in his hands to relieve himself without being beholding to them?

If perhaps the Kings themselves were ignorant of this great prerogative, which cannot be imagined, had they not always about them wise counsellors to assist them, and such as for the procuring of favour to themselves would not have failed to put them in mind of it? Nay, if they had known any such lawful prerogative, had they not been bound in conscience so to have done?

*   *   *   *   *   *

From the end of the reign of E. 3 till the reign of Queen Mary, ...being the space of 170 years or thereabouts, it hath been confessed by all those that have argued in maintenance of his Majesty's right to impose, that there hath not been found one record that proves any one imposition to have been laid. There are indeed in our printed books some three or four statutes during that time in which mention is made of impositions, but they are, as I shall prove, impositions of another nature than those are which we complain of, and so make nothing at all to the proof of his Majesty's right; or if they were such as ours are, yet are they nowhere found mentioned but with disgrace and to the end to be taken away; which may be the reason that, notwithstanding the great use that might have been made of three or four precedents of impositions in these times for the patching up of a continuance of the practice, which otherwise by this long continuance receives a great blemish, those which argued for impositions did not take hold of these, but chose rather to confess that no impositions at all were laid during all this time, and laboured to seek out the reasons of the discontinuance.

*   *   *   *   *

The King may, say they, restrain the passage of merchants at his pleasure.... Upon which they infer that if he may restrain a merchant that he shall not pass at all, he may much more so restrain him that he shall not pass except he pay a certain sum of money; for this, say they, is less than totally to restrain him, and *cui licet quod majus licet etiam quod minus*.... In answer of which I will consider how far the King may restrain the passage of merchants, and then will examine the consequence of the argument.

For my part, I think the King cannot restrain the passage of merchants but for some special cause; wherein to define certainly and resolutely, to say for what causes he may and for what not, I will not undertake. Only let me inform you that there is not one of these precedents vouched by them to prove the King's power to restrain but they are upon special reasons: as by reason of enmity with such a nation from whence they are restrained, or because such a commodity may not be spared within the kingdom. Besides, they are not restraints from all places and of all manner of merchandises, but from certain places only and for certain sorts of merchandises. And for my part, I think that restraints in all these cases, and of like nature, are by the Common Law left to the King's absolute power; for if it were otherwise, it should be in the power of a merchant for a little private lucre to enrich the King's enemies, or to furnish them with munition to be employed against the State, or utterly to ruin the commonwealth, by carrying out a commodity which may not be spared or by bringing in of some that may be hurtful. Nay, which is more, such may be the occasion that the King may, I doubt not, stop the passages of all merchants from all places for a short time, as upon the death of the late Queen it was put in practice to prevent intelligence. There may likewise be such necessary use of their ships, as the want of them upon some sudden attempts may be a cause of the overthrow of the whole State. In such cases as these, if the Common Law did not give the King leave to restrain their passage by his absolute power, it were very improvident in the highest points, which cannot be imagined of so wise a law.... But is the consequence good that because the King may restrain therefore he may impose upon such as pass?... But admitting that the very laying of an imposition did imply a restraint, yet I deny the consequence, because the King may restrain totally, that therefore he may restrain for a time, or from certain places, or certain commodities, or certain merchants; this indeed is a good argument *a majori ad minus*. But because he may restrain totally, therefore that he may give passage for money, is no good consequence; for in our case there is no restraint at all, but it is rather a passage for money. If there be just occasion of restraint, the law giveth the King power to restrain. But when merchants may without hurt to the State have passage, as in our case, to enforce them to pay for that passage is in my opinion as unlawful as to enforce any man whatsoever to pay for doing that which he may lawfully do. Merchants have, as I may so say, as good inheritance in their trade as any man in his lands; and when it may stand with the good of the State that they may pass, they ought to pass as freely, without charge imposed on them, as any man ought to hold his inheritance, or any artificer or other tradesman ought to exercise their lawful trades and means of living free from burdens to be laid on by the King's absolute power. If all others should be free, and only merchants, who adventure their persons and estates in so many dangers, to bring us from far places such things as without which we cannot subsist and to return us profit for our superfluities, should be subject to involuntary burdens, their estate were of all other men's most unhappy and slavish which, of all other trades, is indeed the noblest and most worthy to be cherished.

* * * * * *

I little doubt but the King upon some occasion may lawfully restrain the passage of all men through the gates of London; as for the purpose, when the city shall be besieged, or in the time of an extreme plague. Nay, is it not by authority derived only from him that the gates are shut every night? Doth it follow therefore that because he may do it upon some extraordinary occasion or at some time, that he may shut up the passage for ever; or that pre-supposing such a restraint by his absolute power, he may lay an imposition upon every burden of anything brought in or carried out, as the Duke of Florence and many other States in Italy and Germany do, or upon every man by the poll that shall pass through the gates?

You see the weakness and danger of the consequence of this argument, and how it tends to justify impositions within the land. And so I leave it, and proceed to the next.

'The ports and haven towns of England are,' say they, 'the King's, and in regard thereof he may open and shut them upon what conditions he pleaseth.' I answer, 1. That the position that all the ports are the King's is not generally true; for subjects may also be owners of ports.... But admitting the truth of the position, yet is the consequence as weak and dangerous as of any of the rest of their arguments. For are not all the gates of cities and towns, and all the streets and highways in England the King's, and as much subject to be open and shut at his pleasure as the ports are? Nay, whensoever we speak of the highway in any law business we call it *via regia*, the King's highway; and the King in his commissions, speaking of London or any other city, calls it *civitas nostra*....Doth it follow therefore that the King may lay impositions upon every man or upon all commodities that shall pass through any of these places? Nay, the gates of the King's own house, for the purpose his palace of Westminster, are his in a far nearer degree than any of these. May he therefore by his proclamation impose upon every man that shall pass in or out at Westminster Hall door a sum of money? Doubtless he may not; because the King is a person public, and his subjects ought to have access to him as to the fountain of justice, and to the courts of justice sitting by his authority. I make little doubt but his Majesty may upon just occasion cause any of these passages to be shut, as he may also the passage at the havens. But when the passage may without danger to the State be open and that the subjects may pass, his Majesty may not then exact money for their passage; for the law hath given the King power over these things for the good of the commonwealth, and not thereby to charge and burden the subject. If the King may not exact money for passage in and out of his Court gates because of the publicness of his person, nor for passage through the gates of cities, much less may he for passage out at the ports, which are the great gates of the kingdom, and which the subject ought as freely to enjoy as the air or the water.

Another of their arguments is this. 'The King is bound to protect merchants from spoil by the enemy; he ought to fortify the havens, that their ships may there abide in safety; he ought, if occasion be, to send ambassadors to foreign princes to negotiate for them;' and many the like charges is the King by the law to undergo for the protection of his merchants. It is reason therefore that his expense be defrayed out of the profit made by merchants, and consequently that he may impose upon merchandise a moderate charge thereby to repay himself. The consequence of this argument is thus far true. The law expects that the King should protect merchants. Therefore it alloweth him out of merchandise a revenue for the maintenance of his charge, which is the old custom due, as at first I said, by the Common Law. But it is no good consequence that therefore he may take what he list, no more than he may at his pleasure increase that old revenue which the law giveth him for protecting of subjects in their suits or for protecting wards, etc.

Another argument of theirs is this. 'All other princes of the world may impose upon merchandise at their pleasure, and so may make our merchandises less vendible with them, by laying an imposition upon them to be paid by us when they are brought into their territories, whereby their own commodities of the same nature may be sold more to the gain of their merchants, and our merchant impoverished or driven from his trade. They may also lay impositions upon our merchants fetching commodities from thence, and leave their own merchants free from any imposition in the same case; by which their merchants shall reap all the profit by that commodity in affording it better cheap to us here than we can fetch it, and consequently our merchants shall be undone.' Many the like cases have been put to prove that if the King of England may not impose as other princes may, they shall be able at their pleasure to destroy our trading..., and yet we hear not of any imposition laid by any of our Kings by their absolute power; which may give any man assurance that they took some other course to meet with the inconvenience, and indeed the means are divers which these our Kings used to prevent it. First, they were careful in all their leagues and treaties with foreign princes especially to provide for it; as may appear by the records of the ancient leagues....And yet for further security our Kings have always had ambassadors resident in the courts of such foreign princes, to put them in mind of their leagues if upon any occasion our merchants have in that case happened to be never so little wronged by them; and if upon complaint of the ambassador our merchants have not found redress, our Kings have held the league as broken, and denounced war or seized all the goods of the same prince's subjects within England; and I dare say there have been more wars undertaken by our princes against foreign nations only for this cause than for any one other cause whatsoever.

Besides, our Kings have in this case sometimes made use of that their prerogative of restraint, either by prohibiting our merchants from carrying our commodities into those parts where they are charged with impositions, that so by the want of our commodities foreign princes might be enforced to abate their impositions laid upon them, or by restraining the merchants of foreign princes to import or export commodities from hence; by which means foreign princes have been compelled to deal favourably with our merchants for the good of their own subjects.

All these are lawful and ordinary means to prevent or redress the inconvenience which may grow by the impositions of other princes. If all these ordinary means should happen to fail, which can hardly so fall out, and that the laying of impositions be indeed the only means that is left to redress the inconvenience, why should not that be done by Act of Parliament...?

These are the chief reasons made in maintenance of impositions. The weakness of them and their dangerous consequence you cannot but perceive; for by the same reasons taxes within the land may be as well proved to be lawful. On the contrary part, you have heard the reasons against impositions fortified by many records and statutes in the point. So as I conclude that impositions, neither in the time of war or other the greatest necessity or occasion that may be, much less in the time of peace, neither upon foreign nor inland commodities of whatsoever nature, be they never so superfluous or unnecessary, neither upon merchants strangers nor denizens, may be laid by the King's absolute power without assent of Parliament, be it for never so short a time, much less to endure for ever, as ours. Though this be now my opinion, yet am not I so obstinate therein but if yet I hear better reason I will once again change my mind. In the mean while you see I had reason to alter my first opinion, as being grounded upon very weak reasons as now they appear unto me; and so I suppose they do also unto you.

State Trials, ii, 407–76.

Mr Whitelocke's Argument[1]

*   *   *   *   *   *

The occasion of this question was given by the Book of Rates lately set out,...in which book, besides the rates, is set down every kind of merchandise, exported and imported, for the true answering of subsidy to the King according to the Statute of Tonnage and Poundage....

The case in terms is this. The King, by his letters patents before recited, hath ordained, willed, and commanded that these new impositions contained in that Book of Rates shall be for ever hereafter paid unto him his heirs and successors upon pain of his displeasure. Hereupon the question ariseth, whether by this edict and ordinance so made by the King himself by his letters patents of his own power and will absolute, without assent of Parliament, he be so lawfully intituled to that he doth impose as

---

[1] In the *State Trials* this speech is assigned in error to Yelverton.

that thereby he doth alter the property of his subjects' goods and is enabled to recover these impositions by course of law.

I think he cannot, and I ground my opinion upon these four reasons. 1. It is against the natural frame and constitution of the policy of this kingdom, which is *jus publicum regni*, and so subverteth the fundamental law of the realm and induceth a new form of State and government. 2. It is against the municipal law of the land, which is *jus privatum*, the law of property and of private right. 3. It is against divers statutes made to restrain our King in this point. 4. It is against the practice and action of our commonwealth, *contra morem majorem*, and this is the modestest rule to limit both King's prerogatives and subjects' liberties....

For the first, it will be admitted for a rule and ground of State that in every commonwealth and government there be some rights of sovereignty, *jura majestatis*, which regularly and of common right do belong to the sovereign power of that State, unless custom or the provisional ordinance of that State do otherwise dispose of them; which sovereign power is *potestas suprema*, a power that can control all other powers and cannot be controlled but by itself. It will not be denied that the power of imposing hath so great a trust in it, by reason of the mischiefs may grow to the commonwealth by the abuses of it, that it hath ever been ranked among those rights of sovereign power. Then is there no further question to be made but to examine where the sovereign power is in this kingdom, for there is the right of imposition. The sovereign power is agreed to be in the King: but in the King is a twofold power,—the one in Parliament, as he is assisted with the consent of the whole State; the other out of Parliament, as he is sole and singular, guided merely by his own will. And if of these two powers in the King, one is greater than the other and can direct and control the other, that is *suprema potestas*, the sovereign power, and the other is *subordinata*. It will then be easily proved that the power of the King in Parliament is greater than his power out of Parliament, and doth rule and control it....If a judgment be given in the King's Bench by the King himself, as may be and by the law is intended, a writ of error to reverse this judgment may be sued before the King in Parliament....So you see the appeal is from the King out of the Parliament to the King in Parliament; the writ is in his name; the rectifying and correcting the errors is by him, but with the assent of the Lords and Commons, than which there can be no stronger evidence to prove that his power out of

Parliament is subordinate to his power in Parliament; for in Acts of Parliament, be they laws, grounds, or whatsoever else, the act and power is the King's, but with the assent of the Lords and Commons, which maketh it the most sovereign and supreme power above all and controllable by none. Besides this right of imposing, there be others in the kingdom of the same nature: as the power to make laws, the power of naturalization, the power of erection of arbitrary government, the power to judge without appeal, the power to legitimate; all which do belong to the King only in Parliament. Others there be of the same nature that the King may exercise out of Parliament, which right is grown unto him in them more in those others by the use and practice of the commonwealth, as denization, coinage, making war; which power the King hath time out of mind practised without the gainsaying and murmuring of his subjects. But these other powers before mentioned have ever been executed by him in Parliament, and not otherwise but with the reluctation[1] of the whole kingdom. . . .

It hath been alleged that those which in this cause have enforced their reasons from this maxim of ours, that the King cannot alter the law, have diverted from the question. I say under favour, they have not, for that in effect is the very question now in hand; for if he alone out of Parliament may impose, he altereth the law of England in one of these two main fundamental points. He must either take his subjects' goods from them without assent of the party, which is against the law; or else he must give his own letters patents the force of a law to alter the property of his subjects' goods, which is also against the law. . . .

*   *   *   *   *   *

So we see that the power of imposing and power of making laws are *convertibilia et coincidentia*, and whatsoever can do the one can do the other. And this was the opinion of Sir John Fortescue[2]. . . . He maketh these two powers of making law and imposing to be concomitant in the same hand, and that the one of them is not without the other. He giveth the same reason for this as we do now, but in other words: because (as he saith) in England it is *principatus mixtus et politicus*, the King hath his sovereign power in Parliament, assisted and strengthened with the consent of the whole kingdom, and therefore these powers are to be exercised by him only in Parliament. In other countries they admit the ground of the Civil Law, *quod principi placuerit legis habet vigorem.*

---

[1] Opposition.   [2] Lord Chief Justice of the King's Bench, 1442.

Because they have an absolute power to make law they have also a power to impose, which hath the force of a law in transferring property. Philip Comines...taketh notice of this policy of England, and commends it above all other States as settled in most security; and further to our purpose, layeth this ground, that a King cannot take one penny from his subjects without their consent but it is violence. And you may there note the mischiefs that grew to the Kingdom of France by the voluntary impositions first brought in by Charles 7 and ever since continued and increased, to the utter impoverishment of the common people and the loss of their free Council of Three Estates. And if this power of imposing were quietly settled in our Kings, considering what is the greatest use they make of assembling of Parliaments, which is, the supply of money, I do not see any likelihood to hope for often meetings in that kind because they would provide themselves by that other means....

* * * * * *

That which hath been most insisted upon is this, that the King by his prerogative royal hath the custody of the havens and ports of this island, being the very gates of this kingdom; that he in his royal function and office is only trusted with the keys of these gates; that he alone hath power to shut them and to open them when and to whom he in his princely wisdom shall see good; that by the law of England he may restrain the persons of any from going out of the land or from coming into it; that he may of his own power and discretion prohibit exportation and importation of goods and merchandises; and out of his prerogative and preeminence the power of imposing, as being derivative, doth arise and result, for *cui quod majus est licet, et ei quod est minus licitum est*. So their reason briefly is this: the King may restrain the passage of the person and of the goods; therefore he may suffer them not to pass but *sub modo*, paying such an imposition for his sufferance as he shall set upon them....Admit the King had *custodium portuum*; yet he hath but the custody, which is trust, and not *dominium utile*. He hath power to open and shut upon consideration of public good to the people and State, but not to make gain and benefit by it. The one is protection, the other is expilation[1]. The ports in their own nature are public, free for all to go in and out; yet for the common good this liberty is restrainable by the wisdom and policy of the prince, who is put in trust to discern the times when this natural liberty

---

[1] Spoliation.

shall be restrained.... So in point of government, and common good of the realm, he may restrain the person. But to conclude therefore he may take money not to restrain, is to sell government, trust, and common justice, and most unworthy the divine office of a King.

* * * * * *

The last assault made against the right of the kingdom was an objection grounded upon policy and matter of State: as that it may so fall out that an imposition may be set by a foreign prince that may wring our people, in which case the counterpoise is, to set on the like here upon the subjects of that prince; which policy, if it be not speedily executed but stayed until a Parliament, may in the mean time prove vain and idle, and much damage may be sustained that cannot afterwards be remedied. This strain of policy maketh nothing to the point of right. Our rule is, in this plain commonwealth of ours, *oportet neminem esse sapientiorem legibus*. If there be an inconvenience, it is fitter to have it removed by a lawful means than by an unlawful. But this is rather a mischief than an inconvenience; that is, a prejudice in present of some few, but not hurtful to the commonwealth. And it is more tolerable to suffer an hurt to some few for a short time, than to give way to the breach and violation of the right of the whole nation; for that is the true inconvenience. Neither need it be so difficult or tedious to have the consent of the Parliament, if they were held as they ought or might be....

Much hath been learnedly uttered upon this argument in the maintenance of the people's right and in answering that which hath been pressed on the contrary. But my meaning is not to express in this discourse all that hath or may be said on either side, but only to make a remembrance somewhat larger of that which I myself offered as my *symbolum* towards the making up of this great reckoning of the commonwealth, which if it be not well audited, may in time cost the subjects of England very dear. My hope is of others that laboured very worthily in this business, that they will not suffer their pains to die, and therefore I have forborne to enter into their province. I will end with that saying of that true and honest counsellor, Philip Comines, ... that it is more honourable for a King to say, 'I have so faithful and obedient subjects that they deny me nothing I demand,' than to say, 'I levy what me list, and I have privileges so to do.'

State Trials, ii, 477–520.

(3) Coke on Impositions, c. 1610 (?)

Customs, Subsidies, and Impositions

...Upon conference between Popham, Chief Justice, and myself upon a judgment given lately in the Exchequer concerning the imposition of currants,...it appeared to us...that the King may charge his people of this realm, without special assent of the Commons, to do a thing which may be of profit to the common people but not to their charge.... The effect of which is, that every merchant of this realm, or other, may freely buy, sell, and pass the sea with all their merchandises, paying the customs of ancient time used.

* * * * * *

Upon all which, and divers records which we had seen, it appeared to us that the King cannot at his pleasure put any imposition upon any merchandise to be imported into this kingdom or exported, unless it be for advancement of trade and traffic, which is the life of every island, *pro bono publico*. As if in foreign parts any imposition is put upon the merchandises of our merchants *non pro bono publico*; and for to make equality for the purpose to advance trade and traffic, the King may put an imposition upon their merchandises, for this is not against any of the statutes which were made for advancement of merchandise or of the statutes of Magna Charta,...for the end of all such restraints is *salus populi*.

* * * * * *

Coke, *Twelfth Report* (edition of 1777).

(4) Sir Walter Raleigh on Impositions, c. 1615

This extract is from *The Prerogative of Parliaments in England*, an argument in favour of Parliamentary institutions suggested by the proceedings against one Oliver St John, a gentleman of Marlborough, in the Star Chamber in April, 1615, for attacking the Benevolence levied in the previous year[1]. It takes the form of a Dialogue between a Councillor of State and a Justice of the Peace. This St John is not to be confused with his more famous namesake who was counsel for John Hampden.

* * * * * *

Councillor. Why, Sir? Do you not think it best to compound a Parliament of the King's servants, and others that shall in all obey the King's desires?

Justice. Certainly no; for it hath never succeeded well....

Councillor. But you know they will presently[2] be in hand with those impositions which the King hath laid by his own royal prerogative.

Justice. Perchance not, my Lord; but rather with those

[1] Gardiner, ii, 268–70.   [2] Immediately.

impositions that have been by some of your Lordships laid upon
the King; which did not some of your Lordships fear more than
you do the impositions laid upon the subjects, you would never
dissuade his Majesty from a Parliament. For no man doubted
but that his Majesty was advised to lay those impositions by his
Council;[1] and for particular things on which they were laid, the
advice came from petty fellows (though now great ones) belonging
to the Custom-house. Now, my Lord, what prejudice hath his
Majesty (his revenue being kept up) if the impositions that were
laid were laid by the General Council of the Kingdom, which
takes off all grudging and complaint?

Councillor. Yes, Sir; but that which is done by the King with
the advice of his private or Privy Council is done by the King's
absolute power.

Justice. And by whose power is it done in Parliament but by
the King's absolute power? Mistake it not, my Lord, the Three
Estates do but advise, as the Privy Council doth, which advice if
the King embrace, it becomes the King's own act in the one and
the King's law in the other; for without the King's acceptation
both the public and private advices be but as empty egg-shells.
And what doth his Majesty lose if some of those things which
concern the poorer sort be made free again, and the revenue
kept up upon that which is superfluous? Is it a loss to the King
to be beloved of the commons? If it be revenue which the King
seeks, is it not better to take it of those that laugh than those
that cry? Yea, if all be content to pay upon moderation and
change of the species, is it not more honourable and more safe
for the King that the subject pay by persuasion than to have
them constrained?.... Besides that, when impositions are laid by
Parliament they are gathered by the authority of the law, which,
as aforesaid, rejecteth all complaints and stoppeth every mutinous
mouth. It shall ever be my prayer that the King embrace the counsel
of honour and safety, and let other princes embrace that of force.

*   *   *   *   *   *

Raleigh, *Works*, viii, 212–13.

§ 4. The Parliament of 1614

During the interval between his first and second Parliament James fell
into bad hands. In 1612 his wise adviser Cecil died, and his place in the
King's confidence was taken—not by the wiser Bacon, who was in favour of

[1] The critics of the Stuart kings sometimes overlook the importance of the Privy
Council. As is the case with modern governments, the Crown could always command the best expert advice, and some of the responsibility for both policy and
administration must be assigned to the Council.

calling another Parliament, but by the Scottish upstart Carr, a man without experience and without ideas. Under his influence James postponed Parliament for three years, in the mean time trying to meet his financial necessities by every wasteful and irritating expedient that the ingenuity of his officials could suggest. But the task was an impossible one, and in 1614 he was compelled to summon his second Parliament.

Before it met, Bacon urged the King to adopt a programme of conciliation, making such concessions as would serve to bring in supplies without endangering the more important parts of the prerogative. But James preferred the alternative policy of procuring a submissive Parliament by influencing the elections[1]. He entered into communication with influential persons in every district, who 'undertook' to secure the election in their own localities of members pledged to supply the King's needs. But the scheme leaked out; it could be represented as a conspiracy against the independence of Parliament; and the candidates of the 'undertakers' as they were nicknamed, were everywhere rejected. Of the members elected, we are told, three parts 'were such as had never been of any former Parliament, and many of them young men and not of any great estate or qualities.' 'Many sat there,' wrote one of Sir Dudley Carleton's correspondents, 'who were more fit to have been among roaring boys than in that assembly.' Thus the King's policy only had the effect of replacing the country gentlemen of position by new men, with whom compromises and bargains would be more difficult, and who would be less susceptible to the influence of the Court. Nevertheless, the great names of the next reign were not altogether absent, for Wentworth sat for Yorkshire, Eliot for St Germans in Cornwall, and John Pym for the borough of Calne in Wiltshire.

The King attempted to resume Cecil's policy of financial bargaining with Parliament; but the Commons replied by raising the question of impositions, and demanding the reinstatement of the clergy who had been deprived of their livings in 1604. James pressed them in vain to proceed to supply; they insisted on dealing first with grievances—and after a two months' session he dissolved Parliament. As it passed no Act and granted no supplies, it came to be known as the 'Addled Parliament.'

The *Journals* of this Parliament are brief, disjointed, and incomplete, but the extracts given below [p. **267**] shew that although the composition of the Lower House had changed greatly, the views of the members upon the question of the legality of impositions remained the same as they had been in 1610.

(1) James I on the Undertakers

The following sentence occurs in the King's Speech at the opening of his Third Parliament on 30 January, 1621.

* * * * * *

I confess I have been liberal in my grants, but if I be informed I will amend all hurtful grievances. But who shall hasten after grievances and desire to make himself popular, he hath the

---

[1] About this there was, of course, nothing new. Elections had long been influenced by great persons, and of these the Crown was in some ways the most influential. The novelty lies in the systematic character of the King's proceedings.

spirit of Satan. If I may know my errors I will reform them. I was in my first Parliament a novice; and in my last there was a kind of beasts called 'Undertakers' a dozen of whom undertook to govern the last Parliament, and they led me. I shall thank you for your good office, and desire that the world may say well of our agreement.

Rushworth, *Historical Collections*, i, 23.

(2) The Parliament of 1614 on Impositions

[18 April, 1614]....An Act concerning taxes and impositions upon merchants.

Sir Maurice Berkeley. That no Bill so acceptable as this; none so grievous as this to the subject. That this depriveth the King of the money, and of much of the love of the subjects. That the case of currants in the Exchequer opened the flood-gate of these impositions. Hopeth it will pass the Lords....

* * * * * *

Sir Herbert Croftes. For the Bill, for that, impositions standing, no man certain of the property but only of the use of his own goods....

Mr Brooke.....This matter of imposition never ruled by law till the unhappy case in the Exchequer. If the King may impose by his absolute power, then no man certain what he hath, for it shall be subject to the King's pleasure. Not to leave our posterity in worse case than our ancestors have left us.

* * * * * *

Mr Middleton. Strange that the King requiring supply, we should take from him. That the danger lest the impositions now covering the sea should break over and overflow the land. That if it be considered what the merchant hath paid for impositions, if the King have received it he should not need to require supply now.

Sir Dudley Digges. That the fall of a merchant a feather pulled away from the commonwealth. That the judgment in the Exchequer erroneous. No reason of imposition upon goods upon the sea more than upon the land. That if imposition had been required by Parliament upon divers unnecessary things, he should have furthered it....Edward the Confessor, upon sight of 20,000*l.* of Danegeld, his conscience struck him; and commanded no more should be gathered. Hopes upon examination a little devil may be seen sitting upon these impositions which will take them away.

Mr Hakewill. . . . That 472 or thereabouts of the House: of these above 300 new, not of the last Parliament, whereof divers young. Desireth now they may understand the true state of their right, to leave it for hereafter to posterity.

*   *   *   *   *   *

This Bill to be committed to the whole House in this House to-morrow fortnight. Sir William Strowde moveth all the lawyers of the House that day attend the Committee, without any excuse.

Commons' Journals, i, 466–7.

[5 May 1614]. . . *Sir Edwin Sandys*. . . . That some other princes had imposed, but never claimed any right; now the King had claimed it in open Parliament: they, upon four or five; the King, upon more than so many hundred: they, but for a few months, and at the prayer of the Commons in Parliament put down; here, made perpetual by letters patents. That this liberty of imposing holden to trench to the foundation of all our interests: that maketh us bondmen; giveth use but no propriety. May by the same reason make laws without Parliament. . . . No good counsellors, that advised our most gracious and benign King to impose these and make them perpetual.

*   *   *   *   *   *

Mr Middleton. That the consent of merchants never required to the King's imposing. Thinketh the lion a thorn in his foot which we here to pull out, and wisheth we may do it mannerly, and with respect to the country. Moveth for a present supply of a subsidy, to be gathering whilst we are treating of the great things here to pull out the thorn. Then if thorns pulled out of our feet too, we apply balm to heal the whole sore. That but one can be gathered at once.

*   *   *   *   *   *

Commons' Journals, i, 472–4.

§ 5. PARLIAMENT AND MONOPOLIES

The question of monopolies which had vexed the closing years of the reign of Elizabeth[1] was destined to disturb her successor. Four days after his arrival in London on 3 May, 1603, James, acting upon the advice of his Council, had called in a great part of the existing monopolies, but they soon began once more to increase and multiply. 'For proclamations and patents,' wrote Chamberlain to Carleton on 8 July, 1620, 'they are become so ordinary that there is no end, every day bringing forth some new project or other. In truth, the world doth even groan under the burden of these

[1] *Tudor Constitutional Documents*, p. 557.

perpetual patents, which are become so frequent that whereas at the King's coming in there were complaints of some eight or nine monopolies then in being, they are now said to be multiplied by so many scores.'[1] In 1614 the House of Commons included among their grievances the grant of a patent for the manufacture of glass. The patent of 1617 for licensing inns and that of 1618 for alehouses were strongly objected to as infringing the jurisdiction of the justices of the peace; and when in 1618 the manufacture of gold and silver thread, already regulated by patent, was taken entirely into the King's hands and private manufacturers were fined and imprisoned, there was a great outcry in the City of London. In the Parliament of 1621 Noy and Coke moved for an enquiry into monopolies which led to the proceedings against Sir Giles Mompesson [p. **322**], and on 16 March Coke brought in a Bill against them which got as far as a second reading. James bowed to the storm, and on 30 March he cancelled by proclamation the patents for gold and silver thread, the patent for inns, and another for concealed lands[2]. In May other monopolies were voted by the Commons to be grievances, among them patents for the engrossing of wills, for the levying of lighthouse tolls, for the importation of salmon and lobsters, and for the manufacture of gold leaf[3].

It was reserved for the Parliament of 1624 to legislate on the subject, and the Monopolies Act, while accepting the long established principle that inventors or introducers of a new process were entitled to a monopoly of it for a limited time, placed the control of monopolies under the Courts of Common Law in place of the Council or special commissioners appointed by the Crown.

The Monopolies Act, 1624

An Act concerning Monopolies and Dispensations with penal laws and the forfeiture thereof

I. Forasmuch as your most excellent Majesty in your royal judgment and of your blessed disposition to the weal and quiet of your subjects did, in the year of our Lord God one thousand six hundred and ten, publish in print to the whole realm and to all posterity that all grants of monopolies...are contrary to your Majesty's laws, which your Majesty's declaration is truly consonant and agreeable to the ancient and fundamental laws of this your realm: And whereas your Majesty was further graciously pleased expressly to command that no suitor should presume to move your Majesty for matters of that nature; yet nevertheless upon misinformations and untrue pretences of public good many such grants have been unduly obtained and unlawfully put in execution, to the great grievance and inconvenience of your Majesty's subjects, contrary to the laws of this your realm and contrary to your Majesty's royal and blessed intention so published

---

[1] Gardiner, iv, 1.   [2] *Ib.* iv, 85.   [3] *Ib.* iv, 125.

as aforesaid: For avoiding whereof, and preventing of the like in time to come, may it please your most excellent Majesty, at the humble suit of the Lords Spiritual and Temporal and the Commons in this present Parliament assembled, That it may be declared and enacted...that all monopolies and all commissions, grants, licences, charters, and letters patents heretofore made or granted, or hereafter to be made or granted, to any person or persons, bodies politic or corporate whatsoever, of or for the sole buying, selling, making, working, or using of anything within this realm or the Dominion of Wales, or of any other monopolies, or of power, liberty, or faculty to dispense with any others, or to give licence or toleration to do, use, or exercise anything against the tenor or purport of any law or statute, or to give or make any warrant for any such dispensation, licence, or toleration to be had or made, or to agree or compound with any others for any penalty or forfeitures limited by any statute, or of any grant or promise of the benefit, profit, or commodity of any forfeiture, penalty, or sum of money that is or shall be due by any statute before judgment thereupon had, and all proclamations, inhibitions, restraints, warrants of assistance, and all other matters and things whatsoever any way tending to the instituting, erecting, strengthening, furthering, or countenancing of the same or any of them, are altogether contrary to the laws of this realm, and so are and shall be utterly void and of none effect, and in no wise to be put in ure[1] or execution.

II. And be it further declared and enacted....That all monopolies...and the force and validity of them...ought to be and shall be for ever hereafter examined, heard, tried, and determined by and according to the common laws of this realm, and not otherwise.

III. And be it further enacted....That all person and persons, bodies politic and corporate whatsoever which now are or hereafter shall be, shall stand and be disabled and uncapable to have, use, exercise, or put in ure[1] any monopoly, or any such commission, grant, licence, charters, letters patents, proclamation, inhibition, restraint, warrant of assistance, or other matter or thing tending as aforesaid, or any liberty, power, or faculty grounded or pretended to be grounded upon them or any of them.

IV. And be it further enacted....That if any person... shall be hindered, grieved, disturbed, or disquieted, or his... goods or chattels any way seized, attached, distrained, taken, carried away, or detained by occasion or pretext of any mono-

[1] Put in practice.

poly...and will sue to be relieved,...that then...the same person...shall and may have his...remedy for the same at the Common Law by any action or actions to be grounded upon this Statute, the same action and actions to be heard and determined in the Courts of King's Bench, Common Pleas, and Exchequer or in any of them, against him or them by whom he...shall be so hindered, [etc.]...or against him or them by whom his...goods or chattels shall be so seized, [etc.]..., wherein...every such person...shall recover three times so much as the damages which he...sustained,...and double costs....

V. Provided nevertheless, and be it declared and enacted, That any declaration before mentioned shall not extend to any letters patents and grants of privilege for the term of one and twenty years or under heretofore made, of the sole working or making of any manner of new manufacture within this realm, to the first and true inventor or inventors of such manufactures which others at the time of the making of such letters patents and grants did not use, so they be not contrary to the law nor mischievous to the State by raising of the prices of commodities at home, or hurt of trade, or generally inconvenient....

VI. Provided also, and be it declared and enacted, That any declaration before mentioned shall not extend to any letters patents and grants of privilege for the term of fourteen years or under hereafter to be made of the sole working or making of any manner of new manufactures within this realm to the true and first inventor and inventors of such manufactures....

*   *   *   *   *   *

IX. Provided also, and it is hereby further intended, declared, and enacted, That this Act or anything therein contained shall not in any wise extend or be prejudicial unto the City of London, or to any city, borough, or town corporate within this realm for or concerning any grants, charters, or letters patents to them or any of them made or granted, or for or concerning any custom or customs used by or within them or any of them, or unto any corporations, companies, or fellowships of any art, trade, occupation, or mystery, or to any companies or societies of merchants within this realm erected for the maintenance, enlargement, or ordering of any trade of merchandise, but that the same charters, customs, corporations, companies, fellowships, and societies, and their liberties, privileges, power, and immunities, shall be and continue of such force and effect as they were before the making of this Act, and of none other; Anything before in this Act contained to the contrary in any wise notwithstanding[1].

*   *   *   *   *   *

21 & 22 Jac. I. c. 3; *Statutes of the Realm*, iv, 1212.

§6. THE PRIVILEGE OF PARLIAMENT

The privilege claimed by the House of Commons of examining election returns has been already discussed in a different connexion [p. 201]. The reign of James I also witnessed the further development of the older privileges of freedom of speech and freedom from arrest, and cases arising under the head of the right of Parliament to punish.

(a) The Speaker's claim of Privilege[2]

The claim of Privilege made by the Speaker, Sir Edward Phelips, at the opening of James I's first Parliament in 1604 comes at the end of a somewhat flowery speech of welcome to the new monarch, and it differs in important respects from the Tudor form, being less comprehensive. Thus, the right of access, which in 1559 had been claimed for the whole House[3], is now restricted to, or at any rate only claimed by, the Speaker himself; and the petition for freedom of arrest has disappeared altogether, although it is possible that this is due to an accidental omission in the report of the speech[4].

The Speaker's Petition, 1604

[22 March, 1604] His Majesty's speech ended, Mr Speaker, with an eloquent ovation on the Commons' behalf and his own, presented himself to his Majesty.

*   *   *   *   *   *

And now since God, to whose only prerogative the inthronizing and disthronizing of Kings appertaineth, hath by the setting of her sun raised and spread the beams of your glory, and by calling her[5] to his heavenly service hath freed her from her temporal regiment[6], and hath out of his Divine Providence crowned you with the same crown, blessed you with the same religion, enriched you with the same dominions, and strengthened you with the hearts of the self-same subjects and people, [we pray] that, as she did, so your Majesty will be pleased to protect us in our religion, to favour us in our loyalties, to cherish us in

---

[1] § 9 of this Statute was destined to become of great importance later on, for it was under cover of the exception contained in it that in 1632 monopolies were revived by the device of establishing chartered companies to control manufactures.

[2] See Appendix, p. 382 below.

[3] *Tudor Constitutional Documents*, pp. 550, 551.

[4] See note on p. 274 below.

[5] Queen Elizabeth.   [6] Government.

our obedience, and to nourish us in our faithful subjection. And as to her, so to you, we faithfully prostrate and subject ourselves, our state, and lives, to be disposed and sacrificed for and in your Majesty's service, religiously praying that your Highness's government and our subjection may be to God pleasing, to you our Sovereign absolute, to enemies and traitors powerful and fearful, and to all true, devoted subjects fruitful and comfortable. Then shall God be glorified, your Majesty renowned, religion advanced, and your State and people secured from Popes' cursings, enemies' oppressions, and traitors' treacheries; whereunto all true English hearts say Amen.

And thus being by the rules of discretion foretold that to offend your sacred ears with *multa*, since to satisfy your gracious expectation with *multum* is denied me, were an error, of errors the most erroneous: Therefore, since I retain not the virtue of the one, give me leave, most magnificent Sovereign, to prevent the error of the other; and in these few words be pleased to receive as much as can be conceived may proceed from a man and mind truly and wholly devoted to your service, who desireth no longer to breathe than so to breathe that his breath may breathe out to your Majesty loyalty, faith, and obedience, whereof his life and death shall be his pawn and pledge. Who here, upon the knees of my duty, in all humility do present to your gracious consideration five petitions, the benefit of three whereof are peculiar to mine own particular, the other two to the knights, burgesses, and members of the Lower House of Parliament.

The first whereof is, That if in your gracious eyes, ears, or judgment, during the time of this mine employment and service, I have, do, or shall, through my imperfections (which already appear to your Majesty to be too, too many) either in manner, form, or matter, neglect that which I ought to have performed, or err in that which I ought not to have done, that your Majesty will be pleased out of your clemency rather to commiserate the same than out of your justice therein to correct my unwilling committed errors.

Secondly, That if any by private information endeavour to possess your sacred ears with matter of blemish or detraction concerning my course of proceeding, that your gracious censure thereof may be suspended until by your pleasure I be called to my trial and your judgment; for that many things may be either miscarried or misconceived in causes of this nature.

Thirdly, That, as occasion shall move, I may by your royal favour be permitted access to your princely presence in places and times convenient for such negotiations as the duty of my place shall require.

Fourthly, [For that those conclusions are in councils approved best where freedom of disputation is permitted, that your Majesty will vouchsafe to the members of the Lower House liberty of modest and comely speech in their debating of such things as then shall be propounded.

Thus I end to speak, but never to wish and pray that God will give you *senatum fidelem, exercitus firmos, domum latam, populum probum, mundum quietum, vitam prolixam, et quaecumque sunt hominis et principis vota*][1].

Commons' Journals, i, 148–9.

(b) The Privilege of Freedom of Speech

The attitude of the Parliament of 1621 was profoundly affected by considerations of foreign policy. In 1618 the Thirty Years' War had broken out on the Continent, and the success which was everywhere attending the arms of the Catholic League had already caused in England a revival of that panic fear for Protestantism which had been so frequent a political phenomenon in the days of Elizabeth. On the recovery of the Palatinate both King and people were in accord, for James's daughter Elizabeth, like his son Henry who died in 1612, was greatly beloved, and her husband, Frederick Elector Palatine, was a Calvinist. It was for slighting words about the Elector Palatine and his wife that the Parliament of 1621 laid upon Floyd the most ferocious series of punishments ever inflicted in England for a political offence [p. 319]. But James's plan for recovering the Palatinate by diplomatic representations at the Court of Spain, supported by a scheme for a Spanish marriage for his heir, appeared to Parliament dangerous in the highest degree; and under the pressure of this sense of danger the Commons were provoked to the annexation of a new province. They drew up a petition to the King on matters of foreign policy [p. 276].

The attitude of James towards this innovation was precisely the attitude of Elizabeth. 'Mr Speaker,' he wrote, on 3 December, 1621 [p. 279], 'we have heard by divers reports, to our great grief, that our distance from the Houses of Parliament caused by our indisposition of health' (he was at Newmarket), 'hath emboldened some fiery and popular spirits of some of the House of Commons to argue and debate publicly of the matters far above their reach and capacity, tending to our high dishonour and breach of prerogative royal. These are therefore to command you to make known in

[1] The entry in the *Commons' Journals* ends at the word 'Fourthly.' The passage in square brackets is supplied from the British Museum MS. Lansdowne 491, fo. 208, printed in *English Historical Review*, October 1929, by Professor F. G. Marcham, to whom the editor is indebted for permission to reproduce it here.

The reference in the text to 'five petitions' is not clear. In 1559 there were four petitions only (*Tudor Constitutional Documents*, p. 551). If a fifth petition is missing, it must be the claim to freedom from arrest, which was included in 1559 but does not appear in 1604.

our name unto the House, that none therein shall presume henceforth to meddle with anything concerning our Government or deep matters of State, and namely, not to deal with our dearest son's match with the daughter of Spain.' In Elizabeth's reign such a royal message would have led to the offender's being clapped up in the Tower by order of the House itself. Now, the Commons persisted in their petition [p. 280], with an added protest against the King's attempt 'to abridge us of the ancient liberty of Parliament for freedom of speech, jurisdiction, and just censure of the House' [p. 283].

The King's rejoinder to this [p. 283] profoundly stirred the Commons. After exhorting them 'to remember that we are an old and experienced King, needing no such lessons,' he proceeded to take the ground which they could never allow him to occupy without a protest,—that their privileges were not, as the House had called them, an 'ancient and undoubted right and inheritance,' but only 'derived from the grace and permission of our ancestors and us.' The same position was also taken up by the King in a message sent on 16 December to the House by one of the Secretaries of State [p. 287]. In his proclamation of 6 January, 1622, for the dissolution of Parliament [p. 289], James appealed from the House of Commons to public opinion outside it. This tendency to self-justification on the part of the Sovereign, so alien to the ideas of the Tudors, suggests that public opinion was no longer the almost negligible factor which it had been under Elizabeth; and in the later phases of the constitutional conflict the Parliament also, as in the Grand Remonstrance of 1641, is to be found attaching great importance to an appeal to the country.

The result of the controversy concerning privilege was that on 18 December, 1621, the whole House concurred in a famous Protestation [p. 288] which was said to have been torn from the Journals by the King's own hand. The note in the Journals is, 'rent out,' and this has given to the King's action in the eyes of historians the character of a temporary outburst of passion which it did not possess. As a matter of fact the whole proceeding was characterised by extraordinary solemnity and deliberation. It appears from a report in the Privy Council Register[1] that at the end of December the King came in person to the Council, 'the Prince his Highness and all the Lords and others of his Majesty's Privy Council sitting about him, and all the Judges then in London, which were six in number, there attending upon his Majesty,' and sent for the Journal which contained the Protestation. He declared himself 'justly offended' with it, but nevertheless 'in a most gracious manner' announced that he had never had any intention of depriving the House of Commons of privileges to which they were really entitled; 'but this Protestation of the Commons' House, so contrived and carried as it was, his Majesty thought fit to be razed out of all memorials and utterly to be annihilated, both in respect of the manner by which it was gained and the matter therein contained.' He therefore, 'in the full assembly of his Council and in presence of the Judges,' declared the Protestation to be 'invalid, annulled, void, and of no effect, and did further, *manu sua propria*, take the said Protestation out of the Journal Book of the Clerk of the Commons' House of Parliament, and commanded an Act of Council to be made thereupon, and this Act to be entered in the Register of Council

---

[1] Printed in Turner, i, 204.

causes.' The King might annul the Protestation, but he could not alter the fact that the Commons, here the real revolutionaries, had now thrown over all the Tudor limitations which warned them off matters of State or the forbidden ground of the Royal Supremacy in matters of religion, and had brought within the scope of their survey all 'arduous and urgent affairs concerning the King, State, and defence of the realm and of the Church of England.'

James I's fourth Parliament met in 1624 under different auspices. In October, 1623, Charles and Buckingham had returned from Madrid without the Infanta, an event which was celebrated by bonfires in the streets of London, and a special anthem in St Paul's: 'When I shall come out of Egypt, and the house of Jacob (*Jacobi*) from amongst the barbarous people.'[1] When Parliament met, it was to hear with joy that the treaties with Spain were dissolved and to grant large supplies for the impending war; but the addresses presented to the King by both Houses [pp. 296 and 299] shew that they were still maintaining their interest in and concern with foreign policy.

(1) Commons' Petition, 3 December, 1621

Most gracious and dread Sovereign: We, your Majesty's most humble and loyal subjects, the knights, citizens, and burgesses now assembled in Parliament, who represent the commons of your realm, full of hearty sorrow to be deprived of the comfort of your royal presence, the rather for that it proceeds from the want of your health, wherein we all unfeignedly do suffer; in all humble manner calling to mind your gracious answer to our former petition concerning religion[2], which, notwithstanding your Majesty's pious and princely intentions, hath not produced that good effect which the danger of these times doth seem to us to require; and finding how ill your Majesty's goodness hath been requited by princes of different religion, who even in time of treaty have taken opportunity to advance their own ends, tending to the subversion of religion and disadvantage of your affairs and the estate of your children; by reason whereof your ill-affected subjects at home, the Popish recusants, have taken too much encouragement and are dangerously increased in their number and in their insolencies; we cannot but be sensible thereof, and therefore humbly represent what we conceive to be the causes of so great and growing mischiefs, and what be the remedies.

1. The vigilancy and ambition of the Pope of Rome and his dearest son; the one aiming at as large a temporal monarchy as the other at a spiritual supremacy. 2. The devilish positions and doctrines whereon Popery is built, and taught with authority to their followers for advancement of their temporal ends. 3. The

---

[1] John Nichols, *The Progresses of King James I*, iv, 928–9.   [2] See p. 278.

distressed and miserable estate of the professors of true religion in foreign parts. 4. The disastrous accidents to your Majesty's children abroad, expressed with rejoicing, and even with contempt of their persons. 5. The strange confederacy of the princes of the Popish religion, aiming mainly at the advancement of theirs and subverting of ours, and taking the advantages conducing to that end upon all occasions. 6. The great and many armies raised and maintained at the charge of the King of Spain, the chief of that league. 7. The expectation of the Popish recusants of the match with Spain, and feeding themselves with great hopes of the consequences thereof. 8. The interposing of foreign princes and their agents in the behalf of Popish recusants for connivance and favour unto them. 9. Their open and usual resort to the houses and, which is worse, to the chapels of foreign ambassadors. 10. Their more than usual concourse to the City, and their frequent conventicles and conferences there. 11. The education of their children in many several seminaries and houses of their religion in foreign parts appropriated to the English fugitives. 12. The grants of their just forfeitures intended by your Majesty as a reward of service to the grantees but, beyond your Majesty's intention, transferred or compounded for at such mean rates as will amount to little less than a toleration. 13. The licentious printing and dispersing of Popish and seditious books, even in the time of Parliament. 14. The swarms of priests and Jesuits, the common incendiaries of all Christendom, dispersed in all parts of your kingdom.

And from these causes, as bitter roots, we humbly offer to your Majesty that we foresee and fear there will necessarily follow very dangerous effects both to Church and State. For, 1. The Popish religion is incompatible with ours in respect of their positions. 2. It draweth with it an unavoidable dependency on foreign princes. 3. It openeth too wide a gap for popularity to any who shall draw too great a party. 4. It hath a restless spirit, and will strive by these gradations: if it once get but a connivancy, it will press for a toleration; if that should be obtained, they must have an equality; from thence they will aspire to superiority, and will never rest till they get a subversion of the true religion.

The remedies against these growing evils, which in all humility we offer unto your most excellent Majesty, are these. 1. That seeing this inevitable necessity is fallen upon your Majesty which no wisdom or providence of a peaceable and pious King can avoid, your Majesty would not omit this just occasion speedily and effectually to take your sword into your hand. 2. That once undertaken upon so honourable and just grounds, your Majesty would resolve to pursue and more publicly avow the aiding of those of our religion in foreign parts; which doubtless would reunite the Princes and States of the Union, by these disasters disheartened and disbanded[1]. 3. That your Majesty would propose to yourself to manage this war with the best advantage, by a diversion or otherwise, as in your deep judgment shall be found fittest, and not to rest upon a war in these parts only, which will consume your treasure and discourage your people. 4. That the bent of this war and point of your sword may be against that prince (whatsoever opinion of potency he hath) whose armies and treasures have first diverted and since maintained the war in the Palatinate. 5. That for securing of our peace at home, your Majesty would be pleased to review the parts of our petition formerly delivered unto your Majesty and hereunto annexed, and to put in execution, by the care of choice commissioners to be thereunto especially appointed, the laws already and hereafter to be made for preventing of dangers by Popish recusants and their wonted evasions. 6. That to frustrate their hopes for a future age, our most noble Prince may be timely and happily married to one of our own religion. 7. That the children of the nobility and gentry of this kingdom, and of others ill-affected and suspected in their religion, now beyond the seas, may be forthwith called home by your means and at the charge of their parents or governors. 8. That the children of Popish recusants, or such whose wives are Popish recusants, be brought up during their minority with Protestant schoolmasters and teachers, who may sow in their tender years the seeds of true religion. 9. That your Majesty will be pleased speedily to revoke all former licences for such children and youth to travel beyond the seas, and not grant any such licence hereafter. 10. That your Majesty's learned counsel may receive commandment from your Highness carefully to look into former grants of recusants' lands, and to avoid them if by law they can; and that your Majesty will stay your hand from passing any such grants hereafter.

This is the sum and effect of our humble declaration, which we (no ways intending to press upon your Majesty's undoubted and regal prerogative) do with the fullness of our duty and obedience humbly submit to your most princely consideration: the glory of God, whose cause it is; the zeal of our true religion, in which we have been born and wherein (by God's grace) we are

---

[1] The Union of Protestant Princes had been dissolved in April 1621 (Gardiner, iv, 191).

resolved to die; the safety of your Majesty's person, who is the very life of your people; the happiness of your children and posterity; the honour and good of the Church and State, dearer unto us than our own lives, having kindled these affections truly devoted to your Majesty.

*   *   *   *   *   *

Rushworth, *Historical Collections*, i, 40.

(2) King's letter to the Speaker, 3 December, 1621

This was in reply to the preceding petition of the same date, a copy of which James had seen. It was written without waiting for the formal presentation of the petition.

Mr Speaker,

We have heard by divers reports, to our great grief, that our distance from the Houses of Parliament caused by our indisposition of health hath emboldened some fiery and popular spirits of some of the House of Commons to argue and debate publicly of the matters far above their reach and capacity, tending to our high dishonour and breach of prerogative royal. These are therefore to command you to make known in our name unto the House, that none therein shall presume henceforth to meddle with anything concerning our government or deep matters of State, and namely not to deal with our dearest son's match with the daughter of Spain, nor to touch the honour of that King or any other our friends and confederates; and also not to meddle with any man's particulars which have their due motion in our ordinary courts of justice. And whereas we hear they have sent a message to Sir Edward [*sic*] Sandys to know the reasons of his late restraint, you shall in our name resolve them[1], that it was not for any misdemeanour of his in Parliament[2]; but to put them out of doubt of any question of that nature that may arise among them hereafter, you shall resolve them[1] in our name that we think ourself very free and able to punish any man's misdemeanours in Parliament, as well during their sitting as after. Which we mean not to spare hereafter upon any occasion of any man's insolent behaviour there that shall be ministered unto us. And if they have already touched any of these points which we have forbidden in any petition of theirs which is to be sent unto us, it is our pleasure

[1] 'Resolve them' in the sense of 'inform them,' a common use at this time.

[2] Sir Edwin Sandys had been imprisoned in the Tower on 16 July, 1621, for his proceedings in connexion with Virginia, although the Commons leaped to the conclusion that the real cause was the nature of his speeches in Parliament.

that you shall tell them that except they reform it before it come to our hands we will not deign the hearing nor answering of it.

Dated at Newmarket, 3 December 1621.

Rushworth, *Historical Collections*, i, 43.

(3) Commons' Petition of 9 December, 1621

This is an explanatory document intended to modify the effect of the petition of 3 December which had been so much resented by the King. It was presented to the King at Newmarket on 11 December. It was on this occasion that James uttered the famous saying, 'Bring stools for the ambassadors.'

Most dread and gracious Sovereign,

We your most humble and loyal subjects, the knights, citizens, and burgesses assembled in the Commons' House of Parliament, full of grief and unspeakable sorrow through the true sense of your Majesty's displeasure expressed by your letter lately sent to our Speaker and by him related and read unto us[1], yet comforted again with the assurance of your grace and goodness and of the sincerity of our own intentions and proceedings, whereon with confidence we can rely, in all humbleness beseech your most excellent Majesty that the loyalty and dutifulness of as faithful and loving subjects as ever served or lived under a gracious Sovereign may not undeservedly suffer by the mis-information of partial and uncertain reports, which are ever unfaithful intelligencers, but that your Majesty would, in the clearness of your own judgment, first vouchsafe to understand from ourselves and not from others what our humble declaration and petition (resolved upon by the universal voice of the House, and proposed with your gracious favour to be presented unto your sacred Majesty) doth contain, upon what occasion we entered into consideration of those things which are therein contained, with what dutiful respect to your Majesty and your service we did consider thereof, and what was our true intention thereby. And that when your Majesty shall thereby truly discern our dutiful affections, you will in your royal judgment free us from those heavy charges wherewith some of our members are burdened and wherein the whole House is involved.

And we humbly beseech your Majesty that you would not hereafter give credit to private reports against all or any of the members of our House whom the whole have not censured, until your Majesty have been truly informed thereof from ourselves; and that in the mean time, and ever, we may stand upright in

---

[1] See p. 279 above.

your Majesty's grace and good opinion, than which no worldly consideration is or can be dearer unto us.

When your Majesty had reassembled us in Parliament by your royal commandment sooner than we expected, and did vouchsafe by the mouths of three honourable Lords to impart unto us the weighty occasions moving your Majesty thereunto; and from them we did understand these particulars:

That notwithstanding your princely and pious endeavours to procure peace, the time is now come that Janus' Temple must be opened.

That the voice of Bellona must be heard, and not the voice of the turtle.

That there was no hope of peace, nor any truce to be obtained, no, not for a few days.

That your Majesty must either abandon your own children or engage yourself in a war, wherein consideration is to be had, what foot, what horse, what money will be sufficient.

That the Lower Palatinate was seized upon by the army of the King of Spain as executor of the ban there in quality of the Duke of Burgundy, as the Upper Palatinate was by the Duke of Bavaria.

That the King of Spain at his own charge had now at least five armies on foot.

That the Princes of the Union were disbanded but the Catholic League remained firm, whereby those princes so dissevered were in danger one by one to be ruined.

That the estate of those of the Religion in foreign parts was miserable; and that out of these considerations we were called to a war, and forthwith to advise for a supply for keeping the forces in the Palatinate from disbanding, and to foresee the means for raising and maintaining the body of an army for the war against the spring. We therefore, out of our zeal to your Majesty and your posterity, with more alacrity and celerity than ever was precedented in Parliament, did address ourselves to the service commended unto us. And although we cannot conceive that the honour and safety of your Majesty and your posterity, the patrimony of your children invaded and possessed by their enemies, the welfare of religion, and state of your kingdom, are matters at any time unfit for our deepest consideration in time of Parliament; and although before this time we were in some of these points silent, yet now being invited thereunto and led on by so just an occasion, we thought it our duties to provide for the present supply thereof, and not only to turn our eyes on a war abroad but to take care for the securing of our peace at home, which the dangerous increase and insolency of Popish recusants apparently, visibly, and sensibly did lead us unto. The consideration whereof did necessarily draw us truly to represent unto your Majesty what we conceive to be the causes, what we feared would be the effects, and what we hoped might be the remedies of these growing evils; among which, as incident and unavoidable, we fell upon some things which seem to touch upon the King of Spain, as they have relation to Popish recusants at home, to the wars by him maintained in the Palatinate against your Majesty's children, and to his several armies now on foot; yet, as we conceived, without touch of dishonour to that King or any other prince your Majesty's confederate.

In the discourse whereof we did not assume to ourselves any power to determine of any part thereof, nor intend to encroach or intrude upon the sacred bounds of your royal authority, to whom and to whom only we acknowledge it doth belong to resolve of peace and war and of the marriage of the most noble Prince your son: but as your most loyal and humble subjects and servants, representing the whole commons of your kingdom (who have a large interest in the happy and prosperous estate of your Majesty and your royal posterity, and of the flourishing estate of our Church and commonwealth), did resolve out of our cares and fears truly and plainly to demonstrate these things to your Majesty which we were not assured could otherwise come so fully and clearly to your knowledge; and that being done, to lay the same down at your Majesty's feet, without expectation of any other answer of your Majesty touching these higher points than what at your good pleasure and in your own time should be held fit.

This being the effect of that we had formerly resolved upon, and these the occasions and reasons inducing the same, our humble suit to your Majesty and confidence is, that your Majesty will be graciously pleased to receive at the hands of these our messengers our former humble declaration and petition, and vouchsafe to read and favourably to interpret the same[1]; and that to so much thereof as containeth our humble petition concerning Jesuits, priests, and Popish recusants, the passage of bills, and granting your royal pardon, you will vouchsafe an answer unto us.

[1] On the receipt of the King's angry letter of 3 December the messengers who had been sent to present the Commons' petition to him had been at once recalled, so there had been no formal presentation (Gardiner, iv, 249, 251).

And whereas your Majesty by the general words of your letter seemeth to restrain us from intermeddling with matters of government, or particulars which have their motion in the courts of justice, the generality of which words in the largeness of the extent thereof (as we hope beyond your Majesty's intention) might involve those things which are the proper subjects of Parliamentary occasions and discourse.

And whereas your Majesty doth seem to abridge us of the ancient liberty of Parliament for freedom of speech, jurisdiction, and just censure of the House, and other proceedings there (wherein we trust in God we shall never transgress the bounds of loyal and dutiful subjects), a liberty which we assure ourselves so wise and so just a king will not infringe, the same being our ancient and undoubted right, and an inheritance received from our ancestors; without which we cannot freely debate nor clearly discern of things in question before us, nor truly inform your Majesty; in which we have been confirmed by your Majesty's most gracious former speeches and messages. We are therefore now again inforced in all humbleness to pray your Majesty to allow the same, and thereby to take away the doubts and scruples your Majesty's late letter to our Speaker hath wrought upon us.

So shall we your loyal and loving subjects ever acknowledge your Majesty's justice, grace, and goodness, and be ready to perform that service to your Majesty which in the true affection of our hearts we profess, and pour out our daily and devout prayers to the Almighty for your Majesty's long life, happy and religious reign, and prosperous estate, and for your royal posterity after you for ever.

Rushworth, *Historical Collections*, i, 44–6.

(4) King's Answer of 11 December, 1621

This was the King's reply to the petition of 9 December when it was presented to him at Newmarket. Gardiner (iv, 253) calls it 'a long, rambling letter.'

We must here begin in the same fashion that we would have done if the first petition had come to our hands before we had made a stay thereof, which is to repeat the first words of the late Queen of famous memory used by her in an answer to an insolent proposition made by a Polonian ambassador unto her: that is, *Legatum expectabamus, heraldum accipimus.* For we had great reason to expect that the first message from your House should have been a message of thanksgiving for our continued gracious behaviour towards our people since your last recess, not only by our proclamation of grace, wherein were contained six or seven and thirty articles, all of several points of grace to the people, but also by the labour we took for the satisfaction of both Houses in those three articles recommended unto us in both their names by the Right Reverend Father in God the Archbishop of Canterbury, and likewise for the good government of Ireland we are now in hand with at your request: but not only have we heard no news of all this, but contrary, great complaints of the danger of religion within this kingdom, tacitly implying our ill government in this point. And we leave you to judge whether it be your duties, that are the representative body of our people, so to distaste them with our government; whereas by the contrary it is your duty with all your endeavours to kindle more and more a dutiful and thankful love in the people's hearts towards us for our just and gracious government.

Now whereas, in the very beginning of this your apology, you tax us in fair terms of trusting uncertain reports and partial informations concerning your proceedings, we wish you to remember that we are an old and experienced King needing no such lessons, being in our conscience freest of any king alive from hearing or trusting idle reports, which so many of your House as are nearest us can bear witness unto you if you would give as good ear to them as you do to some tribunitial orators among you.... In the body of your petition you usurp upon our prerogative royal, and meddle with things far above your reach, and then in the conclusion you protest the contrary; as if a robber would take a man's purse and then protest he meant not to rob him. For first, you presume to give us your advice concerning the match of our dearest son with some Protestant (we cannot say princess, for we know none of these fit for him) and dissuade us from his match with Spain, urging us to a present war with that king; and yet in the conclusion, forsooth, ye protest ye intend not to press upon our most undoubted and regal prerogative, as if the petitioning of us in matters that yourselves confess ye ought not to meddle with were not a meddling with them.

And whereas ye pretend that ye were invited to this course by the speeches of three honourable Lords, yet by so much as yourselves repeat of the speeches, nothing can be concluded but that we were resolved by war to regain the Palatinate if otherwise we could not attain unto it. And you were invited to advise forthwith upon a supply for keeping the forces in the Palatinate from disbanding, and to foresee the means for the raising and maintenance of the body of an army for that war against the spring. Now what inference can be made upon this, that therefore we must presently[1] denounce war against the King of Spain, break our dearest son's match, and match him to one of our religion, let the world judge. The difference is no greater than if we would tell a merchant that we had great need to borrow money from him for raising an army, that thereupon it would follow that we were bound to follow his advice in the direction of the war and all things depending thereupon. But yet not contenting yourselves with this excuse of yours, which indeed cannot hold water, ye come after to a direct contradiction to the conclusion of your former petition, saying that the honour and safety of us and our posterity and the patrimony of our children invaded and possessed by their enemies, the welfare of religion, and state of our kingdom, are matters at any time not unfit for your deepest considerations in Parliament. To this generality we answer with the logicians, that where all things are contained, nothing is omitted; so as this plenipotency of yours invests you in all power upon earth, lacking nothing but the Pope's to have the keys also both of heaven and purgatory. And to this vast generality of yours we can give no other answer, for it will trouble all the best lawyers in the House to make a good commentary upon it. For so did the Puritan ministers in Scotland bring all kinds of causes within the compass of their jurisdiction, saying that it was the Church's office to judge of slander, and there could no kind of crime or fault be committed but there was a slander in it, either against God, the King, or their neighbour; and by this means they hooked in to themselves the cognizance of all causes: or like Bellarmine's distinction of the Pope's power over Kings *in ordine ad spiritualia*, whereby he gives them all temporal jurisdiction over them.

*   *   *   *   *   *

And touching your excuse of not determining anything concerning the match of our dearest son, but only to tell your opinion and lay it down at our feet: first, we desire to know how you could have presumed to determine in that point without committing of high treason? And next, you cannot deny but your talking of his match after that manner was a direct breach of our commandment and declaration out of our own mouth at the first sitting down of this Parliament, where we plainly professed that we were in treaty of this match with Spain, and wished you to have that confidence in our religion and wisdom that we would so manage it as our religion should receive no prejudice by it. And

---

[1] Immediately.

the same we now repeat unto you, professing that we are so far engaged in that match as we cannot in honour go back, except the King of Spain perform not such things as we expect at his hands. And therefore we are sorry that ye should shew to have so great distrust in us as to conceive that we should be cold in our religion; otherwise we cannot imagine how our former public declaration should not have stopped your mouths in this point.

And as to your request that we would now receive your former petition, we wonder what could make you presume that we would receive it, whereas in our former letter we plainly declared the contrary unto you. And therefore we have justly rejected that suit of yours; for what have you left unattempted in the highest points of sovereignty in that petition of yours except the striking of coin? For it contains the violation of leagues, the particular way how to govern a war, and the marriage of our dearest son, both negative with Spain, nay, with any other Popish princess, and also affirmatively as to the matching with one of our religion; which we confess is a strain beyond any providence or wisdom God hath given us, as things now stand.

These are unfit things to be handled in Parliament except your King should require it of you; for who can have wisdom to judge of things of that nature but such as are daily acquainted with the particulars of treaties and of the variable and fixed connexion of affairs of State, together with the knowledge of the secret ways, ends, and intentions of princes in their several negotiations? Otherwise a small mistaking of matters of this nature may produce more effects than can be imagined: and therefore *Ne sutor ultra crepidam*....

* * * * * *

But we cannot omit to shew you how strange we think it that you should make so bad and unjust a commentary upon some words of our former letter, as if we meant to restrain you thereby of your ancient privileges and liberties in Parliament....

And although we cannot allow of the style, calling it 'your ancient and undoubted right and inheritance,' but could rather have wished that ye had said that your privileges were derived from the grace and permission of our ancestors and us (for most of them grow from precedents, which shews rather a toleration than inheritance), yet we are pleased to give you our royal assurance that as long as you contain yourselves within the limits of your duty, we will be as careful to maintain and preserve your lawful liberties and privileges as ever any of our predecessors were, nay, as to preserve our own royal prerogative. So as your

House shall only have need to beware to trench upon the prerogative of the Crown; which would enforce us, or any just king, to retrench them of their privileges that would pare his prerogative and flowers of the Crown. But of this we hope there shall never be cause given. Dated at Newmarket, the eleventh day of December, 1621.

Rushworth, Historical Collections, i, 46–52.

(5) King's Letter of 16 December, 1621

To our trusty and well-beloved Counsellor Sir George Calvert, knight,
one of our Principal Secretaries

Jacobus Rex—Right trusty and well-beloved counsellor, We greet you well. We are sorry to hear that notwithstanding our reiterated messages to our House of Commons for going on in their businesses, in regard of the shortness of time betwixt this and Christmas and of their own earnest desire that we should now conclude a session by making of good and profitable laws, they continue to lose time, and now of late, upon our gracious answer sent unto them, have taken occasion to make more delay in appointing a committee to-morrow to consider upon the points of our answer, and especially concerning that point in it which maketh mention of their privileges. Our pleasure therefore is, that you shall in our name tell them that we are so loth to have time mis-spent, which is so precious a thing, in the well using whereof our people may receive so great a benefit, as we are thus far contented to descend from our royal dignity by explaining at this time our meaning in our said answer touching that point; that all our good subjects in that House that intend nothing but our honour and the weal of the commonwealth may clearly see our intention.

Whereas in our said answer we told them that we could not allow of the style, calling it their ancient and undoubted right and inheritance, but could rather have wished that they had said their privileges were derived from the grace and permission of our ancestors and us (for most of them grow from precedents, which sheweth rather a toleration than inheritance), the plain truth is, that we cannot with patience endure our subjects to use such anti-monarchical words to us concerning their liberties, except they had subjoined that they were granted unto them by the grace and favour of our predecessors. But as for our intention herein, God knows we never meant to deny them any lawful privileges that ever that House enjoyed in our predecessors' times, as we expected our said answer should have sufficiently cleared them; neither in justice, whatever they have undoubted right unto, nor in grace, whatever our predecessors or we have graciously permitted unto them. And therefore we made that distinction of the most part: for whatsoever liberties or privileges they enjoy by any law or statute shall be ever inviolably preserved by us, and we hope our posterity will imitate our footsteps therein. And whatsoever privileges they enjoy by long custom and uncontrolled and lawful precedents we will likewise be as careful to preserve them, and transmit the care thereof to our posterity; neither was it any way in our mind to think of any particular point wherein we meant to disallow of their liberties; so as in justice we confess ourself to be bound to maintain them in their rights, and in grace we are rather minded to increase than infringe any of them, if they shall so deserve at our hands. To end therefore as we began: let them go on cheerfully in their businesses, rejecting the curious wrangling of lawyers upon words and syllables; otherwise (which God forbid) the world shall see how often and how earnestly we have pressed them to go on according to their calling with those things that are fit to be done for the weal of our Crown and Kingdom; and how many various shifts have been from time to time maliciously found out to frustrate us of our good purpose and hinder them from the performance of that service which they owe to us and to our whole kingdom; whereof when the country shall come to be truly informed, they will give the authors thereof little thanks. Given at our Court at Royston, the 16th of December, 1621.

Mr Secretary Calvert then said that it was not strange that the business of the House (which was so commonly spoken of abroad in the town) doth come to his Majesty's ear; and he thinketh whosoever hath informed his Majesty hereof hath done a good office to the House. He desireth that his Majesty's letter may be entered here in the House, and that we may go on with business. It was thereupon ordered that this letter from his Majesty shall be here entered in the House, and that everyone that will may have copies thereof. *Parliamentary History*, i, 1350–2.

(6) The Commons Protestation of 18 December, 1621

The Commons now assembled in Parliament, being justly occasioned thereunto concerning sundry liberties, franchises, and privileges of Parliament, amongst others here mentioned, do make this Protestation following, That the liberties, franchises, privileges, and jurisdictions of Parliament are the ancient and undoubted birthright and inheritance of the subjects of England; and that the arduous and urgent affairs concerning the King, State, and defence of the realm and of the Church of England, and the maintenance and making of laws, and redress of mischiefs and grievances which daily happen within this realm, are proper subjects and matter of counsel and debate in Parliament; and that in the handling and proceeding of those businesses every member of the House of Parliament hath, and of right ought to have, freedom of speech to propound, treat, reason, and bring to conclusion the same; and that the Commons in Parliament have like liberty and freedom of speech to propound, treat, reason, and bring to conclusion the same; and that the Commons in Parliament have like liberty and freedom to treat of these matters in such order as in their judgments shall seem fittest; and that every member of the said House hath like freedom from all impeachment, imprisonment, and molestation (other than by censure of the House itself) for or concerning any speaking, reasoning, or declaring of any matter or matters touching the Parliament or Parliament-business; and that if any of the said members be complained of and questioned for anything done or said in Parliament, the same is to be shewed to the King by the advice and assent of all the Commons assembled in Parliament, before the King give credence to any private information.

Rushworth, *Historical Collections*, i, 53.

(7) Proclamation for the Dissolution, 6 January, 1622

De Proclamatione Regia pro Dissolutione Conventionis Parliamenti

Albeit the assembling, continuing, and dissolving of Parliaments be a prerogative so peculiarly belonging to our Imperial Crown, and the times and seasons thereof so absolutely in our own power that we need not give accompt thereof unto any; yet, according to our continual custom to make our good subjects acquainted with the reasons of all our public resolutions and actions, we have thought it expedient at this time to declare not only our pleasure and resolution therein, grounded upon mature deliberation, with the advice and uniform consent of our whole Privy Council, but therewith also to note some especial proceedings moving us to this resolution, and that chiefly to this end: that as God so the world may witness with us that it was our intent to have made this the happiest Parliament that ever was in our time, and that the let and impediment thereof being discerned, all misunderstandings and jealousies might be removed, and all our people may know and believe that we are as far from imputing any of those ill accidents that have happened in Parliament to any want or neglect of duty or good affection toward us by them in general, or by the greater or better number of Parliament men, as we are confident, the true causes discovered, they will be far from imputing it to any default in us, there having in the beginning of this late assembly passed greater and more infallible tokens of love and duty from our subjects to us their Sovereign, and more remarkable testimonies from us of our princely care and zeal of their welfare than have byn[1] in any Parliament met in any former age.

The Parliament was by us called as for making good and profitable laws, so more especially in this time of miserable distraction throughout Christendom for the better settling of peace and religion and restoring our children[2] to their ancient and lawful patrimony, which we attempted to procure by peaceable treaty at our own excessive charge, thereby to save and prevent the effusion of Christian blood, the miserable effect of war and dissension; yet with full purpose, if that succeeded not, to recover it by the sword, and therefore as a necessary means conducing to those ends the supply of our treasures was to be provided for.

This Parliament, beginning in January last, proceeded some months with such harmony between us and our people as cannot be paralleled by any former time, for as the House of Commons at the first, both in the manner of their supply and otherwise, shewed greater love and more respect than ever any House of Commons did to us, or as we think to any King before us, so we upon all their complaints have afforded them such memorable and rare examples of justice as many ages past cannot shew the like; wherein, that we preferred the weal of our people before all particular respects, the things themselves do sufficiently prove, our justice being extended not only to persons of ordinary rank and quality but even to the prime officer of our kingdom[3], and although, after their first recess at Easter, we found that they mis-spent a great deal of time rather upon the enlarging of the limits of their liberties, and divers other curious and unprofitable

---

[1] An obsolete form of part of the verb 'to be.'

[2] James's daughter Elizabeth and her husband, Frederick Elector Palatine.

[3] This is a reference to the proceedings against Lord Chancellor Bacon for bribery in 1621.

things, than upon the framing and proponing[1] of good and profitable laws, yet we gave them time and scope for their Parliamentary proceedings and prolonged the session to an unusual length, continuing it until the eight and twentieth day of May before we signified our purpose for their recess, and then we declared that we would make a recess on the fourth day of June next following, but only for a time, and in such manner as might be without disturbance to any their businesses in hand; expressing out of our grace, though we needed not, the causes of that our purpose, which were, the season of the year, usually hot and unfit for great assemblies; our progress approaching, the necessity we had to make use of our Council attending in both Houses both to settle our weighty affairs of State before we went and to attend us when we went our progress; the disfurnishing our ordinary Courts of Justice so many terms together; the long absence of Justices of Peace and Deputy-Lieutenants whose presence was needful for making and returning of musters and for subordinate government of the country; And therefore we appointed to adjourn the Parliament on the fourth day of June, giving that warning longer than usual that they might set in order their business and prepare their grievances, which we promised both to hear and answer before that recess, for presenting whereof we appointed them a time.

This message, graciously intended by us, was not so well entertained by some who in a short time dispersed and spread their jealousies unto others, and thereby occasioned discontentment in the House for being adjourned without passing of bills, yet made not their address to us as byn meet, but desired a conference with the Lords, and at that conference the nine and twentieth of May, under colour of desiring to petition us for some further time to perfect and pass some special bills, were emboldened not only to dispute but to refell[2] all the reasons that we had given for the adjournment; which being made known unto us, we again signified our pleasure to both Houses that on the fourth day of June the Parliament should rise, but we would then give our royal assent to such bills as were or should be ready and fit to be then passed, continuing all other businesses in [the] state they were, by a special Act to be framed for that purpose.

The Lords with all duty and respect submitted to our resolution, passed the Act, and sent it with special recommendation to the House of Commons, but they neither read it nor proceeded with business but, forgetting that the time was ours

---

[1] Setting forth for consideration.   [2] Refute.

and not theirs, continued their discontent as they pretended for being so soon dismissed.

We, though it were strange to observe such averseness for our resolving upon such weighty reasons that wherein we needed not be measured by any other rule but our own princely will, yet were contented to descend from our right to alter our resolution and to continue the session for a fortnight more, wherein they might perfect such public bills as were esteemed of most importance, for which purpose we ourself came in person unto the Higher House of Parliament and made offer thereof unto them, which being in effect as much as the Commons had formerly desired, was no sooner offered but, yielding thanks to us, the said Commons resolved the same day, directly contrary to their former desire, to refuse it, and to accept our first resolution of an adjournment, but attending us at Greenwich, presented no grievances.

This inconstancy as we passed by with a gentle admonition, so for the matter of grievances as well of England as Ireland we promised to take them into our own care though not presented to us, and really performed the same so far forth as time and the advice of our Council of each kingdom could enable us, as is witnessed by our several proclamations published in both realms, as likewise in granting at the same time those three suits which were propounded unto us by the Archbishop of Canterbury at the request and in the name of both the Houses; but in conclusion the House of Commons making it their choice, we made a recess by adjournment of the Parliament the fourth day of June, though indeed we must do them this right that at the said recess, taking into their serious consideration the present estate of our children abroad and the general afflicted estate of the true professors of religion in foreign parts, they did with one unanimous consent, in the name of themselves and the whole body of the kingdom, make a most dutiful and solemn protestation that if our pious endeavours by treaty to procure their peace and safety should not take that good effect which was desired in the treaty, whereof they humbly besought us not to suffer any long delay, then upon signification of our pleasure in Parliament, they would be ready to the uttermost of their powers, both with lives and fortunes, to assist us, so as that, by the divine help of Almighty God, we might be able to do that by our sword which by peaceable courses should not be effected.

But during the time of this long recess, having to our great charges mediated with the Emperor by the means of our

Ambassador the Lord Digby, and having found those hopes to fail which we had to prevail by treaty, we in confidence of the assistance of our people, thus freely promised and protested in Parliament, did instantly shorten the time of the recess, which we had before appointed to continue until the eighth day of February, and did reassemble our Parliament the twentieth day of November last, and made known unto them the true state and necessity of our children's affairs; declaring our resolution unto them of taking upon us the defence of our children's patrimony by way of arms since we could not compass it by an amicable treaty, and therefore expected the fruit of that their declaration whereby we were invited unto this course.

Wherein, howbeit we are well satisfied of the good inclination of most part of our House of Commons, testified by their ready assent to the speedy payment of a subsidy newly to be granted, yet upon this occasion some particular members of that House took such inordinate liberty, not only to treat of our high prerogatives and of sundry things that without our special direction were no fit subjects to be treated of in Parliament, but also to speak with less respect of foreign princes our allies than were fit for any subject to do of any anointed King, though in enmity and hostility with us.

And when upon this occasion we used some reprehension towards those miscarriages, requiring them not to proceed but in such things as were within the capacity of that House according to the continual custom of our predecessors, then by the means of some evil-affected and discontented persons such heat and distemper was raised in the House that, albeit themselves had sued unto us for a session and for a general pardon, unto both which at their earnest suit we assented, yet after this fire kindled they rejected both, and setting apart all businesses of consequence and weight notwithstanding our admonition and earnest pressing them to go forward, they either sat as silent or spent the time in disputing of privileges, descanting upon the words and syllables of our letters and messages, which for better clearing of truth and satisfaction of all men we are about to publish in print so soon as possibly we can; and although in our answer to their petition we gave them full assurance that we would be as careful of the preservation of their privileges as of our own royal prerogative, and in our explanation after sent unto them by our letters written unto our Secretary we told them that we never meant to deny them any lawful privileges that ever that House enjoyed in our predecessors' times, and that whatsoever privileges or liberties they enjoyed by any law or statute should ever be inviolably preserved by us, and we hoped our posterity would imitate our footsteps therein, and whatsoever privileges they enjoyed by long custom and uncontrolled and lawful precedents we would likewise be as careful to preserve them, and transmit the care thereof to our posterity, confessing ourselves in justice to be bound to maintain them in their rights, and in grace that we were rather minded to increase than infringe any of them if they should so deserve at our hands, which might satisfy any reasonable man that we were far from violating their privileges.

And although by our letters written to their Speaker we advised them to proceed and make this a session, to the end our good and loving subjects might have some taste as well of our grace and goodness towards them by our free pardon and good laws to be passed as they had both by the great and unusual examples of justice since this meeting and the so many eases and comforts given unto them by proclamation, and although we had given order for the pardon to go on, and that in a more gracious and liberal manner than had passed in many years before, and signified our willingness that, rather than time should be mis- spent, they might lay aside the thought of the subsidy and go on with an Act for continuance of statutes and the general pardon; but all this prevailed not to satisfy them, either for their pretended privileges or to persuade them to proceed with bills for the good of themselves and those that sent them. But as the session and pardon were by them well desired at first, so were they as ill rejected at the last, and notwithstanding the sincerity of our protestations not to invade their privileges, yet by persuasion of such as had been the cause of all these distempers they fall to carve for themselves, and pretending causelessly to be occasioned thereunto, in an unseasonable hour of the day and a very thin House, contrary to their own customs in all matters of weight, conclude and enter a protestation for their liberties in such ambiguous and general words as might serve for future times to invade most of our inseparable rights and prerogatives annexed to our Imperial Crown whereof, not only in the times of other our progenitors but in the blessed reign of our late predecessor that renowned Queen Elizabeth, we found our Crown actually possessed, an usurpation that the majesty of a King can no means endure.

By all which may appear that howsoever in the general proceedings of that House there are many footsteps of loving and well-affected duty towards us, yet some ill-tempered spirits have sowed tares among the corn, and thereby frustrated the hope of that plentiful and good harvest which might have multiplied the wealth and welfare of this whole land, and by their cunning diversions have imposed upon us a necessity of discontinuing this present Parliament without putting unto it the name or period of a session.

And therefore, whereas the said assembly of Parliament was by our commission adjourned until the eighth day of February now next ensuing, we minding not to continue the same any longer, and therefore not holding it fit to cause the prelates, noblemen, and States of this our realm or the knights, citizens, and burgesses of the same Parliament to travail thereabout, have thought fit to signify this our resolution with the reasons thereof unto all our subjects inhabiting in all parts of this realm, willing and requiring the said prelates, noblemen, and States, and also the said knights, citizens, and burgesses, and all others to whom in this case it shall appertain, that they forbear to attend at the day and place prefixed by the said adjournment, and in so doing they are and shall be discharged thereof against us: and we do hereby further declare that the said convention of Parliament neither is, nor after the cessing[1] and breaking thereof shall be nor ought, to be esteemed, adjudged, or taken to be or make any session of Parliament.

And albeit we are at this time enforced to break off this convention of Parliament, yet our will and desire is that all our subjects should take notice, for avoiding of all sinister suspicions and jealousies, that our intent and full resolution is to govern our people in the same manner as our progenitors and predecessors, Kings and Queens of this realm, of best government have heretofore done, and that we shall be careful, both in our own person and by charging our Privy Council, our Judges, and other our ministers in their several places respectively, to distribute true justice and right unto all our people, and that we shall be as glad to lay hold on the first occasion in due and convenient time, which we hope shall not be long, to call and assemble our Parliament with confidence of the true and hearty love and affection of our subjects as either we or any of our progenitors have at any time heretofore.

Given at our Palace of Westminster the sixth day of January [1622.] *Per ipsum Regem.*

Rymer, *Foedera*, (edition of 1704–35), xvii, 344–7.

1 'Cess' is used here in the quasi-technical sense of ceasing to perform a legal duty.

(8) Address of both Houses, 8 March, 1624

May it please your most excellent Majesty,—We are come unto you employed from your most faithful subjects and servants the Lords and Commons assembled in this present Parliament.

And first, they and we do give most humble and hearty thanks unto Almighty God that out of his gracious goodness he hath been pleased now at last to dispel that cloud and mist which for so many years hath dimmed the eyes of a great part of Christendom in that business whereof we do now consult.

And secondly, we acknowledge ourselves most bound unto your Majesty that you have been pleased to require the humble advice of us your obedient subjects in a cause so important as this which hitherto dependeth between your Majesty and the King of Spain, which we jointly offer from both Houses, no one person therein dissenting or disagreeing from the rest.

And that is, That upon mature consideration, and weighing many particulars of sundry natures, finding so much want of sincerity in all their proceedings, we, *super totam materiam*, present this our humble advice unto your Majesty, That the treaties, both for the marriage and for the Palatinate, may not any longer be continued with the honour of your Majesty, the safety of your people, the welfare of your children and posterity, as also the assurance of your ancient allies and confederates.

Lords' Journals, iii, 250.

(9) The King's Answer, 8 March, 1624

This illustrates the strength of James I's personal and dynastic feeling, and the way in which it was bound to influence the foreign policy of the Crown.

My Lords and Gentlemen all,—I have cause first to thank God with my heart and all the faculties of my mind, that my speech which I delivered in Parliament hath taken so good effect amongst you as that with an unanimous consent you have freely and speedily given me your advice in this great business, for which I also thank you all as heartily as I can. I also give my particular thanks to the gentlemen of the Lower House for that I heard, when some amongst you would have cast jealousies and doubts between me and my people, you presently[1] quelled those motions, which otherwise might have hindered the happy agreement I hope to find in this Parliament.

You give me your advice to break off both the treaties, as well concerning the match as the Palatinate; and now give me leave as

---

[1] *I.e.* immediately.

an old King to propound my doubts and hereafter to give you my answer.

First, it is true that I, who have been all the days of my life a peaceable King, and have had the honour in my titles and impresses[1] to be styled *Rex Pacificus*, should without necessity embroil myself in war, is so far from my nature and from the honour which I have had at home and abroad in endeavouring to avoid the effusion of Christian blood (of which too much hath been shed, and so much against my heart), that, unless it be upon such a necessity that I may call it, as some say merrily of women, *malum necessarium*, I should be loth to enter into it. And I must likewise acquaint you that I have had no small hopes given me of obtaining better conditions for the restitution of the Palatinate, and that even since the sitting down of the Parliament: but be not jealous, nor think me such a King that would, under pretext of asking your advice, put a scorn upon you by disdaining and rejecting it. For you remember that in my first speech unto you, for proof of my love to my people, I craved your advice in these great and weighty affairs; but in a matter of this weight I must first consider how this course may agree with my conscience and honour; and next (according to the parable uttered by our Saviour), after I have resolved of the necessity and justness of the cause, to consider how I shall be enabled to raise forces for this purpose.

As concerning the case of my children, I am now old, and would be glad, as Moses saw the land of promise from a high mountain (though he had not leave to set his foot in it), so would it be a great comfort to me that God would but so long prolong my days as if I might not see the restitution yet at least to be assured that it would be; that then I might with old Simeon say, *Nunc dimittis servum tuum, Domine*, etc., otherwise it would be a great regret unto me, and I should die with a heavy and discomforted heart.

I have often said, and particularly in the last Parliament, and I shall be ever of that mind, that as I am not ambitious of any other men's goods or lands, so I desire not to brook[2] a furrow of land in England, Scotland, or Ireland without restitution of the Palatinate; and in this mind I will live and die.

But let me acquaint you a little with the difficulties of this case. He is an unhappy man that shall advise a King, and it is an unchristian thing to seek that by blood which may be had by peace. Besides, I think your intentions are not to engage me in a

---

[1] Emblems, devices. [2] Possess or enjoy.

war, but withal you will consider how many things are requisite thereunto. I omit to speak of my own necessities; they are too well known; sure I am I have had the least help in Parliaments of any King that reigned over you these many years. I must let you know that my disabilities are increased by the charge of my son's journey into Spain which I was at for his honour and the honour of this nation; by sending of ambassadors, by maintenance of my children, and by assisting of the Palatinate, I have incurred a great debt to the King of Denmark which I am not yet able to pay. The Low Countries, who in regard of their nearness are fittest to help for the recovery of the Palatinate, are at so low an ebb that if I assist them not they are scarce able to subsist. The Princes of Germany that should do me any good are all poor, wrecked, and disheartened, and do expect assistance from hence. For Ireland, I leave it to you if that be not a back-door fit to be secured. For the Navy, I thank God it is now in better case than ever it was; yet more must be done, and before it can be prepared as it ought to be, it will require a new charge as well for its own strength as for securing my coasts. My children, I vow to God, eat no bread but by my means. I must maintain them, and not see them want in the mean time till the Palatinate be recovered. My customs are the best part of my revenue, and in effect the substance of all I have to live on; all which are farmed out upon that condition, that if there be war, those bargains are to be annulled, which will enforce a great defalcation. Subsidies ask a great time to bring them in. Now, if you assist me that way, I must take them up beforehand upon credit, which will eat up a great part of them.

This being my case, to enter into a war without sufficient means to support it were to shew my teeth and do no more. In the mean time I heartily thank you for your advice and will seriously think upon it; as I pray you to consider of these other parts. My Treasurer, to whose office it appertains, shall more at large inform you of those things that concern my estate. Thus freely do I open my heart unto you, and having your hearts I cannot want your helps; for it is the heart that opens the purse and not the purse the heart. I will deal frankly with you. Shew me the means how I may do what you would have me, and if I take a resolution, upon your advice, to enter into a war, then yourselves by your own deputies shall have the disposing of the money; I will not meddle with it, but you shall appoint your own treasurers[1]. I say not this with a purpose to invite you to open your purses and

---

[1] See p. 374 below.

then to slight you so much as not to follow your counsel; for I will not take your money unless I take your counsel, nor engage you before I be engaged myself. Give me what you will for my own means; but I protest none of the money which you shall give for those uses shall be issued but for those ends, and by men elected by yourselves. If upon your offer I shall find the means to make the war honourable and safe, and that I resolve to embrace your advice, then I promise you in the word of a King that although war and peace be the peculiar prerogatives of Kings, yet as I have advised with you in the treaties on which war may ensue, so I will not treat nor accept of a peace without first acquainting you with it and hearing your advice, and therein go the proper way of Parliament in conferring and consulting with you in such great and weighty affairs; and haply conditions of peace will be the better when we are prepared for war, according to the old proverb that weapons bode peace.

Your kind carriage gives me much contentment; and that comforts me which my Lord of Canterbury said, There was not a contrary voice amongst you all; like the seventy interpreters, who were led by the breath of God. I am so desirous to forget all rends[1] in former Parliaments that it shall not be my default if I be not in love with Parliaments, and call them often, and desire to end my life in that intercourse between me and my people for the making of good laws, reforming of such abuses as I cannot be well informed of but in Parliament, and maintaining the good government of the commonwealth.

Therefore go on cheerfully and advise of these points, and my resolution shall then be declared.

Lords' Journals, iii, 250–1.

(10) Address of both Houses, 22 March, 1624

Most gracious Sovereign,—We your Majesty's most humble and loyal subjects, the Lords and Commons in this present Parliament assembled, do first render unto your sacred Majesty our most dutiful thanks for that, to our unspeakable comfort, you have vouchsafed to express yourself so well satisfied with our late declaration made to your Majesty of our general resolution in pursuit of our humble advice to assist your Majesty in a Parliamentary way with our persons and abilities.

And whereas your Majesty in your great wisdom and judgment

---

[1] *I.e.* all divisions.

foreseeing that it would make a deeper impression both in the enemies of that cause and in your friends and allies if they shall not only hear of the cheerful offers but also see the real performance of your subjects towards so great a work, your Majesty was pleased to descend to a particular proposition for the advancement of this great business, we in all humbleness most ready and willing to give your Majesty and the whole world an ample testimony of our sincere and dutiful intentions herein, have upon mature advice and deliberation as well of the weight and importance of this great affair as of the present estate of this your kingdom (the weal and safety whereof is in our judgments apparently threatened if your Majesty's resolution for the dissolving of the treaties now in question be longer deferred, and that provision for defence of your realm and aid of your friends and allies be not seasonably made), with a cheerful consent of us your Commons (no one dissenting) and with a full and cheerful consent of us the Lords resolved, That upon your Majesty's public declaration of the utter dissolution and discharge of the two treaties of the marriage and Palatinate, in pursuit of our advice therein, and towards the support of the war which is likely to ensue, and more particularly for those four points proposed by your Majesty, namely, the defence of this realm, the securing of Ireland, the assistance of your neighbours the States of the United Provinces and others your Majesty's friends and allies, and for the setting forth of your royal Navy, we will grant for the present the greatest aid which was ever granted in Parliament to be levied in so short a time: that is, three entire subsidies and three fifteenths, to be all paid within the compass of one whole year after your Majesty shall be pleased to make the said declaration; the money to be paid into the hands and expended by the direction of such Committees or Commissioners as hereafter shall be agreed upon in this present session of Parliament.

And we most humbly beseech your Majesty graciously to accept of these firstfruits of our hearty oblation, dedicated to that work which we infinitely desire may prosper and be advanced; and for the future to rest confidently assured that if you shall be engaged in a real war, we your loyal and loving subjects will never fail to assist your Majesty in a Parliamentary way in so royal a design, wherein your own honour, and the honour of your most noble son the Prince, and the ancient renown of this nation, the welfare and very substance of your noble and only daughter and her consort and their posterity, the safety of your own kingdoms and people, and the prosperity of your neighbours and allies, are so deeply engaged.

Lords' Journals, iii, 275.

(11) Address of both Houses, 10 April, 1624

May it please your most excellent Majesty,—It having pleased your Majesty, upon our humble suit and advice, to dissolve both the treaties, to our great joy and comfort, we your Majesty's most faithful and loyal subjects, the Lords and Commons assembled in Parliament, do in all humbleness offer unto your sacred Majesty these two petitions following:

First, That for the more safety of your realms and better keeping your subjects in their due obedience, and other important reasons of State, your Majesty will be pleased, by some such course as your Majesty shall think fit, to give present order that all the laws be put in due execution which have been made and do stand in force against Jesuits, seminary priests, and all others having taken orders by authority derived from the See of Rome, and generally against all Popish recusants; and as for disarming, that it may be according to the laws and according to former acts and directions of State in the like case; and yet that it may appear to all the world the favour and clemency your Majesty useth towards all your subjects of what condition soever, and to the intent the Jesuits and priests now in the realm may not pretend to be surprised, that a speedy and certain day may be prefixed by your Majesty's proclamation, before which day they shall depart out of this realm and all other your Highness's dominions, and neither they nor any other to return or come hither again upon peril of the severest penalties of the laws now in force against them; and that all your Majesty's subjects may thereby also be admonished not to receive, entertain, comfort, or conceal any of them, upon the penalties and forfeitures which by the laws may be imposed on them.

Secondly, (seeing we are thus happily delivered from that danger which those treaties now dissolved, and that use which your ill-affected subjects made thereof, would certainly have drawn upon us, and yet cannot but foresee and fear lest the like may hereafter happen, which would inevitably bring such peril unto your Majesty's kingdoms), we are most humble suitors to your gracious Majesty to secure the hearts of your good subjects by the engagement of your royal word unto them that upon no occasion of marriage or treaty or other request in that behalf from any foreign Prince or State whatsoever, you will take away or slacken the execution of your laws against Jesuits, priests, and Popish recusants.

To which our humble petitions, proceeding from our most loyal and dutiful affections towards your Majesty, our care of our country's good, and our own confident persuasion that these will much advance the glory of Almighty God, the everlasting honour of your Majesty, the safety of your kingdoms, and the encouragement of all your good subjects, we do most humbly beseech your Majesty to vouchsafe a gracious answer.

Lords' Journals, iii, 298.

(c) The Privilege of Freedom from Arrest

The final form of the privilege of freedom from arrest was fixed in 1604 by Shirley's case [p. 303].

Sir Thomas Shirley was elected member for Steyning, but before Parliament met he was arrested at the suit of a City alderman and imprisoned in the Fleet. The Commons summoned the Warden of the Fleet to the Bar; but he refused to release the prisoner on the ground that he himself would thereby become liable for Shirley's debt. The House committed the creditor to the Tower for breach of privilege, as well as the bailiff who had made the arrest, and introduced a special Bill to protect the Warden from any liability which he might incur by releasing Shirley; and when he refused to act until the Bill had actually passed, they sent him also to the Tower. He was eventually prevailed upon to release his prisoner, but not until the House had committed him 'to the prison called Little Ease within the Tower' where he was very uncomfortable[1]. He was then required to confess his fault upon his knees before being pardoned and discharged [p. 315].

The proceedings in Shirley's case led to the passing of a general Act [p. 317] enabling creditors whose prisoners should be set at liberty by privilege of Parliament to sue out new writs against them as soon as the time of privilege expired, and protecting the officers who arrested them from the legal consequences of surrendering them in obedience to a claim of privilege. In addition to this general Act,[2] a private Act was also passed entitled 'An Act to secure the debt of Simpson and others, and save harmless the Warden of the Fleet in Sir Thomas Shirley's case.'[3] This recognised that the members had 'ever used to enjoy the freedom in coming to and returning from the Parliament and sitting there without restraint or molestation, and it concerneth your Commons greatly to have this freedom and privilege inviolably observed; yet to the end that no person be prejudiced or damnified hereby,' it was provided (1) that those persons who had had Shirley in their custody should be protected against the legal consequences of having liberated him; and (2) that as soon as the time of privilege expired, Shirley's creditors might sue out and execute a new judgment for his debt.

---

[1] See note on p. 315 below.
[2] May, *Parliamentary Practice* (10th edition), p. 104.
[3] 1 Jac. I, Private Acts, cap. 10: printed in Prothero, p. 324.

(1) Shirley's Case, 1604

The human interest of the proceedings in Shirley's case centres in the tenacious resistance of the Warden of the Fleet to the demands of the House of Commons, and the loyal support given to her husband by the Warden's wife.

[22 March, 1604]... This being a motion tending to matter of privilege, was seconded by another by Mr Serjeant Shirley touching an arrest made the 15th of March last, the day of his Majesty's solemn entrance through London and four days before the sitting of the Parliament, upon the body of Sir Thomas Shirley, elected one of the burgesses for the borough of Steyning in the county of Sussex, at the suit of one Giles Simpson a goldsmith, dwelling in Lombard Street, London, by one William Watkins a serjeant-at-mace and Thomas Aram his yeoman; and prayed that the body of the said Sir Thomas might be freed, according to the known privilege of the House.

Hereupon the House in affirmation of their own privilege assented, and ordered that a warrant according to the ancient form should be directed under the hand of Mr Speaker to the Clerk of the Crown for the granting of a writ of *habeas corpus* to bring the body of the said Sir Thomas into the House upon Tuesday next at eight a clock in the morning. The form of the warrant was:

Jovis, 22 Martii, 1603[-4.]

It is this day ordered and required by the Commons' House of Parliament that a writ of *habeas corpus* be awarded for the bringing of the body of Sir Thomas Shirley knight, one of the members of this House and now prisoner in the Fleet, into the said House upon Tuesday next at eight a clock in the morning, according to the ancient privilege and custom in that behalf used. And this shall be your warrant.

Your loving Friend,

EDWARD PHELIPS, *Speaker.*

Directed to my very loving friend Sir George Coppin, knight, Clerk of the Crown in his Majesty's High Court of Chancery. *In pede*, RA. EWENS.

Upon this warrant issued a writ of *habeas corpus* in this form:

Jacobus, Dei gratia Angliae, Scotiae, Franciae, et Hiberniae Rex, Fidei Defensor, etc., Guardiano Prisonae nostrae de le Fleet, salutem. Praecipimus tibi quod habeas coram nobis in praesenti Parliamento nostro apud Westmonasterium in die Martis, octavo die instantis mensis Maii, circa horam octavam ante meridiem ejusdem diei, corpus Thomae Shirley militis, capt. et in prisona nostra sub custodia tua ut dicitur detent. quocunque nomine seu cognomine idem Thomas censeatur, una cum causa captionis et detentionis ejusdem Thomae, ad respondendum super hiis quae sibi tunc ibidem objicientur, et ad faciendum ulterius et recipiendum quod per nos in Parliamento nostro praedicto consideratum et ordinatum fuerit: Et hoc nullatenus omittas, sicut nobis inde respondere volueris. Et habeas ibi hoc breve. Teste meipso apud Westmonasterium septimo die Maii, anno regni nostri Angliae, Franciae, et Hiberniae secundo et Scotiae tricesimo septimo.

The Serjeant of the House was also commanded by the House to bring in at the same time the bodies of William Watkins the serjeant and Thomas Aram his yeoman...(p. 149).

[27 March, 1604]...This day the writ of *habeas corpus* formerly awarded by order of the House for the bringing in of the body of Sir Thomas Shirley, one of the members of the House and prisoner in the Fleet, was returned by the Warden of the Fleet, the prisoner himself brought to the Bar, and Simpson the goldsmith and Watkins the serjeant-at-mace as delinquents brought in by the Serjeant of the House....

Mr Speaker proposed divers questions to be answered by the said offenders: by whose relation it was averred that the writ of execution was taken forth the thirtieth of January; was delivered to the serjeant the eleventh of February, before Sir Thomas was elected burgess; that Simpson and the serjeant, in the interim before the arrest, had no conference or privity one with the other; that the serjeant knew nothing at all of Sir Thomas his election, but understood by his Majesty's proclamation that no person outlawed for treason, felony, debt, or any other trespass, ought to be admitted a member of the Parliament, and was thereupon induced to think that Sir Thomas Shirley, standing outlawed, should not be elected or admitted a burgess, which if he had known or suspected, he would have been very careful not to have given offence to this honourable House by any such arrest.

To this Sir Thomas was admitted to answer, who affirmed that the arrest was made the fifteenth day of March, the day of his Majesty's first and solemn entrance through London, at what time he was going by commandment to wait upon his Majesty; whereof, upon the first offer to touch him, he wished the serjeant to take knowledge; as also that he was elected a burgess for the borough of Steyning in the county of Sussex to serve at this present Parliament; that, notwithstanding, they persisted in the arrest, and carried his body to the prison of the Compter.

The case being understood by the House, and the parties withdrawn, sundry learned members delivered their opinion, both in the point of privilege and in the point of law, for the state of the debt, the party being delivered out of execution by privilege.

For matter of privilege, it was avouched by one as an ancient ground that it was to be allowed to every member of the House *eundo, sedendo, morando, redeundo*; by others that there was some difference whether the party be sworn and admitted or not sworn at the time of his arrest. For matter in law, it was disputed whether Sir Thomas were subject to the execution after the Parliament, and whether the remedy were to be taken against the Sheriff or the debtor; and a difference put between a discharge by act of the party and a discharge by act in law: in the one case, the execution altogether discharged; in the other, not. Other manner of discharges also remembered, as discharge by suspension, discharge by authority, and sundry cases put upon them; and the whole case, after long dispute, summarily considered in three particulars, viz., 1. privilege to a member; 2. interest reserved to a stranger; 3. punishment of the offender. Which being the grounds of all the subsequent arguments in this case, the dispute ended for this day, with caution that the House should so proceed as they gave not way and encouragement to others to practise to be arrested upon execution with a purpose by pretence of privilege to discharge the debt; and a motion that a special committee might be named for the consideration of all the questions and doubts in this case...(p. 155).

[11 April, 1604]...Mr Hitcham reporteth the travail of the committees in Sir Thomas Shirley's case; wherein (he said) they took into consideration two things: 1. The contempt and the punishment of the offenders; 2. Whether the debt were extinguished. They found that Simpson was guilty of the contempt wittingly; that Lightbone the serjeant-at-mace made the arrest wittingly, willingly, and wilfully: which both were made appear by these circumstances: 1. It was found that the writ of execution was procured to be made of a clerk that had no authority to do it; that Sir Thomas, being first arrested upon a *latitat*[1], said he was a burgess of Parliament and therefore willed the serjeant to beware. The serjeant answered that Mr Simpson knew that, and he

---

1 'A writ which supposed the defendant to lie concealed, and which summoned him to answer in the King's Bench' (*Oxford Dictionary*).

himself knew it well enough. Sir Thomas being in the Compter, and the execution laid upon him, sent again to Simpson and told him as before. Simpson answered, he could but lie by it.

Upon this report the question was moved, and made by Mr Speaker: *Question.* Whether Simpson, the serjeant, and his yeoman should be committed, viz., to the Tower, the proper prison of the House? *Resolved,* That they should be committed. But the House being informed that my Lord Chancellor, before the sitting of the House, had committed them, Sir Edward Hobby and Mr Francis Moore were appointed to acquaint his Lordship with the judgment of the House for their remove to the prison of the Tower....And the House...ordered, That the counsel of all parties should be heard on Friday morning following....

According to former order, a warrant for a writ of *habeas corpus* to bring in the body of Sir Thomas Shirley issued in this form:

Whereas Sir Thomas Shirley knight, one of the members of the Commons' House of Parliament, is arrested upon an execution at the suit of Giles Simpson of London, goldsmith, and now remaineth prisoner in the Fleet, to the great contempt of the privilege of this Parliament; it is ordered and required by the said House that a writ of *habeas corpus* be forthwith awarded for his remove out of prison and for his appearance in the House upon Friday next at eight a clock in the morning. And this shall be your warrant.

ED. PHELIPS, *Speaker.*

Directed, To my very loving friend, Sir Geo. Coppin, knight, Clerk of the Crown in the Chancery.

A warrant was also directed for the bringing in of Simpson the goldsmith at whose suit, and Watkins the serjeant that made the arrest, to this effect:

Whereas Giles Simpson and William Watkins have committed a manifest contempt against the privileges of this Parliament, and now remain prisoners in the Fleet; it is required by the Commons' House of the said Parliament that you take the bodies of the said Giles and William into your custody, and bring them into the said House upon Friday the thirteenth of this month at eight a clock in the morning to answer to such matters as shall be objected against them. And this shall be your warrant.

Directed, To my loving friend, Mr Roger Wood Esquire, one of his Majesty's Serjeants-at-Arms and Serjeant of the Commons' House of Parliament...(pp. 167–8).

[13 April, 1604]...Counsel in Sir Thomas Shirley's case came to the Bar. Mr George Crooke, for the privilege of Sir Thomas Shirley, said it was but a suspension of the debt *pro tempore*: cited precedents....Mr Stafferton for the Warden of the Fleet....

Ordered upon this argument, That Simpson at whose suit, and Watkins the serjeant that made the arrest, should be committed to the prison of the Tower...(p. 171).

[16 April, 1604]...Moved, that a Bill might be drawn in the matter of Sir Thomas Shirley; wherein was to be considered only two things: justice of privilege and justice to the party.

For better information of the House and direction to the committees, certain ancient precedents of petitions to the Kings of this realm, with answer and assent from the said Kings, in the very point of privilege and of arrest upon execution, taken out of the Parliament records in the Tower, upon this occasion were produced and read to the House, in number three, as followeth:

* * * * * *

After these precedents read, and some consideration had what was to be done, the House agreed upon three questions: 1. Whether Sir Thomas Shirley shall have privilege? 2. Whether presently [*i.e.* immediately], or be deferred till further order? 3. Whether we shall be petitioners to his Majesty (according to former precedents) for some course of securing the debt to the party and saving harmless the Warden of the Fleet?

These questions being severally put, were all resolved in the affirmative; and so left for this day...(pp. 173–5).

[17 April, 1604]...Sir John Shirley offereth to the House a Bill drawn by the Committee in Sir Thomas Shirley's case, intituled, An Act to secure Simpson's debt and save harmless the Warden of the Fleet in Sir Thomas Shirley's case... (p. 175).

[20 April, 1604]...To secure Simpson's debt, etc., reported from the Committee by Mr Francis Moore with amendments; which being twice read, the Bill upon question ordered to be ingrossed...(p. 179).

[21 April, 1604]...To secure Simpson's debt and save harmless the Warden of the Fleet in Sir Thomas Shirley's case, upon a third reading and the question, passed....

Bills sent up to the Lords by Mr Vice-Chamberlain to his Majesty, *viz*: An Act to secure Simpson's debt [etc.]...(p. 181).

[28 April, 1604]...Mr Secretary Herbert returneth from the Lords....

Sir Edward Hobby. That the Bill concerning Sir Thomas Shirley was twice read and committed: That upon the return from the Committee they would give it a third reading so soon as should become the gravity of that House. For his Highness's royal assent to the Bill, whether the King should come in person or be done by commission, they doubted: Both too much in the case of a private person; but this a matter of privilege concerning the whole House. It were fit a petition were exhibited to his Majesty from the House that he would be pleased to give his royal assent, leaving the manner to himself...(p. 189).

[4 May, 1604]...A petition tendered, and read in the House, to be exhibited to his Majesty for his royal assent to Sir Thomas Shirley's Bill presently to be had. Upon the reading it was not approved, nor thought fit by the House to proceed in that manner, being, as was conceived, some impeachment to the privilege of the House....

*   *   *   *   *   *

By this occasion a question was resolved on and made, Whether Sir Thomas Shirley shall presently be delivered? Resolved.

Ordered, upon this question, That a writ of *habeas corpus* shall presently be awarded for the bringing of his body, being prisoner in the Fleet, into the House to-morrow at eight a clock in the morning; and a warrant containing the effect of the order, under the hand of Mr Speaker, directed to the Clerk of the Crown accordingly...(p. 198).

[7 May, 1604]...[The House] was informed that the Warden of the Fleet denied to execute the writ of *habeas corpus* lately awarded for bringing of the body of Sir Thomas Shirley into the House before the King's royal assent be procured to the Bill for the security of Simpson and himself.

The Warden himself at the Bar examined upon oath whether any intercourse or dealing between Simpson and him; any reward or promise of reward by Simpson, or other hope from him or his friends, was there for the detaining and not delivering of Sir Thomas Shirley.

He answered resolutely, That he had no hope, directly or indirectly.

Being urged whether upon a new writ he will yield his body, he denied it as before.

The Warden retired, and upon some debate the order was,

That the Warden shall remain in the custody of the Serjeant; the prison of the Fleet in the mean while be set in safety; and if to-morrow upon a new writ of *habeas corpus cum causa* he do not yield, that then without further hearing or appearance in the House he be delivered over to the Lieutenant of the Tower as the House's prisoner and there kept until further order...(p. 200).

[8 May, 1604]...The Warden of the Fleet was brought to the Bar by the Serjeant; and being charged with his obstinacy and contempt, he offereth the writ of *habeas corpus* with the return, which was read as followeth:

Jacobus...Rex...Gardiano prisonae nostrae de la Fleete, salutem. Praecipimus tibi quod habeas coram nobis in praesenti Parliamento nostro apud Westm. in die Martis, octavo die instantis mensis Maii, circa horam octavam ante meridiem ejusdem diei, corpus Thomae Shirley militis, capt. et in prisona nostra sub custodia tua ut dicitur detent. quocunque nomine aut cognomine idem Thomas censeatur, una cum causa captionis et detentionis ejusdem Thomae, ad respondendum super hiis quae sibi tunc ibidem objicientur, et ad faciendum ulterius et recipiendum quod per nos in Parliamento nostro praedicto consideratum et ordinatum fuerit; et hoc nullatenus omittas, sicut nobis inde respondere volueris. Et habeas ibi hoc breve. Teste meipso apud Westm. septimo die Maii, anno regni nostri Angliae, Franciae, et Hiberniae secundo, et Scotiae tricesimo septimo.

COPPIN.

Responsum Johannis Trench armigeri, Gardiani:

Ego Johannes Trench armiger, Gardianus prisonae Domini Regis de le Fleet, Domino Regi in Parliamento suo certifico, quod istud breve adeo tarde mihi advenit, quod corpus infra nominati Thomae Shirley ad diem, horam, et locum infra content. habere non potui, prout interius mihi praecipitur.

Being demanded who drew the return:

Answer. Himself conceived it; one Kempe wrote it. He affirmed he received the writ after eight a clock.

The Warden retired to the door; and Baskerville, servant to Sir Thomas, produced upon oath, saith he offered it long before eight at the Lord Chancellor's house, and delivered it half an hour before eight at the Fleet. Mr Speaker observeth that the writ was not well made, being *circa horam octavam.*

The Warden brought in again and asked, if this writ had come in convenient time, or if another shall come, whether he would deliver him?

Answer. He could make no other answer than yesterday.

Question. Why he dealt so severely with Sir Thomas Shirley?
Answer. Sir Thomas refuseth to give security.
Question. Why he restrained any to come to him?
Answer. He kept the like restraint upon others.

Mr Speaker pressed him to understand the case by sundry precedents;...but it did not move.

After this he desired to be heard; and demanded whether the Act to be assented unto by the King will discharge him.

Answer. That it would.

He replied, he would discharge Sir Thomas if by a writ directed unto him for that purpose he were brought before the Lord Chancellor; and so retired again....

At length ordered, upon two several questions: 1. To commit the Warden of the Fleet to the Tower close prisoner; 2. To send the Serjeant to-morrow...to require the delivery of Sir Thomas Shirley...(p. 203).

[9 May, 1604]...The Serjeant returneth from the Fleet: said he demanded the body of Sir Thomas Shirley three times, and called upon him at his chamber window. That the Warden's wife had taken all the keys and discharged her servants from attendance on the prisoners. Cried out, that if they would call her husband he would satisfy the House. He was loth to use violence, neither had he any such commandment, therefore returned without him.

Mr Secretary Herbert reporteth, that his Majesty, upon the reading of the precedent of Ferrers[1], was graciously pleased to leave it to their liberty to proceed in the case of Sir Thomas Shirley as they thought fit; with care and caution for the other prisoners....

...Mr Recorder...moved, that six gentlemen of the House might be selected and sent to the Fleet with the Serjeant and his mace to attend them, and there require the delivery of Sir Thomas Shirley; and if it were denied, to press to his chamber and, providing for the safety of the prison and prisoners, to free him with force and bring him away with them to the House.

This motion was put to question, and the House divided upon it:

With the Yea, 176 } Difference, 23.
With the No, 153 }

Resolved, they should be sent, with direction and authority as before.

---

[1] See *Tudor Constitutional Documents*, pp. 579–83. In Ferrers's case in 1543 the House of Commons had already made use of Little Ease.

After this question, Mr Speaker putteth the House in mind that all such as were sent, and did enter the prison in that manner, were by the law subject to an action upon the case; and thereupon thought meet to stay that proceeding...(pp. 204–5).

[10 May, 1604]...The debate renewed touching Sir Thomas Shirley.

Moved, That a new Bill might be drawn; and that the Lord Chancellor in the mean time might, *de bene esse*, deliver him. The former Bill passed both Houses and after found faulty; and therefore a new Bill to be thought on.

Sir Henry Mountagu bringeth in a new Bill.

[This Bill was read twice, ordered to be ingrossed, and was 'presently[1] ingrossed by the Clerk's servant, attending to that purpose at the door;' read a third time and passed, and 'instantly sent up to the Lords.']

Sir Roger Aston delivereth from the King that, *in verbo Principis*, he will give his royal assent at the end of the session....

...The House understanding that the Warden of the Fleet had the liberty of the prison, and was not kept close prisoner according to the order of the House, it was now, upon question, ordered, That he shall be put in close prison; and the Lieutenant to attend here to-morrow, bringing with him all such as have had or now have the custody of the said Warden, to render a reason of his said setting at liberty against order.

A letter from Mrs Trench, wife of the Warden of the Fleet, directed to Mr Speaker and the House, published and read in the House in these words:

May it please you, Mr Speaker, and the rest of the honourable House of Parliament: The perplexity I have dwelt in since it pleased your honourable Court to commit my husband to the Tower moveth me your distressed petitioner[2] humbly to prefer my miseries to your merciful considerations. The Serjeant-at-Arms was yesterday at the Fleet, and demanded the body of Sir Thomas Shirley. I confess I dared not absolutely bid the Serjeant take him. I had the commandment of my husband on Monday last (since which time it pleased you by close imprisonment to divorce me his presence) to the contrary. His Majesty's prison is disordered, wanting him or a deputy of trust (which he never had), and I am only left, without either guide or counsel and ignorant of all men's causes. There is murmuring and muttering; many, I fear, plotting to escape, and I and my

---

[1] *I.e.* immediately.
[2] The *Journals* read 'prisoner.'

children thereby utterly undone. I am so far from contempt of this Court as, if it seem pleasing unto you to certify me, under the hand of the three Chief Justices, that it is no escape, or to send for Simpson and persuade him to release all escapes, or Sir Thomas Shirley to put in good security for his true imprisonment, or to invent any ways for my safety whereby I and mine perish not in the street, I am in all willingness ready to obey, and discharge him in an hour's warning, and shall think myself everlastingly bound unto you for the same. And so humbly praying your favours in the premises, craving pardon for my boldness, and submitting myself as shall seem best unto you, I humbly take my leave.

From the Fleet this present Thursday, written with tears.

The distressed and oppressed wife of
the Warden of the Fleet,
ANNE TRENCH ... (pp. 205–6).

[11 May, 1604] The Serjeant with his mace sent to the Fleet for Sir Thomas Shirley.

Sir George Harvey, the Lieutenant of the Tower, being present in the House according to appointment, excuseth the liberty of the Warden now in his custody; saying that where the prisoner is committed for treason or *crimen laesae majestatis*, his manner is to keep him close; where but for contempts or misdemeanours, he giveth him the liberty of the prison. For the first, the prisoner hath his diet in his chamber; for the other, he cometh to the Lieutenant's table.

*　　*　　*　　*　　*　　*

The Serjeant returneth from the Fleet and reporteth that, meeting with Mr Warden's wife, he told her of the favour of the House and of his Majesty's gracious message for giving his royal assent to the Bill (which was beyond his commission, for which he prayed pardon), he demanded the body of Sir Thomas Shirley. She answered, If she might hear from Mr Trench she would deliver him; otherwise not. He called at Sir Thomas's chamber, wishing him to come: She said, If he carried away Sir Thomas, he should carry her dead. He offered to take her by the hand: She fell down and began to cry aloud, 'Sir Thomas Shirley,' etc. But he, having no commission to use violence, desisted.

Moved, That the Warden might be sent for and once again

terrified with the prison of Little Ease; and if he did not yield, then to proceed for his commitment to that place.

* * * * * *

The Warden of the Fleet being brought from the Tower to the Bar by his keeper, was by Mr Speaker put in mind of the favourable course of the House held with him and of the greatness of his contempt, and terrified with further punishment, etc., and then demanded if he would yield, etc. He refused as before, and by direction of the House being retired to the door, it was disputed whether it might be fit to intimate the particulars of the House's proceeding to him in care and favour of his case, and Mr Speaker's opinion required, who said it could not be much derogatory to let him know some particulars....The Warden brought to the Bar again,...and the House finding him still perverse in refusing to deliver Sir Thomas Shirley, Mr Speaker pronounced his judgment,...that as he doth increase his contempt so the House thought fit to increase his punishment, and that their [sentence] was now, he should be committed to the prison called Little Ease within the Tower...(pp. 206–7).

[12 May, 1604]...A Letter from Mr Lieutenant of the Tower to Mr Speaker touching the Warden of the Fleet: Sir— I determined this morning to have attended the House, but having been sick this night I crave pardon hereby to certify you that upon conference with the Warden of the Fleet he now hath some feeling of his own error and obstinacy; and because, as he now apprehendeth, it pleased you yesterday to open unto him the grace which he received from both the Houses of Parliament in providing for his security, his humble desire is that by some of the House...he may be resolved therein; whereupon he will, as he saith, most humbly submit himself upon Monday in the morning to deliver the body of Sir Thomas Shirley unto the Serjeant if it shall please you to send him. Whereof I have thought good to certify you, with desire that it may be made known unto the House; and so do take my leave. From the Tower, this twelfth of May, 1604.

Your poor Friend to be commanded,

G. HERVEY, *Locumt. Turr.*....(p. 208).

[14 May, 1604]...Sir Herbert Crofts reporteth the proceeding of the gentlemen appointed the last day to repair to the Tower, etc.—the loathsomeness of the place called Little Ease, an engine devised by Mr Skevington[1], some time Lieutenant of the Tower, called Skevington's Daughters or Little Ease; the Warden's insolent carriage; the care and demeanour of the Lieutenant, etc.; with other circumstances of their endeavour to see the order of the House performed.

It appeared by the report that the Lieutenant had not, with the care which was expected, satisfied the desire and pleasure of the House for the Warden's restraint: Whereupon himself being present stood up and made a relation, from the beginning, of his manner of proceeding with the Warden, and desired his name might not without cause be taxed or mentioned in this matter. This his justification was delivered with a low voice, and therefore it was moved that Mr Speaker might open it to the House; which he presently did.... Great fault in the Lieutenant that he did not make clean and ready the place called Little Ease (being reported to be very loathsome, unclean, and not used a long time either for prison or other cleanly purpose) as the order of the House might have been performed in time.

...In the end several questions agreed and made; and ordered, upon question,

1. That a warrant be directed for a new writ of *habeas corpus cum causa*.

2. That the Serjeant go with the writ.

3. That the Warden be brought to the Fleet door by Mr Lieutenant himself, and there the writ be delivered unto him and the commandment of the House by the Serjeant for the executing of it.

4. That the Warden in the mean time, and that presently [*i.e.* immediately], be committed to the dungeon in the Tower called Little Ease; and after this done, to be returned to the dungeon again.

The form of the warrant for the *habeas corpus*, etc., was this:

Whereas by order of the Commons' House of Parliament there have been several writs of *habeas corpus* and *habeas corpus cum causa* awarded for the delivery of the body of Sir Thomas Shirley, now prisoner in the Fleet, which the Warden of the Fleet hath from time to time contemptuously refused to execute; it is this day again ordered, to the end he may be left without all excuse, that another writ of *habeas corpus cum causa* be forthwith

---

[1] 'Skevington's Daughter' was the invention of Leonard, a son of Sir William Skevington or Skeffington, Master of the Ordnance and Lord Deputy of Ireland under Henry VIII, but it is described as an instrument of torture (*D.N.B.* lii, 325), whereas 'Little Ease' was evidently a dungeon.

awarded for the bringing of the body of the said Sir Thomas Shirley into the House to-morrow in the forenoon, *sedente curia*; and that the Serjeant deliver the writ to the Warden, and withal in the name of the House command him to bring forth the body of the said Sir Thomas according to known and ancient privilege and the tenor of the writ.

EDW. PHELIPS, *Speaker*.

Memorandum, It was observed that Mr Vice-Chamberlain to the King was privately instructed to go to the King and humbly desire that he would be pleased to command the Warden on his allegiance to deliver Sir Thomas—not as petitioned by the House but as of himself found fit in his own gracious judgment...(pp. 209–10).

[15 May, 1604]...Mr Speaker desireth the counsel might retire to the door, and so interposeth that Mr Lieutenant of the Tower had writ unto him yesterday with two letters[1] enclosed from the Warden of the Fleet,...both expressing his penitency for his former obstinacy and his willingness to deliver the prisoner; desiring withal that he might be spared from the dungeon until this morning; that he might lie in the Fleet the last night for providing some money which he had to pay the next day.

He answered (he said) the Lieutenant by writing, that if the Warden would yield the prisoner presently, he would take upon him that he might be spared from the dungeon till this morning. Upon that answer he caused Sir Thomas to be delivered.

Immediately upon this report, Sir Thomas was said to attend at the door. Sir Edward Hobby, being one of the Lord Steward's deputies, went forth to give him the oath of supremacy, and after the oath taken, he was instantly admitted to sit in the House...(p. 210).

[19 May, 1604]...The Warden of the Fleet attending at the door was called in; and on his knees at the Bar confessed his error and presumption, and professed that he was unfeignedly sorry that he had so offended this honourable House. Upon this his submission, Mr Speaker (by direction of the House) pronounced his pardon and discharge, paying ordinary fees to the Clerk and Serjeant.

A petition from Watkins, the serjeant-at-mace that first arrested Sir Thomas Shirley, read in the House:

[1] In one of these letters the prisoner complains, 'I remain still in Little Ease; I have come in no bed these three nights; my wife is barred access to me, and no servant of mine to minister to my wants' (*C.J.* i, 211).

To the Right Worshipful Sir Edward Phillippes, Knight, Speaker for the Common House of Parliament, and to the rest of that honourable and grave Society.

The most humble petition of William Watkin, Serjeant of the Mace in the City of London.

That in a compassionate respect of the miserable and poor estate of your poor suppliant, who most humbly prostrateth his error to your mercy, having now endured eight weeks' imprisonment, never having purpose, as he is ready to depose upon his knees at the Bar, to offend that honourable House nor the liberties thereof; it will please you, in commiseration of a poor man's estate, to consider of these articles following, most humbly submitted to your wisdoms.

First, he protesteth, and will take his corporal oath, that before he had arrested Sir Thomas Shirley he did not hear that he was elected for the Parliament; but true it is that Sir Thomas did presently tell your orator that he was so, and then your orator, having the execution about him, durst not part with him, being bound to the Sheriff in five hundred pounds with great surety.

2. It is supposed, as your poor orator hath heard, that your orator hath some promise or security from Simpson, which your suppliant will deny upon his oath; with this further, that he thinketh Simpson neither hath means, will, nor honesty so to do.

3. Your poor orator hath long been a suitor to some of that honourable House, but their answer was, they would first have Sir Thomas Shirley.

Your poor suppliant keepeth of alms and charity four fatherless children of his dead brother's who are otherwise left to the world, and a blind sister of your orator's who otherwise must either beg or perish, whose whole relief, and your orator's, is nothing else but his labour in attending his said function.

All which considered, he most humbly beseecheth that honourable House for Christ's sake to have compassion upon him.

Your most humble petitioner for compassion,

WILLIAM WATKIN...(p. 215).

[22 May, 1604]...Moved by Sir Edward Hobby, That since he found the House much inclined to mercy, that they would be pleased to extend their mercy to Watkins, the poor serjeant that arrested Sir Thomas Shirley; who hath patiently endured the censure and punishment of the House a long time, and is very penitent for his offence.

The House upon this motion was pleased to discharge him, without calling to the Bar or other submission...(p. 222).

Commons' Journals, i, 149–222.

(2) General Act in Shirley's case, 1604

An Act for new executions to be sued against any which shall hereafter be delivered out of execution by Privilege of Parliament, and for discharge of them out of whose custody such persons shall be delivered

Forasmuch as heretofore doubt hath been made if any person being arrested in execution, and by privilege of either of the Houses of Parliament set at liberty, whether the party at whose suit such execution was pursued be for ever after barred and disabled to sue forth a new writ of execution in that case: For the avoiding of all further doubt and trouble which in like cases may hereafter ensue, Be it enacted by the King's most excellent Majesty, by the Lords Spiritual and Temporal, and by the Commons in this present Parliament assembled, That from henceforth the party at or by whose suit such writ of execution was pursued, his executors or administrators, after such time as the privilege of that session of Parliament in which such privilege shall be so granted shall cease, may sue forth and execute a new writ or writs of execution in such manner and form as by the law of this realm he or they might have done if no such former execution had been taken forth or served: And that from henceforth no sheriff, bailiff, or other officer from whose arrest or custody any such person so arrested in execution shall be delivered by any such privilege shall be charged or chargeable with or by any action whatsoever for delivering out of execution any such privileged person so as is aforesaid by such privilege of Parliament set at liberty; Any law, custom, or privilege heretofore to the contrary notwithstanding. Provided always, That this Act or anything therein contained shall not extend to the diminishing of any punishment to be hereafter by censure in Parliament inflicted upon any person which hereafter shall make or procure to be made any such arrest as is aforesaid.

1 & 2 Jac. I, c. 13: *Statutes of the Realm,* iv, 1029.

(d) *The Expulsion of Members*

The right of the House of Commons to expel a member of its own body was asserted on 21 March 1621, by the expulsion of Sir Robert Floyd the monopolist [p. 318].

Sir Robert Floyd's Case, 1621

[21 March, 1621]...Sir Edward Coke from the Committee for Grievances. The patent for dispensing with pedlars, rogues, ruled by the Committee to be a patent of grievance....The last, for wills ingrossing, the worst of all. Every man dying either maketh his will or dieth intestate. The subject hath liberty by the law to ingross his own will; if intestate, the subject hath liberty to write his own inventory or get any other to do it. Now every of these must come to Sir Robert Floyd. He the sole ingrossing of all wills and inventories, so as the subject cannot write his own will or inventory. The consequence hereof will extend to confining to some certain scrivener, butcher, brewer. 3d. for every line, which double as much as before....

...*Sir Robert Floyd.* That he no projector, nor ever was any; will give his voice against any ill thing. Wisheth all his life may be examined; wisheth all the kingdom heard him. Was neither projector nor petitioner in this business....That the King hath granted this patent for reformation of the exactions of proctors[1]; upon full hearing of great counsel this granted. That great learned lawyers and divers of the judges of opinion for this patent. That the proctors maintained by their counsel that the subjects could not ingross their own wills; if they did, yet they were to pay them. That none complained but the proctors; no subject complaineth. That this beneficial for avoiding exactions. That he is to ingross more for 5s. than is, in many other offices, for 5l. Moveth the certificates may be heard read, and he be heard by his counsel in this House. Will make the extortion of the proctors appear.

*   *   *   *   *   *

Mr Solicitor. Satisfied that it cannot be defended for this patent that the subjects should not ingross their own wills....

Upon question, Resolved, The patent to Sir Robert Floyd, of the sole ingrossing of wills and inventories a patent of grievance, in the original and execution; without one negative.

*   *   *   *   *   *

Upon question, Sir Robert Floyd to be removed out of the House for being a projector[2], and maintainer of this patent....

...Sir Robert Floyd called to the Bar (not kneeling): Mr Speaker pronounceth his sentence, That he is to be no longer any member of this House, but to be removed; and that his patent a grievance in the original.

Commons' Journals, i, 565–7.

---

[1] These were the advocates practising in the ecclesiastical courts.
[2] Used invidiously of a schemer or speculator.

(e) *The Punishment of Non-members*

The leading case for the reign of James I is that of Edward Floyd, a Roman Catholic barrister, who for slighting words against the Elector Palatine and his wife the Princess Elizabeth of Bohemia, James's daughter, was sentenced by the House of Commons in 1621 to a fine and the pillory.

In this case the Commons clearly exceeded their jurisdiction[1]. The House of Lords, after an intermission of more than a century and a half, had just revived their criminal jurisdiction in Mompesson's case[2], but there were no precedents under which the Commons could claim similar rights, and there was no answer to the position taken up by the King, that they could not act as a judicial body in cases in which their privileges were not concerned. Unless he were handed over to the Lords, as James suggested, Floyd could only be tried in the Star Chamber, the King's Bench, or by a Commission of Oyer and Terminer[3], and as none of these leisurely methods satisfied the indignation of the Commons, they eventually adopted the proposal of the King. The Lords were quite alive to the importance of maintaining their exclusive privilege, and while shewing the utmost consideration for the susceptibilities of the Lower House, took care to stipulate that their action in Floyd's case should not be drawn into a precedent.

The unfortunate Floyd would have fared better if his case had remained in the hands of the Commons. They had only condemned him 'to pay a fine of £1000, to stand in the pillory in three different places for two hours each time, and to be carried from place to place upon a horse without a saddle, with his face towards the horse's tail, and holding the tail in his hand'; but the sentence of the Lords was that he should be 'degraded from the estate of a gentleman; his testimony not to be received; he was to be branded, whipped at the cart's tail, to pay £5000, and to be imprisoned in Newgate for life.'[4]

Edward Floyd's Case, 1621

Proceedings in the House of Lords.

[5 May, 1621]...The House being moved to take consideration of an act lately done by the Commons in conventing before them the person of one Edward Floud [Floyd], in examining of witnesses, and giving judgment upon him, and entering this as an act with them, the which doth trench deep into the privileges of this House, for that all judgments do properly and only belong unto this House; the Lords resolved not to suffer anything to pass which might prejudice their right in this point of judicature...(p. 110).

[7 May, 1621]...The Lords having considered of the

---

[1] May, *Parliamentary Practice* (10th edition), p. 90.
[2] See below (p. 321) under 'Impeachment.'
[3] *Notes of the Debates in the House of Lords...1621, 1625, and 1628...*Ed. Miss F. H. Relf (Royal Historical Society, 1929), p. xvii.
[4] *D.N.B.* xix, 343.

precedents alleged by the Commons at the last conference, 5 May, they found that they tended to prove:

1. That the House of Commons is a Court of Record.

2. That they have ministered an oath in matters concerning themselves.

3. That they have inflicted punishments on delinquents where the cause hath concerned a member of their House or the privileges thereof.

And their Lordships having determined that the question at this time is not whether that House be a Court of Record, nor whether the oath by them alleged to be ministered in a matter concerning that House was ministered by that House or by a Master of the Chancery (then being one of that House), nor whether thay have right of judicature in matters concerning themselves; but the question is, whether that House may proceed to sentence any man who is not a member of that House, and for a matter which concerns not that House; for which the Commons alleged no proofs nor produced any precedent.

Their Lordships agreed to pray a re-conference about the same...(p. 113).

[12 May, 1621]...The Archbishop of Canterbury reported the conference yesterday...to this effect, *videlicet*:

1. They shewed their constant resolution to maintain the love and good correspondency between both Houses.

2. Their resolution not to invade the privileges of this House, that have dealt so nobly with them.

3. That out of their zeal they sentenced Floud; but they leave him to the Lords, with an intimation of their hope that this House will censure him also.

They propounded a protestation to be entered with them, for a mean to accommodate the business between both Houses.

That the Lords' sub-committees, returning into this House, considered of the proposition and conceived a form of a protestation in writing....The protestation was read twice, and no exceptions taken unto it. It followeth *in haec verba*, *videlicet*:

A protestation to be entered, by consent of the House of Commons, to this purpose: That the proceedings lately passed in that House against Edward Floud be not at any time hereafter drawn or used as a precedent, to the enlarging or diminishing of the lawful rights or privileges of either House; but that the rights and privileges of both Houses shall remain in the self-same state and plight as before...(p. 119).

[16 May, 1621]...Message from the House of Commons by Sir Edward Coke and others: That where they received from the Lords a copy of a protestation which concerned the accommodating of the business of that wicked and wretched man Floud, they do approve it in all things, without addition or alteration... (p. 124).

[18 May, 1621]...Message to the House of Commons by Mr Serjeant Hitcham and Sir Charles Caesar: The Lords desire the trunk of writings which concerneth Floud's cause may be sent up unto this House for the better proceeding in that cause... (p. 127).

[26 May, 1621]...Edward Floud being brought to the Bar, Mr Attorney charged him with notorious misdemeanours and high presumption, *videlicet*:

1. For rejoicing at the losses happened to the King's daughter and her children.

2. For discouraging of others which bear good affection unto them.

3. For speaking basely of them.

4. For taking upon him to judge of the rights of kingdoms. ...Mr Attorney shewed that the said Floud, taking occasion to speak of these matters, did term the Prince and Princess Palatine (the King's daughter) by the ignominious and despiteful terms of 'Goodman Palsgrave' and 'Goodwife Palsgrave,' and termed him 'that poor lad'...(pp. 133-4).

Lords' Journals, iii, 110-34.

§7. PARLIAMENT AND IMPEACHMENT

Since the trial of Lord Stanley in 1459, there had been no case of impeachment and trial before the Lords at the suit of the Commons, for the Lords had ceased to act as a judicial body. Even the punishment of traitors had come to be a legislative process, in which the House of Commons took part with the Lords by reading, debating, and passing Bills of Attainder. The revival of impeachment in 1621 was not a far-sighted political measure aimed at the removal of Ministers of State but a natural result of the exercise of the traditional function of the Lower House in searching out and redressing grievances. In 1621 the Commons wanted to get at Sir Giles Mompesson the monopolist [p. 322], but if they proceeded against him in their own House it could only be for a breach of privilege, and the worst punishment they could inflict upon him would be to send him to the Tower for 'an indignity to the House.'[1] A committee was appointed to search for precedents 'to shew how far and for what offences the power of this House doth

[1] Relf, p. xiii.

extend to punish delinquents against the State as well as those who offend against this House,' but they could only report 'that we must join with the Lords for the punishing of Sir Giles Mompesson, it being no offence against our particular House or any member of it, but a general grievance.'[1] It was this discovery of their own impotence that sent the Commons to the Lords with the suggestion that they should try the case at the Commons' suit, and so revive the ancient procedure of Parliamentary impeachment. To this the King, who came down in person to the House of Lords on 10 March[2], was disposed to object. He pointed out to them that the question of monopolies 'was not for a subject: you put of them into the King's hand you were best. The Lower House have dealt temperately, modestly; they have not taken upon them to judge, neither can they, being no Court of Record.' It would be best for the House to refer the question of law to the Judges. 'I will give accompt to God and to my people declaratively, and he that will have all done by Parliament is an enemy to monarchy and a traitor to the King of England.' 'You are a House of Record, but how far you may punish, what your privileges be, is a question.' But James could find no very strong ground for objection, and the Lords proceeded with the case.

The impeachment of Mompesson for monopolies and of Bacon for bribery [p. 324] in 1621 was followed in 1624 by that of the financier Cranfield, now Earl of Middlesex [p. 334]. Bacon's case is of special constitutional importance, for James proposed that he should be tried by a commission of the King's selection, consisting of six Lords and twelve members of the House of Commons, but the Lower House resisted the temptation, and supported the claim of the Lords to act as judges of an impeachment[3]. The trial of a monopolist was without political importance, but in the cases of Bacon and Cranfield a great official was overthrown. And moreover, impeachment was an assertion of the responsibility of ministers to the law, whereas the autocracy of the Tudors rested on the principle that ministers were responsible to the Sovereign alone[4]. Thus was refurbished the rusty constitutional weapon which was to be used hereafter with fatal effect against Strafford and Laud.

Associated with the revival of impeachment was the right now claimed by the Lords to act as a judicial body apart from the Commons or the King, and to hear civil cases upon petition. Of this there are only a few instances in the reign of James I, and the growth of this jurisdiction belongs for the most part to a later chapter of history[5].

(1) Impeachment of Sir Giles Mompesson, 1621

The House of Commons began to enquire into Mompesson's offences as early as 20 February, 1621, but it was not until 15 March that the impeachment was sent up to the Lords. Meanwhile on 3 March the accused had made good his escape to France.

*   *   *   *   *   *

[March 26]. . . The collection of offences and abuses committed by Sir Giles Mompesson in the three patents which were

---

[1] Relf, pp. xiii–xiv.   [2] Ib. pp. 12–16.
[3] See p. 324 below; also C. H. Firth, The House of Lords during the Civil War, p. 38.
[4] Goldwin Smith, i, 466.   [5] On this see Relf, pp. xviii–xxxii.

granted to him being all read, it was resolved by the whole House, That it did appear to the Lords, and they were fully satisfied, Sir Giles Mompesson had erected a court without warrant, and also that he imprisoned the King's subjects and exacted bonds from them by threats, without warrant; and afterwards by undue practices procured a proclamation and other warrants to colour such his doings. And yet that he executed all these ills, and seized the goods of divers persons, contrary to such authority so unduly procured by him. That he neither paid the 10*l.* reserved rent to the King nor brought in the 5000*l.* of bullion yearly, as he pretended and covenanted to have done. And that all his other offences and abuses had been fully proved against him.. . .

[In the afternoon] the whole House met again. The Lords were in their robes, in order to give sentence against the offender. It was much debated first among them what punishment Sir Giles deserved for his high crimes; and because the punishment inflicted heretofore on Empson and Dudley was much spoken of, the Lords desired to hear their indictments.. . .After a long debate, the Lords agreed upon a judgment.. . .Accordingly a message was sent from the Lords to the Commons, That if they and their Speaker, according to the ancient custom of Parliaments, come to demand of the Lords that judgment be given against Sir Giles for the heinous offences by him committed, they shall be heard.. . .

The knights, citizens, and burgesses of the House of Commons with their Speaker being come up to the Bar, the Speaker repeated the last message which the Lords had sent unto them, and said, 'The Commons by me their Speaker demand judgment against Sir Giles Mompesson as the heinousness of his offences doth require.'

The Lord Chief Justice, as Speaker of the House of Peers, answered: 'Mr Speaker, the Lords Spiritual and Temporal have taken knowledge of the great pains the Commons have been at to inform their Lordships of many complaints brought unto them against Sir Giles Mompesson and others, whereof their Lordships received several instructions from them; and thereupon, proceeding by examination of divers witnesses upon oath, they find Sir Giles and several others guilty of many heinous crimes against the King's Majesty and against the commonwealth. Time will not permit their Lordships to deal with all the offenders now; therefore they proceed to give judgment against Sir Giles according to your demand, and hereafter their Lordships will proceed against the other offenders. The judgment of the Lords against the said Sir Giles is, and the Lords Spiritual and Temporal of this High Court of Parliament do award and adjudge: 1. That Sir Giles shall from henceforth be degraded of the Order of Knighthood, with reservation to his wife and children; the ceremonies of degradation to be performed by direction of the Earl Marshal's Court whensoever he shall be taken. 2. That he shall stand perpetually in the degree of a person outlawed for misdemeanours and trespasses. 3. That his testimony be received in no court; and that he shall be of no assize, inquisition, or jury. 4. That he shall be excepted out of all general pardons to be hereafter granted. 5. That he shall be imprisoned during life. 6. That he shall not approach within 12 miles of the Courts of the King or Prince, nor of the King's high courts usually holden at Westminster. 7. That the King's Majesty shall have the profits of his lands for life, and shall have all his goods and chattels as forfeited; and he shall undergo fine and ransom, which their Lordships assess at 10,000*l*. 8. That he shall be disabled to hold or receive any office under the King or for the commonwealth. 9. Lastly, that he be ever held an infamous person.'

March 27. The Lord Admiral delivered his Majesty's hearty thanks to the Lords for their sentence given yesterday against Mompesson, it being so just and yet moderate in respect of the heinousness of the offence; and said that the King, out of regard to his people and detestation of the said crimes, is pleased *ex abundante* to inflict perpetual banishment on the said Mompesson out of all his Majesty's dominions. . . .

State Trials, ii, 1130–2.

(2) Impeachment of Lord Chancellor Bacon, 1621

On his appointment to the office of Lord Chancellor in 1618 Sir Francis Bacon had been created Baron Verulam, and in 1621, just before his impeachment, he had been made Viscount St Albans.

[19 March, 1621]. . . Mr Secretary from the King. . . . That the King taking notice of the accusations against the Lord Chancellor; that the King very sorry a person so much advanced by him, and sitting in so high a place, should be suspected; that he cannot answer for all others under him; his care in his choice of Judges hath been great; that his Majesty, if the accusation shall be proved, will punish it to the full.

That his Majesty will, if [it] shall be thought fit here, grant out a Commission under the Great Seal of England to examine all upon oath, all that can speak in this business; the Commissioners, six of the Upper House to be chosen by them, and twelve here to be chosen here. . . .

Sir Edw. Coke. That this gracious message taketh not away our Parliamentary proceeding. . . . To return no answer to the King till the like message to the Lords.

Sir Edw. Sackville. To have no divorce between the Lords and us. That Mr Secretary let the King know we desire the same message be sent by him to the Lords; and to have their consent before we give any answer to the point of the Commission.

* * * * * *

Mr Secretary from the King:—That he acquainted the King with the thanks of the House for his gracious licence to the House to adjourn this session for some small time, and that the House desireth he will be pleased to send a message to the Lords about the Commission and receive their answer, that so they and this House may proceed with an unanimous assent, as hitherto they have done.

Sir Ro. Phillippes. That he acquainted the Lords that where this House had made inquisitions into the Courts of Justice within this kingdom, they had met with some complaints against some Lords of that House, and that therefore they desired a conference with the Lords, where they would acquaint them with the particulars.

Answer: That the Lords would afford a conference with the whole House in the Painted Chamber this afternoon.

Commons' Journals, i, 563.

[20 March, 1621] . . . The Lord Treasurer reported the conference yesterday with the Commons.

At which conference was delivered the desire of the Commons to inform their Lordships of the great abuses of the Courts of Justice, the information whereof was divided into three parts: 1. Of the persons accused. 2. Of the matters objected against them. 3. Their proof. The persons are, the Lord Chancellor of England and the now Lord Bishop of Llandaff[1]. . . . The incomparable good parts of the Lord Chancellor were highly commended, his place he holds magnified, from whence bounty, justice, and mercy were to be distributed to the subjects, with which he was solely trusted; whither all great causes were drawn, and from whence no appeal lay for any injustice or wrong done, save to the Parliament.

---

[1] Theophilus Field had been Bacon's chaplain, and in 1619 he was made Bishop of Llandaff. He was afterwards Bishop of St David's, and finally of Hereford.

That the Lord Chancellor is accused of great bribery and corruption committed by him in this eminent place, whereof two cases were alleged.

*   *   *   *   *   *

...The Commons do purpose that if any more of this kind happen to be complained of before them, they will present the same to your Lordships: wherein they shall follow the ancient precedents, which shew that great personages have been accused for the like in Parliament.

They humbly desire that, forasmuch as this concerns a person of so great eminency, it may not depend long before your Lordships; that the examination of the proofs may be expedited; and if he be found guilty, then to be punished; if not guilty, the accusers to be punished.

This report ended, the Lord Admiral declared that he had been twice with the Lord Chancellor to visit him, being sent to him by the King. The first time he found his Lordship very sick and heavy; the second time he found him better, and much comforted for that he heard that the complaint of the grievances of the Commons against him were come into this House, where he assured himself to find honourable justice; in confidence whereof, his Lordship had written a letter to the House. The which letter the Lord Admiral presented to the House to be read, the tenor whereof followeth:

To the Right Honourable his very good Lords, the Lords Spiritual and Temporal in the Upper House of Parliament assembled.

My very good Lords,

I humbly pray your Lordships all to make a favourable and true construction of my absence. It is no feigning nor fainting, but sickness both of my heart and of my back; though joined with that comfort of mind that persuadeth me that I am not far from Heaven, whereof I feel the firstfruits. And because, whether I live or die, I would be glad to preserve my honour and fame as far as I am worthy, hearing that some complaints of base bribery are come before your Lordships, my requests unto your Lordships are: First, that you will maintain me in your good opinion, without prejudice, until my cause be heard; Secondly, that in regard I have sequestered my mind at this time in great part from worldly matters, thinking of my account and answer in a Higher Court, your Lordships would give me some convenient time, according to the course of other Courts, to advise with my counsel and to make my answer, wherein nevertheless my counsel's part will be the least, for I shall not, by the grace of God, trick up an innocency with cavillations, but plainly and ingenuously (as your Lordships know my manner is) declare what I know or remember; Thirdly, that according to the course of justice I may be allowed to except to the witnesses brought against me and to move questions to your Lordships for their cross-examination, and likewise to produce my own witnesses for discovery of the truth: And lastly, if there come any more petitions of like nature, that your Lordships would be pleased not to take any prejudice or apprehension of any number or muster of them, especially against a Judge that makes two thousand decrees and orders in a year (not to speak of the courses that have been taken for hunting out complaints against me), but that I may answer them, according to the rules of justice, severally and respectively. These requests I hope appear to your Lordships no other than just. And so, thinking myself happy to have so noble Peers and reverend Prelates to discern of my cause, and desiring no privilege of greatness for subterfuge of guiltiness, but meaning (as I said) to deal fairly and plainly with your Lordships and to put myself upon your honours and favours, I pray God to bless your counsels and your persons; and rest,

Your Lordships' humble Servant,

FR. ST ALBAN, Canc.

19th March, 1620[–1].

The Clerk, having read the letter, delivered the same to the Lord Chief Justice, who by repetition read the same also.

*   *   *   *   *   *

...Agreed, That an answer should be sent to my Lord Chancellor's letter; whereupon message is sent to the Lord Chancellor...to this effect: That the Lords received his Lordship's letter delivered unto them by the Lord Admiral; they intend to proceed in his cause (now before their Lordships) according to the right rule of justice, and they shall be glad if his Lordship shall clear his honour therein; to which end they pray his Lordship to provide for his defence...(pp. 53–5).

*   *   *   *   *   *

[22 March, 1621]...The Lord Treasurer signified that in the interim of this cessation the Lord Chancellor was an humble suitor unto his Majesty that he might see his Majesty and speak with him; and although his Majesty, in respect of the Lord

Chancellor's person and of the place he holds, might have given his Lordship that favour, yet for that his Lordship is under the trial of this House his Majesty would not on the sudden grant it.

That on Sunday last the King, calling all the Lords of this House which were of his Council before him, it pleased his Majesty to shew their Lordships what was desired by the Lord Chancellor, demanding their Lordships' advice therein. The Lords did not presume to advise his Majesty, for that his Majesty did suddenly propound such a course as all the world could not advise a better; which was, that his Majesty would speak with him privately.

That yesterday, his Majesty admitting the Lord Chancellor to his presence, his Lordship desired that he might have a particular of those matters wherewith he is charged before the Lords of this House; for that it was not possible for him who passed so many orders and decrees in a year to remember all things that fell out in them, and that this being granted, his Lordship would desire two requests of his Majesty: 1. That where his answers should be fair and clear to those things objected against him, his Lordship might stand upon his innocency; 2. Where his answer should not be so fair and clear, there his Lordship might be admitted to the extenuation of the charge; and where the proofs were full and undeniable, his Lordship would ingenuously confess them and put himself upon the mercy of the Lords. Unto all which his Majesty's answer was, He referred him to the Lords of this House; and thereof his Majesty willed his Lordship to make report to their Lordships.

It was thereupon ordered, That the Lord Treasurer should signify unto his Majesty that the Lords do thankfully acknowledge this his Majesty's favour, and hold themselves highly bound unto his Majesty for the same...(p. 75).

[24 April, 1621]...The Prince his Highness signified unto the Lords that the Lord Chancellor had sent a submission unto their Lordships, the which was presently read. It follows *in haec verba*:

To the Right Honourable the Lords of Parliament in the Upper House assembled. The humble submission and supplication of the Lord Chancellor.

It may please your Lordships, I shall humbly crave at your Lordships' hands a benign interpretation of that which I shall now write. For words that come from wasted spirits and an oppressed mind are more safe in being deposited in a noble construction than in being circled in any reserved caution. This being moved, and as I hope obtained, in the nature of a protection to all that I shall say, I shall now make into the rest of that wherewith I shall at this time trouble your Lordships a very strange entrance. For in the midst of a state of as great affliction as I think a mortal man can endure (honour being above life), I shall begin with the professing of gladness in some things.

The first is, that hereafter the greatness of a Judge or magistrate shall be no sanctuary or protection of guiltiness, which (in few words) is the beginning of a golden world.

The next, that after this example, it is like that Judges will fly from anything that is in the likeness of corruption (though it were at a great distance) as from a serpent; which tendeth to the purging of the Courts of Justice and the reducing them to their true honour and splendour.

And in these two points God is my witness that, though it be my fortune to be the anvil upon which these good effects are beaten and wrought, I take no small comfort.

But to pass from the motions of my heart whereof God is only judge, to the merits of my cause whereof your Lordships are judges under God and his Lieutenant; I do understand there hath been heretofore expected from me some justification, and therefore I have chosen one only justification instead of all other, out of the justifications of Job. For after the clear submission and confession which I shall now make unto your Lordships, I hope I may say and justify with Job in these words: 'I have not hid my sin as did Adam, nor concealed my faults in my bosom.' This is the only justification which I will use. It resteth therefore that, without fig-leaves, I do ingenuously confess and acknowledge that having understood the particulars of the charge, not formally from the House but enough to inform my conscience and memory, I find matter sufficient and full both to move me to desert the defence and to move your Lordships to condemn and censure me. Neither will I trouble your Lordships by singling those particulars which I think may fall off,

Quid te exemta juvat spinis de pluribus una?

Neither will I prompt your Lordships to observe upon the proofs where they come not home, or the scruples touching the credits of the witnesses; neither will I represent unto your Lordships how far a defence might in divers things extenuate the offence in respect of the time or manner of the gift, or the like circumstances, but only leave these things to spring out of your own noble thoughts and observations of the evidence and examinations themselves, and charitably to wind about the particulars of the charge here and there, as God shall put into your mind; and so submit myself wholly to your piety and grace.

And now that I have spoken to your Lordships as Judges, I shall say a few words to you as Peers and Prelates, humbly commending my cause to your noble minds and magnanimous affections.

Your Lordships are not simple judges but Parliamentary judges; you have a further extent of arbitrary power than other Courts; and if your Lordships be not tied by the ordinary course of Courts or precedents in points of strictness and severity, much more in points of mercy and mitigation. And yet if anything which I shall move might be contrary to your honourable and worthy ends to introduce a reformation, I should not seek it. But herein I beseech your Lordships to give me leave to tell you a story. Titus Manlius took his son's life for giving battle against the prohibition of his general; not many years after, the like severity was pursued by Papirius Cursor the Dictator against Quintus Maximus, who being upon the point to be sentenced, by the intercession of some principal persons of the Senate was spared; whereupon Livy maketh this grave and gracious observation: *Neque minus firmata est disciplina militaris periculo Quinti Maximi quam miserabili supplicio Titi Manlii.* The discipline of war was no less established by the questioning of Quintus Maximus than by the punishment of Titus Manlius; and the same reason is of the reformation of Justice, for the questioning of men of eminent place hath the same terror though not the same rigour with the punishment. But my case standeth not there. For my humble desire is that his Majesty would take the Seal into his hands, which is a great downfall, and may serve I hope in itself for an expiation of my faults. Therefore if mercy and mitigation be in your power and do no ways cross your ends, why should I not hope of your Lordships' favour and commiseration?

Your Lordships will be pleased to behold your chief pattern the King our Sovereign, a King of incomparable clemency and whose heart is inscrutable for wisdom and goodness. Your Lordships will remember that there sat not these hundred years before a Prince in your House, and never such a Prince, whose presence deserveth to be made memorable by records and acts mixed of mercy and justice. Yourselves are either nobles (and compassion ever beateth in the veins of noble blood), or reverend prelates, who are the servants of Him that would not break the bruised reed nor quench smoking flax. You all sit upon one high stage, and therefore cannot but be more sensible of the changes of the world and of the fall of any of high place. Neither will your Lordships forget that there are *vitia temporis* as well as *vitia hominis*, and that the beginning of reformations hath the contrary power of the Pool of Bethesda; for that had strength to cure only him that was first cast in, and this hath commonly strength to hurt him only that is first cast in; and for my part I wish it may stay there and go no further.

Lastly, I assure myself your Lordships have a noble feeling of me, as a member of your own body, and one that in this very session had some taste of your loving affections, which I hope was not a lightning before the death of them but rather a spark of that grace which now in the conclusion will more appear. And therefore my humble suit to your Lordships is, That my penitent submission may be my sentence and the loss of the Seal my punishment; and that your Lordships will spare any further sentence, but recommend me to his Majesty's grace and pardon for all that is past. God's Holy Spirit be amongst you.

Your Lordships' humble servant and suppliant,

FR. ST ALBAN, *Canc.*

22 April, 1621.

The which submission being read,...the House was adjourned *ad libitum*, to the end, the whole House being a Committee, it might be the better debated whether the said submission were a sufficient confession for the Lords to ground their censure on.

Their Lordships being all agreed that the Lord Chancellor's submission gave not satisfaction to their Lordships, for that his Lordship's confession therein was not fully nor particularly set down, and for many other exceptions against the submission itself, the same in sort extenuating his confession and his Lordship seeming to prescribe the sentence to be given against him by the House; their Lordships resolved, That the Lord Chancellor should be charged particularly with the briberies and corruptions complained of against him, and that his Lordship should make a particular answer thereunto; but whether his Lordship shall be brought to the Bar to hear the charge, or that respect being had to his person (as yet having the King's Great Seal) the charge shall be sent unto his Lordship in writing, it was much debated. And the Lord Chief Justice returning to the Lord Chancellor's place, his Lordship put it to the question, *videlicet*, Whether the charge shall be sent to the Lord Chancellor in writing, or the Lord

Chancellor brought to the Bar to hear the same; and agreed by most voices the charge to be sent to his Lordship.

Memorandum. That during the time the whole House was a Committee, the collections of corruptions charged upon the Lord Chancellor and the proofs thereof...was read by Mr Attorney-General. And the said collection (without the proofs) was...then sent to the Lord Chancellor...with this message from their Lordships: That the Lord Chancellor's confession is not fully set down by his Lordship in the said submission, for three causes: 1. His Lordship confesseth not any particular bribe nor corruption; 2. Nor sheweth how his Lordship heard of the charge thereof; 3. The confession, such as it is, is afterwards extenuated in the same submission: and therefore the Lords have sent him a particular of the charge, and do expect his answer to the same with all convenient expedition.

Here followeth the said collection: *videlicet*, corruptions charged upon the Lord Chancellor, with the proofs thereof... (pp. 84–6).

[There follow in the *Journals* 23 instances of bribery and corruption, with the names of the witnesses testifying to them.]

[30 April, 1621]...The Lord Chief Justice...signified that he had received from the Lord Chancellor a paper roll sealed up, which was delivered to the Clerk; and being opened and found directed to their Lordships, it was also read; which follows *in haec verba*:...

[In this document, which is described as 'The Confession and humble Submission of me, the Lord Chancellor,' and the contents of which are set out in the *Journals*, Bacon recites 28 Articles of accusation and formally confesses to each, with the exception of the 15th. The Confession then continues as follows:]

This Declaration I have made to your Lordships with a sincere mind, humbly craving that if there should be any mistaking, your Lordships would impute it to want of memory and not to any desire of mine to obscure truth or palliate anything; for I do again confess that in the points charged upon me, although they should be taken as myself have declared them, there is a great deal of corruption and neglect; for which I am heartily and penitently sorry, and submit myself to the judgment, grace, and mercy of the Court.

For extenuation I will use none concerning the matters themselves; only it may please your Lordships out of your nobleness so cast your eyes of compassion upon my person and estate. I was never noted for an avaricious man; and the Apostle saith that covetousness is the root of all evil. I hope also that your Lordships do the rather find me in the state of grace, for that in all these particulars there are few or none that are not almost two years old, whereas those that have an habit of corruption do commonly wax worse and worse; so that it hath pleased God to prepare me, by precedent degrees of amendment, to my present penitency. And for my estate, it is so mean and poor as my care is now chiefly to satisfy my debts.

And so, fearing I have troubled your Lordships too long, I shall conclude with an humble suit unto you, That if your Lordships proceed to sentence, your sentence may not be heavy to my ruin but gracious and mixed with mercy; and not only so, but that you would be noble intercessors for me to his Majesty likewise for his grace and favour.

Your Lordships' humble servant and suppliant,

FR. ST ALBAN, *Canc.*

This confession and submission being read, it was agreed... to tell him that the Lords do conceive it to be an ingenuous and full confession....

...It was agreed by the House to move his Majesty to sequester the Seal...(pp. 98–101).

[3 May, 1621]...The Lords, having agreed upon the sentence to be given against the Lord Chancellor, did send a message to the House of Commons....That the Lords are ready to give judgment against the Lord Viscount St Alban, Lord Chancellor, if they with their Speaker will come to demand it.

In the mean time the Lords put on their robes, and answer being returned of this message, the Commons come. The Speaker came to the Bar, and making three low obeisances said: 'The knights, citizens, and burgesses of the Commons' House of Parliament have made complaint unto your Lordships of many exorbitant offences of bribery and corruption committed by the Lord Chancellor. We understand that your Lordships are ready to give judgment upon him for the same. Wherefore I their Speaker in their name do humbly demand and pray judgment against him the Lord Chancellor, as the nature of his offence and demerits do require.'

The Lord Chief Justice answered: 'Mr Speaker, upon the complaint of the Commons against the Lord Viscount St Alban, Lord Chancellor, this High Court hath thereby, and by his own confession, found him guilty of the crimes and corruptions complained of by the Commons, and of sundry other crimes and corruptions of like nature. And therefore this High Court (having first summoned him to attend, and having received his excuse of not attending by reason of infirmity and sickness, which he protested was not feigned or else he would most willingly have attended) doth nevertheless think fit to proceed to judgment; and therefore this High Court doth adjudge:

1. That the Lord Viscount St Alban, Lord Chancellor of England, shall undergo fine and ransom of forty thousand pounds.

2. That he shall be imprisoned in the Tower during the King's pleasure.

3. That he shall for ever be incapable of any office, place, or employment in the State or commonwealth.

4. That he shall never sit in Parliament nor come within the verge[1] of the Court.

This is the judgment and resolution of this High Court.'

The Prince his Highness was entreated by the House that, accompanied with divers of the Lords of this House, he would be pleased to present this sentence given against the late Lord Chancellor unto his Majesty. His Highness was pleased to yield unto this request...(p. 106).

(3) Impeachment of Lionel Cranfield, Earl of Middlesex, 1624

Sentence against the Lord Treasurer

Then a message was sent to the Commons that the Lords were now ready to give judgment against the Lord Treasurer if they with their Speaker will come and demand the same.... Accordingly, the Lords being all in their robes, to the number of 62, the Lord Treasurer was brought to the Bar by the Gentleman Usher and the Serjeant-at-Arms; when his Lordship, making a low reverence, kneeled, until the Lord Keeper willed him to stand up. The Commons came in with their Speaker, and the Serjeant attending him let down his mace, when the Speaker addressed himself to the Lords as follows:

'The knights, citizens, and burgesses in this Parliament assembled have heretofore transmitted unto your Lordships

---

[1] This was the area of twelve miles round the Court which was subject to the jurisdiction of the Lord Steward.

several offences against the Right Honourable Lionel, Earl of Middlesex, Lord High Treasurer of England, for bribery, extortions, oppressions, and other grievous misdemeanours committed by his Lordship; and now the Commons, by me their Speaker, demand judgment against him for the same.'

The Lord Keeper answered, 'This High Court of Parliament doth adjudge that Lionel, Earl of Middlesex, now Lord Treasurer of England, shall lose all his offices which he holds in this kingdom; and shall hereafter be made incapable of any office, place, or employment in the State and commonwealth. That he shall be imprisoned in the Tower of London during the King's pleasure. That he shall pay unto our Sovereign Lord the King a fine of 50,000*l.* That he shall never sit in Parliament any more, and that he shall never come within the verge of the Court.'[1]

May 14. A committee of Lords was appointed by the House to attend the King and to acquaint him with the judgment awarded by the Lords against the Earl of Middlesex, and to desire his Majesty to take away the staff, and the seal of the Court of Wards from him. Ordered also, That the King's counsel do draw up a bill and present the same to the House to make the lands of the Earl of Middlesex liable unto his debts; unto his fine to the King; unto accounts to the King hereafter; and to restitution to such whom he had wronged, as shall be allowed by the House. Which bill afterwards passed into a law.

State Trials, ii, 1250.

[1] See note, p. 334.

Finance

Financially, the Stuart Kings fell on evil days. The permanent revenue of the Crown, even under the careful management of Elizabeth, did not produce enough to meet the ordinary expenses of government, and yet the expenses of government continually tended to increase. It was not that the country as a whole was poorer; in fact the contrary was the case. After the defeat of the Armada, and the clearing of the cloud of uncertainty and danger which had hung so black over England in the earlier years of the great Queen's reign, there had been an immense improvement in the general financial position. This is the period of the manor-house—what someone alludes to as 'all that great bravery of building that set in in the times of Elizabeth.' It is pre-eminently the period of plate, in which the savings of all classes were accumulated, almost as a peasant of India lays money by in the form of silver ornaments and jewels. The foreign trade of England also was making a considerable start. In the earlier years of James I's reign both the East India Company and the Levant Company did remarkably well, and later the Thirty Years' War on the Continent threw a great deal of trade into English hands. The difficulty was that under existing constitutional arrangements the Crown did not sufficiently share in this increase in the country's wealth. It is true that the revenue of James I benefited through the customs by the increase in foreign trade, and the remarkable increase in the yield to custom was his salvation from bankruptcy. But the Crown gained little from the increasing wealth of the country in general, because the assessment for subsidy remained unchanged. We find Sir Walter Raleigh protesting in Elizabeth's Parliament of 1601 against the absurd under-assessment of persons of large fortune. 'Our estates that be £30 or £40 in the Queen's books are not the hundredth part of our wealth.'[1] And yet it was not in practice possible to go behind the subsidy books or to break down the tenacious custom which governed the entries there.

Although the Stuart Kings succeeded to the poverty of Elizabeth, they did not inherit her saving spirit. Speaking generally, they were wasteful Kings, and this is true of James I as well as of Charles II. The ordinary peace expenditure of Elizabeth had been about £220,000 a year; in 1607 James spent £500,000. It is true that the Irish troubles were a constant drain on the Exchequer, and that the rise in wages and prices was always putting Government, as a large employer and purchaser, at a disadvantage— but a considerable part of the increase was due to an extravagant household, pensions to courtiers, and preposterous purchases of plate and jewels[2]. On the whole we may take it, that where Elizabeth had only been pressed for money, James and Charles were on the verge of bankruptcy and that this sinister change in the situation was due—in part at least—to wasteful administration.

[1] *Parliamentary History*, i, 920.
[2] In the first four years of his reign James spent £92,000 on jewels alone (*Parliamentary Debates of* 1610, p. xv).

This poverty of the Stuart Kings is a fundamental fact in the history of the period, because it established a vicious circle. (1) It compelled the Crown to summon frequent Parliaments, and to ask for subsidies to meet ordinary expenditure, in violation of the theory of the Constitution, which made Parliament meet on great occasions only, to vote supplies for the emergencies of war or rebellion. (2) Frequent Parliaments meant facilities for Parliamentary organisation and Parliamentary criticism which had not existed in the days of the Tudors when Parliament met seldom and sat for a short time. (3) When a Stuart Parliament met, it found itself confronted by ecclesiastical grievances of sufficient magnitude to justify it in pressing the Crown for their redress, and for this a powerful lever now lay ready to its hand, for it could insist that redress of grievances should precede supply. (4) It thus became an object of the first importance with the Crown to increase its ordinary or extra-Parliamentary revenue, even although in order to do so it was necessary to press its legal rights against individuals much further than Elizabeth had done. But (5) this was to make fresh grievances for Parliament to redress, and so to embitter still further its relations with the Crown.

§ 1. BATE'S CASE IN THE EXCHEQUER

In the reign of Elizabeth a monopolist company called the Levant Company had been established to trade with Venice in currants and oil. The Company paid £4000 a year to the Crown for its charter, and recouped itself by levying a custom of 5s. 6d. a cwt. on currants and a similar duty on oil from all merchants engaged in the trade who were not members of the Company. But in consequence of the outcry against monopolies, the Company surrendered its charter, a decision to which it was also encouraged by losses in trade, and the Crown, to recoup itself for the loss of the £4000 a year, though it threw the trade open to all merchants, levied upon all the custom of 5s. 6d. For a time this was cheerfully paid, but in 1606 a Turkey merchant named John Bate or Bates suddenly professed to discover that the custom was illegal, and refused to pay it upon his operations in currants: he was therefore sued in the Court of Exchequer, and the case was heard before the four Exchequer Barons [p. 338].

From the legal point of view Bate had no case, and even the Parliamentarian Hakewill admitted afterwards that at the time, when he was listening to the judgments which the Exchequer Barons gave in favour of the Crown, he had been perfectly satisfied with their arguments. Hallam's attack upon the impartiality of the judges—'some corrupt with the hope of promotion, many more fearful of removal or awestruck by the frowns of power'[1]—is singularly devoid of foundation in respect of a case which preceded by ten years the dismissal of Chief Justice Coke. The constitutional interest of Bate's case lies—not in the decision but in the grounds on which the decision was given. The language used by the judges shews that the doctrine of absolute power had penetrated to the Law Courts. Baron Clarke argued that no King can bind his successors; and Chief Baron Fleming drew a distinction between the King's ordinary and absolute power, relegated im-

[1] Constitutional History, i, 318.

positions to the province of his absolute power, and maintained that he was therefore free to make what charges he pleased. Fleming meets very ingeniously the argument which was to be made so much of later on, that if the King might impose 5s. 6d. on currants, he might by the same principle impose what he pleased upon anything else, and so all the goods of the subject would be at his mercy. 'Many things,' he said, 'are left to' the King's 'wisdom for the ordering of his power, rather than that his power shall be restrained. The King may pardon any felon; but it may be objected that if he pardon one felon he may pardon all, to the damage of the commonwealth, and yet none will doubt but that is left in his wisdom' [p. 344]. Perhaps we are in danger of exaggerating the importance of this element in the decision in Bate's case. It was very usual in this period for judges whose real conclusions were based upon the narrowest and most technical grounds to embellish their judgments with vague philosophy, and here there was no need to go to absolute power to prove that James was right in law. The Tudor precedents were quite enough.

Judgments in Bate's Case, 1606

Baron Clarke's Judgment

... This case being of so great consequence, great respect and consideration is to be had, and it seemeth to me strange that any subjects would contend with the King in this high point of prerogative, but such is the King's grace that he had shewed his intent to be that this matter shall be disputed and adjudged by us according to the ancient law and custom of the realm; and because that the judgment of this matter cannot be well directed by any learning delivered in our books of law, the best directions herein are precedents of antiquity, and the course of this Court wherein all actions of this nature are to be judged, and the Acts of Parliament recited in arguments of this case prove nothing to this purpose.... And as it is not a kingdom without subjects and government, so he is not a King without revenues, for without them he cannot preserve his dominions in peace, he cannot maintain war, nor reward his servants according to the state and honour of a King; and the revenue of the Crown is the very essential part of the Crown, and he who rendeth that from the King pulleth also his crown from his head, for it cannot be separated from the Crown. And such great prerogatives of the Crown, without which it cannot be, ought not to be disputed; and in these cases of prerogative the judgment shall not be according to the rules of the Common Law, but according to the precedents of this Court wherein these matters are disputable and determinable.

*   *   *   *   *   *

King Edward the Third in the sixteenth year of his reign
proclaimed that no man should sell wool-fells or leather under
such a price, so that these staple commodities might not be
debased, and this at no place but Northampton and Alnwick.. ..
And for precedents in this matter of impost, there are many of
antiquity.. . . In 16 E. I. the custom for a tun of wine was 4*s*.. . .
and it was increased.. . . And after, in the 4th of Mary, it was
increased to 4 marks; and as it appears by the records of this
court, it was answered upon accompt for all this time according
to that rate. And it is apparent that no Act of Parliament gave
this to the King, but that it was imposed by his absolute power: and
shall it now be doubted if it be lawful? God defend.. . . The
Statute of the 45 E. 3 cap. 4 which hath been so much urged,
that no new imposition shall be imposed upon wool-fells, wool, or
leather, but only the custom and subsidy granted to the King,
this extends only to the King himself, and shall not bind his
successors; for it is a principal part of the Crown of England,
which the King cannot diminish. And the same King, 24th of
his reign, granted divers exemptions to certain persons, and
because that it was in derogation of his State Imperial, he himself
recalled and annulled the same. As to that which was objected,
that the defendant had paid poundage granted by the Statute of
the first of the King, that is nothing to this purpose, for that is a
subsidy and not a custom; for when any imposition is granted by
Parliament it is only a subsidy and not a custom, for the nature
thereof is changed, and the impost of wine is paid over and above
the poundage, and so should it be here. And whereas it was
objected that if it were in the time of war it is sufferable, but in
peace not, this seems no reason, for the King cannot be furnished
to make defence in war if he provide not in peace, and the
provision is too late made when it ought to be used. And as to
that which was said, that the subject ought to have recompense
and valuable satisfaction, it seemeth to me that he hath; for he
hath the King's protection within his ports, and his safe conduct
upon the land, and his defence upon the sea. And all the ports of
the realm belong to the King, and in this court there is a precedent
where one in the time of Queen Eliz. claimed to have a port to
himself as his own, and it was adjudged that he could not, for it
belonged to the Queen and it could not be severed; and the King
only shall have the customs for landing throughout all the land.
And in the 17th of E. 3 there is a notable precedent, where he
reciteth all the benefits which the subject had in his foreign
traffic by the King's power and protection, and therefore he

imposed a new impost. The writ of *ne exeat regno* comprehends a prohibition to him to whom it is directed that he shall not go beyond the seas, and this may be directed at the King's pleasure to any man who is his subject, and so consequently may he prohibit all merchants; and as he may prohibit the persons so may he the goods of any man, viz., that he shall export or import, at his pleasure. And if the King may generally inhibit that such goods shall not be imported, then by the same reason may he prohibit them upon condition or *sub modo*, viz., that if they import such goods that then they shall pay, etc. And if the general be lawful, the particular cannot be unjust....And so for all these reasons judgment shall be given for the King.

State Trials, ii, 382–7.

Chief Baron Fleming's Judgment

...For the matter, it is of great consequence, and hath two powerful objects which it principally respecteth. The one is the King, his power and prerogative, his treasure and the revenues of his Crown; and to impair and derogate from any of these was a part most undutiful in any subject. The other is the trade and traffic of merchandise, transportation in and out of the land of commodities, which further public benefit ought much to be respected, and nourished as much as may be. The state of the question is touching a new custom. The impositions or customs are duties or sums of money newly imposed by the King without Parliament upon merchandise for the augmentation of his revenues. All the questions arising in the case are *aut de personis, de rebus, vel de actionibus*, viz., form and proceeding. The persons are, first the King, his power and authority; secondly, not Bates the defendant nor the Venetians, but all men who import currants. The imposition is properly upon currants and for them, and is not upon the defendant, nor his goods, who is a merchant; for upon him no imposition shall be but by Parliament. The things are currants, a foreign commodity and a victual; the 5s. for impost, which is said to be great. The action formed, or process is the command by the Great Seal....And first, for the person of the King, *omnis potestas a Deo, et non est potestas nisi pro bono*. To the King is committed the government of the realm and his people; and Bracton saith that for his discharge of his office God had given to him power, the act of government and the power to govern. The King's power is double, ordinary and absolute, and they have several laws and ends. That of the ordinary is for the profit of

particular subjects, for the execution of civil justice, the determining of *meum*; and this is exercised by equity and justice in
ordinary Courts, and by the Civilians is nominated *jus privatum* and
with us Common Law: and these laws cannot be changed without
Parliament, and although that their form and course may be
changed and interrupted, yet they can never be changed in
substance. The absolute power of the King is not that which is
converted or executed to private use, to the benefit of any particular person, but is only that which is applied to the general
benefit of the people and is *salus populi*; as the people is the body
and the King the head; and this power is [not] guided by the rules
which direct only at the Common Law, and is most properly
named policy and government; and as the constitution of this body
varieth with the time, so varieth this absolute law according to the
wisdom of the King for the common good; and these being
general rules and true as they are, all things done within these
rules are lawful. The matter in question is material matter of
State, and ought to be ruled by the rules of policy; and if it be
so, the King hath done well to execute his extraordinary power.
All customs, be they old or new, are no other but the effects
and issues of trades and commerce with foreign nations; but
all commerce and affairs with foreigners, all wars and peace, all
acceptance and admitting for current, foreign coin, all parties and
treaties whatsoever, are made by the absolute power of the King;
and he who hath power of causes hath power also of effects. No
exportation or importation can be but at the King's ports. They
are the gates of the King, and he hath absolute power by them to
include or exclude whom he shall please; and ports to merchants
are their harbours and repose, and for their better security he is
compelled to provide bulwarks and fortresses, and to maintain for
the collection of his customs and duties collectors and customers;
and for that charge it is reason that he should have this benefit.
He is also to defend the merchants from pirates at sea in their
passage. Also by the power of the King they are to be relieved if
they are oppressed by foreign princes, for they shall have his treaty
and embassage; and if he be not remedied thereby, then *lex talionis*
shall be executed, goods for goods and tax for tax; and if this will
not redress the matter, then war is to be attempted for the cause of
merchants. In all the King's Courts, and of other princes, the
judges in them are paid by the King and maintained by him to do
justice to the subjects, and therefore he hath the profits of the said
Courts. It is reasonable that the King should have as much power
over foreigners and their goods as over his own subjects; and if

the King cannot impose upon foreign commodities a custom as well as foreigners may upon their own commodities and upon the commodities of this land when they come to them, then foreign States shall be enriched and the King impoverished, and he shall not have equal profit with them; and yet it will not be denied but his power herein is equal with other States....

It is said that an imposition may not be upon a subject without Parliament. That the King may impose upon a subject I omit; for it is not here the question if the King may impose upon the subject or his goods, but the impost here is not upon a subject but here it is upon Bates, as upon a merchant who imports goods within this land charged before by the King; and at the time when the impost was imposed upon them they were the goods of the Venetians and not the goods of a subject, nor within the land, but only upon those which shall be after imported; and so all the arguments which were made for the subject fail. And where it is said that he is a merchant, and that he ought to have the sea open and free for him, and that trades of merchants and merchandise are necessary to export the surplus of our commodities and then to import other necessaries, and so is favourably to be respected; as to that, it is well known that the end of every private merchant is not the common good but his particular profit, which is only the means which induceth him to trade and traffic. And the impost to him is nothing, for he rateth his merchandise according to that. The impost is imposed upon currants, and he who will buy them shall have them subject to that charge; and it is a great contempt to deny the payment....

I will give a brief answer to all the statutes alleged on the contrary part, with this exposition, that the subjects and merchants are to be freed of 'maletolt,' and this was toll unjustly exacted by London, Southampton, and other ports within this realm; but they are with this saving, that they pay the duties and customs due, or which hereafter shall be due, to the King, which is a full answer to all the statutes. The commodity of currants is no commodity of this land, but foreign. And whereas it is said that it is victual and necessary food, it is no more necessary than wine, and impost for that hath been always paid without contradiction; and without doubt there are many drinkers of wine who are also eaters of currants. That which should be said victual for the commonwealth is that which ariseth from agriculture and of the earth within this land, and not nice and delicate things imported by merchants, such as these currants are. They are rather delicacy or medicine than a victual; and it is no reason that so many of our good and staple commodities should be exported to Venice for such a slight delicacy, and that all the impost shall be paid to the Venetians for them, and the King should have none for their commodity: and although that the price be thereby raised, this hurteth not the merchant nor no other, but only a small number of delicate persons, and those also who are of most able and best estate, for their pleasure. But when the King is in want, he is to be relieved by a general imposition or subsidy upon all the subjects. The imposition which is here is said to be so great and intolerable as an evil precedent; for if he may do so much, he may do it *in infinitum* and upon all other merchandise. For the imposition, I say that it is reasonable, for it is no more than four times so much than was before, and that there hath been as much done in ancient time in other imposts, as in that of wool, which was at first but a noble[1] a sack and is now at 50s. The impost of wine was in ancient time 3s. 4d. a tun and now is four marks[2]. The lessening of custom and impost is much to be guided by intelligence from foreign nations, for the usage and behaviour of a foreign prince may impose a necessity of raising custom of these commodities. And so it was in the particular of currants. The Duke of Venice imposed upon them a ducat[3] by the hundred, which by the wisdom of the State was foreseen to be a means that in time will waste and consume the treasure of the land; whereupon the Queen writ to the Duke that he would abate his custom, which he refused. Wherefore to prevent that so great a quantity of this commodity should not be imported into the land, the Queen granted to the Company of Merchants of the Levant that none should bring in currants but by their licence; and those merchants imposed upon them who did import which were not of their Company, if he were denizen 5s., if he were a stranger 10s. And this was paid by the merchants without contradiction. But there was a clause in the patent that when the Duke of Venice abated his impost that the patent should be void, and after[4] the Duke was solicited again that he would abate the impost, but he refused and the first commission was recalled, and after[4] a new grant was made, which was executed all the Queen's lifetime, which was as aforesaid.

And whereas it is said that if the King may impose, he may impose any quantity what he pleases, true it is that this is to be referred to the wisdom of the King, who guideth all under God by

---

[1] Usually 6s. 8d.   [2] A mark was 13s. 4d.
[3] A Venetian ducat was valued at about 4s. as money of account.
[4] *I.e.* afterwards.

his wisdom, and this is not to be disputed by a subject; and many things are left to his wisdom for the ordering of his power, rather than his power shall be restrained. The King may pardon any felon; but it may be objected that if he pardon one felon he may pardon all, to the damage of the commonwealth, and yet none will doubt but that is left in his wisdom. And as the King may grant a protection for one year, so it may be said that he may grant it for many years, which is a mischief, and so ought to grant none, which will not be denied but that he may. So it may be said that the Queen may grant a safe-conduct to a stranger, for if she may do that, then she may grant to all, which would be burdensome to the inhabitants; and yet it will not be denied but that she may grant to any or all as in her wisdom shall seem convenient. And the wisdom and providence of the King is not to be disputed by the subject; for by intendment they cannot be severed from his person, and to argue *a posse ad actum* to restrain the King and his power because that by his power he may do ill, is no argument for a subject. To prove the power of the King by precedents of antiquity in a case of this nature may easily be done, and if it were lawful in ancient times it is lawful now, for the authority of the King is not diminished and the Crown hath the same attributes that then it had. And in ancient time such imposts were never denied; and that which is given by Parliament is not an impost but a subsidy. In ancient time small traffic or intercourse was betwixt the inhabitants of this land and foreign nations, so that the principal custom was of the commodities of this land, which were woolfells and leather; and that the custom for wools, which was a noble for a sack, was an imposition, appears by the Statute of the 14th Ed. III, stat. 1, cap. 21[1].

It is objected that merchants cannot be restrained, but only persons suspected, as the writ of *ne exeat regno* is. But...it is without doubt that the cause is not traversable[2] and that the King may inhibit any man; for if it be not traversable it is not material. And the reason wherefore any man may be restrained is for the defence of the realm, and it may be done by privy seal, privy signet, great seal, or proclamation; and that appears by the writ of *licencia transportandi* in the register, which containeth licence for one to travel, and limits him to what place he shall go,

---

[1] This statute, which granted to the King an additional subsidy for a limited period on wool, woolfells, and other merchandise exported, contained a clause providing that only the old custom should be levied after the period expired. On wool this was half a mark a sack.

[2] In Law, capable of being traversed or formally denied.

and when he shall return, and with what goods, so that the King may prohibit body and goods. And when a man is beyond the seas, the King may command him to return; and if he doth not obey such command he shall forfeit his goods.

Now for restraint of commodities many precedents are to prove it. In the time of H. 3 and E. 1 it was forbidden that the wool should be transported into Flanders; and in E. 1 a commission was awarded to enquire who had done against this ordinance, and the goods of one Freeston were seized, and therefore an attachment awarded against the ships of Hull for transporting contrary to the ordinance. In the 22 E. 1 it was forbidden that no merchant should trade with France; for trade with foreigners is a foreign thing which is only referred to the King. In the 17 H. 6 all merchants were forbidden to import wares from Flanders into this land; and the citizens of London complained of certain merchants which had done contrary to this ordinance to the Lords of the Privy Council, which I have here ready; . . .   *State Trials*, ii, 387–92.

§ 2. THE GREAT CONTRACT

The 'Great Contract' of the session of 1610, like the compromise with the Commons concerning impositions, was an arrangement with the King which was never carried into effect. As a form of taxation the feudal dues payable to the Crown had long been obsolete. As fiefs were no longer spheres of government but only landed estates, there was now no reason why the King should take over the property of a minor under the name of wardship. As the monarchy was no longer itinerant, but had 'a fixed seat and constant access to fair markets,'[1] the reason for purveyance had disappeared. It was therefore proposed to convert all military tenures into free socage, and to compound for wardship and other feudal dues by granting £200,000 a year to the King as part of his permanent revenue. The dissolution of Parliament in 1611 prevented the bargain from being completed, and military tenures were not abolished until the Restoration.

(1) Memorial concerning the Great Contract, 1610

This is dated 26 March, 1610.

Memorial concerning the Great Contract with his Majesty touching Tenures, with the dependents, Purveyance, etc., delivered by the Committees of the Commons' House unto the Lords

Demands in matter of tenures, etc. The desire in general is to have all knight's service turned into free and common socage.

1 Goldwin Smith, i, 446.

In particular, some tenures more properly concern the person, some the possession.

Grand Serjeanty: wherein though the tenure be taken away yet the service of honour to be saved. And the tenure *per Baroniam*, as it may concern Bishops or Barons or men in Parliament, to be considered.

Petty Serjeanty: escuage[1], certain and uncertain, to be taken away.

Castle Guard: that castle guard which rests in rent to be saved.

All Knight's Services generally, both of King and common person, to be taken away. The rents and annual services to be saved.

Homage ancestral[2] and ordinary, with the respite of them. Both these to be taken away; only the coronation homage to be saved, not in respect of tenure but of honour.

Fealty: the form of doing fealty not yet resolved of.

Wardship of body, marriage of the heir, of the widow. These to be taken away.

Respite of fealty to be taken away.

Wardship and custody of lands likewise to be taken away.

Primer Seizin to cease. Livery, Ouster-le-main[3], to be taken away so far as they concern tenures, or seizure by reason of tenures, other than for escheats.

Licence of alienation upon fines, feoffments, leases for life, and other conveyances.

Pardon of alienation, pleading, *Diem clausit extremum*, *Mandamus*, *Quae plura devenerunt*, offices *post mortem*, inquisitions *ex officio*, except for escheats.

Also all concealed wards *de futuro*, all intrusions, all alienations past, all bonds and covenants for performance of what tends to knight's service. All these to be determined[4].

All wards now in being, or found by office[5], or which shall be found by office before the conclusion of this Contract, shall be found, and whose ancestors died within three years before. Those to be saved.

Relief upon knight's service to cease.

Patentees that pay a sum in gross, or pay tenths, or fee farmers. These not to double their rents upon a relief to be paid.

[1] A money payment in lieu of military service = scutage.

[2] 'Homage ancestral' is applied to cases where the ancestors of a feudal tenant have held their lands by homage from time immemorial.

[3] 'Ouster-le-main' was a livery of land out of the hands of the sovereign or a surrender by a guardian on a ward's coming of age. The reference here appears to be a payment.

[4] *I.e.* brought to an end.   [5] *I.e.* by an official enquiry.

Escheats, heriots, suit of court, rents, work-days, and such services. These all to remain.

Aid to the King to remain, but limited in certain to twenty-five thousand pounds, *cum acciderit*.

Aids to common persons to cease.

* * * * * *

All purveyance and takings for his Majesty, the Queen, the Prince and all other the King's children, and for all offices, officers, courts, councils, and societies whatsoever to be utterly taken away, as well purveyance and takings for household, stable, navy, servants, labourers, and all other provisions, as also for carts, horses, and carriages, both by land and water; and generally, all purveyances and takings, for whomsoever or whatsoever, of what name or nature soever, to be for ever extinguished; the composition for the same to be all dissolved and released. The Clerk of the Market and all other to be disabled for setting any prices. The power and prerogative of pre-emption to be determined, not intending hereby the pre-emption of tin.

* * * * * *

That whereas the House of Commons have already, among their grievances, preferred a petition to his Majesty, as of right and justice, that the four English counties[1] may have a trial by law concerning their inheritance to the Common Laws of this Realm, and so to be exempted from the jurisdiction of the President and Council of Wales (a matter wherein the whole realm is deeply interested); notwithstanding, upon occasion of this Great Contract, the House of Commons doth humbly petition his Majesty, as of grace, that without further suit, trial, or trouble, those counties may be restored to that their ancient right, the same being no way prejudicial to his Majesty's honour in point of sovereignty (as we conceive), as being alike to his Majesty in which of his Courts his subjects have their trials, and in profit much less; but rather being a matter of greater benefit to his Majesty in the duties due for suits in his Courts at Westminster, and to his Majesty's loving subjects there it will be a matter of great comfort, and of enabling them the better to perform their part of this Contract, by easing them of much causeless vexation and charges which in trifling suits they now bear and endure.

* * * * * *

---

[1] The four English counties were Shropshire, Worcester, Hereford, and Gloucester.

(2) Sir Julius Caesar on the Great Contract, 1610

This imaginary conversation bearing on the Great Contract was found among Sir Julius Caesar's papers. *C.* probably stands for Caesar himself. The document suggests that the scheme was not without its critics, who described it as a losing bargain for the Crown. Caesar was at this time Chancellor of the Exchequer, and had been employed in estimating the value of the feudal incidents for the purposes of the Contract.

17th August, 1610. *Quaeritur*, whether that this contract between the King and the two Houses of Parliament be profitable for the King or no?

A. It appeareth that the King shall gain thereby a yearly addition to his other revenue . . . 200,000*l.*

C. True, did it not also appear that this bargain taketh yearly from the King, which before he held uncontrollably by his just prerogative, the wards and tenures, with their incidents, alienations, pre-fines and post-fines, respite of homage, etc., worth yearly to the King . . . . 44,000*l.*

The purveyances of the King's house and stable by commission, composition, and caretaking . . . 50,000*l.*

Assarts[1], defective titles, informations upon penal statutes, and such other lawful advantages and prerogatives quitted[2] and released in the several retributions[3] yielded unto on his Majesty's behalf . . . . 21,000*l.*

All which amount unto . . . . 115,000*l.*

Which taken out of the said . . . 200,000*l.*

There will remain to the King towards the increase of his yearly revenue but . . . . . 85,000*l.*

But with the loss of such power and command over his subjects in so high points of prerogative as never yet could be obtained from any of his progenitors, Kings or Queens of this realm.

Now the question will be, whether the King may not, without wronging the subjects, raise that 85,000*l.* by improvement of those things so parted with by this bargain? And questionless it seemeth that he may. For no man can doubt that the wards and alienations will yield, without wrong to the subjects, more than heretofore to the King's yearly purse by . . 40,000*l.*

Likewise penal statutes executed lawfully and mercifully will yield more than heretofore yearly by . . 12,000*l.*

By the law not only the King but the King's children have the benefit of purveyance, which might very well be enlarged to the value of . . . . 20,000*l.*

---

[1] *I.e.* the clearing of forest land to convert it into arable.
[2] Remitted or cancelled.   [3] Repayments.

Neither can it be doubted but that assarts[1], defective titles, purprestures[2], outlawries, forfeitures of felons and traitors, and such advantages as are clearly acquitted[3] by his Majesty will, above that which heretofore they have yielded, rise to a yearly increase of   .   .   .   .   .   .   13,000*l.*

All which maketh up the sum of   .   .   85,000*l.*

A. Well! admit all to be true as you say, yet certainly it cannot be denied but in the said increase by improvements in those kinds the subjects, who complain already for the present profit made of those natures, will double their complaints hereafter; which, though causeless in the King's right, yet the same may grow so heavy to the subjects by the rigour of the executioners thereof that the people may be stirred, if not to rebellion yet to such a coldness of future contributions that may justly occasion a despair in the King never to receive relief hereafter from his subjects by fifteenths, subsidies, or the like; which if it come to pass, consider your present estate, and see in what case you stand without some relief from the Commons at this time, and how you can without their help better the same hereafter.

At the beginning of the last session of Parliament your want yearly in the ordinary was   .   .   .   .   50,000*l.*

For the extraordinary   .   .   .   .   100,000*l.*

To which you must add these sums following, taken from the ordinary receipts since that time, viz.

To the Prince	20,000*l.*
Some of the new impositions . .	20,000*l.*
Sea-coals of Sunderland and Blyth . .	300*l.*
Part of the pre-emption of tin . . .	2,000*l.*
Logwood	1,700*l.*
Alehouses	4,000*l.*
All which amount unto . . .	48,000*l.*

Which, added to the two former sums, make the yearly want at this present   .   .   .   .   .   .   198,000*l.*

Now for your debts, did you not owe at the beginning of the said session   .   .   .   .   .   .   300,000*l.*

And did you not need for necessary provisions for the King and State   .   .   .   .   .   .   150,000*l.*

And for a stock to remain ready for any future peril 150,000*l.*

Whereupon there was necessarily demanded supply of
                                         600,000*l.*

---

[1] See note on p. 348 above.
[2] 'Purprestures' are illegal encroachments upon the land or property of others.
[3] Cancelled.

And is not your debt since increased, by addition of 110,000*l.* new debt, to . . . . . . 410,000*l.*

And have you yet obtained more to the discharge thereof than one subsidy and one fifteenth, to the value of 110,000*l.*

And do you suppose that without proceeding in the said contract, or giving them better contentment in their proposed grievances, you shall be able to draw from them one penny more for your supplies? No, surely. And then behold your money state. You want yearly . . . . 198,000*l.*

You want in present money, over and above 110,000*l.* to be discharged by the said subsidy and fifteenth 600,000*l.*

Now if you, or any man living, can tell me how to supply the said two wants without the help of Parliament, or abating of expenses, or improving the King's lands and some forests, parks, and chases, *eris mihi magnus Apollo.*

Now for the abating of the expenses, admit that you may abate yearly:

In the King's House	10,000*l.*
In Ireland	20,000*l.*
In the Wardrobe	3,000*l.*
In the Navy	8,000*l.*
In ambassadors	4,000*l.*
In works	10,000*l.*
In the jewel-house	4,000*l.*
In parks, pales, rails, and lodges	2,000*l.*
In rewards for officers and messengers	2,000*l.*
In the Tower and other prisons	1,000*l.*
All that amounteth but to	64,000*l.*

Which I fear will never be done, but if it be, yet there will be still wanting yearly . . . . . . 134,000*l.*

To which if you will add that the King will be content to spare in his extraordinary expenses yearly . 50,000*l.*

Yet there will be wanting yearly . . 84,000*l.*

So that abating of expenses, though that might be, will not serve the turn desired, and prove to him perhaps more distasteful than the parting with the said prerogatives to his people.

Now then for the improving of the King's lands, and some remote forests, parks, and chases, the latter I fear his Majesty will dislike, and the former by no means will yield him above 84,000*l.*

So that if neither improving of the King's lands nor abating of expenses will either of them singly by itself supply the yearly

want, then both jointly must do it, or else the King must resolve
to depend upon the help and assistance of his people in Parliament. And both those jointly together without help of Parliament
will never be able to furnish your yearly want, and withal discharge the said huge debt and provide those necessary sums
which, otherwise provided[1], will draw with them upon the King a
daily and yearly interest which will miserably increase the yearly
wants and calamities of this estate.

    C. Then, after your long discourse, thus much have I gotten
of you, that the King may, by these two means jointly, relieve his
estate for yearly wants without his Parliament, but not to pay his
present debts or to make provision of money for the present
necessity and use of the King and State. But how shall the
Parliament do that, unless they will supply the residue of the
yearly want of 200,000*l.* and supply the sum of 600,000*l.* first
demanded of them?

    A. It may well be that his Majesty, by yielding them content
in some of their grievances wherein they are not yet satisfied with
the late answers, may win from them three subsidies and six
fifteenths to be paid in three years to begin after the last payment of
the subsidy already granted, which will amount unto   450,000*l.*

    But certainly they will never be persuaded to any yearly
support further than they have offered already.

    C. If they will do as you say, yet the said 450,000*l.* will be
no more in that time than if they should give presently 350,000*l.*,
by reason of the continual interest still growing upon us for want
of ready money. So we shall still want of that we need

                                                250,000*l.*

    Which, if not prevented, will bring us in very short time to
the former misery.

    Now then it appeareth that albeit you give that 200,000*l.* by
way of bargain, and give four subsidies and seven fifteenths, yet
we shall still want for support of yearly charges .   115,000*l.*

    And for payment of our debts and necessary provision in
money .   .   .   .   250,000*l.*

    And also by this contract the King shall be stripped and
divested of those imperial prerogatives and flowers of his Crown
that never King of England yet did or would part with upon any
condition.

    A. I must confess that you have said truly; but if the greatest
Kings in the world will in their expenses exceed the bounds of
their revenue, *non admirentur si paupertate graventur.* And

---

[1] *I.e.* by loan.

consequently they then will find it true that poverty in a King is the most disadvantageous and distasteful sickness that can assail him, and commonly proveth a miserable disaster to King and people; and therefore you must hereafter *non aliunde quod a te potes petere*, and learn by good husbandry in improving your own certain revenue, and abating your ordinary expenses and avoiding of extraordinary, to repair the ruins of this decayed estate.

C. I find now the end of worldly friendship, either not to relieve, or to do it sparingly, or in lieu thereof to give good counsel. I will therefore accept of the last, and endeavour to make trial how the said twofold necessity may be supplied without the said contract or further help of Parliament at this time.

It appeareth by the premisses that the King's yearly want is

198,000*l.*

For support whereof the improvements of the wards, alienations, and the other kinds for which we should have contracted, will amount to . . . . . . 85,000*l.*

The improvements of the King's lands, not meddling with his forests, parks, and chases . . . . 84,000*l.*

The abatement of expenses in the King's House 10,000*l.*

In the works . . . . . 5,000*l.*

In the allowance of Ireland . . . 5,000*l.*

In the jewel-house . . . . 4,000*l.*

In repairing parks, pales, and lodges . . 2,000*l.*

In rewards to officers and messengers . 2,000*l.*

In prisons . . . . . . 1,000*l.*

All which amounteth to . . . 198,000*l.*

Now let us try what means may be taken for the supplying of so much as may satisfy the great debt of . 600,000*l.*

There was left 4,044*l.* of refuse land unbought and turned back by the late contractors, which to be sold after the rate of twenty-five years' purchase will amount unto . . . . . 101,100*l.*

There was left in fee farms reserved upon parsonages impropriate 7,000*l.* a year, which to be sold at fifteen years' purchase will yield . . . . 105,000*l.*

There was left in fee farms reserved upon mills 1,500*l.* a year, which to be sold after fifteen years' purchase cometh to 22,500*l.*

There is returned back by the contractors for mills 1,026*l.* yearly, which to be sold in fee simple at twenty-five years' purchase will amount unto . .   25,650*l.*

There was left in fee farms by the first contractors for lands, Garaway, etc., 700*l.* a year reserved to the King, which to be sold after the rate of fifteen years' purchase amounteth to . .   10,500*l.*

The interest of lands inned[1] and recovered from the sea since 32 H. 8 in fines, besides a reservation of a fee farm rent to the Crown . . . .   40,000*l.*

The interest of lands escheated to the King, either by bastardy of the pretended owners, or by dying without heirs, or being purchased by aliens not denized[2] . . . . .   10,000*l.*

The interest of lands entailed upon the Crown either generally or specially whereof the entail is spent . .   30,000*l.*

The interest of lands where two manors have been carried away from the King for one, where rectories appropriate have been carried away for advowsons, where whole chantries and chapels and the lands of the same have been carried away under colour of an advowson .   10,000*l.*

There is to be returned from the contractors for parsonages at least 2,000*l.* a year, which to be sold at twenty-two years' purchase in fee simple is worth   44,000*l.*

The King will forbear the desired stock (which would have tended to the safety of the whole realm if conveniently it might have been had), viz. . .   150,000*l.*

And, because the Commons are so sure of their safety as that they refuse to enlarge themselves to the provision of things necessary for the maintenance of the name of England—the Office of Ord-

[1] Enclosed.
[2] Not made denizens. The verb to denize was in use at this time.

nance and the like—the King must be
pleased to forbear some part of that
provision, which will have towards the
balancing of the said great sum . 51,300*l.*

Total 600,000*l.* [*sic*]
[600,050]

A. Now I perceive the old proverb to be true that haste
makes waste, for in making up your yearly wants of 198,000*l.*
you reckon the improvement of the King's lands at 84,000*l.*,
whereby you take yearly from the King in the fines of copyholders 2,000*l.*, in the fines of leases 2,000*l.*, and in fines,
heriots, and perquisites of courts 1,000*l.*, all . 5,000*l.*

And in making up your sum of 600,000*l.*, you take away in
fee simple and fee farm rents out of the King's present standing
revenue yearly . . . . . 17,000*l.*
Both which sums amount to . . . 22,000*l.*

C. I see you take me at every turn; but to give you a full
answer, the King will be pleased to abate yearly in the charges of
his Navy . . . . . . 2,000*l.*
And of his extraordinary expenses . . 20,000*l.*
Both which sums amount to yearly . . 22,000*l.*

And now I trust you are satisfied that the King is not in such
extreme need of the Commons' help to relieve his present wants,
but that he can by his own means, and without taking any
desperate course, relieve himself.

A. I see it and am glad of it, and I thank God for it....

* * * * * *

Parliamentary Debates in 1610 (ed. S. R. Gardiner:
Camden Society, 1861), pp. 163–79.

§ 3. REVENUE AND EXPENDITURE

'The only disease and consumption which I can ever apprehend as likeliest to endanger me,' wrote James to his Council in 1607, 'is this eating
canker of want, which being removed, I could think myself as happy in all
other respects as any other king or monarch that ever was since the birth of
Christ.'[1] At this time his financial position seemed almost hopeless. In spite of
her careful husbandry, Elizabeth had been forced during the last five years of
her reign to sell Crown property to the amount of £372,000, and had incurred
a debt of at least £300,000[2]. James required about £290,700 to meet his
normal annual expenditure, and during the first year of his reign he received
only £264,000 from sources other than Parliamentary, so failing Parliament
he was faced with a recurring deficit of £26,700[3]. He had also incurred an

[1] Strype, *Annals of the Reformation* (edition of 1824), iv, 560.
[2] *Parliamentary Debates in* 1610, ed. S. R. Gardiner, p. ix. [3] *Ib.* p. x.

exceptional expenditure of about £100,000 in respect of the change of Sovereign. Expenses connected with the colonisation of Ireland were also to prove very heavy, and, unlike Elizabeth, James had a family to provide for. Thus in 1606 the debt had risen to £735,000[1], while a Parliamentary grant of £375,000 spread over four years had done little to relieve the situation. By 1608, owing mainly to the notable improvement in the yield to land revenue and custom, the ordinary revenue of 1603 had risen from £264,000 to £366,000, but expenditure was advancing still more rapidly, and the estimate for 1610 shewed an increase on 1603 from £290,700 to £509,524[2]. It should be observed that gifts to favourites, and especially to Scots, only partly explain the deficits. From the King's accession until 29 November, 1610, Scotchmen received in annuities £10,614 a year and in cash payments £221,380; during the same period the annuities granted to Englishmen amounted to about £20,000 a year, but the grants in cash were quite small[3].

When Robert Cecil, Earl of Salisbury, became Lord Treasurer in 1608, the debts of the Crown stood at nearly a million, due partly to a general increase in the luxury of the Court and partly to the laxity with which expenditure was supervised in an age long before the modern development of Treasury control[4]. In two years Salisbury's wise administration reduced the debt to £300,000; but it was also of the utmost importance to reduce the annual deficit, and it was for this purpose that he proposed to increase impositions[5]. These only brought in £70,000, and that was why it became necessary to appeal to Parliament. A speech by Salisbury explaining the financial position and an extract from the report of the subsequent debate thereon in the House of Commons are printed below [pp. 357 and 358].

One of the devices of Salisbury's Treasurership was the creation and sale of baronetcies. This was not the shameless prostitution of honours which it was afterwards represented to be[6]. The cost of the army in Ireland far exceeded the whole revenue of the country, for it came to £35,810 as against a revenue of £24,000 a year[7], and the English Exchequer had to meet the difference. As far back as 1606, in his Discourse on the Plantation in Ireland, the fertile mind of Bacon had thrown out a suggestion from which the idea of the baronetcy may very well have developed,—'knighthood to such persons as have not attained it; or otherwise knighthood with some new difference and precedence; it may no doubt work with many.'[8] The order of baronets constituted in 1611 (the earliest patents are dated 22 May of that year) was to 'consist entirely of gentlemen of good family and estate, who should bind themselves to pay into the Exchequer a sum sufficient to

1 F. C. Montague, *Political History of England* 1603–1660, p. 33.
2 *Debates of 1610*, p. xii.   3 *Ib.* p. xiii.
4 *Ib.* p. xv.   5 *Ib.* pp. xvii–xx.
6 'This institution of the order of Baronet is commonly spoken of as a disgraceful proceeding on the part of the King. Why, I have never been able to understand or conjecture. The object was a good one; the conditions were open and honourable; the persons selected were no way unfit or disreputable; the order itself has never fallen into disgrace. To invite contributions and other assistance towards the settlement and civilisation of what was then the most unsettled part of Ireland from the class of persons likeliest to do the work effectually, cannot be considered an unworthy act on the King's part' (James Spedding in Bacon, *Letters and Life*, vi, 138).
7 Gardiner, ii, 112.   8 *Letters and Life*, iv, 121.

maintain 30 foot-soldiers in Ireland for three years, at the same time declaring on oath that they had not directly or indirectly paid anything else for the honour.'[1] The sum required for this purpose, which was payable in three instalments, amounted altogether to £3,240, and in this way as much as £90,000 was raised in the course of the next three years[2].

In 1612 the Earl of Salisbury died, leaving the finances in a position somewhat less favourable than in 1610 [pp. 359-60] and the Treasury was placed in commission; but under the wasteful influence of the favourite Robert Carr, the debt had risen by 1613 to £680,000, while the expenditure had come to exceed the revenue by something like £200,000 a year. A feudal aid for the marriage of the King's daughter Elizabeth was levied in 1612 [p. 360], but by 1614 the position was serious [p. 361]. The Parliament of that year granted no supplies, and a clerical loan [p. 362] could do little to relieve the situation, so that by 1615 the amount of the debt was £700,000[3]. James was therefore thrown back on a number of irritating expedients for raising money. After the dissolution of Parliament a voluntary benevolence produced £23,000[4], but a general appeal to the country by letters from the Council met with a poor response, and an application to the City of London for a loan of £100,000 provoked the reply that they would rather give £10,000 than lend £100,000[5].

A review of the financial position made in 1617 by Bacon [p. 363], who had been appointed Lord Keeper of the Great Seal, suggests that a considerable improvement had taken place; and it is clear from his correspondence [p. 366] that economies were being effected in the cost of the Court and the Household. In fact it may be said that the King's financial difficulties were now drawing to an end, for in 1618 he was fortunate enough to discover a financier in the person of Lionel Cranfield, a merchant of the City of London, afterwards Earl of Middlesex, who took over the task of reform. He was so successful in reducing expenditure and making the most of revenue that by the time James met his third Parliament in 1621, although he was not solvent, he was at any rate in a much better position than in 1614. The supplies granted by that Parliament were not, however, much worth considering, and in 1622 an appeal for a benevolence was sent out to both clergy and laity [p. 370].

The beginning of the reign of James I witnessed an important advance in the unification of the customs administration. In Burghley's time a system had been gradually built up under which government officials were replacing the private persons to whom taxes were farmed out at a fixed rent. But when he died in 1598, the needs of the war in Ireland forced his successors to clutch at any expedient that would bring in money quickly, and this led to a revival of farming in particular cases, although no general scheme was in contemplation. The combination of government administration with a multiplicity of farms was not satisfactory, because it meant a fluctuating yield when a constant yield was what the administration needed most; and moreover it was not easy to audit the accounts in such a way as to prevent loss. The new reign saw 'an avalanche of minor

---

[1] *Letters and Life*, vi, 136.   [2] Gardiner, ii, 112.
[2] *Calendar of State Papers* (*Domestic*), 1611–18, p. 310.
[3] Gardiner, ii, 261.   [5] *Ib.*

leases'[1] which were setting up fresh complications, and it was therefore decided in 1605 to group together all the customs in London and the outports, as far as existing contracts allowed, and to let them as a single farm, government supervision and control being, however, still retained.

(1) The Lord Treasurer's Speech on Finance, 1610

This speech was delivered at a conference of the two Houses on 15 February, 1610. The debate that follows took place on 19 February. These papers shew the close connexion between the Great Contract and the levy of Impositions as methods of solving the King's financial difficulties.

*   *   *   *   *   *

...The King's wants and estate he described in three several times:—1. At the time when he came to the Crown; 2. From that time till Michaelmas was twelvemonth, when his estate was at the lowest ebb[2]; 3. A progression from that time till now.

Queen Elizabeth entered into the Irish wars having 700,000*l.* in her coffers. From [August 1598]...until her death the charge of Ireland cost 1,600,000*l.* ....When the King came to the Crown he could not possibly dissolve the army upon a sudden, so that the charge of Ireland in his time hath cost 600,000*l.* Besides which he hath redeemed the lands (cost 63,000*l.*) mortgaged by the late Queen, hath taken away the copper money, the exchange of Ireland, and paid divers debts of the Queen's; all amounting to 300,000*l.*

The Low Countries hath cost him 250,000*l.*

The obsequies of the Queen; the King's entrance; the entrance of the Queen and her children; the coronation; the entertainment of the King of Denmark; embassages and gratulations sent and received: 500,000*l.*

In tertio Jacobi, when the last Lord Treasurer accompted, the gross debt of the King was 700,000*l.*; since which time his Majesty hath been at great charge in the rebellion of Sir Cahir O'Dogharty[3].

In maintaining the charge of the Prince, in
building of ships, and paying interest for
money borrowed; so that at Michaelmas
1603 he owed *in toto*   .   .   .   1,400,000*l.*

---

[1] Professor F. C. Dietz on 'Elizabethan Customs Administration' in *E.H.R.* xlv, 57; in this article the whole question of the organisation of the customs is discussed.
[2] *I.e.* 29 September, 1608; Salisbury had been appointed Lord Treasurer on 6 May.   [3] In 1608.

At that time also his yearly expenses did ex-
    ceed his receipts   .   .   .   .   31,000*l.*
Since which time there hath been an allevia-
    tion of his debt and charge, so that the
    King's debt is now drawn down to   .   300,000*l.*
And his yearly expenses do now exceed his
    receipts: *per annum*   .   .   .   .   46,000*l.*
Towards the discharge of all these payments he hath received
as followeth, (viz)—
    Of the subsidies due in the Queen's time   300,000*l.*
    Of the subsidies last given   .   .   .   450,000*l.*
    Of the aid   .   .   .   .   .   22,000*l.*
        Whereof the nobility paid 4,000*l.* and
        the City of London 1,000*l.*
    He hath received upon privy seals   .   .   120,000*l.*
        The most whereof is already repaid.
This debt and charge was thus drawn down
    by means of the last subsidy, which was   .   450,000*l.*
Sales of land and mills   .   .   .   .   400,000*l.*
Copyholders, freed woods, and assarts[1]   .   100,000*l.*
Old debts to the Crown   .   .   .   200,000*l.*
So that the debt remaining is 300,000*l.* But the King's certain
charge is 1,400*l. per diem,* which is 511,000*l. per annum.*

      *   *   *   *   *   *

Parliamentary Debates in 1610 (ed. S. R. Gardiner:
Camden Society, 1861), pp. 1–9.

*Debate on the Earl of Salisbury's appeal for
supplies,* 19 *Feb.* 1610

Upon this speech the matter was debated often in the House.
Whereupon it was generally conceived that for the matter of
subsidy, it was a thing not intended by the Lords; first, for that
it would not give satisfaction to his Majesty, for though it
might discharge his debts yet it would do no good for the yearly
supply of the defect of his receipts, which was 46 thousand
pounds *per annum*; and also for that a subsidy is never spoken of
until the end of the Parliament, and doth voluntarily proceed
from the Commons, who will not be deprived of the thanks for it
by any motion from the Lords....
    ...So that, leaving the debate of subsidies, they entered
into consideration of the yearly contribution desired, and of the
retribution to proceed from the King to the subjects, which

[1] See note 1 on p. 348 above.

being referred to the General Committee of Grievances, divers means of supply were proposed, whereof the first was,

1. The due execution of the laws against Papists and recusants, and the entailing of the lands to the Crown which should come by attainder....

2. ...A resumption of the patents and grants of the King's customs and imposts, which are very profitable to the farmers....

3. ...The taking away of the purveyance, wherein such course may be taken as the King may be provided for by a market at the Court gate at reasonable prices for ready money without troubling the country—for which the subjects would yield to his Majesty a great yearly allowance.

4. The discharge of tenures and wardships, whereby the subjects should receive a great ease and contentment, and our laws should be more agreeable to the Law of God. And the King also should have in lieu thereof an yearly rent out of the lands held of him, without charging the poorer sort who have no lands.

5. Another motion was made concerning wardships, that the whole benefit might come to the King's purse and not unto the Committee's, but that motion was not seconded by any other.

6. Lastly, it was said that all these courses would be to no purpose except it would please the King to resume his pensions granted to courtiers out of the Exchequer, and to diminish his charge and expenses. For (says he[1]) to what purpose is it for us to draw a silver stream out of the country into the royal cistern, if it shall daily run out thence by private cocks? Or to what end is it to bring daily sacrifices, if others (like Baal's priests) steal it away in the night? And for his part he said that he would never give his consent to take money from a poor frieze jerkin to trap a courtier's horse withal. And therefore he wished that we might join in humble petition to his Majesty that he would diminish his charge and live of his own, without exacting of his poor subjects....

*   *   *   *   *   *

Parliamentary Debates in 1610 (ed. S. R. Gardiner: Camden Society, 1861), pp. 9–11.

(2) Financial Statement, 1612

18 *May*, 1612

In June last, presently[2] after the death of the Lord Treasurer Salisbury, the Chancellor of the Exchequer acquainted his sacred Majesty with the estate of his revenue and receipt, which was, that his yearly ordinary expenses exceeded his yearly ordinary

1 Thomas Wentworth, member for the City of Oxford.   2 Immediately.

revenues by 160,000*l.* or thereabouts; and that his present debt was 500,000*l.* or near thereabouts.

That between that Midsummer and Michaelmas following, there was necessarily to be provided for the maintenance of the ordinary expenses, 60,000*l.*

No way else presently left for to do it but the sale of the mills, pasturages, and other lands left out of the entail or annexation. That the same was to be done fruitfully. Which done, yet the debt remained 500,000*l.*, and would increase by the quarterly inequality of the ordinary receipts with extraordinary, which would tend to a plain ruin if it were not prevented.

*   *   *   *   *   *

Lansdowne MSS. 165, f. 223.

(3) Feudal Aid of 1612

Super Auxilio propter Maritagium Dominae
Elizabethae levando

Whereas our eldest daughter Elizabeth hath long since accomplished the age of seven years, by reason whereof there is due unto us by the laws and statutes of this our realm of England reasonable Aid, to be had and levied of all our immediate tenants by knight's service and in socage for her marriage,

These are therefore to will and require you our Chancellor to cause to be made and sealed under our Great Seal of England as well several Commissions to be directed into all the counties of this our said realm, according to the form of a draught of a Commission for that purpose to these presents annexed, as also several Commissions for the Cinque Ports, and for compounding with all the Lords Spiritual and Temporal of this our realm, and with the Masters, Governors, Principals, Guardians, and other the Heads of Houses, Halls, and Colleges of our Universities of Oxford and Cambridge, according to several draughts hereto likewise annexed, changing such things therein as are to be changed, and to direct them to such Commissioners as you, with the Lord Privy Seal and our Chancellor of our Exchequer, shall name and appoint, returnable at the days in the several draughts prefixed, and the same several Commissions to renew to the same Commissioners or any others according to your directions as often as need shall require; and also to name and choose any two of the said Commissioners in every county respectively to be Collectors for the same Aid; and this shall be our sufficient warrant in that behalf.

Given under our Signet at Woodstock the thirtieth day of August in the tenth year of our reign of England, France, and Ireland, and of Scotland the six-and-fortieth.

Per ipsum Regem.

Rymer, *Foedera* (edition of 1704–35), xvi, 724.

(4) Financial Statement, 1614

2 *May*, 1614. *Debts, Foreign*

	l.
Ireland	32,000
Low Countries	5,000
Ambassadors	9,000
Lady Elizabeth's portion[1] . . .	20,000
Horatio Palavicino[2]	13,000
	79,000

Domestical Debts touching the honour and safety of the State

	l.
Navy	38,000
Marine victuals	2,000
Ordnance	4,000
Gunpowder	2,000
Armoury, castles, forts, Tower, prisons .	16,000
Master of the posts	2,000
Waterworks, Middleton, Barwick Bridge	6,000
Fetching in of pirates . . .	3,000
	73,000

Debts Domestical concerning the persons of the King, Queen, and Prince

	l.
Cofferers	21,000
Wardrobes and Robes . . .	85,000
Band of Pensioners . . .	2,000
Treasurer of the Chamber . . .	15,000
Works	9,000
Jewel-house for plate, chains, and medals	15,000
To Jeweller for jewels . . .	18,000

[1] Princess Elizabeth had been married to the Elector Palatine on 14 February, 1613.

[2] When Sir Horatio Palavicino, the merchant and political agent, died in 1600 Queen Elizabeth owed him nearly £29,000, which was never paid in full by her successor (*D.N.B.* xliii, 98).

Fees and annuities	.	.	.	.	71,000
Queen's creditors	.	.	.	.	70,000
Late Prince's debts	.	.	.	.	30,000
					336,000

Domestical Debts touching loans upon Privy Seals and money anticipated from the ordinary revenues

				l.
Loans upon privy seals	.	.	.	125,000
Anticipated from the ordinary revenues		.		67,000
				192,000
[Total]				680,000

Lansdowne MSS. 165, f. 257.

(5) Clerical Loan, 1614
The Archbishop of Canterbury to the Bishop of London
[Desires him to assist in raising a loan for the King, upon the Parliament refusing it.]

June 1614

My very good Lord,

I doubt not but you have heard what was the issue of this late Parliament, and how, by the harsh courses of some men, his Majesty received no kind of satisfaction in that great cause wherefore he called them, that is to say, for the supplying of his necessities. This event producing a great damp on all sides, it pleased God to put into the mind of my Lords the Bishops, after the expiring of the Convocation, to think upon some course how they might in some measure testify their duty unto their Sovereign by some free-will offering.

The matter whereupon they resolved was, that every Bishop should voluntarily send unto the King the best piece of plate which he had; and if his Majesty should be pleased to accept of this, then we promised to move the civilians, and others of the abler sort of the clergy, according to their proportion, to do the like. In brief, his Majesty graciously accepted it, conceiving that it would produce that effect whereat we principally aimed, that this our example would bring on the Lords and others of the Temporalty to do the like. And, verily, God blessed our intendments, for his Highness immediately making it known in the Court, the Lords of the Council and the rest of the nobility presently[1] took it up, and not only themselves do perform the same, but

[1] Immediately.

sent forthwith to the Judges, to the Lord Mayor and Aldermen, together with other persons of special note, so that I trust the harvest will be great throughout the better sort of the whole kingdom. We of the Bishops that were here presently[1] sent in our gifts, myself leading the way; and some of our company, not having any piece of plate sufficient to express their zeal to this service, sent in some one of smaller worth, but filled with gold, so that it made a present of reasonable value. The desire of us all is, that your Lordship will bear a part in this work, and that you will move the clergy in your diocese to send in such a voluntary gratification, whereunto those which were here in Convocation already prepared, out of this ground, that if the Parliament had obtained the expected success, they might well have conceived that they should have granted no less that three or four subsidies. Our meaning in this is, that no poor man should be grated on, but that it should come freely from the purses of those who are of ability, and shall part with that which is of ornament and luxury rather than of necessity; and where men are unwilling to part with their plate, they may send in some convenient sum of money as a redemption for the same. I pray your Lordship, with all diligence and dexterity, to set yourself to this work, wherein I trust all good men will concur with alacrity; for it is a shame unto our whole nation that so good and gracious a King should be driven to necessity, when we his people do live in plenty. And I know it was a singular comfort unto his Majesty that when some have been unrespective of him, there were not wanting others which remembered their duty, and that so opportunely. So ceasing to be any way further troublesome unto your Lordship, with my hearty commendations,

I rest, your so very loving brother,

G. Cant.[2]

Goodman, The Court of King James, p. 157.

(6) Bacon's Financial Statement, 1617

This document should probably be assigned to a date a little before 27 September, 1617.

A Memorial for your Majesty

Although I doubt not but your Majesty's own memory and care of your affairs will put you in mind of all things convenient against you shall meet with your Council, yet some particulars

---

[1] Immediately. [2] Dr George Abbot.

I thought it not unfit to represent unto your Majesty, because they passed the labour of your Council.

I. Some time before your departure, here was delivered unto you by the officers of your Exchequer a computation of your revenue and expense, wherein was expressed that your revenue ordinary was not only equal to your expense but did somewhat exceed it, though not much. In this point, because the half-year will now be expired at Michaelmas, it shall be fit that your Majesty call to account whether that equality hath held for this half-year; and if not, what the causes have been, and whether the course prescribed hath been kept, that the ordinary expense hath been borne out of the ordinary revenue and the extraordinary only out of such money as hath come in by extraordinary means, or else your state cannot clearly appear.

II. To maintain this equality, and to cause your Majesty's state to subsist in some reasonable manner till further supply might be had, it was found to be necessary that 200,000*l.* of your Majesty's most pregnant and pressing debts should be discharged; and after consideration of the means how to do that, two ways were resolved on. One, that 100,000*l.* should be discharged to the farmers of your customs by 25,000*l.* yearly, they having for their security power to defalk[1] so much of their rent in their own hands; but because if that should be defalked then your ordinary should want of so much, it was agreed that the farmers should be paid the 25,000*l.* yearly in the sale of woods. In this point it is fit for your Majesty to be informed what hath been done, and whether order hath been taken with the farmers for it, and what debts were assigned to them so to discharge; for of the particulars of that course I never heard yet. And because it is apparent that the woodfalls this year do not amount to half that sum of 25,000*l.*, your Majesty is to give charge that consideration be had how the same shall be supplied by some other extraordinary for the present year, or else here will follow a fracture of the whole assignments. *Item*, your Majesty may please to call for information how that money raised upon the woods is employed, so much as is already received, and to be wary that no part hereof be suffered to go for extraordinaries, but to be employed only for the use for which it is assigned, or else a greater rupture will follow in your assignments. *Item*, if special consideration is to be had, what course shall be taken for the rest of the years with the wood sales for supply of this 25,000*l.* yearly.

[1] Deduct.

III. The other hundred thousand pound was agreed to be borrowed, and an allotment made by my Lords of the Council at the Table how the same should be employed, and for what special services, whereof I deliver to your Majesty herewith a copy. In which point it may please your Majesty to cause yourself to be informed how that allotment hath been observed, and because it is likely that a good part of it hath gone towards the charges of this your journey to Scotland[1] (at least so it is paid), your Majesty is to call for the particulars of that charge, that you may see how much of that hundred thousand it taketh up. And then consideration is to be had how it may be supplied with some extraordinary comings-in, as namely, the moneys to come from the Merchant Adventurers, that the same be allotted to none other use but to perform this allotment, that so the foundation laid may be maintained, or else all will be to seek; and if there be any other extraordinary means to come to your Majesty, that they may be reserved to that use. And because care must be had to keep your credit in London for this money borrowed, your Majesty may please to call for information what is done in the matter of the forests, and what sum, and in what reasonable time, is like to be made thereof.

The extraordinaries which it is like will be alleged for this year:

Your Majesty's journey into Scotland.
The Lord Hay's employment into France[2].
The Lord Roos into Spain[3].
The Baron de Tour extraordinary from France.
Sir John Bennet to the Archduke[4].
The enlarging of your park at Theobalds.
Sir John Digby's sending into Spain[5].

Of all which when your Majesty hath seen an estimate what they amount unto, and what money hath been already delivered towards them, which I fear will fall to be out of the moneys borrowed at London; then is it to be considered what extra-

[1] James spent the summer of 1617 in Scotland.
[2] In July, 1616, Lord Hay of Sawley was sent on a mission to Paris.
[3] Lord Roos, the grandson of the Earl of Exeter, was sent to Madrid in 1616.
[4] Early in April, 1617, Sir John Bennet the civil lawyer was sent on a special mission to Brussels to the Archduke Albert to obtain the punishment of Henri Dupuy, the author of a pamphlet *Corona Regis* which satirised James I and his Court; in this he was unsuccessful (*D.N.B.* iv, 234).
[5] In 1617 Sir John Digby, afterwards first Earl of Bristol, had been sent into Spain in connexion with the negotiations for the Spanish Match.

ordinaries are any ways to come in which may supply these extraordinaries laid out, and be employed for the uses for which the moneys borrowed were intended.

Bacon, *Letters and Life* (ed. J. Spedding), vi, 254–6.

(7) Reform of the Household, 1617

There are references in this correspondence to Lionel Cranfield as in cooperation with Bacon and the Council in schemes for reducing expenditure on the King's Household. He was appointed Master of the Great Wardrobe in the following year.

Lord Keeper Bacon to the Earl of Buckingham, 19 November, 1617

The liking which his Majesty hath of our proceeding concerning his Household telleth me that his Majesty cannot but dislike the declining and tergiversation of the inferior officers; which by this time he understandeth.

There be but four kinds of retrenchments: 1. The union of tables; 2. The putting down of tables; 3. The abatement of dishes to tables; 4. The cutting off new diets and allowance lately raised; and yet perhaps such as are more necessary than some of the old.

In my opinion the first is the best and most feasible. The Lord Chamberlain's table is the principal table of state. The Lord Steward's table I think is much frequented by Scottish gentlemen. Your Lordship's table hath a great attendance; and the Groom of the Stole's table is much resorted to by the Bed-chamber. These would not be touched. But for the rest (his Majesty's case considered) I think they may well be united into one.

These things are out of my element, but my care runneth where the King's state most laboureth. Sir Lionel Cranfield is yet sick, for which I am very sorry; for methinks his Majesty, upon these tossings over of his business from one to others, hath an apt occasion to go on with sub-committees...(p. 275).

The same to the same, 22 November, 1617

Yesterday at afternoon were read at the Table his Majesty's two letters, written with his own hand; the matter worthy the hand, for they were written *ex arte imperandi*, if I can judge. And I hope they and the like will disenchant us of the opinion which yet sticks with us, that to-day will be as yesterday and to-morrow as to-day; so that these things will be (as he saith) *acribus initiis, fine incurioso*.

I hold my opinion given in my former letter, that the uniting of some tables is the most passable way. But that is not all; for when that is done, the King may save greatly in that which remaineth. For if it be set down what tables shall be fixed and what diet allowed to them, my steward (as ill a *mesnager* as I am) or my Lord Mayor's steward, can go near to tell what charge will maintain that proportion. Then add to that some large allowance for waste (because the King shall not lose his prerogative to be deceived more than other men) and yet no question there will be a great retrenchment. But against this last abatement will be fronted the payment of arrears. But I confess I would be glad that I might see, or rather that a Parliament may see, and chiefly that the King (for his own quiet) may see, that upon such a sum paid such an annual retrenchment will follow; for things will never be done in act except they be first done in conceit. ...

As soon as I find any possibility of health in Sir Lionel Cranfield to execute a sub-commission, I will by conference with him frame a draught of a letter from his Majesty, for which there is the fairest occasion in the world and the King hath prepared it as well as is possible...(p. 276).

The same to the same, 27 November, 1617

...I send your Lordship a draught of a letter touching the sub-commission, written in wide lines because it may be the better amended by his Majesty. I think it is so penned as none can except to it, no, nor imagine anything of it. For the Household business there was given a fortnight's day; for the pensions, the course which I first propounded, of abating of a third throughout, and some wholly, seemeth well entered into. These be no ill beginnings. But this course of the sub-commission thrids all the King's business. ...

Draught of the Sub-Commission

My Lords[1],—In this first and greatest branch of our charge concerning our House, we do find what difficulties are made and what time is lost in disputing and devising upon the manner of doing that whereof the matter must be and is so fully resolved. Neither can we but see in this, as in a glass, the like event to follow in the rest upon like reason. For the inferior officers in every kind who are best able for skill to propound the retrenchments will, out of interest or fearfulness, make dainty[2] to do ser-

---

[1] Of the Council.
[2] To 'make dainty to do' anything is to be chary or loth to do it.

vice; and that which is done with an ill will will never be well done. Again, to make it the act of the whole Table for the particular propositions and reckonings will be too tedious for you, and will draw the business itself into length; and to make any particular committees of yourselves were to impose that upon a few which requireth to be carried indifferently as the act of you all. For since the great officers themselves think it too heavy for them, as our state now is, to deal in it without bringing it to the Table, with much more reason may any particular persons of you be loth to meddle in it but at the Board. In all which respects we have thought fit (neither do we see any other way) that you send unto us the names of the officers of our Exchequer and our Custom-house and Auditors, out of which we will make choice of some few best qualified to be sub-committees, for the better ease and the speeding of the business by their continual travails and meetings; whose part and employment we incline to be to attend the principal officers in their several charges, and join themselves to some of the inferior officers, and so take upon them the mechanic and laborious part of every business, thereby to facilitate and prepare it for your consultations, according to the directions and instructions they shall receive from you from time to time.

The Earl of Buckingham to Lord Keeper Bacon; 2 December, 1617

His Majesty liketh very well of the draught your Lordship sent of the letter for the sub-commission, and hath signed it as it was, without any alteration, and sent it to the Lords...(pp. 279–81).

The Council to the King; 5 December, 1617

May it please your Majesty,—Being yesterday assembled in Council to proceed in the course we had begun for retrenchment of your Majesty's expenses, we received your princely letters whereby we are directed to send to your Majesty the names of the officers of the Exchequer, Custom-house, and Auditors out of which you purpose to make choice of some to be sub-committed to handle the mechanic and laborious part of that which your Majesty had appointed to our care; we have, according to our duty, sent unto your Majesty the names of the several officers of your Majesty in those places, to be ordered as your wisdom shall think best to direct. But withal, we thought it appertenant[1] to our

---

[1] For appurtenant = appertaining.

duties to inform your Majesty how far we have proceeded in the several heads of retrenchments by your Majesty at your departure committed unto us, that when you know in what estate our labours are, your judgment may the better direct any further course as shall be meet.

The matter of the Household was by us, some days since, committed peremptorily to the officers of the House as matter of commandment from your Majesty and of duty in them, to reduce the expense of your House to a limited charge of fifty thousand pounds by the year, besides the benefit of the compositions; and they have ever sithence painfully (as we are informed) travailed in it and will be ready on Sunday next, which was the day given them, to present some models of retrenchments of divers kinds all aiming at your Majesty's service.

In the point of pensions, we have made a beginning by suspending some wholly for a time and of others of a third part, in which course we are still going on until we make it fit to be presented to your Majesty; in like manner the Lord Chamberlain and the Lord Hay did yesterday report unto us what their travail had ordered in the Wardrobe; and although some doubt did arise unto us whether your Majesty's letters intended a stay of our labours until you had made choice of the sub-committee intended by you, yet presuming that such a course by sub-committee was purposed rather for a furtherance than let to that work, we did resolve to go on still till your Majesty's further directions shall come unto us, and then according to our duty we will proceed as we shall be by your Majesty commanded... (pp. 281–2).

Lord Keeper Bacon to the Earl of Buckingham,
6 December, 1617

* * * * * *

For the present my advice is, his Majesty would be pleased to write back to the Table that he doth well approve that we did not put back or retard the good ways we were in of ourselves, and that we understood his Majesty right that his late direction was to give help and not hindrance to the former courses, and that he doth expect the propositions we have in hand when they are finished. And that for the sub-commissioners, he hath sent us the names he hath chosen out of those by us sent and propounded, and that he leaveth the particular directions from time to time in the use of the sub-commissioners wholly to the Table.

This I conceive to be the fairest way: first to seal the sub-commission without opening the nature of their employments, and without seeming that they should have any immediate dependence upon his Majesty, but merely upon the Table.

As for that which is to be kept in breast, and to come forth by parts, the degrees are these:

First, to employ the sub-commissioners in the reconsidering of those branches which the several officers shall propound.

Next, in taking consideration of other branches of retrenchment besides those which shall be propounded.

The third, to take into consideration the great and huge arrears and debts in every office; whether there be cause to abate them upon deceit or abuse, and at least how to settle them best both for the King's honour and avoiding of clamour, and for the taking away (as much as may be) that same ill influence and effect whereby the arrear past destroys the good husbandry and reformation to come.

The fourth is to proceed from the consideration of the retrenchments and arrears to the improvements.

All these four, at least the last three, I wish not to be stirred in till his Majesty's coming... (pp. 283–4).

Bacon, *Letters and Life*, vi, 275–85.

(8) The Benevolence of 1622

Circular letters were sent from the Council to the Judges, Sheriffs, Justices of the Peace, and magistrates of the cities and boroughs, requiring them to urge upon their districts the duty of contributing to the King's necessities and to certify to the Council the names of those who shewed themselves unwilling. The first of the letters printed below is in the form addressed to the Judges; the second, signed by the Archbishop of Canterbury and thirteen Bishops, and dated 21 January, 1622, quotes a letter from the King to the Bishops of 14 January, and was intended for circulation among the other Bishops who were then to 'incite' their clergy to contribute. The Benevolence was expected to bring in £200,000; the actual yield for the year was £88,000.

Letters from the Privy Council to the Justices of the Courts at Westminster and to the Barons of the Exchequer

What endeavours his Majesty hath used by treaty and by all fair and amiable ways to recover the patrimony of his children in Germany, now for the most part withholden from them by force, is not unknown to all his loving subjects, since his Majesty was pleased to communicate to them in Parliament his whole proceedings in that business: of which treaty being of late frustrate[1], he was inforced to take other resolutions, namely, to recover that

---

[1] Disappointed.

by the sword which by other means he saw no likelihood to compass. For which purpose it was expected by his Majesty that his people in Parliament would (in a cause so nearly concerning his and his children's interest) have cheerfully contributed thereunto. But the same unfortunately failing, his Majesty is constrained, in a case of so great necessity, to try the dutiful affections of his loving subjects in another way, as his predecessors have done in former times, by propounding unto them a voluntary contribution. And therefore, as yourselves have already given a liberal and worthy example (which his Majesty doth take in very gracious part) so his pleasure is, and we do accordingly hereby authorise and require your Lordships as well to countenance and assist the service by your best means in your next circuits in the several counties where you hold General Assizes, as also now presently, with all convenient expedition, to call before you all the officers and attorneys belonging to any his Majesty's Courts of Justice, and also all such others of the Houses and Societies of Court, or that otherwise have dependence upon the Law, as are meet to treated withal in this kind and have not already contributed, and to move them to join willingly in this contribution in some good measure, answerable to that yourselves and others have done before us, according to their means and fortunes: wherein his Majesty doubteth not but, beside the interest of his children and his own crown and dignity, the religion professed by his Majesty and happily flourishing under him within this kingdom (having a great part in the success of this business) will be a special motive to incite and persuade them thereunto. Nevertheless, if any person shall, out of obstinacy or disaffection, refuse to contribute herein proportionably to their estates and means, you are to certify their names unto this Board.

And so recommending this service to your best care and endeavour, and praying you to return unto us notes of the names of such as shall contribute and of the sums offered by them, We bid, etc.

Rushworth, *Historical Collections*, i, 60.

Letters to the Bishops

Right Reverend Father in God, our very good Lord and Brother. We have lately received from his Majesty certain letters directed unto us, the Lord Archbishop of Canterbury and the Lord Bishop of Lincoln, Lord Keeper of the Great Seal, but referring to the rest whose names are underwritten, the tenor whereof here ensueth:

Right Reverend Fathers in God, right trusty and well beloved counsellors, we greet you well. What endeavours we have used, by treaty and by all fair and amicable ways, to recover the patrimony of our children in Germany, now for the most part withholden from them by force, is not unknown unto all our loving subjects, since we were pleased to communicate unto them in Parliament our whole proceedings in that business: of which treaty our hopes being at the last frustrate, we were enforced to take other resolutions, namely, to recover that by the sword which by other means we see no likelihood to compass. For which purpose we did expect that our people would, in a cause so nearly concerning our children's interest and ours, have cheerfully contributed thereunto, as indeed they did by promise and de-claration to the proportion of one subsidy at their last meeting before Christmas: but the same failing to be legally perfected by the wayward divisions of some few, we are constrained in a case of so great necessity to try the dutiful affections of our subjects in another way, as our predecessors have done in former times, by propounding a voluntary contribution unto them; and knowing the faithful and loving service performed unto us by the clergy of this realm at all times upon the like urgent occasion, have thought good to make use thereof at this present, and do therefore require you to give notice thereof to all the Bishops who are not as yet departed from the City of London, and together with them to write your letters to all the Bishops of both Provinces for the speedy collecting and receiving of the voluntary contributions of the whole clergy towards the support of this so necessary and justifiable a warlike defence, wherein not only our crown and dignity but the true religion also, which you and they teach and profess, is so much interested. And we do further require that you and the other Bishops do likewise move the same to all the schoolmasters which have license to teach within your or their several dioceses, not doubting of either your care or their forward-ness in this so necessary a service. Given under our signet at our Palace of Westminster, the 14th day of January in the nineteenth year of our reign of England, France, and Ireland, and of Scotland the five and fiftieth.

Your Lordship by these letters may see how far it concerneth his Majesty in honour and the realm in safety that the patrimony of the King's children should be recovered again by force of war, since it cannot be obtained by treaty. And inasmuch as arms are not maintained but by large expense, and his Majesty hath not lately received such supply as otherways was expected, it may well stand with our most bounden duty that in this time of necessity we of the clergy should by way of voluntary contribution testify our observance and loyal respect unto so gracious a prince. We therefore, who upon the receipt of these his Majesty's letters have met together and duly considered what was most convenient to be done, have resolved that three shillings and tenpence in the pound is as little as we can possibly offer towards so great an enterprise; yet hoping that such as be of ability will exceed the same. You shall therefore do well, by all forcible reason drawn from the defence of religion and justice, to incite all your clergy, as well within peculiars as otherwise, as all the lecturers and licensed schoolmasters within your diocese, that with all readiness they do contribute unto this noble action. And whereas there be divers commendatories[1], dignitaries, prebendaries, and double-beneficed men that have livings in several dioceses, we hold it fit that for every one of these within your Lordship's diocese the contribution be rateable, so that the moneys in such sort given may be brought to London by the tenth day of March next, to be delivered to the hands of such receivers as for that purpose shall be appointed. And to the end that true notice may be taken of such as are best disposed to this so good a service, we expect that your Lordship send up to the Lord Archbishop of Canterbury the several sums and names of all those who contribute; and lastly, your Lordship shall do right well also, that inasmuch as the laity are like to be moved for such contribution in the country, wherein many about London already have begun and given good example, that you cause the preachers within your diocese in a grave and discreet fashion to excite the people, that when occasion shall serve, they do extend their liberalities to so Christian and worthy an enterprise: wherein not doubting but your Lordship will use all your best, prudent, and most careful endeavours, we leave you to the Almighty. From Lambeth, 21 Januarii, MDCXXI[2] *juxta* etc.

Your Lordship's very loving brethren,

G. Cant.	Tho. Coven. et Lich.
Jo. Lincoln, C.S.[3]	Arthur Bath. et Wellen.
G. London.	Lu. Bangor.
R. Dunelm.	Nic. Elien.
L. Winton.	Theo. Landaven.
Jo. Wigorn.	Will. Meneven.
Jo. Roffen.	Jo. Cestren.

Cardwell, *Documentary Annals*, ii, 141.

---

[1] *I.e.* holders of benefices *in commendam*.   [2] *I.e.* 1621–2.
[3] *Custos Sigilli.*

§ 4. The Subsidy Act of 1624, and the Council of War

When the Parliament of 1624 met, the Commons were ready to vote large supplies if they could be sure that the money would really be devoted to providing for the impending war with Spain. To secure this they adopted the novel constitutional expedient of settling the money they voted upon the war by means of unprecedented clauses introduced into the Subsidy Bill of 1624 [below]. These provide (1) that the sums raised under the Bill should be paid to treasurers appointed by Parliament, who should only pay it over on warrants from the Council of War [p. 379]; (2) that the money should be appropriated to certain specified purposes all directly or indirectly connected with the war which it was hoped that James would declare upon Spain—'the defence of this your realm of England, the securing of your kingdom of Ireland, the assistance of your neighbours the States of the United Provinces and other your Majesty's friends and allies, and for the setting forth of your royal navy'; (3) it was expressly declared that both the treasurers and the Council of War should be responsible to Parliament, which should have power to commit them prisoners to the Tower of London in case of default; and (4) as a guarantee for their performance of the duties laid upon them, both the treasurers and the Council of War were to take oath faithfully to discharge their offices according to the tenor of the Act.

The Council of War of 1624 was not the first to be established. On 13 January, 1621, with a view to armed intervention in the Palatinate, the Earls of Oxford, Essex, and Leicester and others had been appointed by Order in Council 'to sit as a Council of War for the affairs of the Palatinate, and to report on all matters submitted to them, with power to advise with experienced persons.'[1] This was not a committee of the Council, for it included members who were not Privy Councillors; but it differed constitutionally from the War Council of 1624, which derived its authority from a direct commission from the King, and functioned under conditions laid down in an Act of Parliament.

(1) The Subsidy Act of 1624

An Act for payment of Three Subsidies and Three Fifteenths by the Temporalty

I. Most gracious Sovereign, We your Majesty's most humble, faithful, and loving subjects, by your royal authority now assembled in your High Court of Parliament, having entered into serious and due consideration of the weighty and most important causes which at this time more than at any other time heretofore do press your Majesty to a much greater expense and charge than your own treasure alone can at this present support and maintain, and likewise of the injuries and indignities which have

---

[1] *Calendar of State Papers (Domestic)*, 1619–23, p. 214.

been lately offered to your Majesty and your children, under colour and during the time of the treaties for the marriage with Spain and the restitution of the Palatinate, which in this Parliament have been clearly discovered and laid open unto us; And withal what humble advice with one consent and voice we have given unto your Majesty to dissolve those treaties, which your Majesty hath been graciously pleased, to our exceeding joy and comfort, fully to yield unto, and accordingly have made your public declaration for the real and utter dissolution of them, by means whereof your Majesty may haply be engaged in a sudden war: We in all humbleness most ready and willing to give unto your Majesty and the whole world an ample testimony of our dutiful affections and sincere intentions to assist you therein for the maintenance of that war that may hereupon ensue, and more particularly for the defence of this your realm of England, the securing of your kingdom of Ireland, the assistance of your neighbours the States of the United Provinces and other your Majesty's friends and allies, and for the setting forth of your royal Navy, we have resolved to give for the present the greatest Aid which ever was granted in Parliament to be levied in so short a time; And therefore we do humbly beseech your Majesty that it may be declared and enacted, and be it declared by the authority of this present Parliament, that the said two treaties are by your Majesty utterly dissolved; And for the maintenance of the war which may come thereupon, and for the causes aforesaid, Be it enacted that three whole Fifteenths and Tenths shall be paid, taken, and levied of the moveable goods, chattels, and other things usual to such Fifteenths and Tenths to be contributory and chargeable within the shires, cities, boroughs, towns, and other places of this your Majesty's realm, in manner and form aforetime used;...And the same three Fifteenths and Tenths...to be paid unto the hands of Sir Thomas Middleton knight and Alderman of London, Sir Edward Barkham knight and Alderman of London, Sir Paul Baning knight and baronet, Sir Richard Grubham knight, James Campbell, George Whitmore, and Ralph Freeman, Aldermen of London, and Martin Bond citizen and haberdasher of London, Treasurers especially appointed in and by this Act to receive and issue the same....

II. And be it further enacted by the authority aforesaid, That the knights elected and returned of and for the shires within this realm for this present Parliament, citizens of cities, burgesses of boroughs and towns, where Collectors have been used to be named and appointed for the collection of any Fifteenth

and Tenth before this time granted, shall name and appoint...
sufficient and able persons to be Collectors....

*   *   *   *   *   *

IV. And furthermore, for the great and weighty considerations aforesaid, we the Lords Spiritual and Temporal and the
Commons in this present Parliament assembled do...give and
grant to your Highness...three entire Subsidies, to be...levied
...in manner and form following:....As well that every person
born within...the King's dominions as all and every fraternity,
guild, corporation, mystery, brotherhood, and comminalty[1]...
being worth three pounds, for every pound as well in coin...as
also plate, stock of merchandise, all manner of corn and grain,
household stuff, and of all other goods movable,...and of all
such sums of money as to him or them is or shall be owing whereof
he or they trust in his or their conscience surely to be paid, except
and out of the said premisses deducted such sums of money as he
or they owe and in his or their consciences intendeth truly to pay,
and except also the apparel of every such person, their wives, and
children, belonging to their own bodies, saving jewels, gold,
silver, stone, and pearl, shall pay [2s. 8d. in the pound on each of
the three subsidies]....

*   *   *   *   *   *

XXXVI. And be it further enacted by the authority aforesaid, That all the sums of money by this present Act given and
granted to the uses aforesaid shall be paid by the several Collectors
...unto the said Treasurers....

XXXVII. And to the end that all and every the sums of
money by this present Act granted as aforesaid...may be truly
expended for and towards the uses aforesaid and not otherwise.
...Be it further enacted, That the moneys to be received by the
said Treasurers by virtue of this Act shall be issued out and
expended for or towards the uses aforesaid to such person and
persons and in such manner and form as by the warrant of George
Lord Carew[2], Foulke Lord Brooke[3], Oliver Lord Viscount Grandison of Limerick within the realm of Ireland[4], Arthur Lord

[1] *I.e.*, commonalty: here = corporation.
[2] Master-General of the Ordnance 1608–17 (*D.N.B.* ix, 52); afterwards Earl
of Totnes.
[3] Sir Fulke Greville, first Baron Brooke, the poet, Sir Philip Sidney's friend.
He had been Secretary of the Navy under Queen Elizabeth.
[4] Oliver St John, first Viscount Grandison, had been Lord Deputy of Ireland
1616–22.

Chichester[1], Sir Edward Cecil knight[2], Sir Edward Conway knight one of the Principal Secretaries to his Majesty[3], Sir Horace Vere knight[4], Sir Robert Maunsell knight[5], Sir John Ogle knight[6], and Sir Thomas Button knight[7], which ten persons before mentioned his Majesty hath already nominated and hath made choice of to be of his Council for the War[8], or any five or more of them, whereof two of them to be of his Majesty's most honourable Privy Council, under their hands and seals shall be directed and not otherwise; And such warrant and warrants of the said Councillors of War or of any five of them, whereof two to be of the Privy Council as aforesaid, together with the acquittances of those persons who shall receive those moneys according to those warrants or the inrolment thereof to be for that purpose likewise kept by his Majesty's Remembrancer of the said Court of Exchequer, shall be unto the said Treasurers and every of them their heirs, executors, and administrators a full and sufficient discharge.

XXXVIII. And be it enacted, That the said eight Treasurers shall and may out of their receipts retain and be allowed the sum of four hundred pounds for or towards the pains and attendance of such servants as they must necessarily use in and about this service, that is to say, the sum of fifty pounds for the servant or servants of every of those eight Treasurers.

XXXIX. And be it further enacted, That as well the said Treasurers as the said persons appointed for the Council of War as aforesaid, and all other persons who shall be trusted with the receiving, issuing, bestowing, and employing of these moneys or any part thereof, their heirs, executors, and administrators, shall be answerable and accountable for their doings or proceedings herein to the Commons in Parliament when they shall be thereunto required by warrant under the hand of the Speaker of the House of Commons for the time being, and there they and every of them, according to their several places and employments, shall give a true and real declaration and accompt of their several and

---

[1] Lord Deputy of Ireland 1605–15.

[2] Sir Edward Cecil, afterwards Viscount Wimbledon, had a high reputation as a military commander until his mismanagement of the expedition to Cadiz in 1625.

[3] Secretary of State 1623–30.

[4] A distinguished soldier who had commanded the troops sent to the relief of the Palatinate in 1620. He was appointed Master-General of the Ordnance in 1623, and created Baron Vere in 1625.

[5] Sir Robert Mansell, afterwards Vice-Admiral of England.

[6] Sir John Ogle had served in the Low Countries.

[7] Admiral.

[8] It should be noted that they had all had experience of service on land or sea.

respective dealings, doings, and proceedings therein; and that the said Commons in Parliament shall have power by this Act to hear and determine the said accompt and all things thereto appertaining.

XL. And be it further enacted, That for the better preparation of these things for the examination of the House of Commons, and for the more frugal expending of the moneys given by this Act, that the said Council of War or any five or more of them as aforesaid, or such person or persons as they or any five or more of them shall under their hands nominate and appoint, shall by virtue of this Act have power, and by virtue of this Act are required, from time to time to take accompt of all person and persons of and for all such sums of money as shall be issued to any person or persons to the uses aforesaid, and how they have expended and bestowed the same: Provided always, That such accompt be[ing] taken by the said Council of War as aforesaid shall not exclude the power of the House of Commons to examine the said accompts and determine the same as aforesaid.

XLI. And be it further enacted, That when the Commons in Parliament have heard, examined, and determined the dealings, doings, and proceedings of any the persons aforesaid according to the true intent and meaning of this Act, that then and in every such case the offender or offenders being no Lord or Lords of Parliament shall by the House of Commons be committed to the Tower of London, there to remain close prisoners until by order of the House of Commons they be delivered; and if any the Lords of Parliament shall be found offenders, then the Commons in Parliament shall present their offence to the Lords in Parliament, and thereupon the Lords in Parliament shall have power by virtue of this Act to hear, examine, and determine the offence so presented, and to commit them likewise to the Tower of London, there to remain close prisoners until by order of that House they shall be delivered.

XLII. And be it further enacted, That the offender and offenders in every such case shall undergo such further censure and punishment as to justice shall appertain, according to the quality of the offence and according to the judgment of either House respectively.

XLIII. And to the end that as well the said Council of War as the said Treasurers may the better observe and perform the trust aforesaid committed unto them, Be it further enacted, That they shall severally and distinctly take these respective oaths following, that is to say, the said Treasurers shall take this oath following: You shall swear that you, being appointed one of the Treasurers for the receiving of the three Subsidies and three Fifteenths and Tenths granted by the Temporalty, shall not issue any part of those moneys which shall be paid into your hands, or unto the hands of any other by your appointment or consent, without the special warrant of those persons which are by his Majesty appointed to be of his Council for the Wars and in this Act nominated, or of five of them at the least, whereof two of them to be such as are of his Majesty's Privy Council, under their hands; in every of such warrant or warrants there shall be expressed that those moneys for which such warrant is given are to be issued for some of those ends mentioned in this present Act. And the said Council of War shall take this oath following: You shall swear that you, being one of the Council of War chosen by his Majesty and nominated in this Act, shall make no warrant for any moneys to be issued which are given by this present Act but for some of those ends which are expressed in this Act, and that all such warrants as shall be made by you shall mention in them that those moneys are to be employed according to the true meaning of this Act, and to the best of your means you shall employ the same accordingly. Both the said oaths to be taken before the Lord Keeper of the Great Seal or Master of the Rolls for the time being, within one week after the end of this present session of Parliament, and the taking of their oath to be entered of record in Chancery.

XLIV. And be it further enacted, That for all and every the several services or purposes mentioned in this Act to be performed in any part beyond the seas, the charge thereof shall be defrayed from time to time out of the treasure raised and given by this Act and not otherwise, either for arms, coat or conduct money[1], or otherwise; And that no part of this money shall be disposed of but for the ends mentioned in this Act, and not for the satisfying of any arrearages due before the beginning of this Parliament; And because these moneys are given for the public service of the whole kingdom and not for any private end, that therefore there shall be no fees required by any person whatsoever for the collecting, receiving, issuing, expending, or disposing of any part of these moneys given or granted by this Act, but that the same shall be done freely, without any fee, reward, allowance, or defalcation[2] whatsoever, other than is particularly mentioned in this Act.

21 & 22 Jac. I, c. 33: *Statutes of the Realm*, iv, 1247.

[1] Money to provide each man enlisted with a coat, and to cover the expense of conducting him to a rendezvous.   [2] Deduction.

(2) Commission for the Council of War, 1624

A Commission in the same terms had already been issued on 21 April 1621.

De Commissione Olivero Vicecomiti Grandison et aliis

James, by the grace of God, etc., to our right trusty and well-beloved cousin and Councillor, Oliver Viscount Grandison; And to our right trusty and well-beloved Councillors, George Lord Carew, Master of our Ordnance[1], Fulke Lord Brooke, Arthur Lord Chichester; and to our right trusty and well-beloved Henry Lord Dockwra[2]; and to our trusty and right well-beloved Councillor, Sir Edward Conway knight, one of our Principal Secretaries of State; and to our trusty and well-beloved Sir Edward Cecil knight, Sir Horace Vere knight, Sir Robert Mansfield[3] knight, Sir John Ogle knight, and Sir Thomas Button[4] knight, Greeting.

Whereas we are now to take such ways and means as shall be most requisite for securing our realm of Ireland, with the rest of our dominions, and putting our Navy Royal in readiness, we have thought good to nominate and appoint a Council of War for this purpose; and of the knowledge we have of your wisdom, integrity, and experience in matters of this nature, we have made special choice of you, and do hereby require and authorise you, or any six or more of you, to assemble and meet together from time to time as there shall be cause, to call unto you such persons of experience whose advice and opinion you shall find cause to make use of, and to advise of such ways and means as may further and give advancement to our foresaid ends of assisting our allies, specially the Low Countries, securing Ireland and the rest of our dominions, and putting our Navy in readiness and safety, together with what else shall be recommended to you from us for your advice towards the furtherance of our service; and upon mature deliberation of such things as shall fall into debate with you, you are to set down in writing your opinions, and make speedy representation to us of such things as shall be fit for our knowledge, and likewise to offer unto our Privy Council

[1] But see note 2 on p. 376 above; in 1624 the office was being held by Sir Horace Vere (*D.N.B.* lviii. 237).

[2] Sir Henry Dockwra, first Baron Dockwra, had had a distinguished military career in Ireland. His is the only name in the Commission which is not in § 37 of the Subsidy Act.

[3] Mansell: see note 5 on p. 377 above.

[4] The text reads Dutton in error.

such propositions as may be meet for their consideration or to be by them put in execution: And these our letters shall be your sufficient warrant and discharge in this behalf. In witness whereof, etc.

Witness ourself at Nonsuch, the twentieth day of July.

Per ipsum Regem.

Rymer, *Foedera* (edition of 1704–35), xvii, 615.

Appendix

The Speaker's claim of Privilege
(see p. 272 above)

(see p. 272 above)

The earliest instance of the Speaker's claim of Privilege including anything of the nature of freedom of speech for members of the House has hitherto been assigned to 1542[1]; but Professor J. E. Neale has called the editor's attention to a remarkable passage in the *Life of Sir Thomas More*[2] which shews vague ideas beginning to take shape as early as 1523 which were afterwards to find briefer and more precise expression. The petition for favourable interpretation for the House, as stated by More, is not far off being a claim for freedom of speech in the sense in which the sixteenth century understood it, although it is not the freedom to discuss any subject which the Commons were trying to secure in the reign of James I. The passage runs as follows:

In the 14th year of his gracious reign there was a Parliament holden whereof Sir Thomas More was elected Speaker. Who being very loth to take this room upon him, made an oration not now extant to the King for his discharge thereof. Whereunto when the King would not consent, he spake unto his Grace in form following:

'Sith I perceive, most redoubted Sovereign, that it standeth not with your pleasure to re-form this election and cause it to be changed, but have, by the mouth of the most reverend Father in God my Lord Legate, your Highness's Chancellor, thereunto given your royal assent, and have of your benignity determined far above that I may bear to enable me and for this office to repute me meet, rather than you should seem to impute unto your Commons that they had made an unfit choice, I am therefore, and always shall be, ready obediently to conform myself to the accomplishment of your Highness's pleasure and commandment; in most humble wise beseeching your most noble Majesty that I may, with your Grace's favour, before I farther enter thereinto, make my humble intercession for two lowly petitions: the one privately concerning myself, the other the whole assembly of your Commons' House.

'For myself, gracious Sovereign, that if it mishap me, in anything hereafter that is on the behalf of your Commons in your high presence to be declared, to mistake my message, and in the lack of good utterance by my misrehearsal to pervert or impair their prudent instructions, that it may then like your most noble Majesty of your abundant grace, with the eye of your wonted pity, to pardon my simpleness, giving me leave to repair again to the Commons' House, and there to confer with them, and to take their substantial advice what things and in what wise I shall on their behalf utter and speak before your noble Grace, to th'intent their prudent devices and affairs be not by my simpleness and folly hindered or impaired. Which thing if it should so happen, as it were like to mishappen me[3] if your gracious benignity

[1] *Tudor Constitutional Documents*, p. 551.
[2] William Roper, *The Life of Sir Thomas More* (edition of 1817), p. 15.
[3] *I.e.* inflict on me a misfortune.

relieved not my oversight, it could not fail to be during my life a perpetual grudge and heaviness to my heart. The help and remedy whereof in manner afore remembered is (my gracious Sovereign) my first lowly suit and humble petition unto your noble Grace.

'My other humble request, most excellent Prince, is this. Forasmuch as there be of your Commons here by your high commandment assembled for your Parliament a great number which are after your accustomed manner appointed in the Commons' House to entreat and advise of the common affairs among themselves apart; and albeit, most dear liege Lord, that according to your prudent advice by your honourable writs everywhere declared there hath been as due diligence used in sending up to your Highness's Court of Parliament the most discreet persons out of every quarter that men could esteem most meet thereunto, whereby it is not to be doubted that there is a very substantial assembly of right wise, meet, and politique persons; yet, most virtuous Prince, sith among so many wise men neither is every man wise alike, nor among so many alike well-witted every man alike well-spoken, and it often happeneth that likewise as much folly is uttered with painted, polished speech, so many boisterous and rude in language see deep indeed and give right substantial counsel; and sith also in matters of great importance the mind is so often occupied in the matter that a man rather studieth what to say than how, by reason whereof the wisest man and best spoken in a whole country fortuneth while his mind is fervent in the matter somewhat to speak in such wise as he would afterward wish to have been uttered otherwise, and yet no worse will had he when he spake it than he had when he would so gladly change it; therefore, most gracious Sovereign, considering that in your High Court of Parliament is nothing treated but matters of weight and importance concerning your realm and your royal estate, it could not fail to let and put to silence from the giving of their advice and counsel many of your discreet Commons, to the great hindrance of the common affairs, except that every one of your Commons were utterly discharged of all doubts and fears how anything that it should happen them to speak should happen of your Highness to be taken. And in this point, though your well-known and proved benignity putteth every man in good hope, yet such is the weight of the matter, such is the reverent dread that the timorous hearts of your natural subjects conceive towards your high Majesty our most redoubted King and undoubted Sovereign, that they cannot in this point find themselves satisfied except your gracious bounty therein declared put away the scruple of their timorous minds and animate and encourage them and put them out of doubt. It may therefore like your most abundant grace, our most benign and godly King, to give all your Commons here assembled your most gracious license and pardon, freely without doubt of your dreadful displeasure, every man to discharge his conscience, and boldly in everything incident among us to declare his advice; and whatsoever happeneth any man to say, that it may like your Majesty of your inestimable goodness to take all in good part, interpreting every man's words, how uncunningly soever they be couched, to proceed yet of good zeal towards the profit of your realm and honour of your royal person, the prosperous estate and preservation whereof, most excellent Sovereign, is the thing which we all, your loving subjects, according to our most bounden duty, of our natural allegiance most highly desire and pray for'.

Index